ON ZION'S MOUNT

ON ZION'S MOUNT

Mormons, Indians, and the American Landscape

JARED FARMER

HARVARD UNIVERSITY PRESS
Cambridge, Massachusetts
London, England
2008

Library of Congress Cataloging-in-Publication Data

Farmer, Jared, 1974–
On Zion's mount : Mormons, Indians, and the American landscape / Jared Farmer.
p.   cm.
Includes bibliographical references and index.
ISBN-13: 978-0-674-02767-1 (cloth : alk. paper)
ISBN-10: 0-674-02767-1 (cloth : alk. paper)
1. Timpanogos, Mount (Utah)—History.   2. Utah Lake (Utah)—History.
3. Ute Indians—History.   4. Mormons—History.   5. Frontier and pioneer life—Utah.
6. Utah—History.   7. Great Basin—Description and travel.   8. Landscape assessment—
United States.   9. Indians in popular culture—United States.   I. Title.
F832.U8F37   2008
979.2'24—dc22   2007034611

For my sister Rachel,
who knows where I'm coming from,
and my daughter, Anna,
who doesn't

Contents

Contents

Illustrations

Illustrations

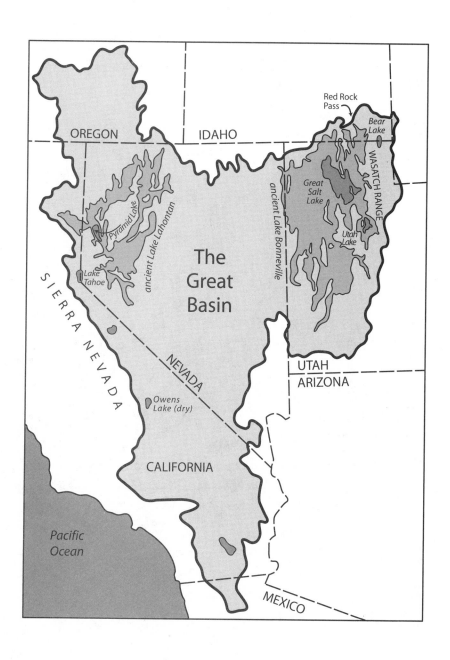

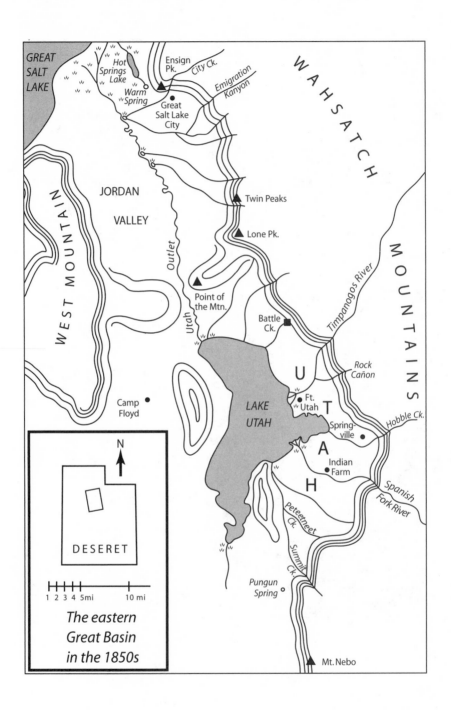

GREAT
SALT
LAKE

Hot
Springs
Lake

Warm
Spring

Ensign
Pk.

City Ck.

Emigration
Kanyon

W A H S A T C H

Great
Salt Lake
City

JORDAN

VALLEY

WEST MOUNTAIN

Twin Peaks

Lone Pk.

Outlet

Point of
the Mtn.

Utah

Battle
Ck.

Timpanogos River

M O U N T A I N S

U

Rock
Cañon

Camp
Floyd

LAKE
UTAH

Ft.
Utah

T

A

Spring-
ville

Hobble Ck.

N

DESERET

Indian
Farm

H

Spanish

Fork River

Peteetneet Ck.

1 2 3 4 5mi   10 mi

Summit Ck.

The eastern
Great Basin
in the 1850s

Pungun
Spring

Mt. Nebo

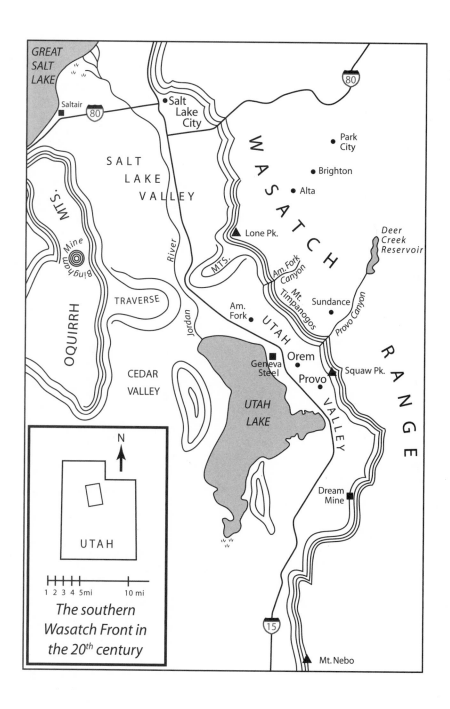

GREAT SALT LAKE

Saltair

Salt Lake City

Park City

Brighton

Alta

SALT LAKE VALLEY

WASATCH

Bingham Mine

OQUIRRH MTS.

TRAVERSE

River

Jordan

MTS.

Lone Pk.

Am. Fork Canyon

Mt. Timpanogos

Deer Creek Reservoir

Sundance

Provo Canyon

CEDAR VALLEY

Am. Fork

UTAH

Geneva Steel

Orem

Provo

Squaw Pk.

UTAH LAKE

RANGE

VALLEY

Dream Mine

N

UTAH

1 2 3 4 5mi   10 mi

The southern Wasatch Front in the 20th century

I-15

Mt. Nebo

Every old part of the country is filled with memorials of our past: tombstones and cottages and churches, names and legends, old roads and trails and abandoned mines, as well as the things we built and used yesterday. All these memorials bring us closer to the past; and, so doing, they bring us closer to our own present; for we are living history as well as recording it; and our memories are as necessary as our anticipations.

—Lewis Mumford (1927)

There is nothing less permanent than geography.

—*United States Democratic Review* (1842)

Thou shalt not remove thy neighbour's landmark, which they of old time have set in thine inheritance, which thou shalt inherit in the land that the LORD thy God giveth thee to possess it.

—Deuteronomy 19:14 (King James Version)

Introduction

Here is the creation story of a landmark—one beloved peak in the American West. In the beginning, this mount had form without meaning. It was not visible, nor haunted; now it is both. Getting to the bottom of the matter requires disorientation. The bedrock is liquid. The landmark's life history begins with the ghost of a lake.

Utah Lake occupies the center of Utah Valley, which occupies the center of Utah County, which occupies the center of Utah. The names expand outward concentrically, with decreasing specificity, for a reason. In the nineteenth century, and for untold ages before, this lake defined a place and a people. Indeed, in its original usage as a place-name, "Utah" signified the lakeside home of the "Utahs." The name was not endemic; colonial invaders—first Spaniards, then Mexicans, then Americans—imposed it. At the time of contact, the natives called themselves Fish-Eaters, Lake People, or the Timpanogos—a name drawn from the river where the lake fish spawned. The Lake of the Timpanogos was a haven in a hard, inconstant land. Even in the thinnest year, the natives (now called Utes) could procure fat trout in spring.

This rich, anomalous ecosystem attracted outsiders. In 1849 a Euro-

American settler population—the Latter-day Saints, or Mormons—began colonizing Utah Valley. These farmers became fish-eaters too as they struggled at first to establish an agrarian economy. Here at the shoreline natives and newcomers coexisted edgily for one generation. Under the guidance of their prophet Brigham Young, the Saints aspired to redeem their "red brethren," the "Lamanites." In practice, hostility supplanted harmony. Settlers and Indians clashed repeatedly at the mouth of the Provo (Timpanogos) River, the best fishing site in the valley. Ultimately, with the federal government's blessing, the Mormons forced the starving remnants of the Timpanogos to move to a distant reservation. Without the Lake People, the lake stopped being the Center Place. Nonetheless, Utah Lake remained significant to the second generation of settlers as an economic and recreational resource. The presence of water still set the valley apart.

In the twentieth century, things changed. Gradually Utah Lake was marginalized. As a result of local overuse and state mismanagement, the trout fishery degenerated into a carp pond. Then, during World War II, the federal government built a colossal steel mill on the lakeshore. The water acquired a reputation—not undeserved—for being polluted. As local recreationists looked elsewhere for fishing, boating, and swimming, Utah Lake lost its centrality. By the end of the century it was perceived as just one element of the valley rather than its essence; Utah's eponymous lake had symbolically shrunk. In 1996, in conjunction with the state centennial, a local newspaper ran the headline "Timpanogos Has Always Dominated Utah Valley." The accompanying story had nothing to do with a lake or a river. It was all about a mountain.

Mount Timpanogos, a limestone massif in the Wasatch Range, is by far the most-loved, most-hiked, most-photographed, most-talked-about mountain in contemporary Utah. Its attractions include the Mount Timpanogos Wilderness Area, the Timpanogos Cave National Monument, and the Sundance Resort, built by movie star Robert Redford. More than a million people (and counting) live within twenty miles of this recreational magnet. Here along the Wasatch

Front, Utah's main population corridor, the overwhelming majority of residents are Mormons—descendents of the pioneers. In conversation, locals refer to the mountain by its endearing diminutive, "Timp."

The bonds of affection are strongest in Utah Valley—otherwise known as the Provo-Orem metropolitan area—where the mountain's name graces a hospital, three public schools, and a Mormon temple. The profile of the massif adorns the masthead of Provo's newspaper, whose publisher sponsors a popular summer contest: guess when the last winter snow will be visible on "Timp." Oil paintings of "Timp" abound in local offices and foyers; picture windows face north toward the rock face. Climbing to the 11,750-foot summit is a local rite of passage—something to do before you grow old. Grandparents entertain their progeny with "Indian stories" about the landform.

The most widespread tale, the Legend of Timpanogos, concerns the lover's leap of an Indian princess. Tour guides at Timpanogos Cave have repeated this yarn for decades. In the 1930s a Provo composer wrote an opera based on the suicide legend; more recently a local ballet troupe adapted it for the stage. Influenced by the story, many valley residents—children in particular—visualize the outline of a dead or sleeping maiden on the crest of the mountain.

People see what they want to see. But vision, like desire, changes over time. In the mid-nineteenth century people didn't see the landmark called "Timp" because it didn't yet exist. Mount Timpanogos didn't even appear as a named feature on maps. To settlers it was just another long ridge in "the mountains," which even in the aggregate didn't merit recognition as Utah Valley's outstanding natural feature. That distinction belonged to the lake.

What caused a mountainous *space* to become the mountain-*place* called "Timp"? Remarkably, it was a promotional campaign. In the 1910s and 1920s, boosters from Brigham Young University (BYU) and its home city, Provo, desired their own celebrated mountain. To realize this goal, they organized mass community hikes to what federal surveyors had determined—mistakenly, it turns out—to be the

Photorealistic aerial view of the southern Wasatch Front: Utah Valley and Utah Lake in the foreground, Salt Lake Valley and Great Salt Lake in the background. (Courtesy of Dr. William A. Bowen, California Geographical Survey, http://geogdata.csun.edu)

highest point in the Wasatch. Promoters pushed a "Wonder Mountain." The point man, BYU athletics director Eugene "Timpanogos" Roberts, wrote and disseminated the original fake Indian legend. Intuitively he understood a geographic principle: great landmarks are storied landmarks. Since Mount Timpanogos possessed no usable past, boosters invented one. Ultimately they failed to turn their legendary mountain into a national landmark, but they succeeded in making a local one. The booster project worked so well as to be forgotten.

In local collective memory, legendary Indians in the rocky highlands replaced historical Utes in the watery lowlands. Notwithstanding the Mormon fixation on pioneer history, the story of Provo's colonization—a violent, intimate chronicle of Mormon-Ute relations—fell to the margins of consciousness by the 1910s, when the Legend of Timpanogos began to circulate. As a memory site, Mount Timpanogos encouraged forgetting. According to the stories told by hikers, the unnamed Indians of olden days were mountain people, too.

In short, the sense of place surrounding "Timp" concealed a double displacement—the literal displacement of the Timpanogos Utes, and the symbolic displacement of their lake. To be understood, this split-level history must be viewed from the bottom as well the top.

The same large-scale historical forces that strengthened one landmark weakened the other. Utah Lake was an emblem of the Aquarian Age—a time when people necessarily developed intimate relationships with their local water resources. Before the twentieth century, fording a stream, carrying water from a well, bathing in a mineral spring, collecting ice were everyday American experiences. In the subsequent Hydraulic Age, water use went indoors even as water knowledge went underground. Today only technocrats and technicians develop familiarity with waterworks. For most residents, it's enough to know that potable water arrives through one set of invisible pipes, and wastewater leaves through another. Visual and recreational contact with faraway nature has largely replaced tactile and workaday contact with nearby nature. In this respect, "Timp" symbolizes our time.[1]

"Timp" is a *landmark*—a legible feature of the landscape where meaning is concentrated. Landmarks come in different shapes and sizes. They can be fabricated (like the tallest skyscraper in the city) or biological (like the oldest tree in the neighborhood) or geomorphic (like the biggest boulder in the park). We must resist the temptation to employ a simpler, two-part schema, the man-made versus the natural; trees can be planted, and boulders can be moved.[2]

The topography of Earth is a hybrid creation. Since ancient times, humans have produced both deliberate and accidental landmarks; burial mounds and shell mounds represent each type, respectively. More often, humans have *enhanced* "natural landmarks" with modifications. Inscription Rock (or El Morro)—a sandstone butte beside a historic thoroughfare in New Mexico—is both a cultural and a physical landmark. Over the centuries, hundreds of wayfarers have carved names and symbols on its walls. Metaphorically, all landmarks bear human inscriptions. Even unmodified terrestrial landmarks like "Timp" are hybrid creations in that they wouldn't exist without the human imagination.[3]

Environmental perception is more concrete than image and representation. Out in the world, as within our bodies, mental causes can produce physical effects. Once people start or stop imagining a landform as a landmark, that landform will receive more or less intensive use. A designated landmark like Mount Rainier—a national park—attracts tourists who expect roads and trails and facilities, all of which leave footprints. Seeing has consequences: "natural landmarks" equate to human marks on the land.

In other words, a perceptual landscape overlaps the physical one. These layers of reality are not glued together in smooth and permanent contiguity; instead, they are fastened together at points. Landmarks are these fastening-points. We use them for orientation. They are the icons of our mental maps. Landmarks fall within a certain size range: big enough that humans can see them, not so big that humans cannot visualize them. Pikes Peak is a landmark; the Rockies, of which it is part, are not. Not everyone "sees" the obvious peak, however. Children are far more aware of the world at their feet than of the world above their heads. From the perspective of adults, children orient themselves strangely. They use smaller, more intimate landmarks. Likewise, old-timers see differently from newcomers. There are as many layers of landscape perception as there are people. Each of these layers has a few unique fastening-points. But major landmarks anchor the perceptions of multiple people—and sometimes of multiple groups of people. These communities of perception may be as small as a family or as large as a nation.[4]

Mount Timpanogos anchors several sizable communities of perception (for example, the users of Sundance, the students at BYU) and also symbolizes one of them. For the permanent residents of the

Mount Timpanogos and related billboard as seen from I-15 in Orem, Utah, 2005. (Author's photo)

Provo-Orem metropolitan area, the mountain is an emblem. A specific sense of place supports a general sense of home. Most cities possess at least one affiliated landmark—something that appears on logos and souvenirs. Thanks to media exposure, certain urban emblems have earned recognition far beyond their locale. Everyone knows that the Golden Gate Bridge stands for San Francisco and the Gateway Arch for St. Louis. From 1973 to 2001 the Twin Towers of the World Trade Center functioned as a landmark for New Yorkers. Mount Timpanogos is Provo's skyscraper.

Civic polities aren't the only communities that create general "place identities" out of specific "place attachments." Ethnic and religious groups sustain landmarks even as the landmarks help sustain those groups. The Pyramid Lake Paiutes of Nevada see themselves reflected in Pyramid Lake and recognize their mother deity in the form of a rock on the eastern shore. The Mormon temple in downtown Salt Lake City—a granite edifice from which the street grid radiates—symbolizes The Church of Jesus Christ of Latter-day Saints (LDS) for its members worldwide.[5]

For good measure, I'll use a negative example. According to my usage, the Grand Canyon is *not* a landmark. Tourists come here to experience *dis*orientation—to feel small and out of place. Like the ocean, the canyon isn't legible as a discrete topographical feature. The eye doesn't focus on one thing; the canyon is a vast overlapping series of scenes. While Grand Canyon National Park is a place, the canyon itself is a space. Only rangers and guides—those exceptional people who know the park not as tourists but as residents—see an array of landmarks when they gaze from the South Rim. The original concessionaire at the park recognized the need for visual anchors. In the early 1900s the Fred Harvey Company built a series of eye-catching stone buildings on the edge of the abyss.[6]

The tourism industry is responsible for creating and maintaining innumerable landmarks. Consider the famous 17-Mile Drive along the Pacific coast near Monterey, California. The highlight of the drive, the only private toll road west of the Mississippi, is the "Lone Cypress." This photogenic tree is the logo and registered trademark of the Pebble Beach Corporation. Although the scenic drive leads past the landmark tree, the tree wouldn't be a landmark without the road. Thanks to the well-publicized work of licensed photographers, auto tourists come prepared to see the cypress long before it comes into view. They overlook other gnarled trees on other rocky outcroppings along the coast of California. Only because of historical contingency—the Pacific Improvement Company, a subsidiary of the Southern Pacific, wanted a scenic drive to complement its resort hotel (and eventual golf course) at Monterey—did this tree become *the* tree.[7]

Not every tree and rock can be a landmark; that would defeat the purpose. Landmarks are supposed to be outstanding. The question is *why* do they stand out? Why do certain landforms become totems while most do not? To some extent, geology and sociobiology determine the selection. Humans are far more ocular than most other creatures; furthermore, certain shapes and color combinations naturally excite the human imagination. Caves (dark recesses) and mountains (bright prominences) are primordial symbols. And of the various types of mountains, volcanoes offer the best visual and imaginative material for landmarks. Lone symmetrical cones demand ocular attention. The heightened sense of place around Mount Hood and Mount Shasta seems easily explicable: these mountains have no visual competition. By contrast, numerous high peaks in the stunning Wasatch Range adjoin Mount Timpanogos. Yet somehow only this massif—not nearby Lone Peak, Cascade Peak, or Mount Nebo—has become a totem. Here, as with most places, historical contingency has far more explanatory power than environmental determinism. "Timp" came to light in a unique historical moment in the early twentieth century. That is a different matter from saying that people arbitrarily fixated on Mount Timpanogos. My point is that landmarks are contingent and timebound. Few are inevitable; fewer are timeless.[8]

Trees die, buildings deteriorate: landmarks come and go like other mortal things. Compared to a human lifespan, a mountain will last forever; but a mountain landmark's community of perception will sooner or later disappear, or relocate, or simply change. As the primary mode of long-distance travel shifted from animals to railroads, and from railroads to automobiles, whole sequences of roadside landmarks became unfastened. In certain cases, obsolescent travelers' landmarks lost their physical as well as their perceptual existence. Utah's Castle Gate once consisted of two pillars on either side of the canyon of the Price River. For late nineteenth-century railroad tourists, this "natural wonder" marked the entrance/exit to Utah. By 1966 the rock formation had become so unimportant that the Utah Department of Transportation razed one side of it to make room for a wider highway.[9]

With assistance, some landmarks outlast their "natural" lifespan. In 1983, when the 3,600-square-foot lighted CITGO sign above Boston's Kenmore Square was scheduled for dismantling, Bostonians rose in defense of the deteriorating fixture. In the years since 1965, when it was first lit, the neon display transcended its intended community of perception and became a beloved landmark for students at Boston University and fans at Fenway Park. Under pressure from citizen groups and the Boston Landmarks Commission, the CITGO Petroleum Corporation agreed to pay for refurbishment and continuing maintenance. To this day, locals repeat the tongue-in-cheek saying "London has Big Ben; Paris has the Eiffel Tower. Boston has the CITGO sign."

Ironically, the electric sign has outlasted New England's original elevated landmark, the Old Man of the Mountain. Starting in the 1820s, this rock formation high above Franconia Notch, New Hampshire, earned fame for its likeness to the profile of a human head. In 1945 New Hampshire officially adopted the Old Man as its emblem. The rock face appeared on letterheads, road signs, license plates, and eventually the state's commemorative quarter. All the while, the megalith was developing structural cracks. Aware of the problem, the state paid for a reinforcement project in 1958. To firm up the granite face, workers applied bolts, cables, and epoxy (all invisible to sightseers below). Even so, in May 2003 the inevitable happened: the Old Man collapsed. People in New Hampshire responded with disbelief and grief, as if a member of the family had died.

Mount Timpanogos is bigger and stronger; it won't fall down. Neither can it be dismantled or blown up. But metaphorically, "Timp"—like all "natural" landmarks—requires its own maintenance, its own cable support. It needs our attention.

⁝⁝⁝ The creation of "Timp" was one small part of two vast, interrelated geographic projects: the mapping of the nation and the shaping of the nation's landscape. Respectively, these projects entailed the representation of terrain as bounded, gridded space and the filling of that space with mappable places—not just cities and roads and properties but things like mountain summits with official names and elevations.

The colonizers of the United States—both settlers and their government allies—wielded geographic power as an extension of military and economic power. The natural landmarks they claimed and mapped and named (or *re*named) manifested that power.[10]

Inescapably, the making of the National Map brought about the unmaking of indigenous geographies. In many cases, native landmarks have been omitted from the map if not literally erased from the scene. For example, Bonneville Dam, The Dalles Dam, and Grand Coulee Dam—the defining features of the modern Columbia River—replaced landmark fishing sites: the Cascades, Celilo Falls, and Kettle Falls. A historical cartographer could create an alternative map of the United States composed entirely of lost places and phantom place-names.[11]

In certain cases Native Americans have contested the destruction or reinscription of old landmarks or protested the creation of new ones. Outside their government-delineated tribal lands, Indian peoples have for the most part been stymied in their campaigns against the desecration or destruction of landmarks. In relation to sacred geography, the American Indian Religious Freedom Act (1978) has proven to be a weak legal instrument. This weakness is most apparent on privately owned land. In the late 1990s, for instance, a gravel company bulldozed away portions of Woodruff Butte, or *Tsimontukwi,* a Hopi pilgrimage site near Holbrook, Arizona. Seen through the property owner's eyes, the butte was merely one of numerous small cinder cones remarkable only for its high-density, low-porosity aggregate ideal for resurfacing I-40. "I didn't realize I was destroying anything but a big ugly pile of rocks out in the big ugly middle of nowhere," he said.[12]

The Black Hills region of Wyoming–South Dakota offers two instructive examples of contested landmarks on public land. Bear Lodge, better known as Devils Tower, has been a symbol for various native peoples as long as the surrounding country has been peopled. (In Steven Spielberg's *Close Encounters of the Third Kind,* even space aliens use the tower as a landmark.) This quarter-mile-high monolith—the relic of a volcanic plume—rises from the earth like a charcoal skyscraper. Because of its "scientific interest" it became America's first national monument in 1906. More recently the tower has become a rock climbers' mecca. In the 1990s climbers and Indians clashed in court over the meaning of the site. One group saw a recreational landmark; the other saw a spiritual landmark.

Similarly, nearby Mount Rushmore has come to mean different things to different peoples. To most tourists—over 2 million per year—the megalith stands for the dignity of the nation. The Park Service has managed the site as a national memorial since 1933, even before sculptor Gutzon Borglum completed his dream project. Later, in the tumultuous 1970s, the memorial attracted protests by the American Indian Movement. The site has been a point of contention ever since. To native activists, Borglum's great white heads represent the conquest of the continent and, more specifically, the theft of the Black Hills from the Lakotas.

Mount Rushmore is potent because it functions simultaneously as a landmark, a symbol, and a mnemonic. It reinforces a framework of collective memory: *great individuals—especially white male leaders, and most especially presidents—have advanced the destiny of America.* More obvious "memory sites" such as history museums and historical markers fill in that scaffolding with details from the past. Whereas museums collect memorabilia for display in exogenous spaces, markers derive their power from endogenous places: "Someone important was born *here* in this house" or "Many people died *here* at this site." The United States is full of such commemorative signs—but not nearly as full as it could be. In the same way that societies don't turn every feature of the Earth into landmarks, they don't turn every aspect of the past into memories. For example, the United States commemorates far more Civil War battlefields than Indian massacre sites.

Collective memory involves forgetting as much as remembering. Societies, like individuals, forget passively when they make no effort to remember or when their attention gets diverted. Less often, societies choose to forget. They erase or suppress historical knowledge considered discomforting or dangerous. Hierarchical churches and totalitarian states excel at memory suppression. A combination of passive and active forgetting explains the fading of the Lake Utes in the collective memory of the second-generation Mormon residents of Utah Valley. The LDS Church and its early official historians—and later folk historians—mythologized Utah's pioneer period. Discordant pieces of the past were discarded incidentally or buried deliberately. The Indianness of Mount Timpanogos resulted from the separate implantation of false memories: *the Indians of Utah Valley were mountain worshipers who lived here sometime in the distant past before the Mormon pioneers planted a stake in a desert wilderness.* "Timp" is a special kind of memory site—a monument to forgetfulness.[13]

I don't mean to be overly negative. Certainly it is good for people to love their home topography. We live in an increasingly "placeless" world in which landscapes are fungible. Like so many other metropolitan areas, the built environment of Provo-Orem has increasingly come to look like "Anywhere, U.S.A."—the familiar matrix of freeways, storage units, strip malls, and chain stores. In this context, the distinctive sense of place constructed and maintained around "Timp" is beneficent. However, beneficent is different from innocent. In settler nations such as the United States, belonging to place is a privilege that comes with possession.[14]

To my knowledge, Utah Indians have not contested the Indianness of "Timp"; to the contrary, certain Utes have recently cooperated in it. That is one irony. Another is that the LDS Church, the main architect of collective memory in Utah, made this book—this countermemorial—possible thanks to its assiduous preservation of archival sources.[15]

::: Everyone engages in place-making and memory-making. The American history offered in the following pages has implications for all nations founded by colonial settler societies. Viewed in national context, "Timp" can be seen as a generic Euro-American settlers' landmark as well as a distinctively Mormon creation. A place, like a person, cannot be understood by itself. A place has no meaning except in relation to other places. That is the reason why much of this book, whose starting point is Utah, looks at landmarks elsewhere, why its concern with local history is framed larger.[16]

By being typical and exceptional at the same time, Utah offers a valuable perspective on the United States. The religious element is of course distinctive, yet the main story of Utah's formation—settlers colonizing Indian land, organizing a territory, dispossessing natives, and achieving statehood—could not be more American. Even so, the Great Basin, the Mormons' region of settlement, remains outside the purview of mainstream American history. This relationship is best explained by geographic metaphors. The Great Basin is that large piece of North America that has no outlet to the sea. Its runoff flows inward, where it pools and evaporates. So it is with Utah history. Because of the LDS stronghold in Utah, and because of the LDS emphasis on history, the state sustains a steady flow of scholarship. However, the water lacks proper turbidity. It's unnaturally pure because so many historians have filtered out non-Mormons and native peoples. Because of provincialism, scholars of Utah rarely push beyond the rim of their basin. They write for an audience of Mormons. History pools at their feet; their stream never reaches the ocean. Meanwhile, in the seaboard cities where opinion generally takes shape, most U.S. historians ignore Utah history *and* Mormon history. In their coast-to-coast historical surveys, scholars may occasionally glance down, may even notice a curious patch of blue—an inland sea of history. Yet whether through prejudice or indifference, they rarely descend for a closer look. They should. The Great Basin is the perfect place to be disorientated and reoriented.[17]

As your guide, I offer an insider-outsider perspective. Ironically, doing local history forced me to leave my home state, Utah. In order to write a biography of a local mountain, I had to learn its remote genealogy; I had to become familiar with precedent landmarks and the people who maintained them. By tracing the lineage of "Timp," I came to a new understanding of my place in the world—not only as an expatriate Utahn but also as an American.

This book revisits the terrain of the past in a sequence of three parallel narratives. Each begins long ago (late eighteenth or early nineteenth century) and continues to the near present. Part I is bioregional history; the setting is the eastern Great Basin—what is now called the Wasatch Front. Here I reconstruct the water-based geography of what used to be called "Utah Lake Valley" and illustrate the former centrality of Utah Lake and its fish to indigenous peoples. I narrate the great American story of the colonization of the Great Basin by the Latter-day Saints under Brigham Young, a migration that had devastating consequences for the Lake Utes. Then I outline the gradual process by which Utah Lake became diluted as a fishery, a resort, and a symbol.

Next I have divided the cultural geomorphology of Mount Timpanogos—Utah Lake's foil—into complementary halves. Part II resembles local history; the main setting is Provo, Utah. After providing background on Mormons and mountains, I explore why and how people from one particular city affiliated themselves with one particular mountain in the early twentieth century. My cast of characters includes surveyors and painters and particularly hikers; the protagonist is Eugene Roberts, director of athletics at BYU in the 1910s and 1920s, who promoted "Timp" through a mass annual hike. I then discuss the enduring legacy of Roberts' promotional project in the late twentieth century.[18]

Part III moves away from the linear and the local. It might be described as *extra*local history. Here I move back and forth in time and space to show how Roberts and his collaborators marked "Timp" with Indianness. Euro-Americans have often expressed their desire to feel native by "playing Indian." This cultural tradition has a geographic component. I discuss numerous U.S. landmarks—some familiar, others forgotten—that have been popularly associated with Native Americans. Many of these places functioned as prototypes for Mount Timpanogos. In this discussion, collective bodies—"American culture" and "Mormon culture"—serve as the chief actors. Formerly divergent, these two cultures converged significantly, though never fully, in the twentieth century. Indians also reappear here—sometimes as actual people but more often as cultural constructions or as ghosts. I underscore how the place-stories and storied places created by colonizers are persistently haunted by the colonized.[19]

In the end, this book is about understanding home. It shows how settlers gave meaning to the lands they settled, and how their progeny developed an attachment to place—in other words, how nonnatives became neonatives.[20] Utah offers a powerful case study because only here can we find a colonial U.S. population that speaks of having a "homeland" in the Native American sense—an endemic spiritual geography. They call it Zion. That the establishment of the Mormon homeland in Utah occurred in tandem with the diminishment of native peoples and places may be discomforting enough. But I must prod further. Mormonism, a religion indigenous to the United States, originally embraced American Indians as spiritual kin, or "Lamanites." Metaphysically and geographically, this religion reserved a privileged place for natives. But prophecies, dreams, and intentions never quite become realities. In high relief, Utah history exposes an unsettling incongruity of U.S. history: the senses of place that make present-day Americans feel at home would not exist without past displacements.

Wherever we live, we live among landmarks—topographic relics from the human past. This book will, I hope, help all of us to survey our homes with new eyes. This matters. What we see affects what we do. The mountains and valleys of the American West have been altered by visions. The great westerner Wallace Stegner wished that his home region might someday have "a society to match its scenery."[21] From my vantage point, I see the reverse. Our scenery has always matched our society—for better and for worse.

I

Liquid Antecedents

Ute Genesis, Mormon Exodus

Long before Mount Timpanogos had its name—or its "Indian" legend—the Timpanogos people lived by Utah Lake and fished from its waters. Compared to the rest of the Great Basin, the homeland of the Fish-Eaters was munificent. Its reputation spread to New Mexico even before 1776, the year that traveling Franciscans put the place on the map. Following this *entrada,* the Lake People became more involved in the Spanish colonial trade system. In exchange for pelts and slaves, they acquired horses. The Timpanogos leader Walkara rode this way of life to fame and wealth and power. This equestrian pioneer ventured as far as the Pacific and the Plains. At spawning time, however, Walkara knew to return to the lake. Even after the horse revolution, this was the place.

In 1847 an exotic group of pioneers began to coalesce in the Great Basin. Led by Brigham Young, these religious refugees came in search of a home. Young wanted a "place apart" where his faction of The Church of Jesus Christ of Latter-day Saints could be made into a people. Strategically, he settled for the next-best place, Salt Lake Valley, located immediately to the north. The Mormon vanguard meant to get acclimated before attempting a full-scale colonization of the Basin, moving next to Utah Lake. In time, Young would "gather" all the Saints—and with them various diseases unfamiliar to Utes. Unwittingly as well as deliberately, the Salt Lake settlers set the stage for a new revolution.

::: The Great Basin, one of North America's most arid regions, is marked by lakes and the absence of lakes. Centered on Nevada, the Basin also includes half of Utah, large pieces of California and Oregon, and bits of Idaho and Wyoming. The southern and northern boundaries are difficult to see with the naked eye, but the western and eastern boundaries—the Sierra Nevada and the Wasatch Range—stand out majestically. The Basin is everything between. This is the interior space of the inland West, a closed system cut off from the drainages of the Columbia and the Colorado. "In this strange region all nature seems to be reversed," wrote a nineteenth-century observer.[1] Many streams go parch in midcourse. The larger, more persevering streams push on to pseudoseas. Pulled by gravity, they descend to their lowest reachable points, or sinks. In some places, like Badwater, Death Valley, the sink lies below sea level. After a storm a salt-encrusted sink may transform into a lagoon, only to revert in the next warm spell. A few wet spots, such as the Great Salt Lake and Pyramid Lake, are nonephemeral. "Permanent" is not quite right, since the shape of these water bodies changes by year and by season. No verdure adorns the brackish, gnat-infested shores. The deathly beautiful lakes of the Great Basin attract less attention than the truly dead ones, called playas. Racers go to the Bonneville Salt Flats of the Great Salt Lake Desert to set land speed records; this flat, stark landscape also lures cinematographers. The annual neohippie festival called Burning Man brings tens of thousands to the Black Rock Desert of Nevada—a dried mudflat, a geomemory of a departed lake.

The land hasn't always been like this. In the wetter, cooler Pleistocene epoch, the Great Basin had literal *playas*—beaches—all around. Sinks filled up, spilled over; coalescence resulted in twin lakes on the scale of the modern Great Lakes. In the west, Lake Lahontan covered 8,700 square miles in the flats beyond present-day Reno. Lahontan's eastern counterpart, Lake Bonneville, topped out at 20,000 square miles with a maximum depth of 1,200 feet. After the ancient Bear River changed its course and became a tributary, Lake Bonneville tried to grow even bigger. Like a squid, it sent tentacles in every direction; one of these pushed its way through a natural levee at Red Rock Pass in southeastern Idaho. Here, about 14,500 years ago, occurred one of the notable floods in Earth's history; in one event, Bonneville lost about one quarter of its surface area. The postdiluvian lake stabilized at the "Provo Level"—still deep enough to submerge Provo and every other modern city on the Wasatch Front. Over the next few thousand years the climate changed, and Bonneville receded, leaving behind residual lakes and one giant bathtub ring called the Provo Bench. It is part of the larger Bonneville Bench—a vertical zone of ancient lake terraces that provides the only transition from the smooth valleys to the steep mountains.

Even today there is a mirrored similarity between the Lahontan and the Bonneville drainage systems. On the Nevada side, an upland freshwater lake (Tahoe) discharges into a river (the Truckee) that descends to the desert, where it empties into a salty inland sea (Pyramid Lake). Likewise, on the Utah side, the deep mountain Bear Lake contributes inflow to the Great Salt Lake. But the modern Bonneville system possesses one striking difference—Utah Lake. This is the one unsalted lake in the lowlands of the Great Basin. Fur traders called it Sweetwater Lake. In a desert characterized as much by salinity as by aridity, Utah Lake remains (relatively) fresh and constant. It benefits from inflow and outflow. After accepting snowmelt from the high country, the lake functions as a catchment basin or natural reservoir for the Great Salt Lake, which sits at a slightly lower elevation.

The land immediately surrounding Utah Lake is now known as Utah Valley. In this case the word "valley" is somewhat misleading, suggesting as it does a fluvial depression between two stretches of high ground. Utah Valley looks more like an enclosure. Immediately to the east of this downfaulted basin—what geologists call a graben or rift valley—the Wasatch Range makes a stupendous vertical ascent of 6,000–7,000 feet. On the western side of the graben, discontinuous hills obstruct the view of the "West Desert" and the Great Salt Lake (to the north). Without these minor uplifts, Utah Valley would look more like the terrain at Boulder, Colorado—a flatland against the peaks. But the western hills are sufficiently large to complete the sense of containment. The enclosed space is crescent-shaped. From tip to tip it runs about forty-five miles; across the middle it measures twelve miles. The base elevation is 4,500 feet above sea level. The west-central section of the crescent is submerged by the lake, which has an area of roughly 150 square miles. The water is shallow, rarely more than 10 feet deep. Two important rivers, the Provo and the Spanish Fork, end their journeys here. Several local streams also discharge their flows. Historically, springs and marshes ringed the lake, providing habitat for migratory birds and wetland mammals. Within the lake, native fish—suckers, chubs, and cutthroat trout—made the water quake. No other area of the Great Basin boasted such a variety of aquatic resources.

It was here in 1844 that the Great Basin received its name. Rumors of a landlocked drainage system had circulated for decades, but few explorers accepted the possibility; the idea seemed "Asiatic," not American. People kept looking for the river that should have been there, some hidden tributary of the Columbia, some long arm of San Francisco Bay. On maps, this mythical river went by the name "Buenaventura" or "Multnomah." Not until John C. Frémont circumambulated the inland West on his Second Expedition were these geographical fantasies put to rest. Returning to his starting point, Utah Lake, on 25 May 1844, Frémont completed his "circuit" and pronounced the existence of a "rare and singular feature—that of the Great interior Basin."[2]

A later explorer, James Simpson, complained that Frémont's terminology was "erroneous." Something called a basin, Simpson wrote, "must, as a whole, present a generally concave surface." He had a point: the Great Basin looks more like a washboard than a sink. A succession of parallel faults between the Sierra Nevada and the Wasatch has created a stunningly repetitive topography of horsts (up-faulted mountains) and grabens (down-faulted valleys). "While the so-called Great Basin is in some small degree a basin of lakes and streams," Simpson continued, "it is pre-eminently a basin of mountains and valleys."[3] No comparable region of the Earth contains more mountain ranges. Nevada alone is home to 314 ranges, all of which trend north-south. Many exceed 10,000 feet in elevation. Just as the Sierra Nevada casts a rain shadow over an entire region, each horst steals moisture from winter Pacific storms away from the next graben to the east. Geologically, the Great Basin belongs to the larger "Basin and Range Province" that stretches from upper Mexico to Oregon. In the southern part of the Great Basin, the ranges are comparatively low, and the vegetation aligns with two "hot deserts"—the Mojave and the Colorado. But the better part of the Basin in Nevada and Utah has its own flora, its own ecozone. Here, in the Great Basin Desert, high-elevation plants have adapted to extreme seasonal fluctuations in temperature. The emblematic plants of this "cold desert" are specimens of toughness: sagebrush, shadscale, juniper, bristlecone.

The native inhabitants of the Basin adapted to this environment of extremes. When the first Europeans arrived, the Great Basin was peopled almost exclusively by members of one linguistic group, the Numa. The Numic language is a branch of the Uto-Aztecan family spoken by peoples from the American Southwest to central Mexico. Numic divides into three groups—Western, Central, and Southern— each of which once included numerous dialects. According to one prominent theory, Numic-speaking peoples migrated northeast from the Death Valley region roughly one millennium ago. Arriving in the eastern Great Basin around 1200, they replaced, displaced, or absorbed the ancient people now called the Fremont Culture. The invaders were the ancestors of today's Utes and Paiutes (Southern Numic speakers) as well as today's Shoshones (Central Numic speakers). Before the introduction of the horse, all the Numa practiced similar economies and traditions. This fact is remarkable: similarities in language do not always align with similarities in culture, nor do shared environments necessarily produce shared cultures. Historically, the Great Basin was one of those rare regions where language, culture, and environment reinforced one another. For this reason, historical anthropologists and archaeologists use the term "Great Basin culture area."[4]

By all four definitions—hydrographic, physiographic, floristic, cultural—Utah Valley belongs to the Great Basin. However, its location at the edge of the Basin made it unusually attractive to the Numa and to American settlers alike. The Basin is not uniform. As Major Frémont wrote, "It is called a *desert*, and, from what I saw of it, sterility may be its prominent characteristic; but where there is so much water, there must be some *oasis*."[5] And indeed there are several oases scattered in the middle (for example, the Ruby Marshes) and two broad oasis zones bordering the Wasatch Range and the Sierra Nevada. This hydrography explains the placement of Salt Lake City–Provo and Reno–Carson City. Even before American settlers arrived, these mountain-front oasis zones sustained relatively large populations; the Numa developed fishing cultures at Pyramid and Utah Lakes. In time, outsiders coveted these well-watered places—or just the water. The Great Basin culture area's most densely populated locale, the valley of Owens Lake, was deprived of its water in the early twentieth century, when Los Angeles breached the Great Basin with giant suction tubes. Over several decades in the same century, federal funding enabled Salt Lake City to engineer the converse, the importation of Colorado River water to supplement its existing oasis.

In short, the Great Basin proved to be permeable at its moist edges—for people as well as for water. Because of its position, Utah Valley was a desirable access point for Indians and Europeans.

⁝⁝⁝ In 1776 officials in New Spain authorized an expedition to find an overland route from Santa Fe, New Mexico, to Monterey, California. Even as the king of England witnessed the erosion of British America, the king of Spain worked to shore up the margins of his American empire. The Spanish entrusted the expedition to two friars, Francisco Atanasio Domínguez and Francisco Silvestre Vélez de Escalante, who also wanted new souls to save. More than most people, the colonial Spanish conflated spiritual and material gain. Since the sixteenth century, quixotic Spaniards had looked for the Seven Cities of Gold on the Southern Plains. This mythical region came to be known as Quivira. West of Quivira and north of New Mexico lay another mythical province, the Land of Teguayo. Supposedly the ancestors of the Aztecs emerged from caverns in this prosperous land beside a great lake called Teguayo or Copala. Rumor had it that the inhabitants of Lake Copala walked around with golden jewelry on their wrists and arms and ears. To the extent that this geographical fantasy had any basis in reality, Copala referred to Utah Lake or the Great Salt Lake. Eventually the Spaniards devised a general name for the owners of this country: the Yutas.[6]

Historically, all Southern Numic speakers referred to themselves as *Nuche,* "The People." However, there was no metasociety to match this meta-identity—no kingdom or nation or confederation. In the protohistoric period, individual Utes had no fixed identity beyond the large-scale speech community and the small-scale family cluster or band. A cluster might be as small as one married couple, their children, and some relatives from both sides. Related bands who practiced the same subsistence strategy in the same locale could be identified by geographic "food names." For example, Numa living in drier areas referred to the various Nuche bands of Utah Lake as "Lake People" *(Pawanutch)* or "Fish-Eaters" *(Tumpanawach).* The Fish-Eaters did not constitute a tribe, however; identity was flexible. Over a lifetime an individual could pass from one band to another, from one place to another, from one subsistence to another, from one name to another, even from one language to another. Southern Numic speakers (Nuche) sometimes crossed over to bands of Central Numic speakers (Neme). The Fish-Eaters of Utah Valley referred to Neme bands collectively as *Kumantsi* (the source of the name "Comanche"), meaning "Left-Handed Ones." The term implied relatedness: left-handed people, though different from right-handed ones, still belonged with The People. Thinking historically, it is useful to imagine a Numic continuum on which boundaries were drawn, erased, redrawn, and eventually made permanent. Until the U.S. government mandated tribal rolls, individuals could move across these boundaries with relative ease.[7]

Lake People/Fish-Eaters clustered along the streams that fed into Utah Lake. The most important fishing and wintering site was the mouth of the Provo River. The bands that used this location as their home base called themselves *Timpanogos,* referring to the "rocky river" in which they fished. Expert fishers, the Timpanogos Nuche used tools of harvest such as woven squawbush nets, willow weirs, spears, and bows. At spawning time in spring, the Timpanogos clubbed masses of fish to death, shot them with arrows, trapped them in weirs, or wrestled them out with bare hands. The fish could be eaten raw, cooked, or dried. Sacks of dried fish were buried for storage. Anthropologists estimate that fish accounted for 30 percent of the Timpanogos diet—twice as much as for the Utes of western Colorado.[8]

Even so, a lot of calories had to come from other sources. Spring was a fleeting season of abundance. In the summer the Timpanogos retreated to the mountains to gather serviceberries and elderberries. In the late summer and fall some of the men stayed in the high country to hunt big game while others returned to the valley to harvest seeds as well as crickets and locusts, using fire to corral the protein-rich insects. The hunters returned to the lake for the fall migration of birds. Winter brought the lean days. For long stretches, the Timpanogos had to get by with dried fish reserves, roots and bulbs, and "desert fruit-cake"—a power bar made of berries, ground insects, and animal fat.

Until the early 1800s Utah Lake and Salt Lake Valleys supported small herds of "Western bison," a smaller form of the Plains bison. Unfortunately, this valuable source of food and raiment fell victim to a double-punch of overhunting and severe weather. The son of one of Utah Valley's prominent Mormon settlers remembered a story told in the 1850s by Sowiette, leader of an equestrian Nuche band: "He said one time when he was a young man, (about forty years previously,) the buffalo and deer were as thick as the Mormons' cattle, sweeping his hand in that direction [toward Utah Lake], but that a deep snow fell as deep as to the ceiling, pointing to the ceiling eight feet high, which killed them all off. The indians camped that winter at the lake border, and by cutting holes thru the ice cought fish, which added to the scant provisions and tided them over the 'cold and cruel winter.'"⁹

Because of its stable fish resource, Utah Valley was the most densely populated place in the eastern Great Basin. The valley supported several (the exact number is unknown) semipermanent villages composed of wickiups made of bulrush and willow. At critical moments in the food calendar, especially winter and late spring, the Timpanogos (Provo) River hosted hundreds of people. Like all major encampments, this one had multiple men of authority—a leader for war, a leader for diplomacy, and at least one to direct subsistence activities like fishing. Every April or May, at spawning time, the riverside village hosted various bands of Nuche from other regions. The gathered peoples (perhaps 1,000 in number) performed the Bear Dance, a sacred springtime festival. This was also a time for marriage and other forms of social reorganization. The family-cluster system permitted countless permutations. The feast-or-famine environment of the Great Basin encouraged social flexibility.¹⁰

Despite its central importance, Utah Lake marked the outer edge of the vast territory inhabited by Nuche. Speakers of Southern Numic could be found as far south as the Colorado River and as far east as the Front Range. People in different subregions experienced different histories. Anthropologists and historians draw a time-bound distinction between the bands in the east (in present-day Colorado) and the bands in the west (in present-day Utah). The distinction turns more on subsistence strategy than on geography. The mountain Utes adopted the horse more quickly and more thoroughly. In 1598 Spaniards (re)introduced equines to North America; in 1680 they lost control of the horse trade when Indians along the Rio Grande revolted against colonial rule. Even before the Pueblo Revolt, local Navajos, Apaches, and Utes made a habit of rustling. In this way the "Eastern Utes" of the Rocky Mountains became horse people well over a century before the "Western Utes" of the Great Basin. After adopting the horse, the eastern bands hunted bison on the Plains and took on some of the features of the new Plains Indian culture. Because of their participation in New Mexican trade networks, these bands were sometimes collectively called "Taos Yutas."[11]

Why did the Utes of the Great Basin take a different path to horse ownership? They certainly did not lack imagination or access. After the Pueblo Revolt, equines spread quickly to the Northern Plains and the Snake River country. The latter region belonged to the Neme. In the eighteenth century some Neme bands used their new mounts to emigrate to the Southern Plains, where they created a new ethnic identity as Comanches. Other Neme bands used horses to consolidate their existing homeland. These equestrians—people now called Northern Shoshones—rubbed against Blackfeet to the north and Utes to the south. Utah Valley lay immediately to the south of Neme territory. And this borderland was also a crossroads. Bison-hunting equestrians used the Provo and Spanish Fork Rivers as pathways to the Wind River country and the Uinta Basin. In short, Utah Valley was hardly isolated. The Lake Utes must have been aware of the benefits and, more importantly, the costs of equestrianism. Horse lords became servants to their steeds, constantly moving in search of fresh grass. Presented with this way of life, the Fish-Eaters remained committed to their tried-and-true homebound subsistence strategy throughout the eighteenth century. But eventually a combination of threat (from Shoshones) and opportunity (from Spaniards) made them rethink their commitment.[12]

The journal of Domínguez and Escalante provides an invaluable glimpse into this time of transition. In 1776 the Lake People still lacked horses, but they had begun to establish trade connections with

New Mexicans and the mounted Taos Yutas. Tellingly, the friars encountered some "Lagunas" (Lake People) a great distance from their *laguna*. In late August, along the Gunnison River in present-day western Colorado, the Spaniards came across a Fish-Eater traveling with some "Sabuagana" Utes. The friars told the group that they came not to trade or plunder but to find a way to the "pueblos" of the Lagunas. The natives warned them about the "Yamparika," hostile mounted warriors whom they would encounter in the Uinta Basin. Worse yet, the way was rough and dry. Domínguez and Escalante needed assistance. With a prepayment of goods, they convinced the Fish-Eater they called Silvestre to guide them on their journey. A few days later the fathers met some more Lagunas, including a boy they called Joaquín who joined the expedition. With Silvestre's help, Domínguez and Escalante traveled safely across the Uinta Basin. This motley group of Spaniards, New Mexicans, and Indians inspired great fear in the locals: when scouts from Utah Valley spied a mounted party headed in their direction, the Lake People defensively started burning the grassland at the mouth of Spanish Fork Canyon.

Anxiety turned to happiness on 23 September 1776. Amid the smoke, Silvestre explained the situation to his people. A general council of the various lakeside villages was called. The friars presented gifts and explained (through Silvestre) that they wished to return and establish a permanent presence in the valley. In exchange for the Indians' acceptance of Christianity, the priests would teach them how to farm and raise livestock. Instead of deerskin and rabbit fur, the *indios* would have clothing just like the Spaniards'. According to Domínguez and Escalante, the Timpanogos people welcomed the offer and told them to come back soon. The natives were "very poor as regards to dress" but exhibited an "easy-going character." As a token of goodwill toward the king of Spain, the Lagunas presented the friars with a painting done in red ocher on deerskin. It depicted the valley's four main leaders with little Christian crosses on their skin. One of the painted figures was none other than Silvestre, whose Numic name meant "Great Talker."[13]

Because of the lateness of the season, Domínguez and Escalante did not tarry as long as they wanted. After buying some dried fish, they turned southward. A few weeks later they abandoned their journey to California and returned—after a near-disastrous fording of the Colorado River—to Santa Fe. Their report comes across not as failed trip to the ocean but as a successful visit to a great lake. The friars had only good things to say about the Lagunas, who were "very simple, docile, gentle, and affectionate." Domínguez and Escalante likewise spoke highly of the Timpanogos homeland, which "abounds in several species of good fish, geese, beavers, and other amphibious creatures." The expedition's cartographer, Bernardo de Miera, was more effusive. In a letter to the king he offered his vision of a "new empire" between Santa Fe and Monterey. The base of operations should be the Lake of the Timpanogos, he wrote, "because this place is the most pleasant, beautiful and fertile in all of New Spain." The valley here could "support a city with as large a population as that of Mexico City."[14]

Needless to say, this vision was not fulfilled. Domínguez and Escalante never even returned to Utah Valley. Crown officials focused their expansion efforts on Alta California, and even that project exceeded their resources. Throughout the Spanish period the Great Basin remained beyond the reach of colonial rule.

It was not, however, immune from the effects of colonialism. By connecting New Mexico to the Great Basin, the *entrada* of Domínguez and Escalante hastened the horse revolution among the Western Utes. Traders followed the friars. Despite repeated edicts prohibiting unlicensed trade with the Yutas, many enterprising New Mexicans brought horses along the Domínguez-Escalante trail. In exchange for the animals, the traders accepted two kinds of commodities: pelts and slaves. In an 1813 court case, Mauricio Arze and several companions admitted they had spent several days trading at Utah Lake. Their testimony suggested that this practice was routine. According to Arze, the Timpanogos wanted only one thing—to trade people for horses. Arze claimed to have refused. In response, the Indians began to slaughter his herd. Thus Arze was "forced" to obtain twelve slaves along with 109 animal skins.[15]

This account demonstrates a key point: the new animal trade between the Great Basin and New Mexico was based on human violence. Sometime around 1800 the Timpanogos Nuche joined the long-established Spanish slave system. Spaniards bought infants, children, and especially adolescent girls, who were often already the victims of rape. Once baptized in New Mexico, the captives joined society as servants. As *genízaros* (detribalized Indians), these homeless ex-captives occupied the bottom rung of the New Mexican caste system. Over time the *genízaros* created a new transethnic community of bewildering diversity. The slave trade ensnared people from every group in the Southern Plains and greater Southwest—Puebloans, Athabaskans, Shoshoneans—before reaching its violent climax in the eastern Great Basin. Once they obtained horses, the Lake People—following the lead of other mounted Yutas—preyed on their Neme and Nuche neighbors in the deserts of present-day western and southwestern Utah. Through coerced purchases or outright kidnappings, hundreds of youngsters lost all contact with home.[16]

These anonymous victims are normally categorized under modern names: "Paiutes" and "Goshutes." Tellingly, these tribal identities originated in the context of slavery. In the new world made by horses, economic difference replaced linguistic difference as the key cultural boundary. Mounted Western Utes became more like their Neme rivals, the mounted Northern Shoshones. Up and down the rim of the Great Basin, horse ownership created a hierarchy of bands. On top stood the full equestrians, collectively known to English speakers as "Utahs" (Utes) and "Snakes" (Shoshones). The horse economy permitted larger, more stable social groupings. Leaders of these horse-rich bands acted more like "chiefs." The second tier was occupied by smaller bands that acquired some horses without becoming horse people. The Nuche of San Pete Valley in south-central Utah exemplified this intermediate lifeway. Certain bands based at Utah Lake may have fitted this profile, too. Pedestrian bands existed at the bottom. On the

Neme side, these horseless groups became known as "Diggers" or "Goshutes"; on the Nuche side, the equivalent terms were "Piedes" or "Paiutes." By the mid-nineteenth century, this native caste system became the basis of fixed ethnic identities. It became harder—though not impossible—for individuals to cross boundaries. For example, pedestrian Paiutes were defined in opposition to equestrian Utes, and vice versa, even though they spoke the same language.

When Americans came on the scene in the 1840s, they misperceived time-bound power relations as the natural order of things. They explained the pedestrian people's timidity and poverty with environmental determinism. The earliest U.S. maps of the Great Basin—then called the Great Sandy Plain—indicated that the interior residents of this wasteland were "the most miserable objects in creation." "The whole idea of such a desert, and such a people, is a novelty in our country, and excites Asiatic, not American ideas," wrote John C. Frémont. He identified these un-American Indians as "Diggers," a word that implied subsistence based on roots and bulbs. Not coincidentally, it rhymed with "Niggers." The epithets were related in meaning. In the 1850s Anglo travelers sometimes likened the people of the western desert to "old negro women" and orangutans. Captain James Simpson believed that the "Goshoots" illustrated a physical truism: *"That the contour, relief, and relative position of the crust of the earth is intimately connected with the development of man."* In the South, Americans used ideas of place and race to defend the enslavement of Africans. In the Great Basin, related ideas of place and race allowed Americans to overlook the effects of Indian slavery.[17]

Horses and guns gave Western Utes the power to enslave; and these same things gave them the power to expand. By the time Mexico gained independence in 1821, it seems, mounted Nuche had wrested control of the Uinta Basin from Shoshone bands. The newfound power of the "Eutaws" was apparent to the American fur traders who infiltrated the eastern Great Basin in the early years of the Mexican period. "They are, by far," wrote Warren Angus Ferris, "the most expert horsemen in the mountains." It became customary for Eutaws to demand tribute from non-Indians passing through their lands. Wise travelers paid up. Armed and mounted, the Eutaws looked intimidating. In 1825, when William Ashley encountered a Western Ute band in the Uinta Basin, he found himself "much supprised at the appearance of these people." They were clothed in buffalo robes, armed with English rifles, and ornamented with pearls and seashells. They met Ashley "with great familiarity and Ease of manner." In August of the next year Jedediah Smith made a treaty with the "principal Chief" of the Lake Utahs "by which the americans are allowed to hunt & trap in and pass through their country unmolested." At the time, these Fish-Eaters were gathering serviceberries in the mountains. Smith stayed two days in their camp, which consisted of thirty-five "lodges" or families, each with "4 or 5 horses." The animals signified wealth and prestige. "The Uta's are cleanly quiet and active and make a nearer approach to civilized life than any Indians I have seen in the Interior," wrote Smith in admiration.[18]

The 1830s marked the decline of the fur trade and the rise of another regional trade system, the "Old Spanish Trail." This name, though ingrained in the historical literature, is anachronistic, since the trail was used mainly between 1830 and 1850—the last two-thirds of the *Mexican* period. The trail connected Santa Fe and Los Angeles through trade. Great annual caravans carried New Mexican serapes to California and returned with horses and mules. Along the way, traders acquired slaves to sell to buyers at both ends of the trail. From its Pacific terminus, the trail went up Cajon Pass, across the Mojave, and along the western escarpment of the central Utah cordillera before making a wide southward turn across the Wasatch high country and along the edges of the canyonlands. After crossing the Green and Colorado Rivers at present-day Green River, Utah, and Moab, Utah, the trail skirted the San Juan Mountains before dropping into Santa Fe. For Western Utes, New Mexico–bound pack trains presented opportunities for tribute, trade, and theft.[19]

Inspired by the sight of healthy, well-fed California steeds, some got the idea of raiding from the source. The most famous of these horse raiders was the Timpanogos leader Walkara. Most of the information on his early life comes secondhand via Dimick Huntington, a Mormon interpreter who dealt extensively with Walkara in the late 1840s and early 1850s. Walkara was born sometime around 1810 in Utah Valley. Chances are his father, a band leader, never traveled far from the lake. The scale of Walkara's world was much larger. After inheriting a position of leadership, he withdrew from the Timpanogos scene. He developed a horse-based rather than a place-based economy. Equestrianism demanded nomadism. Over the decade of the 1840s Walkara, his herd, and his band—a fluid group of men, women, and children that included Nuche from many places—were almost always on the move. In the winter they often raided horses in California; in the summer they sometimes hunted bison on the Plains. At points between they sold horses and slaves. Walkara's band numbered around 100 or 150 people, with changing personnel. When John C. Frémont met them in 1844, they were "all mounted, armed with rifles, and use their rifles well." Frémont considered them "robbers of a higher order" who "conducted their depredations with form, and under the color of trade and toll for passing through their country." Anglo-Americans gave Walkara strange honorifics that expressed a mixture of respect and contempt—"Napoleon of the Desert," "the Indian Land Pirate," "Hawk of the Mountains," "King of the Mountains," "Mr. Eutaw," and "Soldan [Sultan] of the Red Paynims." By one account, Walkara cut a striking figure with "a full suit of the richest broadcloth, generally brown, cut in European fashion, with a shining beaver hat, and a fine cambric shirt" adorned with "gaudy Indian trimmings." His "richly caparisoned horses" shone and tinkled with "gay metal ornaments." When this living legend died in 1855, he was entombed with his belongings, including sacrificial horses and slaves.[20]

Walkara personified the transformation of the Lake People in the half-century following Domínguez and Escalante. But he did not *exemplify* that change. Walkara lived outside the norm. No other Western Ute leader embraced equestrianism and nomadism so thoroughly.

The other mounted bands of Timpanogos Nuche modified but did not abandon their place-based economy. Horses were important, but so were fish. Tellingly, even Walkara's grand circuits pivoted on the pastures and fishing grounds of the Timpanogos River. This was his critical replenishment stop. The springtime spawn remained the central event in the Timpanogos calendar. Even in a time of change, some things didn't change.

⁘ The origin place of the "Utahs" was the frontier between the eastern Great Basin and northern New Mexico. In 1847 a new frontier would be created by the westward exodus of foreigners.

Upstate New York in the mid-1820s was a place of high expectations. A miracle of engineering, the Erie Canal, had been completed with great fanfare. Another kind of miracle seemed imminent. The towns along the western reaches of the canal became known as the "burnt-over district" because so many born-again preachers blazed through. During the Second Great Awakening—a collective term for the episodic but widespread revivals that swept the nation in the early 1800s—evangelicals gained faith in Jesus Christ and in his impending return. The Second Coming would end the world and restart time by ushering in the Millennium. Numerous millenarian groups blossomed in the antebellum United States. The now-forgotten Millerites determined the precise date of Christ's return—22 October 1844 (a day subsequently known as the "Great Disappointment"). The Seventh-Day Adventists trace their lineage to this evangelical enthusiasm for the End Days. So do the Mormons, whose millenarian expectations are reflected in their formal name, The Church of Jesus Christ of Latter-day Saints.

The founder of the LDS Church, Joseph Smith Jr., came of age in Palmyra, New York. A young farm boy with a propensity for spiritual pursuits—including the use of seer stones to seek buried treasure—Joseph felt excited and troubled by the competing revivals. He prayed for guidance. Like many seekers at the time, Smith received a heavenly visitation from the Lord Jesus Christ. But Smith's visions continued for the rest of his life. They were unusually powerful and detailed. He was instructed to reject all preachers. He learned that he had been chosen to found a new church that was really an old one—the original one true church of Christ. John the Baptist and later Peter, James, and John descended from heaven to confer the "keys" of the ancient priesthood to the farmer-prophet. On other occasions Smith met Moses and Elijah. But Joseph Smith's most regular visitor was the Angel Moroni, who showed him where to find the ultimate buried treasure, a bound collection of engraved metal plates that contained a new scriptural record. Smith translated the plates using a seer stone and published the translation as the Book of Mormon in 1830, the same year he organized the LDS Church.

Even in an age of religious innovation, this new religion stood out. It boasted a prophet who received continuous revelation, a scripture that offered proof of his revelatory powers, and nothing less than the restoration of the ancient priesthood and the primitive church. Over the next decade and a half, Smith added even more: a temple ceremony, plural marriage, a radical theology of the afterlife, and a blueprint for a communitarian economy (called the "Law of Consecration" or the "Order of Enoch"). From the perspective of the Great Basin, Smith's most important innovation was "the gathering." In essence, early Mormons were Christian Zionists. The Prophet planned for his followers to gather at one consecrated place where they would build the temple of the New Jerusalem. "It sounds strange to hear of a church having a 'location,'" commented Charles Dickens. "But a 'location' was the term they applied to their place of settlement." More than any other figure associated with the Second Great Awakening, Joseph Smith cared about the geographic component of religion. Other sects determined the *time* of the Second Coming; Latter-day Saints determined the *place*.[21]

According to one of Smith's revelations, the "center place" was Jackson County, Missouri. In the exegesis of disciple Sidney Ridgon, the Promised Land was "situated at about equal distances from the

Atlantic and the Pacific oceans, as well as from the Alleghany and Rocky mountains." In the first days after the Creation this had been the location of the Garden of Eden. Just as history began here, it would end here. Jackson County would be Christ's first stop on his return. But first the Latter-day Saints needed to do their part. Here in the center of North America, on the western edge of the United States, at the "borders of the Lamanites" (Indian Territory), the gathered Saints needed to erect a holy building to usher in the new dispensation. In 1831 Joseph Smith led a vanguard group to Independence, Missouri, where he dedicated a temple site.[22]

Unfortunately, the hoped-for utopia in Missouri suffered from too few assets, too much dissension, and, most important, too much competition. Neighboring settlers bristled at the Latter-day Saints' land claims based on divine right. Claims and prophecies sounded even worse coming from nonslaveholding Yankees. Hostility turned into violence. In 1838–39, under threat of extermination, the Mormons were expelled from the state by order of the governor. Joseph Smith and his followers regrouped in Illinois, where they erected Nauvoo (supposedly a Hebrew word for "beautiful plantation") out of the swamplands of the Mississippi River. They did not intend to stay long; Nauvoo was an interim Zion at best. Joseph Smith promised that Missouri would yet be redeemed. He also hinted that the Saints would first seek refuge in the Rocky Mountains. In order to move forward in a time of postponement, the Prophet enlarged his meaning of Zion: *"The whole of America is Zion itself from north to south, and is described by the Prophets, who declare that it is the Zion where the mountain of the Lord should be, and that it should be in the center of the land."*[23]

This proclamation from March 1844—one of Joseph Smith's last public discourses—allowed the Saints to keep faith in Missouri while moving on to a new gathering place. Doing so became a necessity when Smith once again ran afoul of his neighbors. Acting as church president, city mayor, municipal justice, and militia general, the Prophet had built Nauvoo into a minitheocracy, a forerunner of the

"Kingdom of God." The Mormon "king" was at once anxious and hubristic: in June 1844, when a dissident newspaper in Nauvoo complained about the church-state alliance and published allegations about the then-secret practice of polygamy, Joseph Smith authorized the destruction of the press. This action led to his arrest by Illinois officials. A mob of vigilantes stormed the county jail as Smith awaited trial. After taking multiple bullets to the chest, the Prophet fell from a second-story window, crying "O Lord, my God!" In the tumult following Smith's martyrdom, the LDS Church splintered. Various would-be prophets vied for control as anti-Mormon violence spread. Hundreds of believers followed James J. Strang, who chose Beaver Island in Lake Michigan as his gathering place. Thousands more, including Joseph Smith's family, remained in Nauvoo. In the 1850s many of them coalesced under the banner of "reorganization." The Reorganized Church of Jesus Christ of Latter-day Saints recruited a prophet with a familiar name. Under Joseph Smith III, the RLDS Church disavowed polygamy and "Mormonism."

The Mormon church as such dates to 1845–46, when Nauvoo's majority faction, 12,000–15,000 strong, lined up behind the Quorum of the Twelve Apostles. Its president, Brigham Young, approved the idea that Zion could be relocated to the Rocky Mountains or beyond. Young, a carpenter, was the right man at the right time. In the history of religion, very few sects have outlived their charismatic founders. Wisely, Young did not attempt to fill the void. Brother Brigham portrayed himself not as the new Joseph Smith but as the Prophet's right-hand man. Smith had been uniquely fey, as he had to be. Creating a religion—a new order—takes magic and disorder. Managing a large church requires a different set of skills. Stern and pragmatic, Brigham Young proved to be ideal for the job.

The westward migration did not begin auspiciously, however. After a hasty, haphazard evacuation from Nauvoo in 1846, the strung-out Mormon caravan got bogged down in the spring mud of Iowa. By the time the lead party got to the Missouri River, it was too late to explore westward. The Latter-day Saints had to postpone their great migration; their desperate situation became worse.

Help came from an unlikely source. Back in January, Brigham Young had instructed one of his subordinates to seek aid in Washington, D.C. The man arrived in May, just days after Congress had declared war on Mexico. Given this turn of events, President Polk authorized the Mormons to raise a 500-member battalion to join Colonel Stephen W. Kearney on his march down the Santa Fe Trail. The soldiers would be compensated sixteen dollars per month. In a sense, the "volunteers" would be paid to move to the Far West. Brigham Young accepted the offer with ambivalence. In his mind, he was leading his people to a faraway land—Mexican territory, in fact—because of the failures of state and federal governments to uphold the constitutional right of religious freedom. In his sermons, Young promised eternal damnation for the elected officials who had failed to stop the vigilantes. At the same time, he couldn't refuse the governmental aid.

As the summer turned to fall, the remaining Saints hunkered down wherever they were—Illinois, Iowa, or present-day Nebraska. At the Mormon staging ground, "Winter Quarters," on Omaha Indian land, several thousand Mormon squatters endured a miserable season of disease and death. When the advance party of 143 men (including three slaves), three women, and two children finally embarked for the mountains on 9 April 1847, everything was at stake. Brigham Young left behind a scattered, bankrupt church of downhearted followers. In order to succeed, the "Pioneer Camp of the Saints" had to cross the Plains quickly, find a suitable resting place, plant crops in time for fall, and erect houses in time for winter.

Where would this resting place be? During their final year in Nauvoo, Young and his counselors held meetings at which they pored over maps and read aloud from the reports of John C. Frémont. Texas, California, and Vancouver Island received passing consideration. Though bountiful, these lands did not offer what the Mormons wanted most, a "place apart." As early as mid-1845, the eastern

Great Basin emerged as the favored destination. In August the LDS General Council projected that the headquarters "will probably be in the neighborhood of Lake Tampanagos as that is represented as a most delightful district and no settlement near there." In September the council resolved to organize a company to go to Salt Lake Valley. Then, in 1846, talk shifted to the "Bear River valley" northeast of the Great Salt Lake. The three eligible sites—Utah Valley, Salt Lake Valley, and Cache Valley—were located close enough together that Brigham Young deferred the final decision. He said he would recognize the new promised land when he saw it.[24]

The Pioneer Camp was structured like a religious army, with captains of hundreds, captains of fifties, and captains of tens. Using fire-and-brimstone language, Brigham Young ordered that all the recruits be "reformed." They would get along or else. Their thousand-mile journey was a mission. In his one and only revelation in his thirty years as church leader—"The Word and Will of the Lord"—Brigham Young laid out the camp's organization and its guiding covenant. If the pioneers were righteous, they would succeed. If they were wicked, they would fail. To emphasize the sanctity of the journey further, camp leaders "sealed" camp members to their families through spiritual adoption ceremonies. All of this group-building seemed to work. With negligible conflict (with one another or with Indians), the pioneers made decent time across the Plains despite their sabbatarianism. Only once did their beleaguered leader issue a jeremiad. At Scotts Bluff (near the western border of present-day Nebraska), Brother Brigham excoriated the camp for having fun around the fire—"card playing, chequres & dominoes" as well as "dancing and Nig[g]ering & Hoeing down." Repent or be ruined, he rebuked. Afterward one of the camp members, William Clayton, wrote that "it truly seemed as though the cloud had burst and we had emerged into a new element, a new atmosphere, and a new society." Brigham Young had taught the group to think mythically. This was their Exodus; he was their Moses.[25]

At Fort Laramie the Pioneer Camp rested, resupplied, and unexpectedly took on some new emigrants from an independent Mormon party. Beyond the fort the Saints continued along the North Platte and then the Sweetwater until reaching the Continental Divide at South Pass (in present-day Wyoming). Near here in late June, they encountered two mountain men, Moses Harris and Jim Bridger, in quick succession. Harris steered the Mormons toward Cache Valley. Bridger, who knew the country better, commended the soil of Salt Lake Valley, but given its late and early frosts, he wondered if the valley could support a large agricultural settlement. He reserved higher praise for Utah Valley, but warned against locating there. "The Indians round Utah Lake will strip a man, if they dont kill him," recorded Thomas Bullock. "in the Utes Land you must not stick a Stake. all they r fit for is Slaves." Transcribing the same information, William Clayton wrote, "The Utah tribe of Indians inhabit the region around the Utah Lake and are a bad people . . . They are mostly armed with guns." After this counsel, Brigham Young "felt inclined for the present not to crowd upon the Utes" in their "choice lands on the Utah" until the Saints had "a chance to get acquainted with them and that it would be better to bear toward the region of the Salt Lake rather than the Utah, & find some good place for our seeds & deposit them as speedily as possible, regardless of a future location."[26]

The Pioneer Camp crossed the point of no return after Fort Bridger, where for the first time they left the well-traveled Oregon Trail. Veering southwest, the Mormons took the one-year-old Hastings Cutoff (more or less the present-day path of I-80). The year before, the Donner Party had come this way on its ill-fated journey to California. Even with the benefit of the Donner Party's trail-clearing, this was still by far the roughest, most mountainous part of the trek. It didn't help that many of the Saints, including Brigham Young, came down with fever. Too sick to move, Young directed a small company to race ahead and start planting. The season was getting late, and Salt Lake sounded good enough. Young reserved the right to move the headquarters somewhere else in the future. But when the Mormon leader finally glimpsed the Valley of the Great Salt Lake from the summit of

Big Mountain on 24 July 1847, he "expressed his full satisfaction in the Appearance of the valley as A resting place for the Saints & was Amply repayed for his Journey." His exact words are unknown. No one recorded the legendary utterance "This is the right place; drive on!" However, Young did say something similar on 28 July during an evening meeting on the valley floor. As Levi Jackman wrote in his diary, "the camp was called togeather to say whear the City should be built. After a number had spoken on the subject a voat was calld for [and it was] unanimosiley aggread that this was the spot After that Pres Young said tha[t] he knew that this is the place. he knew it as soon as he came in sight of it and he had seen this vearey spot before."[27]

::: What made this place *the* place? The heart of the matter was climate. The peculiar water of the Great Basin matched the Mormons' identity as Peculiar People.

For Brigham Young, finding a gathering place was one thing; convincing everyone to gather there was another. Now his efforts turned to environmental salesmanship—a task that compelled him to leave the place after only a short acquaintance. In late August Young headed back to Winter Quarters on the Missouri River. En route he passed the "Emigration Camp" or "Big Camp," containing some 1,500 Saints. They had hit the trail in June, two months after the Pioneer Camp. In a "departure of the fittest," the Big Camp had left behind thousands of less fortunate members to face another winter in limbo. Before these marooned Saints lost faith or defected to James Strang, Young needed to rally their hope with good news about the Great Basin. In late December, during the same week that Brother Brigham was officially elevated to the position of prophet, the Church issued a General Epistle to Latter-day Saints worldwide. It called on everyone to gather by the Missouri River in preparation for a general removal to the Valley of the Great Salt Lake. In describing the location, the Epistle was both realistic and optimistic. "The soil of the valley appeared good, but will require irrigation," it said. "The climate is warm, dry, and healthy; good salt abounds at the lake; warm, hot, and cold springs are common; mill sites excellent; but the valley is destitute of timber."[28]

Compared to the Plains, however, the Wasatch Range above the valley seemed well timbered. Pioneer Camp member William Clayton for one was "happily disappointed" in the appearance of the valley. The ebullient Thomas Bullock called the timber shortage the "only draw-back." Waist-high bunch grass—ideal forage for grazing—covered the site of the planned city; the pioneers had to mow the ground with scythes before planting. Sagebrush and shrub oak could be used as firewood. The only serious deficiency was building material, and this problem had a solution—mud. "The children of Israel built of sun-dried bricks," reported George A. Smith; "we have done the same."[29]

The drab adobe buildings contrasted with the lushness of the site in the northeastern corner of the valley, where brooks from various canyons (City Creek, Red Butte, Emigration, Parleys, Mill Creek, Big Cottonwood, and Little Cottonwood) tumbled from the Wasatch. The greater part of the graben to the west and south—originally called Jordan Valley—was much drier, with only the interlake river supporting a twisting corridor of marshes and sloughs. Just beyond the Mormon capital, warm and hot springs bubbled from the earth. Between these springs and the big lake lay an extensive area of salt marshes. Certainly Missouri and Illinois had more water. But the Great Basin had water of unusual quality in the air as well as in the earth. This is why the Epistle called attention to the dry atmosphere and the warm springs.

When mid-nineteenth-century U.S. settlers talked about water, they used a now-lost vocabulary of medical geography. The "climate" of the country denoted far more than weather. Places could be intrinsically "healthy" or "sickly"; diagnosis demanded careful consideration of elevation, vegetation, wind, water, soil, and air. Phrases like "bad air" and "sweet water" were analytical as well as evocative. The color and smell of the water, air, and humus reflected the character of the land. With knowledge it could be read the way a physician read a body. Settlers drew a correspondence between nature outside (on the land) and nature inside (in the body). According to prevailing medical theory, the body, like the Earth, consisted of elemental matter—the "four humors." Blood, phlegm, yellow bile, and the enigmatic black bile were meant to be evenly and smoothly circulated. American settlers gave daily attention to the sights and smells of bodily fluids. When imbalance showed itself through "risings" (tumors, hemorrhoids, acne), people often responded with bleeding or vomiting. The same principle applied to the land. Settlement usually began with the drainage of unwanted fluids.

Although settlers believed that cultivation made any land healthier, not all lands began equal. Just as certain people's "constitutions" made them susceptible to illness, certain environments intrinsically promoted disease. Ideally, individuals and races could be matched to their "proper" environment. In practice, settlers found it difficult to find or create healthy land without getting sick. The "ague" was an inevitable part of "seasoning" in the Mississippi River Valley. Now known as malaria, the ague commonly appeared in cycles of shaking. It was hard to avoid "the chills" because it could arrive on the very air that permeated wooden cabins. Antebellum settlers attributed many of their maladies to "miasma." Noah Webster defined it as "infecting substances floating in the air; the effluvia of any putrefying bodies, rising and floating in the atmosphere." Miasma rose like fog from stagnant, scum-covered pools of "bad water." Settlers lived in a world in which the boundary between water and air was porous.[30]

Miasma had plagued the Mormons. Nauvoo was a sick, swampy, malarial place. Even after the Latter-day Saints conducted extensive draining, the city remained unhealthy. In the summers of 1839, 1840, and 1841, the fever and ague afflicted massive numbers of people. Yet Nauvoo was a sanitarium compared with Winter Quarters. In this shantytown by the Missouri River the Saints suffered from a deadly combination of disease, exposure, and malnutrition. At the time, though, Mormon evacuees speculated that they had inadvertently transplanted pollutants from Nauvoo. Because of its (slightly) higher elevation, Winter Quarters should—according to medical geography—have been healthier. To the contrary, the "Misery Bottoms" of the Missouri sent forth snakes and bugs and bad air. Sickened Saints endured rotting flesh and raging fevers. One of the worst ailments was known as "Black Canker." In modern terms, the refugees suffered from scurvy. Between June 1846 and May 1847 the dead numbered over 700, about half of them infants. Even by the standards of the time, the infant mortality rate was heartbreaking.[31]

Brigham Young promised to find his suffering people a "healthy country." And according to two key nineteenth-century indicators, he delivered on that promise. Salt Lake's elevation was high (4,300 feet above sea level), and its air was dry (with an average humidity of about 50 percent). Early settlers marveled at the atmospheric clarity that allowed them see far into the distance. In his widely used *Latter-day Saints' Emigrants' Guide,* William Clayton reported that the "air is good and pure, sweetened by healthy breezes from the Salt Lake." Unlike freshwater, saltwater did not issue organic contaminants; the Great Salt Lake promoted life precisely because it was lifeless. And it offered an easy, unlimited source of table salt—an important preservative for meat and a vital supplement for livestock. Even the lack of verdure had its advantages: no trees to clear, no danger of pollutants lurking in a tangled growth. Overall, the country made a strong first impression as a "salubrious" environment. A representative view came from Robert Bliss, a member of the Mormon Battalion who arrived in late 1847. "The atmosphere is pure & there has been no sickness as yet among us to speak of," he wrote after a few months in residence. "All are pleased with the climate." As for disadvantages, Bliss mentioned the presence of wolves and a few deep springs in which livestock might drown. These were manageable problems: wolves could be killed, and pools could be filled.[32]

But not all pools. Some were too valuable; some had the power to cure. Hydropathy, like homeopathy, belonged to "regular" (professional) medicine in the first half of the nineteenth century. In folk medicine, the belief in healing springs was deeper and older. Drawing on this storied tradition, U.S. settlers made fine distinctions among types of spring water—fresh, salt, sulfur, soda, iron, and so on. It mattered whether the water emerged from the Earth cold, warm, or hot. Different waters had different medicinal effects, some preventative, some therapeutic. Of all the water types, sulfurous warm springs possessed the greatest healing powers. Their pungent taste and smell suggested their potency.

When the breeze blew off the lake, the pioneers of Great Salt Lake City could smell a trace of sulfur with the brine. Just northwest of the town site, a collection of warm springs (around 100 degrees Fahrenheit) emerged from the ground at the base of the foothills. A little farther north, some hotter and more carbonated springs fed into a small lake separate from the Great Salt Lake. This geothermal area marked the northern boundary of Salt Lake Valley; the north-south trail passed by these steaming, odoriferous landmarks. Before the advent of the railroad, Hot Springs Lake and the warm springs were vastly more important than the Great Salt Lake to the city's recreational life. Because of the extensive mudflats surrounding the big lake, a trip to bathe in the saltwater required an all-day horseback trip to an access point called Black Rock. By comparison, a trip to the warm springs could be accomplished before or after a day's work. It didn't take the Saints long to make a habit of bathing for health. In February 1848 Robert Bliss wrote that the springs "have effected cures & probably will yet be a resort of Thousands."[33]

Early on, the biggest health booster of the springs—and of the gathering place in general—was Thomas Bullock, secretary to Brigham Young. Bullock took his first bath on 26 July 1847 on advice from the camp doctor. During the last mountainous leg of the pioneer trek, Bullock and many others had become sick. The pioneers seem to have attributed their "mountain fever" to the process of acclimatization.

(Most likely they had been bitten by ticks.) Bullock carried out the doctor's advice so often that his friends nicknamed his anodyne "Bullock's warm bathing Spring." In 1848, hale and hearty, Bullock published a series of letters to the Saints in his native England. LDS missionaries had recently converted over 30,000 working-class Britons, a pool of converts now encouraged to gather. Bullock did his best to promote emigration with glowing descriptions of the valley and its healing waters:

> These springs, like the Pool of Siloam [in Jerusalem], heal all who bathe, no matter what their complaints. The air is very salubrious and with these warm springs, I can truly say we have found a healthy country. This will prove the greatest blessing to the rheumatic; cramp, sprains, bruises, itch, every skin disease, and almost every complaint will be healed.[34]

Bullock repeatedly boasted about the valley's mortality rate, going so far as to enumerate the first year's deaths and their causes. The notable fatalities were accidental rather than disease related. In his diary, Robert Bliss similarly noted that "but few Deaths have occurred here & those of Diseases of other climates."[35]

The healthfulness of the valley was apparent even to those less enamored of the new Zion. Writing from Salt Lake in October 1847, Willard Snow complained about the "meanness & barrenness" of the terrain. He reported that the frost had killed the potatoes and that cattle had eaten the turnips. Sarcastically, he called the situation "a right mormon caper." Nonetheless, he encouraged his mother to emigrate. "We have lived to get through & probably shall now live forever for no one dies here for there is a warm spring or pool of water that whoever bathes therein comes out healthy & feels swell without fault[.] we are in a verry healthy climate."[36]

In 1849–50 Salt Lake Mormons shared their wonder-spring with hundreds of dusty gold seekers en route to California. One forty-niner noted that the locals (following Bullock) referred to the spring as "the pool of Silome [*sic*]." Another gold seeker met some men and children who visited the spring "with great frequency." These regulars told the newcomer that Mormons "have great faith in the efficacy of the spring for healing, and as a panacea for diseases in general." Yet another gold-seeking argonaut (as they often called themselves) reported that "the Mormons make a boast of their good health, and attribute it to bathing in those springs: many that I met declaring they came to the valley perfect cripples, and were restored to their health and agility by frequenting them."[37]

In later reminiscences, pioneers shared stories of water cures. "When I got to Salt Lake City, I was in a very dilapidated condition, having so little to eat," wrote James Ririe. "The mosquito bites had festered and I had a touch of mountain fever. When I got plenty to eat and got re-baptized and bathed in the Warm Springs, that soon healed my sores." Thales Haskell remembered the misery of his rheumatoid wife on the overland trail. But "after bathing in the warm springs a few times, [she] was relieved of the rheumatism." Cyrus Tolman looked back to when his sister fell deaf and dumb. "She wrote on a paper that she wanted me to baptize her in warm springs," he wrote. "Father consented and I did so. She came out of the water able to talk and hear."[38]

Early pioneers practiced rebaptism for health and also for identity. It became a rite of passage for newly arrived emigrants to reimmerse their bodies in the waters of the Great Basin, thereby redeclaring their personal faith and their group identity. In the summer of 1847 few things took greater precedence. Soon after damming City Creek to feed their irrigation ditches, the Saints dammed it again to form an outdoor font. In August almost every member of the Pioneer Camp took his or her turn in the water. In the same month the pioneers named the various watercourses in the valley. The discharge from Utah Lake, initially called the Utah Outlet, was renamed the Western Jordan (ultimately shortened to Jordan River) because it connected a virtual Galilee to an American Dead Sea. "The Pool of Siloam" was of course another obvious reference to Palestine.

On a grand scale, too, Mormons saw religious meaning in their new environment: a self-contained drainage, a basin rimmed by mountains—a place set apart. The non-Mormon gold seeker Gordon Cone grasped this notion—and turned it on its head—when he passed through Great Salt Lake City in 1849. "This basin is certainly one of the wonderful curiosities that are found on our continent," he wrote in his diary. "It appears to be a kind of inland continent, capable of carrying on its own affairs independent of the ballance of the globe." He continued: "The mormons have chosen this singular tract of country as the Fortress, from which, the influence that is to Mormonize the World is to eminate—But like Mahomed's, its Koran can only succeed within the pale of ignorance." The forty-niner went on to denigrate the flora and fauna and the horseless Indians of the Great Basin. Only the "Utahs" seemed to impress him.[39]

On the other side of the looking glass, early pioneers saw the Basin as a promised land. Even after the conclusion of the Mexican War in 1848, when all of present-day Utah became U.S. territory, Mormons continued to refer their resting place as "Great Salt Lake City, Great Basin, North America." They processed mail at the "Great Basin Post Office." On 24 July 1849, to celebrate the second anniversary of settlement, the Saints held a community dinner. Dignitaries made twenty-four prepared toasts, the first of which went to "The Great Salt Lake, and the Saints in the Valley of the Great Basin of North America:—May their savor increase till all Israel is saved." These early Utah Saints were attuned to hydrography. Robert Bliss described the "Great Bacin" as a "little World of Blessings"—a place where the streams have "no communication with any Part of the World" and where the mountains "enclose us we hope from mobs & the heavy hand of Percicution that has hithto followed us." Later, when Bliss wrote about the valley's "pure & free air," he had two mutually supportive attributes in mind. The atmosphere was not contaminated with disease, and likewise it was "not contaminated with foul Spirit of Mobocracy & misrule." The spiritual climate seemed to mirror the physical one.[40]

⁝⁝⁝ Mormons and Indians came from different worlds, but they frequented the same water sources. Most of the early cross-cultural interactions took place at creeks and springs and lakes. Lamentably, these interactions have been downplayed in the historical literature. The notion that Salt Lake Valley was a "no-man's land" persists to this day. Certain pioneer documents have contributed to this misperception. For example, in July 1847 Norton Jacob used this language to justify his vote to remain in the valley: "if we went up south to the Utah Lake the country would be occupied by the Indians, while here it was unoccupied." To the pioneers, "unoccupied" meant something different from "unpopulated" or "unpeopled." It meant "unused" or "unclaimed." At the time of settlement, Salt Lake Valley was home to several itinerant bands, including two mounted groups of Neme-Nuche mixed-bloods led by Wanship and Goship. In the eyes of the Saints, these bands did not qualify as a landholding "tribe." Wrongly *and* rightly, the Mormons perceived these people as different from the "tribe" of "Utahs"/"Timpanodes" to the south and the "tribe" of "Shoshones"/"Snakes" to the north. Salt Lake Valley did in fact function as a buffer zone between equestrian Nuche and equestrian Neme. People of both "tribes" started visiting the Mormons within days of their arrival in 1847. On 31 July William Clayton wrote that the Shoshones "appear to be displeased because we have traded with the Utahs and say they own this land, that the Utahs have come over the line, etc."[41]

In the summer of 1848 Walkara—a man who matched the Mormon idea of a "chief"—rode into Great Salt Lake City with hundreds of horses for sale. Sounding a bit like Domínguez and Escalante, Parley P. Pratt made a glowing report: these "good looking, brave, and intelligent" Indians were "much pleased and excited with every thing they saw, and finally expressed a wish to become one people with us, and to live among us and we among them, and to learn to cultivate the earth and live as we do."[42]

From Walkara's point of view, the Mormons presented a business opportunity. As early as 1847, Utes began selling stolen children to Mormons. That fall, one of Walkara's kinsmen succeeded in obtaining a gun in exchange for a teenage Paiute girl after threatening to kill her. The girl became part of Brigham Young's extended family.[43] In their attempt to save children from enslavement, the Saints unwittingly began to replace Mexicans as the main clients in the regional slave system. As Great Basin neophytes, Mormons displayed a general ignorance of local customs. Unlike mountain men, the Pioneer Camp did not extend gifts or tribute for using native land. In fact Brigham Young tried to minimize all encounters with Indians by erecting a stockade and passing a resolution forbidding unauthorized trade.

With the advent of winter, this policy of nonengagement became untenable. The gathered Saints received the ultimate corroboration that they had picked the best place in the valley: a large congregation of local Indians wintered right next to them. City Creek and the warm springs were essential cold-weather campsites. The riparian growth along the creek offered fuel and shelter; the springs offered warmth and medicine.[44]

Throughout North America, the belief in healing waters was a significant point of overlap between native and Euro-American cultures. Shoshones bathed in and drank from thermal waters and used spring-side mineral deposits for internal and topical medicine. More exotically, they sometimes buried their dead in mineral springs so that the remains would calcify. In what is now Colorado, Utes frequented hot springs throughout the Rocky Mountains. Even after tourist-invalids began their invasion, Utes were known to put their sick horses in the hot sulfur springs of Middle Park. Another important place of resort was Pagosa Springs in the San Juan Mountains. In 1878 a U.S. army officer observed that "Indian trails from all directions converge" on this "great natural curiosity." To his knowledge, the Utes had "always regarded the Springs with feelings akin to adoration, conceiving them to be the creation of the Great Spirit for the cure of the sick of all tribes, howsoever afflicted."[45]

In Numic cosmology, the life force of the universe was *puwa*. This kinetic power could be healthful or harmful to humans. The word— and the life force—resembled water *(pa)*. Like ambient moisture, *puwa* was both ubiquitous and diffuse. However, like a cold spring emerging from a deep aquifer, *puwa* took concentrated form at certain sacred locations—many of which were springs.

Some of these sacred water sites presented danger. Sirenlike personages called "water babies" sometimes haunted lakes and springs. Just over the southern divide of Utah Valley, there used to be a spring-fed pool nine feet in diameter called Pang'un or Pun-gun or Punjun. According to William Clayton, "The Indians say it has no bottom and it is said they sometimes worship it." U.S. Captain Howard Stansbury called it Ghost Spring. Another army explorer, John Gunnison, was more specific. "They fancy in this resides a child," he wrote, "that comes to the surface at the setting of the sun; and when one approaches, it cries and screams for help, making most frightful contortions; but should any attempt to aid the child to escape, they would be carried to the lower regions."[46]

Given these Numic beliefs and practices, it seems profoundly sad and ironic that the healthful *puwa* source at the warm springs of Salt Lake became a sick and haunted place. The roughly 300 natives who wintered here in 1848–59 caught foreign diseases from their Mormon neighbors, a densely packed population of 4,500 emigrants. The winter of 1849–50 brought worse agony. For Utes it marked the beginning of a devastating decade of disease. Cyrena Merrill remembered that "the measles broke out among the indians and they would rush past our cabin howling and screaming—run and jump into the warm springs & then take cold and die—then others would bewail and screech—and at all times of day or night their howls or mournings rent the air and my hair would stand on end from fright." John Nebeker, an early officer of the law, retained equally vivid memories: "They died off about as fast as they went into the water. Some they buried and some they didn't bury. I helped bury those that were left unburied. We buried 36 in one grave; and 44 dogs in another. Their custom was to kill their dogs when their masters died. This was the first time measles appeared here. It was a new disease to them, and they didn't know how to cure it, or where they got it."[47]

These reminiscences provide more information than the contemporary recordbooks. Most Mormons had a blind spot for their dying neighbors. To be fair, the Saints suffered their own afflictions during these winters. But their primary problem was hunger, not disease. Settlers apparently did not question the native health of the country in relation to the sickness of the natives.

As the key site of cross-cultural interaction, the sulfur springs would eventually be surpassed in importance by the sweetwater lake to the south. At first the two lake peoples—new and old, native and newcomer—lived contiguously but not connectedly. Occasionally certain Timpanogos Nuche ventured north to trade or raid livestock, and from time to time individual Mormons ventured south to "see the country and git sum fish." As a policy, though, the early pioneers kept a respectful distance in the first year and a half. Latter-day Saints understood Utah Lake Valley to be "occupied." Indian relations would become more complicated once colonists crossed the dividing line at "Point of the Mountain." This expansion was inevitable. In Iowa and England, thousands of placeless Latter-day Saints awaited emigration. Brigham Young projected that Salt Lake Valley was "capable of watering a city of 100,000 inhabitants." And prophecy did not stop there. Great Salt Lake City would become the center stake of a great godly tent covering the entire Great Basin. Unbeknownst to the original lake people, their valley was next for the staking.[48]

2.

Brigham Young and the
Famine of the Fish-Eaters

According to the Book of Mormon, the Indians of America were a fallen branch of Israel. With help, these benighted people of the covenant would be redeemed, after which they would help the Latter-day Saints usher in the Last Days. In the Great Basin, Mormons struggled to translate these beliefs into practice. Utah Lake—specifically the mouth of the Timpanogos, or Provo, River—was the first and most important testing ground. Fatefully, within one year of settlement Mormon militiamen had killed many Timpanogos Nuche. The "Indian war" of 1850 set the stage for continuing conflict with the Timpanogos and other bands of Fish-Eaters.

Conflict notwithstanding, the first half of the 1850s was a time of tentative coexistence and cautious intimacy on the shores of Utah Lake. Mormons and Indians came to know one another on a first-name basis. Ute leaders corresponded with the Mormon "Big Chief," Brigham Young. However, the gradual shutdown of the New Mexican slave trade and the continual arrival of settlers reduced the options for the Lake Utes. By the time federal officials assumed titular control over Utah's Indian affairs in 1855, the Fish-Eaters were starving. The government established an "Indian Farm" in southern Utah

Valley to teach the natives agriculture. The farm failed. The responsible Indian agent fled during the so-called Utah War of 1857–58, when Brigham Young and federal officials clashed over territorial politics.

Following a détente between church and state, Indian policy shifted from farming to removal. In 1865 Ute leaders met near Utah Lake to sign a reservation treaty. Lacking options, the remnants of the Timpanogos Nuche agreed to relocate from Utah Valley to a distant, lakeless region. Although Mormons had envisioned a different and extraordinary outcome for "their" Indians, the outcome here was bleakly conventional.

::: The Mormon-Indian connection goes back to Joseph Smith's teenage imagination. "In the course of our [family's] evening conversations," his mother recalled, "Joseph would give us some of the most amusing recitals which could be imagined. He would describe the ancient inhabitants of this continent—their dress, their manner of traveling, the animals which they rode, the cities that were built by them, the structures of their buildings, with every particular of their mode of warfare, their religious worship as particularly as though he had spent his life with them."[1] In 1830, as a serious adult, Smith produced the Book of Mormon. This 584-page work purported to be a record of the ancient inhabitants of North America.

Among other things, the Book of Mormon narrates the emigration of an Israelite family out of Jerusalem around 600 B.C.E., shortly before the Babylonian captivity. With God's assistance, these Hebrews traveled by boat to the (other) Promised Land. In the Western Hemisphere they fragmented into antagonistic groups—the Nephites and the Lamanites. The latter were cursed with dark skin. The Lamanites lived as nomads, whereas the civilized Nephites built great cities like Zarahemla. Over the centuries the groups repeatedly switched roles as the wicked and the righteous. Only for a brief period did harmony reign across the land. The righteousness came from Christ. The Redeemer himself appeared in the New World during his absence from the tomb. Before his new audience, the resurrected Savior gave the Sermon on the Mount, performed the sacrament, and appointed twelve disciples. In other words, the Book of Mormon describes a second, parallel Christian church in the first century C.E. Over time, however, the Lamanites permanently reverted to wickedness and idolatry. They eliminated all the fair-skinned Nephites and with them all vestiges of Christianity. The last of the Nephite scribes, Moroni, buried the scriptural record in the Hill Cumorah (in what later became upstate New York) before his death around 421 C.E.

Although the details were novel, the premise of the Book of Mormon did not cause astonishment in 1830. Theories about the Hebraic peopling of the Americas—the result of the wandering of the Lost Tribes or the scattering of Babel—were prevalent and uncontroversial. In 1823 a New England minister, Ethan Smith (no relation), published the popular *View of the Hebrews; or the Tribes of Israel in America*. The notion of a lost book by American Hebrews was also commonplace in the 1820s. For these reasons, some accused Joseph Smith of plagiarism or derivativeness. They missed the point. The Book of Mormon resembled nothing else on American bookshelves except the Bible—long, dense, complicated, multivoiced, and prophetic. It was nothing less than an American scripture.

On its original title page, Joseph Smith announced one of the main purposes of the Book of Mormon: "to shew unto the remnant of the House of Israel how great things the LORD hath done for their fathers; and that they may know the covenants of the LORD, that they are not cast off forever." The Book of Mormon showed that the "Lamanites" did *not* come from the Lost Tribes. Instead they originated with Lehi, a descendent of Jacob and of Manasseh, son of Joseph. Even in their degenerate state, the latter-day Lamanites remained part of the covenant. In the Last Days, the "stick of Joseph" would be redeemed. In preparation, missionaries needed to spread the gospel to the natives. Many nineteenth-century Christian groups proselytized to Indians, but only the Mormons had such strange and lofty expectations. Once redeemed, the "remnant of Jacob" would take the lead in building the New Jerusalem, the site of the Second Coming. Repentant "Gentiles"—that is, Mormon converts—would work with the Lamanites as *assistants*. The remaining Gentiles—that is, all the unconverted—would be annihilated in the apocalypse. In addition to earthquakes and floods, Mormons anticipated an army of Lamanites—the "strong arm of Jehovah," the "battle-ax of the Lord"—crushing their enemies like a lion among sheep. The United States would be destroyed in the process. In the midst of this re-creation, the "seed of Israel" would reclaim their former glory, including their fair skin.

In short, the religion of Joseph Smith reserved a paradoxical place for Indians. They were cursed to be inferior yet promised to be superior. They were destined to save the world, yet they couldn't save themselves. These future Christian Israelites didn't know who they were, didn't know their own lineage. Despite their ignorance, these dark-skinned heathens belonged to the Mormon fold as spiritual if not actual kin. Early Mormons saw themselves as "grafts" of Israel. By converting, Latter-day Saints acquired "believing blood." Later, influenced by British Israelism, the Saints would claim to possess literal Hebraic bloodlines. Either way, they had reason to regard Indians as extended family. Tellingly, early church members sometimes referred to native peoples as "Cousin Laman" or "Cousin Lemuel" (after two of Lehi's sons).[2]

Joseph Smith wasted no time trying to fulfill the prophecies in the Book of Mormon. In 1830, shortly after the publication of the scripture and the organization of the church, Smith announced the doctrine of the gathering. The "center place" was supposed to be "on the borders of the Lamanites." Missouri fitted the description. It was located at the center of the continent and at the edge of the United States—right next to Indian Territory. That very year Congress passed the Indian Removal Act, which called for the relocation of thousands of Indians from the East to the West. Early Mormons regarded this coerced migration as providential: the Indians were already being gathered. Long before moving to Missouri, Joseph Smith dispatched four missionaries to Indian Territory. The journey began propitiously in the fall of 1830: en route the missionaries won over the entire Ohio congregation of Signey Rigdon. This mass conversion significantly enlarged the infant church and helped to pull it westward. The new Ohio Saints immediately caught the Lamanite enthusiasm. In meetings they spoke in "Indian" tongues and chanted and danced "like Indians." But the success of the missionaries ended at the borders of the Lamanites. Although the Shawnees and the Delawares seemed receptive at first, the Mormons couldn't get beyond first impressions because the responsible U.S. Indian agent evicted the missionaries for not having a license. Reporting to superintendent William Clark, the agent noted that the "the Men act very strange."[3]

After the failure of the first Indian mission, Joseph Smith turned his attention to other aspects of kingdom-building. Yet he did not lose faith in the destiny of Indians. In 1835, traveling from Ohio to Missouri with an ad hoc army meant to assist persecuted Mormon settlers, Joseph Smith rekindled the Lamanite enthusiasm. When some of his disciples exhumed a skeleton from a burial mound, Smith received a vision. He identified the bones as the remains of Zelph, an uncursed "white Lamanite" who had fallen in battle. Zelph had been a warrior for Omandagus, a prophet whose fame had stretched from the Hill Cumorah to the Rocky Mountains. Impressed by the vision, apostle Wilford Woodruff carried Zelph's thighbone to Missouri. He meant to bury it at the envisaged temple site. But before the temple could be built, Missourians evicted the Latter-day Saints for misconduct. Allegations included "Indian tampering." Rumors of nefarious alliances with Indians would dog the Latter-day Saints for decades. Joseph Smith did in fact work to create soft diplomatic relations with tribes in Missouri and later Iowa (across the river from Nauvoo). And in private, he anticipated plural marriage with Indian women. But the short-term goal was simple conversion. Before any red army could be raised, the Lamanites would have to "blossom as the rose." No one knew the exact timetable. Expelled from the center place, Joseph Smith recognized that the day of prophecy—for Indians *and* Mormons—had been deferred. In 1844, days before his martyrdom, Smith looked forward to finding refuge in the Rocky Mountains, where the Lamanites would serve as a shield.[4]

As they prepared to flee to the far country, Mormons—that is, Brigham Young's majority faction of Smith's church—had their first sustained experience with native peoples. In 1846 Young needed a wintering place to prepare for the migration. He could have set up camp in western Iowa, but the Mormon persecution complex propelled him the across the Missouri River to unorganized territory. Better to live among the red men than among whites. Young knowingly violated a federal law that forbade contact with Indians on reserved land. He went ahead and negotiated his own extralegal treaties with Omahas and Otoes, both of whom claimed the land at Winter Quarters. The Mormon leader also sent a letter to President James Polk asking permission to squat temporarily. The request was denied. Federal Indian agents, understandably annoyed, tried to move the Saints along as soon as possible. Meanwhile Missourians raised new alarms about Mormons colluding with Indians not far from their border. All of this reinforced the idea among Latter-day Saints that the government and the Gentiles were out to get them.

To make things worse, their Indian brethren reneged on their welcome. By accepting thousands of Mormons, Omahas hoped to gain protection from their enemies, particularly Lakotas. The price—the depletion of timber and forage and game—proved to be unexpectedly steep. In response, Omahas felt justified in taking livestock. Frustrated, Brigham Young held many diplomatic sessions with Big Elk, the "chief" of the "tribe." In fact Big Elk did not possess total authority over the Omahas. Likewise, Brigham Young had troubles tending his flock. Despite Young's proscription on trade with the Indians, disobedient Saints sold liquor. Occasionally they robbed graves. Mormon-Indian relations grew testy in 1847. For the most part, violence was avoided, but so was affection. The Saints did not even attempt to proselytize. They abandoned Winter Quarters in 1848 without any bequest—economic or spiritual—to the natives.[5]

The true believers among the Saints did not forget that someday they would have to turn their attention to the welfare of the Lamanites. Immediately after arriving in the Valley of the Great Salt Lake, Brother Brigham reminded the Pioneer Camp of its moral duties. In a sermon on the proper roles of men and women, he exhorted wives to obey the will of their husbands, and husbands to obey the will of the Lord—including the principle of plural marriage. This principle would be extended in time to Indians. According to Thomas Bullock, Young said that "the Elders would marry Wives of every tribe of Indians, and showed how the Lamanites would become a White & delightsome people & how our descendants may live to the age of a tree & be visited & hold communion with the Angels; & bring in the Millenium."[6]

One of the men in the audience, Levi Jackman, pondered Young's words, especially the prophecy about Lamanites. "A part of [our] duty in this world is to bring the Indians from their benighted situation," he wrote after the meeting. "In this place we finde a place and a people to commence with." Yet Jackman wondered how the will of the Lord could be achieved given the "brute" intelligence and "mean" existence of the Indians here:

> thay are the most filthy, degrade[d] and miserable beings probabl[y] that ever assumid the shape of human beings. When I reflect and co[n]sider that thay are of the haus of Isreal, or the stick of Jacob, and the children of the covenent seed, unto whome belongs the priesthood and the oricals of God. when I see the situation which thay are nowe in, and rearelise whot thay must be brought to by the Church of Jesus Christ, I say to myself O Lord who is able to do all this— But the decree has gon foarth and it must be accomplished,

Brigham Young, ca. 1851. (Courtesy of the Church Archives, The Church of Jesus Christ of Latter-day Saints)

and it will be marvilous, not onley to us but to generations yet to come[7]

This document beautifully illustrates the tension in Mormon thought between Indian-as-brother and Indian-as-other; between sympathy and contempt, belief and doubt. Pioneer leaders sincerely meant to *try* to redeem the Lamanites. But first things came first. In 1847–48 all of the Saints' energy went to establishing Great Salt Lake City as a haven for the expected new arrivals. Not until 1849–50, with the colonization of Utah Lake, did Brigham Young begin to develop an Indian policy. To this task he brought both spiritual expectation and real-world experience. The teachings of Joseph Smith now competed with the lessons of Winter Quarters.

::: Immediately before the Mormons invaded Utah Valley as settlers, they came as soldiers. At issue was livestock. Horses and especially cattle had disappeared from herds in Jordan Valley. Local settlers felt as possessive about their cattle as local natives did about their fish. In March 1849 LDS militiamen made their way around "Point of the Mountain" and along the "Western Jordan" to the lakeside village of "Little Chief." Here the Mormons registered their complaint. In his reply—spoken through a half-Ute, half-Spanish interpreter—Little Chief attributed the thievery to a renegade band of "mean Ewtes" related to the mixed-blood Salt Lake bands of Wanship and Goship. He offered his own sons to guide the militia to the hideout, a canyon now called Battle Creek. The militia made its move at night and executed its ambush at dawn. By fighting back, the four adult males "saved themselves the trouble of civil law." In other words, they were slaughtered. When Little Chief heard the news, he reportedly "howled, cried, moaned[,] hollowed, screamed and smote his breast in the greatest agony of mind."[8] Perhaps he regretted his choice to turn on his kinsmen—even though the decision could be defended rationally. By demonstrating his respect for Mormon claims to Jordan Valley and its animals (cattle), Little Chief might have expected the Mormons to show greater respect for his people's claims to Utah Valley and its animals (fish). If so, he was soon disappointed.

In collective memory and popular history, Mormon settlement of the interior West looks like a centrally organized process. Ecclesiastical leaders would "call" a complement of families on a "mission" to colonize. Obediently, these families would uproot from one valley and plant themselves in another, replicating the physical and cultural model of a Mormon village. In this way, the story goes, Mormons systematically worked their way north and south from Salt Lake, creating evenly spaced colonies—the "Mormon Corridor"—all the way from Idaho's Lemhi Valley to San Bernardino, California. This emphasis appeals to Mormon hagiographers and also to anti-Mormons who would like to hold Brigham Young personally responsible for every action (including murders and massacres) in early Utah. The historical truth is messier. Most Mormon towns were not colonies but regular settlements founded by families and individuals acting in their own interest. This process of self-selection sometimes had an ethnic component; Scandinavian Saints gravitated to the San Pete Valley, for example. In the case of Provo—the first and most important community settled after Great Salt Lake City—economic opportunities enticed settlers in 1849. They founded Fort Utah (the original name of Provo) in order to fish and trade by the sweetwater lake.

Although Brigham Young intended to claim this place for the Lord, he preferred to go slowly. The violent spring of 1849 hardly seemed like the best time. Yet just three days after the militia returned from Utah Valley, Alexander Williams and some other family heads in Salt Lake announced their intention to move south. The year before, as a company leader on the Mormon Trail, Williams had been known to be "refractory." He was not one to be stopped. Unenthusiastically, the High Council of the LDS Church gave its imprimatur to the plan; better to have a premature charter than no charter. According to council member John D. Lee, the goals of the "utauh" colony were "to setle & put in spring crops, open a fishery, introduce schools, teach the Natives how to cultivate the Soil, raise catle, & in fine to improve their Morals, to make Fishers of them, & then the Saints can buy the Fish of them for a trifle, which will preserve their feelings good as they claim the right to the Fish."[9]

It seems fair to take the LDS hierarchy at their word: they hoped to uplift the Indians even as they colonized their best land and exploited their fishery. To reconcile the inherent tension between these spiritual and economic goals would require exceptional local leadership. Unfortunately, Fort Utah did not attract that kind of people, and President Young could not dictate otherwise. Like most vanguard settlements throughout America, Fort Utah earned a reputation for rowdiness and rebelliousness. "The fact that the first settlers of Provo went without the advice of the recognized authorities of the people, was proof that they were not the proper persons to plant a successful colony among savages," recalled one church official. "They became too much on a equality with the barbarians."[10]

As of 1849, the Mormons in Utah were mainly composed of three population groups: New England transplants who had known Joseph Smith from the early days of the church; Britons who had emigrated directly to Nauvoo after conversion; and converts from southern and frontier states and territories—rough-and-tumble places like Missouri. Many of the men from the last group were well acquainted with guns, violence, and Indian trading. As census data show, the self-selecting settlers of Fort Utah drew disproportionately from this regional population.[11]

The Indians the settlers encountered seem to have been clustered in five separate population centers, all of them near water. The most important encampment was at the mouth of the Timpanogos River, at Lake Utah in the middle of the valley. Many related bands lived here. The most important leader was "Little Chief." Other leaders included "Highforehead," "Stick-in-the-Head," and "Big Elk" (not to be confused with the Omaha man). South of the Timpanogos River, several more streams emerged from the mountains. Hobble Creek, the Spanish Fork River, Peteetneet Creek, and Summit Creek each supported encampments. (Peteetneet was in fact the name of a band leader.) In addition to its semipermanent inhabitants, Utah Valley intermittently hosted nomadic bands, notably those led by Sowiette (based in the Uinta Basin), Arapene (based in and around San Pete Valley), and Walkara. Depending on the time of year, the valley's Nuche population varied from the high hundreds to the low thousands. At the Timpanogos River, the lakeside natives greatly outnumbered the initial 149 settlers.

On 1 April 1849 the wagon train of colonizers had almost reached their destination when they received a "no trespassing" message. According to one recollection, a Ute teenager "made a mark with his foot across the trail, and then solemnly forbade us from crossing that mark, saying as near as we could understand, that death and destruction would be our portion if we attempted it." In George Bean's memory, the young man threw his buffalo robe across the trail. Another colonizer remembered that the "greatly exited" Indians demanded a treaty for passage: "Dimick B. Huntington (the famous Indian interpreter) was made to raise his right hand and swear by the sun that thay would not drive the Indians from their land." As of 1849 Huntington's translation skills were still a work in progress, but he managed to communicate enough to mollify the Lake Utes. The pioneers continued to the river and camped half a mile from the Indian village. That evening the Mormons—three of whom were professional fishermen—ate like lake people. "Many had suckers (fish) for dinner but father & I had stewed Crane," remembered Bean, who turned eighteen that day.[12]

The next day the settlers went to work planting corn and grain and building fences and cabins. They connected the walls of the cabins to form a fort. Building material was plentiful. Cottonwoods and other water-loving trees abounded in this fertile land where the braided Timpanogos River ended its journey.

By choosing to locate next to the Timpanogos village, the Mormons unwittingly entered an unsettled arena of Indian-Indian conflict. There was a long-standing feud between the bands at Lake Utah and the mixed-blood bands of Salt Lake. In May 1848 Big Elk had taken the life of one of Wanship's sons in cold blood. The Mormons' 1849 police action against the "mean Ewtes"—abetted by Little Chief—exacerbated the bad feelings on the Salt Lake side. Yet on 7 April, less than a week after the settlers arrived, a representative from Goship's band came to the Timpanogos village to make peace. He was rebuffed. "Had we not protected him they would have killed him," said the leader of Fort Utah. Five days later warriors under Wanship and Goship attacked the camp of Little Chief, wounded one of his sons, and made off with all of his horses (about thirty). Devastated by his loss, Little Chief turned to the Mormons, saying, "if we are his friends he wants us to proove it by getting back their horses for them." Unsure of the proper course of action, the leader of Fort Utah wrote to Brigham Young for advice. Evidently Young sent an armed party to Wanship's camp near Great Salt Lake City to argue for the return of the stolen animals. Not persuaded, Wanship left for Fort Bridger, a safe place to sell horses. Little Chief followed in pursuit, having borrowed some steeds from neighboring bands. He caught up with his enemies and killed four of their men and forty of their horses, only to die in the process. The war party returned without a leader. Subsequently Big Elk and Stick-in-the-Head—a man who adorned his hair with mountain mahogany—assumed more authority over the Timpanogos River village.[13]

Shortly after this excitement, the settlers at Fort Utah witnessed another. "We soon found out," recalled George Bean, "that [the] Provo River region was the great place of gathering of all Ute tribes of central Utah valleys, too, on account of the wonderful supply of fish." On 14 May Dimick Huntington reported to Brigham Young that Walkara had arrived with ten lodges. More were on the way. Huntington felt good about his diplomatic overtures. He had given the famous Ute leader a flint gun in exchange for a horse, and invited him to his home for a smoke. "In the evening they felt happy, sung around the Fort—they slept around the Fire," wrote Huntington. "Walker lay in my arms—at night we talked . . . I told them of the Book of Mormon they must be our friends, & we yours."[14]

Brigham Young was more alarmed than pleased by this intimacy. He shot a letter back to Huntington, admonishing the settlers to finish their fort. Do not be deceived by the kindness of Indians, the prophet warned. Keep the Indians out of the fort except in small numbers, and never let them in with weapons. This advice seems to have been ignored. According to George Bean, "our people did a great deal of trading with them giving guns & ammunition." In addition to trading, the Indians made merry with horse-racing, foot-racing, wrestling, and gambling. The teenager "lost no time idle myself, and enjoyed their games and learned much of their language and made friends." In late May, hoping to curb this kind of familiarity, Brigham Young appointed two men—Dimick Huntington and Alexander Williams—to be the colony's sole Indian traders. "It will be better for your settlement not to be so familiar with the Indians," he rebuked again. "It makes them bold, impudent, and saucy and will become a source of trouble and expence to you—keep them at a respectful distance all the time, and they will respect you the more for it."[15]

In early July apostle Parley P. Pratt traveled to Fort Utah to inspect the scene. He, too, noticed the high degree of interaction between settlers and Indians, especially in connection with fishing. "I was at the Utah Lake last week," he wrote to his brother in England, "and of all the fisheries I ever saw, that exceeds all. I saw thousands caught by hand, both by Indians and whites. I could buy a hundred, which would each weigh a pound, for a piece of tobacco as large as my finger. They simply put their hand into the stream, and throw them out as fast as they can pick them up." As settlers waited for their crops to grow, fish provided a welcome food supplement. But farming and fishing did not take up everyone's time on long summer days. Fort Utah had a wild side. This aspect of Mormon life can be inferred from the settlement's first two regulations. Immediately after Pratt's visit, the colonists passed a law "for the Suppression of gambling with the Indians," followed by a law against "Shooting in or near the fort So as to Endanger lives thereby." Considering the volatile human material, relations between Mormons and Utes had started surprisingly well.[16]

A shooting incident in August put an end to this magnanimity. There are two versions of events. The official version states that an Indian called "Old Bishop" (nicknamed for his resemblance to Presiding Bishop Newell Whitney) stole a shirt. While wearing the shirt he ran into three Mormon men walking the lakeshore with a gun. The Mormons attempted to pull the shirt from Old Bishop's back, and ended up putting a bullet in his brain. The killers cut open Old

Bishop's abdomen, ripped out the guts, replaced them with rocks, and dumped the laden corpse in the river. The other version, told retrospectively by settler Thomas Orr, ends the same way but starts differently. Allegedly the Saints and the Timpanogos had made a treaty by which the Indians "agreed not to molest our cattle if we agreed not to kill the wild game which they depended on for a living." When Old Bishop came across the three Mormon men hunting a deer, he objected, and paid with his life. In any event, the corpse didn't sink as planned. Angry and grieving, the dead man's kinsmen confronted the leadership of Fort Utah. The Mormons refused to turn over the killers, so the Utes demanded compensation. In Ute culture, murders could be covered by a sufficiently large payment of goods, animals, or both. Again the settlers refused. To the Utes, this was a shocking display of injustice as well as ingratitude considering that they had been sharing their best pasture and fishery.[17]

The murder and the aftermath greatly soured relations but did not prevent individuals from reaching across cultures. Settlers continued to host "friendly" Indians even as they worked to complete their fort for protection against "saucy" Indians. In September, after George Bean was horribly wounded by the misfiring of a cannon—a weapon the settlers placed on a high platform for intimidation—many Utes stopped by Bean's house to wish him well in his time of trial. Young Bean prayed for his own death as the camp doctor removed some 200 pieces of wood from his body. With time he would interpret his accident as a blessing. Although he lost his left hand, he gained a life skill. During his long convalescence, Bean began to master the Southern Numic dialect. He would go on to become a noted interpreter. One of his regular bedside visitors was a Timpanogos man named Washear—also called Squash or Squash-Head by Mormons because of his deformed head. It's possible that Washear felt special sympathy for the maimed, scabbed, and blinded boy.[18]

As the injustice of Old Bishop's death festered among the Timpanogos bands, certain Utes took revenge. They shot at settlers, stuck arrows into cattle, and stole corn. In October a large-scale armed conflict was narrowly averted. Hotheads on both sides seemed ready to wage war before apostle Charles Rich, who happened to be traveling south, negotiated a peace. Hearing of this situation, Brigham Young sent another stinging letter to Fort Utah. He reprimanded settlers for inviting Indians into their homes and letting their children play with Indian children. "While you mix with them promiscuously, you must continue to receive such treetment from them which they please to give," he foretold. "If you would have dom[in]ion over them, for their good which is the duty of the Elders, you must not treet them as your equals, You cannot exalt them by this process. If they are your equals, you cannot raise them up to you."[19]

The settlers were in a bind. They couldn't afford to be too familiar, yet they couldn't afford to be unfriendly. The Utes had more people and probably more guns, having acquired many new firearms from a third, unexpected population group beside the Timpanogos River. In the late summer and early fall, several parties of forty-niners fattened their animals on lakeside pasture as they waited for the hottest months to pass. These gold seekers had arrived in Great Salt Lake City too late to continue due west for the Sierra Nevada. Instead they opted for the "Southern Route." The forty-niners happily traded guns and ammunition for fresh horses, though some of them complained about Mormons as well as Utes. "They call us Gentiles and regard themselves as entitled to superior privilege," wrote Arthur Shearer. "They are more troublesome beggars than the savages and to take the united voice of the emigrants for it, they are worse thieves."[20]

We cannot know with certainty, but it seems plausible that the Timpanogos band reflected on the relative benefits of transient outsiders versus colonizers as the forty-niners rolled on toward California. The strain of sharing resources with a settler population increased as winter approached; relations between Fort Utah and its native neighbors deteriorated throughout the remainder of the year. Tensions reached a boil in the bitter cold of January 1850. Out of anger and hunger, the Timpanogos appropriated cattle; by the end of the month the settlers had lost between fifty and sixty head. When the settlers demanded restitution, the Indians "bid Defiens to the Mormans and Sade they wolde Eete Mormon Beefe wen they plesde." Occasionally some Utes discharged guns in the direction of the fort; the settlers responded by forbidding all Indians to enter it. George Bean's father later stated that "Old Elk, who was sick with measles, came in for some medicine; he went to Sister Hunt's house, where Alexander Williams saw him and took him by the nape of the neck and kicked him out of the fort." That same evening, three cows went missing from Mrs. Hunt's yard. In the face of such "depredations," the settlers asked Brigham Young for permission to attack. Young gave his standard advice: patrol your people and your animals. "As to the ideas of warring with the Indians and killing them," he wrote, "there is no necessity for it if you act wisely, and if you do kill them, you do it at your own risk." He advised "rebellious" settlers to return to Great Salt Lake City or to leave for the gold mines of California. He then issued a lecture on morality: "Suppose an Indian steals a Shirt, an ox, a Horse or anything else, there appears to be a feeling in the minds of a few individuals to kill them for it on the spot. Suppose a white man commits precisely the same crime, or rooses [ruses], do those individuals or any person feel like killing them for it[?] We leave you to answer this."[21]

When he made this reference to a hypothetical stolen shirt, Young was apparently unaware of the murder of Old Bishop. Later he stated that settlers withheld this information from him. Had he not been deceived, further violence might have been avoided. As it happened, Fort Utah's bishop, Isaac Higbee, traveled to Great Salt Lake City determined to obtain a war order from President Young. In council, Higbee claimed that the occupants of the fort were unanimous: "Evry man and boy held up his hand to kill them off." Parley P. Pratt, recently returned from a southern exploring expedition, sided with Higbee as part of an overall colonization strategy. Without a secure settlement at Lake Utah, there could be no line of communication with future settlements farther south, he said. This was a live issue. Just weeks before, a colonizing party had been sent to San Pete Valley, about 100 miles south of Utah Valley. Apostle Willard Richards needed no more convincing. He said, "My voice is for War and extirminate them." And with that, Brigham Young changed his mind: "I say go and kill them."[22]

Despite his antipathy to the U.S. government, the Mormon prophet desired an imprimatur for his military action. By law, "Indian wars" fell under federal jurisdiction. But the Territory of Utah did not yet exist. The provisional government, called Deseret, was run as an arm of the LDS Church. The nearest federal troops occupied Fort Hall (in present-day Idaho) on the Oregon Trail, a prohibitively great distance given the weather. So Brigham Young turned to the closest thing to a federal official, Captain Howard Stansbury of the U.S. Topographical Engineers. Stansbury had come to the eastern Great Basin in 1849 to map the Great Salt Lake and Utah Lake. The captain gave his "entire approval" to the prophet's decision, in part because the Lake Utes had taken some of his livestock, too. Stansbury offered tactical advice, camp supplies, and the services of his adjutant and his physician. His self-interest was clear: "I was convinced that the completion of the yet unfinished survey of Utah Valley, [in] the coming season, must otherwise be attended with serious difficulty, if not actual hazard" unless "these savage marauders" were eliminated. Stansbury's lieutenant, John Gunnison, called them "red devils."[23]

For his troops Brigham Young relied on the remnants of Joseph Smith's Nauvoo Legion. On 31 January 1850 the church leader authorized his captains to raise two companies totaling 100 men. They also had to muster animals. In order to fight the livestock-stealing Indians, the legionnaires appropriated many horses (for transportation) and cattle (for food) from disgruntled settlers around Salt Lake. After pushing through some heavy snow, the "Minute Men" arrived at Fort Utah on the evening of 7 February. The strategy for the next day seemed simple: encircle the Indian village and destroy its residents with artillery. The order called for the extermination of "all hostile Indians" and any others who "do not separate themselves from their hostile clans, and sue for peace." The soldiers had instruc-

Engraving of Fort Utah, 1850, in Howard Stansbury's *Exploration and Survey of the Valley of the Great Salt Lake of Utah*. Note the cannon raised on a platform by the settlers. The shadowed massif in the left background is today's Mount Timpanogos.

tions to spare women and children except when "demanded by attendant circumstances."[24] By the time the soldiers arrived, some of the Timpanogos Nuche had evacuated to other camping sites in the valley. At least one family cluster sought and found shelter within Fort Utah. These "friendly" Indians included a man named Antonga (called "Black Hawk" by the Mormons) who would later become a major antagonist. But the majority of the late Little Chief's band—perhaps seventy in number—decided to resist under the leadership of Big Elk and Patsowet.

The ensuing scene was unusual—a pitched battle. The Indians had fortified themselves in and around an abandoned cabin adjacent to their village, located about a mile north of the fort. Timpanogos gunmen took positions behind felled trees and piled-up snow. With these defenses, they fought to a stalemate on the first day. The Mormons could not get close enough to achieve accuracy with their guns, and their shrapnel-loaded cannon produced more noise than damage. Thinking quickly, Stansbury's adjutant devised a movable battery. With late-night help from settlers, the soldiers constructed several large wooden shields and mounted them on sledges. These A-shaped barricades were covered with robes and brush, leaving holes for seeing and shooting. About a dozen men could move behind each shield. This offensive strategy paid off. On the second day of battle, the legionnaires took the cabin and advanced close to the Timpanogos village. Around ten Utes died under fire. Rather than accept further defeat, the Indians retreated during the night. In the morning the Mormons sent Black Hawk to scout his damaged village, which was deserted except for the dead.[25]

Stansbury's adjutant, George Howland, detailed the progress of the campaign in a letter to Major General Daniel Wells of the Nauvoo Legion. Howland praised the troops while noting that discouraging comments from certain settlers had "put a damper on their courage and patriotism. It would have been far better for them [the soldiers] to have gone and encamped close by the indians, than to have gone to the Fort and heard such remarks as 'I had sooner the indians should have my cattle than kill them for you to eat' and 'I want them [the cattle] to go to California with.' such remarks as these are not calculated to inspire our men at all."[26]

When Brigham Young got wind of this ingratitude, he was apoplectic. In a heated meeting he cursed the wicked settlers as much as the thieving Indians. Like Yahweh before the Flood, the Mormon prophet sounded as though he wanted to start all over. After referencing an unrecorded prophecy of Joseph Smith that "many of the Lamanites would have to be slain," Young sent Wells to Utah Valley to take charge. Wells galloped through the night carrying an expanded extermination order; as he recalled, he was "not to leave the valley until every Indian was out." At Fort Utah on the morning of 11 February, Wells declared martial law and ordered two troop movements, one to the east and one to the south. With Black Hawk's help, the first division followed a trail of blood-dappled snow to Rock Canyon. En route the soldiers found the frozen body of Big Elk; measles and exposure had done more harm than Mormon bullets. Hoping to wait out the remaining Indians, troops set up guard at the mouth of the steep box canyon. Over the next few days a few of the refugees were killed or captured, but the families of Stick-in-the-Head and Patsowet somehow managed to make an arduous crossing over the mountains on snowshoes.[27]

Meanwhile Daniel Wells led a sweep of the southern half of Utah Valley. With an enlarged force of 110, he descended on the Indian village at the Spanish Fork River. The Indians there had wisely fled. Wells continued on to Peteetneet Creek, where he divided the group into smaller hunting parties. Here the violence shifted from warfare to killing. Far removed from the battleground at the Timpanogos River, it was impossible for Mormons to distinguish between "hostile" and "friendly" Indians. They no longer cared. Numerous innocent people, including a blind old man, were killed in cold blood. The most sanguinary episode occurred at Table Rock, near the mouth of Summit Creek on the southeastern shore of Lake Utah, where one of the hunting parties tracked down a medium-sized Ute band. According to Lieutenant Gunnison of the Stansbury Expedition, the Mormons first captured some women and children; then the men "were induced to come in on the assurance of the whitemen being friendly to them." The Mormons lied. After a cold, sleepless night, the Ute warriors were lined up for a mass execution even as their families watched. Terrified, some of the men broke through the line and started running across the frozen surface of the lake. The Saints pursued them on horseback and shot them dead. The bodies remained where they fell. At least eleven Utes lost their lives on this Valentine's Day massacre. Gunnison heard about the "terrible scene" from a participant who "seemed disposed to paint it in as soft colors as possible." Instead of "kill," the informant used a nonincriminating verb, "ceased to breathe."[28]

The Mormons employed many such euphemisms. The militia had no choice but to "chastize" or "cut off" or "use up" the Indians, they said. Brigham Young was adept at this style of language. Writing to

Wells on the "proper treatment" of prisoners, he said, "We will not suffer Indians, who are Known to be hostile, and have come in your possession because they were sick [with measles] and could not fight . . . Your Surgeon Mr. Blake, is no doubt well provided with medicine, and will be ready to prevent that which will effect that most desirable of all objects, *perfect health*."[29]

Whether or not James Blake—the physician on loan from Stansbury—assisted in this way, he did contribute a gruesome coda to the massacre. Abner Blackburn recalled:

A few days after the last batle with the Indians, a government surgeon wanted James Or[r] and me to take a sley [and] cross over on the ice and secure the Indians heads, for he wanted to send them to Washington to a medical institution. [We] hired a sley [and] crost over on the ice. The weather was bitter cold. The surgeon to[o]k out his box of instruments and comenced. It took him a quarter of an hour to cut off one head. The sun was getting low and frezing cold. Jim and me took the job in our own hands. We were not going to wait on the surgeons slow motion. Jerked our knives out and had them all off in a few minutes. They were frozen and come off easy in our fassion. The surgeon stood back and watched us finish the job.[30]

Blake paid for Blackburn to box up the heads and bring them to Great Salt Lake City. By then the weather had turned warm. According to Blackburn, the "Indian heads smelt loud." Peteetneet, Tabby, and Grospene, three important band leaders in southern Utah Valley, eventually discovered the decapitated bodies. In March they angrily confronted a representative of Fort Utah about the beheadings. Memories of this grisly scene would be passed down for generations. In 1982 a Uinta Ute, Julius R. Murray Jr., related a family story: "Brigham Young wanted [the Utes] all to come down and parlay and leave all your guns at home and they came down and had a big feast on the lake and after that . . . that's when they killed them all. Killed most of them anyway. Shoved them under the ice in Provo."[31] Another twentieth-century account comes from the Koosharem Paiute Band: "A long time ago the soldiers attacked some peaceful Indians at Utah Lake during the winter when the lake was frozen over. Many of the women, children, and aged sought to flee to safety across the ice, but were overrun by soldiers on horseback who cut their heads off with swords."[32]

The massacre at Table Rock was the last major action in the extermination campaign—later called "the first Indian war." The Mormons had made their point: they were prepared to meet specific depredations with general destruction. Only one Latter-day Saint, a son of Isaac Higbee, lost his life. No definitive tally exists for the other side. Most contemporary sources estimate the number of dead at "about forty"—an example of deliberate undercounting. One reminiscent account states that a treaty made in April 1850 acknowledged 102 casualties. There is no official record of this treaty. However, 102 seems like a more reasonable estimate, especially considering that the besieged Utes also suffered from a measles epidemic and a food shortage during the coldest period of an unusually cold year.[33]

This season of misery produced many widows and orphans. When the Nauvoo Legion left Fort Utah—to the singing of a favorite American ballad, "The Girl I Left behind Me"—they carried with them dozens of these refugees. The "squaws" were kept in two tents in Great Salt Lake City before being distributed to various Mormon families. Writing to his wife from Great Salt Lake City, John Gunnison noted that the Mormons "brought in squaws & children which are placed in families as servants to make white people of them. One old woman went off the other night with her new petticoats & some knives,—the old ones will decamp when warm weather comes round no doubt; they may make something of the children." A wayfarer bound for California, George Montgomery, was so disturbed by this scene that he wrote a letter to Washington to report "that there are now held in slavery by the Mormons in the Valley of the Great Salt Lake about

Thirty Utah women & girls who were taken prisoners in a war of extermination waged last winter by the Mormons." Much later Daniel Wells recalled that the Saints of the city "fed and took care of them until spring when they ran back to their Indian camps. Many of them died, not being able to stand our way of living."[34]

The aftershocks of war traveled far and wide. In San Pete Valley, Walkara followed the events with interest and apprehension. Sick with the measles, he and his band relied on the kindness of the brand-new Mormon colony led by Isaac Morley. Diplomatically, Walkara told Bishop Morley that he approved of the war because the Lake Utes had previously killed one of his sons. To demonstrate his friendliness, Walkara allowed himself to be baptized; others soon followed. By summer more than 100 Utes had strategically "converted." To Brigham Young, it seemed that the "spirit of Lord is beginning to operate upon the hearts of the Lamanites." The prophet put a velvet glove on his iron fist. In Utah Valley Mormons made conciliatory gestures to the surviving bands. For example, they granted confiscated horses to Grospene and released the remaining prisoners from Fort Utah. The Saints tried to prop up Black Hawk as the next "chief" of the Timpanogos Nuche, but Washear, Highforehead, and Tintic (the son of Little Chief) would emerge as the key leaders at the Timpanogos River. On the losing side was Patsowet, who resurfaced around Salt Lake in April. Burning with resentment, he killed cattle and horses belonging to the Mormons. He threatened to do the same to Walkara's animals. Walkara called for his assassination—as if the Mormons needed any encouragement. Patsowet was blamed for the "murder" of Isaac Higbee's son. On 29 April he was arrested, "tried," and executed.[35]

With the two main "hostile chiefs" now dead, Brigham Young extended the hand of kindness to "Pe-tete-nete, Walker, Sow-ee-ette, Black Hawk, Tab-bee and other good Indian chiefs." "I know the difference between good Indians and bad Indians," wrote Young in an open letter. Bad Indians stole, killed, and refused to listen. The Mormons could not stand to live with such people: "The Great Spirit says we must kill bad men who kill others." But there was plenty of room for good Indians. Young promised to lift them up: "We will learn good Indians to raise corn. You must bye cows, and raise cattle." The letter invited all the chiefs for a harvest feast in September. The dispatcher, Major General Daniel Wells, also carried powder and lead to distribute as gifts. Young acknowledged in the letter that "the winter has been hard, and the Indians could not hunt, and they have no bread." He also avowed that God controlled the elements and that "God talks to Mormon chief" and therefore "Indians must do as God tells them, through Mormon chief, and be good and learn to work, raise grain, and learn all Mormons know." Young signed the document, "Big Chief."[36]

Young got a chance to meet his fellow "chiefs" a few weeks later at the annual fish rendezvous. After ferrying across the swollen Timpanogos River, Brigham Young's entourage crowded into Walkara's tipi. First there was a handshaking ceremony. Hundreds of Utes filed in to pay their respects to Young, who squatted uncomfortably. Afterward he held a peace meeting with about twenty band leaders, including Arapene, Tabby, Grospene, Stick-in-the-Head, Black Hawk, and Sanpitch. Dimick Huntington acted as interpreter. In his own tent, Walkara did most of the talking. He began by saying that either Snakes or Bannocks had recently killed eight of his relations near the Wind River Mountains. He wanted Young to discover the identity of the killers. After professing his love and friendship, Walkara asked the Mormon prophet not to throw him away. Young promised he wouldn't. He reminded the Indians that his party from Salt Lake had brought wagons of goods to trade. He then had Thomas Bullock read aloud his "Big Chief" letter, which Huntington translated. Afterward Young added, "You are my brother, let us be brothers, we want you all to be brothers." He asked Walkara to send "some of your young men[,] go and build houses and raise grain &c, and if they will send some of their children to school and we will clothe them and we will make settlements for other chiefs if they like and if some of them will go and make farms." Young asked the Indians to help with the harvest; he would pay them in grain. He even offered to employ an Indian to watch his herds. Walkara did not oppose these ideas, but he balked when Young inquired, "Do you wish to sell your land to the Mormons?" His translated reply: "Dont want you to buy it, but settle on it. Mormons love us, we love them, we are hungry now, but let it rest."[37]

After an afternoon meal Young and his counselors called on the other far-famed equestrian band leader, Sowiette. Here in Sowiette's tipi occurred one of the most captivating scenes in all of Utah history. After Brigham Young repeated his points about Utes learning to help with the harvest, he led the LDS brethren in song. For the Indians they performed two hymns, ending with the beloved Mormon anthem of pioneering, "All Is Well" (now known as "Come, Come Ye Saints"). The male chorus rang out:

We'll find the place which God for us prepared,
Far away in the West,
Where none shall come to hurt or make afraid;
There the Saints will be blessed.

After this song Young called the Utahs into a circle and preached:

my friends I want you all to be brothers tho' we are strangers[.] Now, we expect to be intimately acquainted (yes) We have come here to settle on your land but our Father the Great Spirit has plenty of land for you and for the mormons. We want you to learn to raise grain and cattle and not have to go and hunt and be exposed to other Indians, but build houses, raise grain and be happy as we are. If any of you have esteemed us to be your enemies, it is because you have been enemies to us, and what has passed this last winter we want forgotten and not have another occurrence, but be as friends and your children go to school and learn and always do right. We have many things to say to you when you understand them, to tell you of your forefathers, who they were, if you stay here a time and trade.[38]

Overcome with the Great Spirit, Young proceeded to speak in tongues. When he asked the Utes if they understood the mystical language, they all said yes. Young's traveling physician, Samuel Sprague, caught the enthusiasm: he, too, arose and performed glossolalia. Duly impressed, Arapene said the doctor had spoken Sioux. That evening the Indians returned the musical favor. Thomas Bullock recorded that "the Indians made a circle, singing & dancing, while another company were sitting around a fire gambling, they then formed a semi-circle & went singing up to the Fort, & in their manner giving us a serenading." Inside the fort, Dr. Sprague administered botanic medicine to Walkara, who suffered from fever.[39]

After the cruel, violent winter, both peoples tried hard to display goodwill. The settlers gave away many of their provisions to needy Indians. In Brigham Young's apt words, natives and colonizers expected to be "intimately acquainted." Of course, in the prophet's mind, proper intimacy did not include all forms of familiarity. To his irritation, the ungovernable settlers of Fort Utah continued to ignore his counsel. As in the year before, the fish rendezvous became a cross-cultural celebration; and Young left Lake Utah feeling once again "chagrined at the conduct of the settlers there, who had allowed their boys to wrestle, gamble and run horses with the Indians."[40]

And so Fort Utah's unsettled first year ended ambiguously. At the personal level and the political level, Mormon relations with the Lake Utes vacillated between segregation and neighborliness, disdain and respect, war and peace. This intractable dichotomy puzzled the outsider John Gunnison. His own view, one shared by most white Americans, was harsh but simple: the Indians were a "doomed race" that deserved to be extinguished. The Latter-day Saints struggled to be as straightforward. Reflecting on the lakeside violence of 1850, Gunnison wrote:

> It is a curious matter of reflection, that those whose *mission* it is to convert these aborigines by the sword of the spirit, should thus be obliged to destroy them—but they stoutly affirm that these people will yet, under their instruction, fulfil the prophecy that "a nation shall be born in a day"; and when they have completed the destined time, will listen to the truth and become "a fair and delightsome people."[41]

In actuality this belief varied from Saint to Saint and from year to year. The church hierarchy generally cared more about the redemption of the Lamanites than did the laity. As the lay population absorbed more and more English and Scandinavian converts—people with no connection to Joseph Smith and no experience with Native Americans—this divide widened. And even the authorities were not monolithic. Some, like apostle (and future prophet) Wilford Woodruff, unwaveringly believed in Lamanism. The attitude of President Brigham Young, the architect of Mormon Indian policy, was more vacillating and indifferent. He might be described as a skeptical or fair-weather believer. In May 1849 he expressed his doubts that the "old Indians now alive" would enter "the new and ever lasting covenant." It would be "many years" before the Lamanites would be redeemed, he suggested. The old Indians "will not do it, but they will die and be damned." A few days later John D. Lee recorded Young saying to the Deseret legislature that "this presant race of Indians will never be converted." If they were all killed off, "it mattereth not." By May 1850 this callous pessimism had swung to cautious hope, as illustrated by the scene in Sowiette's tent. By November, however, the pendulum had swung back. Young now advocated the total removal of the Utes.[42]

This new idea was born of political expediency. With the Compromise of 1850, the United States divided its war-won western lands into three large pieces: one free state (California) and two territories without immediate restrictions on slavery (Utah and New Mexico).

Lacking an alternative candidate, the U.S. government initially appointed Brigham Young to be Utah's territorial governor and superintendent of Indian affairs. In November, shortly before gaining his new titles, Young wrote to his liaison in Washington, D.C.: "It is our wish that the Indian title should be extinguished, and the Indians removed from our Territory (Utah) and that for the best of reasons, because they are doing no good here to themselves or any body else." The game animals had been hunted out. "There is little left here (abating the white population), save the naked rocks and soil, naked Indians and wolves. The first two we can use to good advantage, the last two are annoying and destructive to property and peace." Young went so far as to call the "wild men" worse by far than the "wild beasts." He argued that LDS efforts to civilize the Indians had been futile: "We would have taught them to plow and sow, and reap and thresh, but they prefer idleness and theft." It would benefit California-bound emigrants on the overland trail to get rid of these people. Again and again Young repeated the call, "Let them be removed." For a reservation, he suggested some region where game was still plentiful—perhaps the Wind River Mountains, the Snake River, or the eastern slope of the Sierra Nevada.[43]

Nothing came of this plan immediately. Mormons colonizers would have to learn to live with their Indian neighbors for the short term. Over the next ten years the key point of contact, conflict, and negotiation would continue to be Utah Valley. Latter-day Saints from Salt Lake at once took advantage of the "Indian war" to make further incursions to the south. In the second half of 1850 settlers planted eight future Utah Valley towns: Alpine, American Fork, Lehi, Pleasant Grove, Lindon, Springville, Spanish Fork, and Payson. The last three settlements abutted established Ute encampments at Hobble Creek, Spanish Fork River, and Peteetneet Creek. Along with Fort Utah—soon to be renamed Provo—these settlements would form the front line of Mormon-Ute relations in the turbulent 1850s. Devastated by war and disease, and constricted by new settlements, the Lake Utes relied ever more on two means of subsistence—fishing from Utah Lake and trading in slaves. Increasingly the Mormons interfered with these activities, too.

⁝⁝⁝ Brigham Young had some tolerance for slavery, but the traffic in slaves repulsed him. Although he couldn't stop Ute slave traders traveling to New Mexico, he could do something about New Mexican slave buyers coming to Utah.

In late 1851 Don Pedro León Luján, a *genízaro* from Abiquiú, New Mexico, led a trading party of about twenty men and 100 horses to the valleys of the southern Wasatch Front. He carried with him a license from the Indian superintendent of New Mexico Territory authorizing him to trade with the Yutas. However, this authorization did not extend to Utah Territory, where most Yutas lived. Upon arrival Luján realized that he needed a different license. Hoping to acquire the papers, Luján went looking for Governor Young. The two men met in San Pete Valley. Although he didn't speak Spanish, Young conveyed that he would not tolerate any trade with Indians in his jurisdiction. Luján apparently meant to follow these orders, and he headed for home. When a Ute band approached him to trade, he said no. Upset by this unexpected rebuff, the Utes seized many of Luján's animals. Determined to recover his property, Luján set off in pursuit. When confronted, the Utes refused to return his horses, offering slaves instead. In this way, allegedly, Luján came into possession of eight children and one adult female.[44]

When local Mormon officials heard of this incident, they arrested Luján. Eventually the case went to Great Salt Lake City for trial. Mormon officials accused Luján of violating the federal Trade and Intercourse Act. The case hinged on a simple but contentious question: had the New Mexicans planned the slave-buying or had it been forced upon them by circumstance? Neither position could be fully corroborated. Nonetheless, the Mormons meant to make an example of Luján. For their prosecution witness, they called Arapene (who spoke through George Bean). Arapene was well known to Mormons as a slave raider, yet he had been baptized, ordained, and blessed with the priesthood. His testimony was probably coached. In any case, on New Year's Day 1852 the all-Mormon jury found Luján guilty. He was fined $500. Bereft of all property, he and his men had to make their way back to New Mexico in the winter on foot. The confiscated slaves were allocated to LDS families.

For some time Brigham Young had been encouraging his people to "buy up" available Indian children. Ironically, the case against Luján highlighted the need to legalize this form of human traffic. In March 1852 the legislature passed "An Act for the Relief of Indian Slaves and Prisoners." By law, Mormons could go to the county court to certify the indenture of any Indian child for up to twenty years, provided they agreed to clothe and educate that child. From the Mormon perspective, the legislature formalized an existing system of benevolent foster care in which ransomed Indians could be Christianized. As Luján surely recognized, this system mirrored the New Mexican system.[45]

It took one more conflict to finally end the long-standing trade relationship between the upper Rio Grande and the eastern Great Basin. In the spring of 1853 a New Mexican caravan rode into San Pete Valley. Hoping to do better than Luján, the licensed traders brought along a Yankee mountaineer named Bowman to be an advocate for their rights. It didn't work: the San Pete settlers disrupted the trading. In response the Mexicans tried to arouse local Utes—including Walkara and Arapene—against the Mormons. Learning of this activity, Young dispatched Dimick Huntington to talk to Walkara. The prophet then left for his own tour of the southern settlements. In Provo he had a run-in with Bowman, who flouted the governor's authority. Not one to be intimidated, Young ordered a militia to arrest every "strolling" or "suspicious" Mexican in the area. Bowman was soon murdered. The Mormons claimed that Indians did it; the Utes claimed the opposite. With his bodyguards, Young traveled to San Pete, where he lectured to the Indians about the evils of slavery.[46]

Having lost their New Mexican buyers, the needy Utes expected

Mormon settlers to purchase all their slaves. The Saints accommodated them to the best of their limited financial ability. Sometimes it wasn't good enough. Around June, when Arapene tried to sell a young slave in Provo, he could not secure the right price. Angry and frustrated, he dashed the child's brains out.[47]

The best window into the Ute mindset comes from a document dated 3 July 1853. M. S. Marlenas, a trilingual veteran of the Taos fur trade, interviewed Walkara at the request of a federal official. Marlenas had been acquainted with Walkara and his kinsmen for "upward thirty years." Thus "they talk freely with me—and express their feelings and wishes without reserve," he wrote. A heartsick Walkara told Marlenas that he never wanted white settlers on his lands; that the initial kindness of Mormons had turned to abuse; that settlers had taken the best hunting grounds; that graves had been desecrated; that Indians had been driven from their ancestral lands; that whites were taking everything and giving nothing in return; and that the Utes could not live in peace with such people. "One prominent cause of the present excitement," commented Marlenas, "is the interference of the Mormons with their long established Spanish-trade, and the killing of an American by the name of Bowman, from Santa Fe, and charging the Murder to the Indians. I greatly fear that much difficulty will grow out of the present excited condition of the Indians,—should the Mormons continue their unkind treatment."[48]

It took less than two weeks for these fears to be realized. The pent-up resentments of the Lake Utes erupted after an altercation that began, emblematically, with fish. On 17 July 1853 a Ute woman came the house of Mrs. James Ivie near Springville to trade three trout for flour. Since flour was then scarce, the Ute woman received a small amount in return for the fish. When the Ute woman's husband followed her into the house to inspect the deal, he lost his temper and began beating his wife. James Ivie, stepping in to stop the abuse, overreacted and dealt the abuser a fatal blow. The dead man belonged to Walkara's band. The next day, acting upon specific and general grievances, a Ute war party murdered a Mormon boy at Payson before pilfering some cattle. A division of the Territorial Militia in Provo was at once sent to the scene. Going on the offensive, the troops killed six Utes. Tit-for-tat violence continued for another half-year in southern Utah Valley and nearby locales. Atrocities were committed on both sides. Having learned a lesson from the Fort Utah fight, the Ute belligerents did not attempt any head-to-head battles. Instead they staged a series of raids and ambushes. For protection, Mormons abandoned their smaller settlements and sent their surplus cattle to Provo. The larger colonies like Springville "forted up." Hoping to stay neutral, Sowiette and Walkara led their bands out of the valley. In December, hoping to end the cycle of violence, Brigham Young offered amnesty to all Utes. The last major incident in the "second Indian war" occurred in early 1854, when Washear's band stole a herd of cattle from Spanish Fork.[49]

As winter softened its grip, peace slowly reemerged. "Friendly" Indians brought back twenty-four of the sixty stolen cattle. On 1 May, having returned from the Colorado River, Walkara sent a letter to Brigham Young via George Bean. The letter called for an end to all restrictions on New Mexican traders. Walkara also wanted gifts of goodwill—oxen, flour, whiskey, guns, and ammunition. How much would Young be willing to pay for a twenty-year lease of selected Ute lands? Walkara wished to discuss these things in person.[50]

Young moved immediately to negotiate. En route, in Provo, Young called on the settlers to donate at least four cattle. When the cattle did not arrive the next day, Young, now in Springville, sent to the bishop of Provo "the very Severest letter." The embarrassed bishop had to strong-arm his people, who used "hard names" on him and the prophet. When the cattle finally appeared, Brigham Young traveled on to Chicken Creek, some fifty miles south of Utah Valley, where about fifteen band leaders—including Washear, Grospene, and Peteetneet—had congregated. "At first Walker appeared dogish & was not disposed to talk," wrote Wilford Woodruff. Brigham waited. Finally, Walkara agreed to smoke the peace pipe provided the Mormons would first sing him a hymn. Although the outstanding issues of land and trade could not be resolved—and although Walkara later complained that Young showed him disrespect by denying him a white concubine—the parties declared mutual friendship. Walkara asked for and received a letter that could be shown to other Mormons as proof of peace. The next day, before leaving, Heber C. Kimball and Daniel Wells laid their hands on a sick Ute child to give a priesthood blessing, while Dr. Sprague distributed medicine to others who were sick. Brigham Young aided a pair of very young slave children the only way he could: he purchased them. These "deplorable objects" sat "on the open snow, digging with their little fingers for grassnuts, or any roots to afford sustenance," an observer recalled. "They were almost living skeletons."[51]

In a matter of weeks the Chicken Creek congregation relocated to Utah Lake for the fish spawn. After some incidents of burglary, the people of Provo requested permission to "chastize" the Indians once again. Young wrote back with a no. The prophet-governor-superintendent had finally settled on an Indian policy: *it is cheaper to feed the Indians than to fight them.* In subsequent years he would repeat these words incessantly. In LDS collective memory, this dictum has wishfully become a description of Mormon-Indian relations. Of all the settlers of the American West, the tradition goes, only the Saints truly cared about the welfare of native peoples. The truth is not the opposite. But neither is it morally neat. Brigham Young believed that the current generation of Utes had to die out before a righteous generation could rise up. As he once phrased it, "They have either got to bow down to the Gospel or be slain." In defensive situations, Young was always prepared to "meet them with death, and send them to hell." But he no longer wanted to go on the offensive. After two inconclusive episodes of warfare in Utah Valley, he decided it was preferable to wait for deaths than to inflict them. Given the ravages of disease, he did not expect to wait long. In the meantime he hoped to gain goodwill by regularly giving away foodstuff. It was the religious duty of the Saints to treat "friendly" Indians with kindness and forbearance.[52]

Abiding by this conciliatory policy, the people of Provo held a feast for over 200 Utes in August 1854. According to the record, "Three beeves were killed, 4 barrels of biscuits furnished, together with a large quantity of vegetables. A large amount of clothing was distributed among them under the direction of George Bean, Indian interpreter, the whole being contributed by the inhabitants of Provo."[53] In the fall the peace survived a tough test when the settlers of Provo found themselves in the midst of an intertribal conflict between Snake bands and Timpanogos bands. Ironically enough, a bigger immediate challenge to the food-based peace policy would prove to be food. The feast of 1854 would not be repeated the next year. By then the people of Provo would themselves be starving.

The famine started with a population explosion—not of people but of insects. Every one to three years from the 1850s to the 1890s, flying swarms of Rocky Mountain locust *(Melanoplus spretus)*—colloquially called grasshoppers—wreaked havoc on Utah's crops. In scale and intensity, the worst "plague" by far occurred in 1855. From Cache County in the north to Iron County in the south, fields of grain disappeared in front of people's eyes. One observer estimated forty insects per stalk of corn. The prodigious hatch emerged in the spring after a mild, dry winter. "They darkened the air like a thick cloud as they came down upon the fields," recalled Robert Thomas of Provo. "They covered the valley of Utah. The crops every where were destroyed. The vallie appeared as through scarched with fire." Thomas refused to give up. He burned grasshopper hatching sites; he let loose sixty chickens onto his fields. Using a heavy rope as a dragline, he drove insects into a ditch. After they fell in, he buried them. Other farmers used willow branches to sweep locusts into canals or streams, where they could be screened out and thrown into coffee bean sacks before being burned or buried.[54]

Despite the heroics, the outcome was hunger. Drought conditions turned the locust crisis into a general food crisis. Families started rationing flour. Game animals, already scarce in the settlement zones, retreated farther into the mountains. Cattle broke down fences trying to find pasture; many died after drinking from stagnant pools. Then the winter of 1855–56 arrived with great severity. To survive until the next harvest, the Mormons had to act more like natives: they gathered edible roots and bulbs and greens—plants such as wild turnip, lamb's quarter, redroot, and pigweed. William Rigby of Utah Valley later declared that "my wife and I ate so many weeds during the summer [of 1856] that our skin became tinted with green." There were cultural limits on dietary change, however. The settlers ingested "weeds" but not "pests," the animal kingdom equivalent. Although Mormons knew from watching the Indians that crickets and locusts could be used as a food resource, they could not bring themselves to eat wicked insects. Instead they focused on a more palatable native food resource—fish.[55]

Previously local settlers had used the Utah Lake fishery as a supplemental rather than a primary resource. But in 1855–56 settlers all along the Wasatch Front turned to it as an indispensable food store. Thousands of pounds of lake fish were donated as tithing to the church/state, which distributed the food to its many public works employees constructing the temple in Great Salt Lake City. Peddlers sold trout, chub, and suckers in the streets of the capital. Meanwhile many farmers-turned-fishers from Salt Lake squatted along the Provo River—the new name for the Timpanogos River—with nets and salting barrels. So many seines lined the river that the city passed a law banning their use at night and on Sundays. Visiting fishers clashed with resident fishers who operated with city charters. "If i where a prophet i would say there will be no fish in 5 years unless we stop Quarreling," commented a local church leader in April 1856. In May Wilford Woodruff described the fish-for-all: "The shores of Utah Lake are crowded like a fair with wagons—there are so many catching and drying fish."[56]

Mormons were not the only needy ones. In 1855, as customarily, local and nonlocal Utes—about forty lodges—congregated at the Provo River at spawning time. Since the usual pasture was unavailable or inaccessible because of drought or fences, the Utes moved into the "Old

Fort Field," the only plot in Provo that had so far been spared by lo-custs. An LDS Indian agent labored mightily to remove the Utes' ani-mals from the wheat, corn, and potatoes. Negotiations broke down when Utes accused Mormons of killing some of their horses; in reply, Mormons accused Utes of taking cattle and harassing women. The ranking military officer in Provo felt disposed to rout the Indians, but the bishop had strict orders from Young not to shed any blood. The Mormons offered a mollifying payment of animals, flour, and cash. The controversy nonetheless continued for another month. The Timpanogos band leaders Tintic, Washear, and Black Hawk felt less inclined to make peace than the visiting band leaders Tabby, Sanpitch, and Grospene. The unusually competitive fishing scene aggravated bad feelings. After the agent heard complaints from the fishing chiefs, he ordered Mormon netters and seiners to desist for the duration of the Utes' stay. When the Indians did not have much luck fishing with their traps and arrows, they had to call on their competitors for help. In one haul, Mormons pulled in about 1,000 suckers for the Utes.[57]

The gift of fish helped to calm the situation. The government agent also secured a promise that the people of Provo would reserve some lakeside pasture for the Utes the next fishing season. That was all the settlers could promise. In his report to Young the agent observed that the colonizers, destitute from locusts and drought, couldn't afford to continue their "former liberality" toward the even more destitute na-tives. The government would have to make up the difference.

A recently arrived federal Indian agent took this idea in a new direc-tion. Next to Brigham Young, Garland Hurt ranks as the most impor-tant architect of Utah Indian policy in the 1850s. He came to the terri-tory in April 1855 as a presidential appointee to the Office of Indian Affairs. The ambitious Hurt immediately formulated an alternative to the fight/feed policy. It was, he thought, better to teach the Indians to feed themselves than to hand out food. He proposed to Young the idea of "Indian Farms"—quasi-reservations where resident Indians would learn husbandry. Though convinced of the "idleness" of Indians, Young agreed to explore the idea. In the fall, before gaining formal approval, Hurt plowed ahead. He laid out three townships—one near Fillmore, one near Manti, and one near Spanish Fork. The Utah Valley farm plot encompassed 640 acres along the Spanish Fork River. Hurt envisioned it as the germ of a 12,000-acre reservation stretching from the river to the southern shore of the lake. It would be the future home for what the government enumerated as four bands of fish-eating "Pah-utes" (Water Utes)—the "*Tim*-pan-oie" band at Provo River, the "*Tim*-pa-up" band near Hobble Creek, the "*Pe*-kip-oy-na-re" band near Peteetneet Creek, and the "*A*-vick-a-ba" band at Summit Creek.[58]

The blueprint reservation could not provide relief during the harsh winter of 1855–56. In February, the time of worst hunger, Mormon officials distributed some meat and grain to the "friendly" Indians of Peteetneet's band. At the same time, a posse went out with arrest warrants for Tintic and Washear of the Tim-pan-oie/Timpanogos. Pushed out of their ancestral wintering ground at the Provo River, these leaders had turned to large-scale cattle raiding in Utah Valley and Cedar Valley. After several skirmishes and deaths (sometimes called the "Tintic War"), Washear ended up in chains in a house in Springville awaiting trial and execution. Before that could happen, his throat was cut from ear to ear. Twelve "judicious men residents" performed an inquest. This jury immediately returned the verdict that the prisoner had committed suicide with his breakfast knife. This claim is not as outrageous as it seems, since Utes were known to view hanging as an ignominious form of death. It is of course more likely that the inquest was rigged. Whatever the case, Washear joined a growing line of Provo River leaders—Little Chief, Big Elk, Patsowet—who met early deaths.[59]

The options of the Timpanogos Nuche had dramatically shrunk in less than a decade. Except during the fishing season, Provo could no longer accommodate large encampments of Utes. When Sowiette visited the town in 1855 after a two-year absence, he said he hardly knew the place, for it had "grown so very big."[60] Out of necessity,

Utah Valley's native center of gravity shifted south to the Spanish Fork River. For the first time in ages, the mouth of the Provo River was no longer a place of refuge and plenty for The People.

⁝⁝⁝ From 1855 to 1865 Indian-white relations in Utah Valley grew more political and ideological. The federal government tried harder to assert itself in territorial affairs even as the Mormons tried harder to promote kingdom-building. Millenarianism and Lamanism revived during the "Mormon Reformation" of 1855–1857. This period of religious excess greatly damaged relations between Great Salt Lake City and Washington, D.C., and in turn hurt Utah Valley's natives. By the time the Civil War diverted national attention from the "Mormon Question," Garland Hurt's farming policy had failed just as surely as Brigham Young's fight/feed policy.

The Reformation had both internal and external causes. In 1852 the LDS Church began facilitating the "gathering" of thousands of converts directly from Great Britain and Denmark through its Perpetual Emigration Fund Company. As resultant settlements grew more dispersed and diverse, the church leadership worried about the weakening of group cohesion. Provo offered a negative example of the desired relationship between the central hierarchy and the outlying laity. Mormon sermons on obedience and recommitment were common even before 1847, but they increased in frequency and intensity after 1854, when Brigham Young promoted the firebrand Jedediah Grant to the First Presidency. The "biblical" plague of locusts, an apparent sign of God's dissatisfaction with the New Israel, enhanced the mood for revival. Another portent came in 1856, when Congress rejected Utah's opening bid for statehood—a repudiation of veiled theocracy and unveiled polygamy.

In the heat of the moment many Mormons anticipated an alternative scenario—an independent LDS nation that would flourish even as the iniquitous United States burned to ashes. As foreseen by Joseph Smith, the Mormon apocalypse included a prominent role for the "remnant of Jacob." Strong faith in the destiny of the Lamanites reemerged during the Reformation. In 1855 Brigham Young demonstrated his renewed conviction by authorizing the establishment of Indian missions—one at the Colorado River near present-day Moab, Utah; one at the Santa Clara River near present-day St. George, Utah; and one at the upper Salmon River in Idaho. Smaller delegations were sent to preach among the Crows, the Cherokees, and other distant tribes. At the same time Young established "home missions" for lapsed and wayward Mormons. Authorities also staged the LDS equivalent of tent revivals. (Early Utah Saints assembled beneath "boweries," simple thatched shelters like large porticos.)

At a special three-day conference in Provo in July 1855—just after the Indian fishing controversy, and in the midst of the grasshopper crisis—a pantheon of pioneer leaders called the settlers to task. "Their is a strange spirit in provo," wrote Wilford Woodruff. "Many do not pray & have not the spirit of God." Brigham Young lectured on the importance of plural marriage and urged more men to accept the principle. Heber C. Kimball interpreted the insect plague as a chastisement from God. Provo's famine came in the seventh year of its settlement; God and the Earth intended to rest, Kimball suggested. If the Saints at Utah Lake weren't prepared, they deserved what they got. Jedediah Grant said he "would like to see the work of the reformation commence" and called on the people to be more righteous. Orson Pratt, Joseph Young, Ezra T. Benson, and Wilford Woodruff each spoke at length about the Lamanites. Pratt reminded the Saints that "this people will be our shield in days to come" and that they "are to be the principal operators in that important work" of building the New Jerusalem. Woodruff recalled the ministry of Joseph Smith, when many Mormons received the gift of tongues in their enthusiasm about the Lamanites. In Utah, however, these same people became "back-sliders from that faith which they then imbibed." Had they preserved their original faith in the Book of Mormon, they would have led the Lamanites into civilization by now. Woodruff castigated the Provo Saints for treating the Indians the way the Gentiles had treated the Mormons. It was only fair to feed and clothe and teach and employ the Lake Utes, he preached.

> You will eat their fish too, on which they depend for a living one part of the year, and every service berry that you can find in the mountains, and still you grumble to let them have a little with you. You don't want the crickets, and therefore they can have the whole of them, but you have secured the antelope and everything else that you could make any kind of use of. Before the whites came, there was plenty of fish and antelope, plenty of game of almost every description; but now the whites have killed off these things, and there is scarcely anything left for the poor natives to live upon.[61]

Remarkably, Woodruff's Sunday admonition had been preceded by some harsh words from a Timpanogos native, Highforehead. Speaking through Lyman Wood, Highforehead addressed the congregation. Before the settlers came, he said, timber grew abundantly by the river. He and his people loved their ancestral land; they could not bear the thought of selling it. He wanted Utes and Mormons to live together. But he complained that many Mormon men pretended to speak the Numic language better than they actually did. They misrepresented the Ute point of view. He found it offensive that translators typically spoke in a garbled mix of English and Numic. The "great spirit does not like it," said Highforehead. The spirit "talks all one way, and wants all his people to talk one way." Then, sounding just like an LDS authority, Highforehead reprimanded those settlers who refused to listen to Brigham Young. According to the interpreter, Highforehead "wants all those who have got no ears to get some, for they should not have any mouths till they have ears."[62]

Highforehead was not the only Ute who displayed a shrewd understanding of the Mormon idiom. In February 1855, shortly after Walkara's unexpected death, Arapene called on some Mormons in San Pete Valley. He wanted them to transcribe a vision he received.

Even assuming a certain amount of unintended and/or wishful mis-translation, the resulting document clearly comes from a Ute point of view. Arapene began by saying that Walkara had appeared to him and told him to be at peace with the Mormons. After that "the Lord" spoke at length. He said the land belonged to him, not to the Mormons or the Indians. After giving Arapene the authority to punish those Indians who stole Mormon cattle, God specified that he never wanted Indians punished by death. If the Mormons disobeyed this command, the Lord would depart from their church meetings. Through Arapene, God indicated that "by & bye when all People was good and at peace he would come and Live on the earth and not go Back." Arapene also claimed to have seen "three personages and there garments where as white as snow and as Briliant as the sun and by and bye all good People would Apear as they did." The Lord explained that he had come to talk to Arapene just as he often spoke to Brigham Young. Arapene concluded by saying that God had instructed the Mormons "give unto me a young cow or heffer But I was to not kill her but to keep her it is the Lord that wants the cow and not me[;] and as the Lord said for me to not talk to[o] much I will relate no more at this time[.] But this is the Lords talk and not mine." It seems safe to presume that Arapene got his desired animal. The Mormons respected his "vision." When the transcript arrived in Young's mailbox, the clerk filed it as "The Lord to arrowpin." Over the next two years, the Ute prophet carried on an active correspondence with the Mormon prophet.[63]

During this upsurge of Lamanism, Young's point man for Indian affairs was Dimick Huntington. In 1857 he had his hands full. In June–July of that year U.S. President James Buchanan ordered a large armed force—2,500 men—to install a non-Mormon appointee to the territorial governorship. Buchanan acted rashly on the exaggerated complaints of runaway officials—federal appointees who had left the territory in frustration with the LDS shadow government. The paranoid style of Mormon rhetoric encouraged the worst suspicions in outsiders. Correspondingly, the deployment of government troops added fuel to the Mormon Reformation. Having been driven from their homes in Missouri and Illinois, the Mormons responded with defiance to the perceived federal invasion. Brigham Young bragged in public about his influence over the Indians and worked to shut down overland mail routes. Huntington conducted negotiations with various Indian leaders, trying to get them to ally with the Mormons instead of "the Americans." In an August meeting at a camp of Shoshones, Huntington "told them that the Lord had come out of his Hiding place & they had to commence their work." He "gave them all the Beef Cattle & horses that was on the Road to Calafornia"—that is, he gave them authorization to raid American emigrants. Ute and Paiute leaders received a similar sanction for the Southern Route. In this atmosphere of misrule, local Mormons and some Paiute accomplices massacred the California-bound Fancher party at Mountain Meadows on 11 September 1857.[64]

Garland Hurt stayed in the territory as long as he could. Compared to most federal appointees, he was an honest man who made a sincere effort to get along with the Latter-day Saints. "I do not wish to excite prejudice or encourage feelings of hostility against these people," Hurt wrote to his commissioner back in 1855. "On the contrary, I think such a course would be unwise and impolitic." Hurt possessed a brilliant sociological understanding of nineteenth-century Mormons: "They always have and ever will thrive by persecution. They know well the effect it has had upon them, and, consequently, crave to be persecuted." Even so, Hurt raised objections about the Indian missions. He disapproved when missionaries tried to draw a distinction in the minds of Utes between Mormons and Americans. This fictive boundary became a real boundary in September 1857. When local officials made moves to arrest Agent Hurt, the several hundred Utes at the Spanish Fork farm rallied to his aid. The Indians outfoxed the Mormon militiamen and shepherded the man they called "the American" to Fort Bridger.[65]

Shortly thereafter the bishop of Springville made a tour of the Indian Farm. "It seemed a perfect scene of waste and confusion," he

C. B. Hancock, *Indian Reserve Scene of Agency & Peeteteeteneete's Band 1857.*
The artist was a local Mormon militiaman. (Courtesy of the Church Archives, The
Church of Jesus Christ of Latter-day Saints)

wrote. In only its second year of operation, the would-be reservation
had been abandoned and plundered. Hurt and the Utes had left behind ten acres of corn, eight acres of potatoes, and forty-nine cattle
branded ID ("Indian Department"). Local Mormons harvested the
crops and corralled the animals, and the farm/reservation went without formal supervision well into 1858 as the territorial conflict—
dubbed the "Utah War" or "Buchanan's Blunder"—dragged on.[66]

In March 1858 Brigham Young implemented the "Move South," a
temporary relocation of the Mormon capital to Provo. Soon afterward the federal army under Albert Sidney Johnston marched into
the deserted streets of Great Salt Lake City. Negotiations ensued. In
June Young accepted the government's terms of peace. In addition to

a Gentile governor, the Mormons agreed to an army presence. The troops moved on to Cedar Valley, west of Lake Utah, where they constructed Camp Floyd. These events added more pressure to the overused Provo River fishing grounds. One veteran of the Move South recalled that "we had to dig holes to get water, and the people began to complain of sickness. The feed had also been all eaten off by the cattle."[67] Mormon refugees ate lake fish as they waited to return home. Afterward enterprising Provoans sold trout to the soldiers at Camp Floyd before the post was evacuated for the Civil War.

Garland Hurt returned with the troops but couldn't prevent 1858 from becoming another year of hunger and sickness for the Utes of Utah Valley. Since the founding of Fort Utah, the native population had been hit successively by measles, cholera, consumption, scarlet fever, whooping cough, and mumps. The Lake Utes believed the settlers bore direct responsibility. When Dimick Huntington went to Spanish Fork to give away food, one of the Ute men angrily jammed a piece of bread into Huntington's mouth, saying, "Eat it for it is poison & you want to kill us." Tabby, the only leader who would converse with Huntington, asked "what it ment they was all sick & [asserted that] Brigham & I had talked to the Great Spirit to make them all sick & die. I told him it was not so for when B & all the good mormons prayed, they prayed for them. he sayed o shit you Lie."[68]

Huntington actually spoke from his heart. Not long afterward he concluded his journal with a prayer: "may God turn away our enemies from us & all that are not of us & Gather Israel. wake up the sons of Laman[;] make them a defence to Zion & Let Zion be redeemd, the Jews be gatherd to Jerusalem & it be rebuilt [and] the 10 tribes come from the North. Amen."[69]

In retrospect, this prayer was a coda to the Reformation rather than a prelude to the Millennium. Throughout the 1860s, Mormon millenarianism and Lamanism waned. And in the settlements of Utah Valley, Indians became a background rather than a foreground presence. In the historical record, they all but disappear. Granted, the historical record privileges episodes of conflict over episodes of coexistence. Only in the published recollections of Don Carlos Johnson, the son of Springville bishop Aaron Johnson, do we get a glimpse of the full picture of intercultural relations. Writing a half-century later, Johnson described Utes serving as washerwomen; Mormons buying and selling slave children; and, most arrestingly, Ute and Mormon boys playing together. In addition to games of swimming, racing, wrestling, jumping, throwing, slinging, and shooting, the children played roughhouse:

> The white boys would meet them [the Indians] down the lane, equally ready for a friendly game or a rough and tumble fight. The hair pulling game consisted in selecting one of the grit[t]iest champions from each side, who at the word went at each other and pulled hair until one cried enough, while the opposing factions stood around yelling encouragements to its champion. Quite often this game ended in a general fight in which all took a free hand.[70]

As for the adults, the last recorded large-scale conflict in Utah Valley proper occurred in late 1858 after members of Tintic's band gang-raped a mother and daughter near Spanish Fork. When soldiers from Camp Floyd tried to arrest the culprits, a general disturbance ensued. After being arrested, Tintic saved himself by turning in two of his kinsmen. The son of Little Chief would not survive for long, however. He expired in March 1859 at the end of a hard winter. "The Indians had a big pow-wow on the occasion, and killed eight horses to accompany him to the Ute world of spirits," reported a Mormon from San Pete Valley. Like all the remaining Timpanogos, Tintic had been spending more time to the south and east of his ancestral home base. Fewer and fewer Lake Utes returned to the mouth of the Provo River. When they did, they found it ever harder to fish. So they begged. Thomas Groneman reiterated a familiar theme of pioneer reminiscences when he spoke of his 1860s childhood in Provo: "As to the Indians all I know about them is that they were great beggars . . . I do remember of going fishing one day and catching a trout which weighed about 12 pounds. On my way home I met some Indians and they begged it from me."[71]

The proposed Spanish Fork reservation might have replaced the lake as a refuge, but a combination of cultural and environmental factors got in the way. Ute men considered harvest work emasculating. Given their preference for an animal-based peripatetic lifestyle, they probably would have responded better to an Indian Ranch than to an Indian Farm. During its moments of production, the Indian Farm paid Mormon farmers to do most of the work. Although 1859 promised to bring a decent yield, a locust infestation destroyed most of the crops. The following winter many local Utes died of starvation and exposure. "It was a common circumstance to find them frozen to death," wrote Andrew Humphreys, the new agent. Garland Hurt had left permanently as a result of political conflict. For whatever reason, Humphreys did not last long either. During his brief tenure he was forced to sell off all the farm equipment in order to buy food to feed the Utes.

Although it was an American article of faith that agriculture provided the surest path to civilization, the U.S. government never matched that faith with sufficient funding. In 1861 the new agent, Frederick Hatch, found the farm in a "deplorable state." The diversion dam was failing; the fences were on the ground. That winter Hatch reported that "not a spoonful of grain or roots has been raised on this farm the past year." The place was "bare as a picked chicken." The "farm" had been reduced to a bankrupt welfare agency. Agent Hatch tried in vain for weeks to get the government to provide food and supplies for the hungry Utes, who at one point numbered up to 200. The goods never came. To make things worse, local Mormons wouldn't sell or contribute. In May 1862 Hatch sent a dispirited letter to Utah's latest superintendent of Indian affairs—the fourth man to hold that job in as many years. "I am strongly in the faith that these Indians here, are worse off to Day, then if they have never seen or herd of a Goverment Agent," he wrote.[72]

U.S. policy turned to removal. In 1861 President Lincoln had au-thorized the interior secretary to set aside the Uinta Basin for the Utes of the Territory of Utah. This land was located in the eastern part of the territory, beyond the Wasatch. Shortly before, a Mormon explor-ing party had evaluated the Basin as "one vast 'contiguity of waste,' and measurably valueless, excepting for nomadic purposes, hunting grounds for Indians and to hold the world together."[73] Finally, in 1864, the wartime Congress dissolved the Indian farms and provided for the extinguishment of Indian title in Utah Territory by treaty. Technically, the Mormons had been squatting on Indian land since the end of Mexican War. The U.S. government had delayed creating a public domain in Utah because it did not want to see the Latter-day Saints acquiring vast landholdings. But the inevitable could be de-layed for only so long. In early 1865 Congress authorized "negotia-tions" with the Utes.

The Utah superintendent of Indian affairs, Colonel O. H. Irish, worked with Brigham Young to assemble sixteen Ute headmen at the Spanish Fork River on 7 June. En route from Great Salt Lake City, Young's entourage passed "large tracts of well cultivated farm-ing land, with the young grain shooting through the genial earth, show[ing] marks of thrift and industry." As of the latest census in 1860, over 8,000 settlers lived in Utah County, and over 40,000 lived in the territory. The lean years of the 1850s belonged to the past. Not so for the Lake Utes. At the treaty session, the remnants of the Tim-panogos—about 300 people—were represented by one Ankartewets and a "sub-chief," Nanp-peads. Black Hawk conspicuously failed to attend.[74]

Irish presented the terms of the treaty as part of a forceful take-it-or-leave presentation. "You stand before [your people] today to lead them into a road of prosperity or one in which they will be poor, and weak and suffering," he told the Utes. Sounding not unlike a Mor-mon, Irish said that the "Great Spirit in Heaven" had wanted Utah Valley to produce grain and therefore had directed the pioneers to set-tle here. Irish portrayed the treaty as a win-win situation: the settlers would gain peace, and the Indians would gain prosperity. The treaty promised sixty years of annual annuities along with infrastructure development on the proposed reservation. With the aid of the government, the Utes would, Irish promised, become successful farmers on individually owned properties in the Uinta Basin. And although they would relinquish their "possessory right of occupation" to all other lands, they would retain visitation and use rights. Article 4 stipulated that "the right of taking fish at usual and accustomed grounds, and stations is further reserved to said Indians in common with all white citizens of the Territory and of erecting temporary houses for the purpose of curing [the fish]." The government still recognized the importance of Utah Lake and its fishery to the identity of these Utes.[75]

Four band leaders—Sowiette, Tabby, Sanpitch, and Kanosh—spoke for the assembled Utes. Two of Provo's original settlers, Dimick Huntington and George Bean, acted as interpreters. Kanosh had some hard words for Irish. This baptized Pahvant Nuche from the Corn Creek Indian Farm praised Brigham Young for his history of forthrightness, in contrast to the "Washington chiefs" with "two tongues and two hearts." Evidently Kanosh did not fully comprehend the federal process of treatymaking or the import of Mormons' and "Americans'" finally cooperating. Kanosh asked (perhaps with sarcasm), "If the Americans buy the land, where would the Mormons, who live here go to? Will the Lord take them up to his country?" He desired that the Mormons and the Utes would continue living together; he did not want to "cut the land in two." Sanpitch was more blunt. "It used to be the Lord's land," he said, "but now it is the Mormons' land and ours." He did not want to "give up my title to the land I occupy." It was "good heavy land, lots of water and rocks."[76]

In order to convince the intransigent Utes, Young—a man of great stature in their eyes—laid out two stark options. If the Indians sold their land, the government would build them schools and houses; if they didn't, the government would just take the land (though the prophet hastened to add that the land would still belong to the Lord). Young praised the treaty provisions as "just and liberal." And he reiterated that the Utes would be welcome to visit Mormon settlements at any time. In response, Tabby indicated that the delegation needed time to talk and smoke and think. "The Indians are not ready now to give up the land; they never thought of such a thing," he said. Through the night the Ute leaders mulled over their predicament. They had no leverage with which to negotiate. Although it must have pained and offended them, all but Sanpitch agreed the next morning (8 June) to accept the treaty and the presents that Irish had brought. Better to get something than nothing. The Nuche headmen signed the treaty—what they called "the paper"—with a mixture of faith and skepticism. Through George Bean, one leader from San Pete Valley said, "I hope there will not another paper come from Washington that will contradict this and bring bad talk." (In fact something worse would happen. In 1869 the Senate rejected the treaty and with it the promise of long-term aid to the Utes.)[77]

In the second half of the 1860s, the majority of Utah's Utes followed the lead of the treaty signers and relocated to the Uinta Basin. A minority engaged in a low-grade guerrilla insurgency in central and southern Utah. The so-called Black Hawk War did not directly affect Utah Valley, but the lead instigator came from a Timpanogos band. Black Hawk (Antonga) had been one of the "friendly" Indians during the original "Indian war" in 1850. Circumstances had darkened his view of Mormons. Driven from his home lake, Black Hawk helped coordinate a pan-Indian alliance of Utes, Paiutes, and Navajos. In the end, however, Black Hawk pleaded for peace and forgiveness. In 1870, mortally diseased, he returned to Utah Valley to die. The leadership line of the Timpanogos Nuche ended when his relatives buried him with his horse. A U.S. Indian agent reported in 1870 that the "Timpanoge Indians formerly resided at and about Spanish Fort [*sic*] reservation, but they are now scattered among other bands, and do not now exist as a separate tribe. Most of these Indians are on the Uintah Valley reservation." Now and then reservation Utes returned to Provo to fish, but they felt like strangers in a foreign town. It was not like the old days when the village of the Timpanogos on the

Timpanogos River at Lake Timpanogos played host to visiting fishers. That water-world belonged to the past.[78]

In 1865 Sowiette made a dark joke about the famine of the Fish-Eaters. Before signing the treaty at Spanish Fork, the infirm and venerated Ute elder was asked to give the meaning of his name. An earlier reputable source had translated "Sowiette" as "the man that picks fish from the water." This seems to have been a common Nuche name. An 1850 list of 126 baptized Utes includes 3 men with essentially the same title: "Sow,a,att," "Sow,a,at,ott,wood," and "Sow,er,att."[79] The name of the Lake Ute leader, Patsowet, was probably related (and may have been closer to the real name, given that *pa* meant water). The ordinariness of this personal designation offers additional evidence of the centrality of lake fish to the Utes of the eastern Great Basin. By the 1860s, however, Mormon settlers had driven the Fish-Eaters from the most productive and reliable fishing site. Sowiette remembered how things used to be. Over his long life, he had regularly visited the valley of Utah Lake. Now, as he prepared to leave the place for the very last time, He-Who-Picks-Fish told George Washington Bean that his name meant "Nearly Starved." Not catching the pun, the Mormon interpreter reported the all-too-accurate falsehood to the government clerk, who inscribed it on the treaty paper. Nearly blind, Sowiette bent over to place an "X" by the name, making it official.

3.

The Desertification of Zion

In the late nineteenth century, Utah became world-famous for its curious people and its curious hydrology. To outsiders and tourists, the waterscape of Salt Lake Valley seemed more remarkable than that of Utah Valley. Where else could you find a mysterious religious capital alongside a sulfurous warm spring and a briny inland sea? According to popular medical theories and the promotions of the tourist trade, Salt Lake City's watering places possessed revitalizing properties. The bathing business peaked after the completion of the transcontinental railroad in 1869. Resorts appeared at Utah Lake, too, but the American Galilee remained known primarily as a commercial fishery. Epicures praised its native cutthroat trout. By the mid-twentieth century, however, things changed: most of Utah's bathing resorts shut down, and the once-prodigious trout fishery collapsed. Concurrently with these two great desiccations—one recreational, one ecological— a related psychic shift took place: in collective memory, post-pioneer Mormons reimagined Utah's land of lakes as a desert, a place where lifegiving aquatic resources—and the natives who once used them— did not belong. By the postwar era very few residents of Utah Valley could recall the vital importance of Utah Lake to their pioneer ancestors or their Indian predecessors. Although the lake continued to occupy the floor of the valley, it no longer occupied the hearts and minds of valley people. Their genius loci had moved to higher ground.

::: The Mormons of Great Salt Lake City began "taking the waters" in the earliest days of settlement. Initially the destination was the warm springs rather than the lake. In 1849 the city authorized the use of tax dollars to erect a bathhouse—one of the earliest instances of public works in Utah. The leading figures of the city attended the dedication in November 1850. Apostle Heber C. Kimball called on God to sanctify the water and to fill it with "life & health—let the Son of peace take up his abode & no foul spi[rit] pass the threashold—never be dishonored. banish wic[k]ed of[f] from this place." Afterward the gathering sang songs, ate dinner, and danced till dawn.[1]

Compared with Hot Springs, Arkansas, and White Sulphur Springs, West Virginia—the nation's two leading thermal resorts—the Salt Lake municipal warm springs was a small enterprise. Even so, it filled local people with pride. The Mormon capital offered visitors the only warm water therapy in a thousand miles. It was here in 1858 that LDS officials held a welcoming reception for incoming territorial governor Alfred Cumming. And in 1865, when Speaker of the House Schuyler Colfax arrived in Salt Lake, his Mormon hosts immediately took him for a sulfur bath in a special basin prepared for him. Colfax's western tour marked the end of the war between North and South and the opening of the "New West" with the construction of the transcontinental railroad. A reporter who accompanied Colfax predicted that the railroad would make Salt Lake City a bigger watering place than Newport, Rhode Island, or Saratoga and Sharon Springs, New York. In full booster mode, he exclaimed: "So ye votaries of fashion, ye rheumatic cripples, ye victims of scrofula and ennui, prepare to pack your trunks at the sound of the first whistle of the train for the Rocky Mountains, for a season at Salt Lake City."[2]

Salt Lake's sanitarium seemed valuable enough to a non-Mormon physician that he risked a confrontation with LDS partisans. In 1865 John King Robinson, a retired army doctor from nearby Fort Douglas, erected a shanty and a fence within the city's eighty-acre warm springs enclosure. Audaciously, King filed for land ownership on the basis of his "improvements" to the city's land. Evidently he hoped to turn his shanty into a hospital. Robinson and other non-Mormon claim-jumpers argued that the city did not actually own the land because the legislative act that included the city's charter had not been submitted to Congress as required by the organic act of the territory. In 1866 Mormon officials ejected Robinson from the warm springs property and tore down his "improvements." Members of the all-Mormon police corps rubbed it in by destroying a "nuisant" building on Robinson's private land. Like all other Americans, the Utah Saints felt possessive about their land—even more so having previously lost their homes in Missouri and Illinois. Even as Robinson sued the city for its property, he prepared a second suit about his own property. He lost the first case in October and shortly thereafter he lost his life in a nighttime gang attack. The Gentiles of Salt Lake City alleged that Church officials had authorized the "assassination"; later they accused the police of a cover-up. However, J. H. Beadle, an anti-Mormon reporter in Salt Lake City who wrote about the "mysteries and crimes of Mormonism" (including the Robinson murder), conceded that the municipal warm springs were "the most praiseworthy of Mormon institutions." "Without the faith of the Mormons," he said, "I can safely agree with them that this pool is 'for the healing of the nations.'"[3]

After the meeting of the Central Pacific and the Union Pacific in 1869, visitation to Utah increased exponentially. Eastern tourists paid to get close to the territory's "sinful" populace as well as its "healthful" climate. Health tourism prospered throughout the high, dry lands of the American West in the railroad era. Hoping to attract both full-time invalids and part-time pleasure-seekers, rail corporations built splendid spas at places such as Colorado Springs, Glenwood Springs, and Las Vegas (New Mexico, not Nevada). In Utah, however, the railroads saw more potential in the salty lake than in the sulfurous springs. Then as today, the tourist trade relied on the perception of novelty. Thermal zones could be found elsewhere. But the Great Salt Lake was singular, just like Temple Square. In the 1880s and 1890s, railroads turned "America's Dead Sea" into Utah's leading natural attraction. Their allies and frequent employees, the travel writers, consistently invoked the Holy Land in their descriptions of Utah. Publicists encouraged tourists to see Mormons as latter-day Hebrews or as latter-day Sodomites. Either way, the environment remained an American Canaan. If polygamists appealed to voyeurism, the Great Salt Lake appealed to nationalism. In 1891 the passenger department of the Denver & Rio Grande printed this representative promotion:

> The most wonderful feature of all this wonderland tour, the mightiest marvel of all-marvelous Utah, an ocean of majestic mystery clad in beauty divine, is Great Salt Lake, the American Dead Sea. Among all earth's weird wonders in water it has but one rival or peer—the miracle-made sea whose waves of doom and oblivion roll[ed] over Sodom and Gomorrah, the Chicagos of forty centuries ago.[4]

The booklet went on to reproduce a map of "Deseret" (the original Mormon name for Utah) alongside a map of "Canaan," with the words "Promised Land" superimposed on both. The map of Palestine was inverted, enlarged, and exaggerated to suggest a perfect correspondence between the Great Salt Lake/Jordan River/Utah Lake and the Dead Sea/Jordan River/Sea of Galilee.

The Denver & Rio Grande did more than motivate and transport lake-bound tourists; it housed them. In 1886 it opened Lake Park, a bathing resort near Farmington. This was the classiest of a series of east-side watering places developed since 1870. The eastern shore had the advantage of contiguity with the main corridor of settlement and transportation. It had the disadvantage of being muddy and marshy. Even without a beach, Lake Park offered what people wanted most—an opportunity to be buoyed by the therapeutic saltwater. Bathers de-

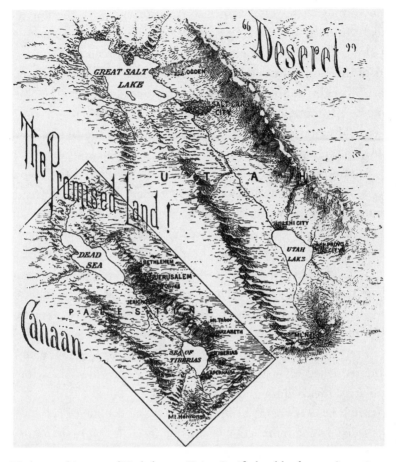

Hydrographic map of Utah from a Union Pacific booklet for tourists, 1891.

scended directly into the water from ladders attached to pavilions built on pilings. The closest thing to a natural beach was situated at Black Rock, a rocky stretch on the less accessible southern shore twenty miles due west of Salt Lake City. The Utah Western Railroad built a spur line here in 1875, and soon afterward a number of small resorts appeared. One of them, Garfield Beach, was later acquired and improved by a subsidiary of the Union Pacific. The UP advertised with a paid promotion from John Muir, who extolled the joys of nude bathing. After his "right lusty relationship with the brave old lake," Muir found himself "a new creature indeed, and went bounding along the beach with blood all aglow, reinforced by the best life salts of the mountains, and ready for any race." As of 1890, Garfield Beach brought in about 100,000 recreationists per year. Unable to compete any more, Lake Park shut down.[5]

Garfield's monopoly did not last long. A new and different kind of resort, Saltair, opened a few miles away in 1893. In addition to bathing, Saltair—the "Coney Island of the West"—offered the "world's largest dance floor," as well as midway games, vaudeville shows, and eventually a Ferris wheel and roller coaster. On the outside, Saltair looked like a fantastical Moorish castle on stilts. Financed by the LDS Church shortly after its repudiation of polygamy, the water resort purposefully demonstrated the mainstreaming of Utah Mormons. Saltair became the state's premier recreational site—especially after the Garfield Beach resort burned down in 1904. In the 1920s up to half a million fun-seekers took the lake-bound train each year. But then a series of setbacks hit Saltair: fire, drought, depression, war. The resort reopened after World War II but never recovered its former popularity. It closed for good in 1958.[6]

At Utah Lake the same history—the rise and decline of pleasure resorts—occurred simultaneously on a smaller scale. More than a dozen watering places operated at various times between the late 1880s and the early 1930s. The three most important resorts were Saratoga, Geneva, and Provo Lake. Each offered bathing, dancing, and picnicking. Before World War II, these east-shore lake resorts functioned as Utah Valley's leading recreational sites. They didn't, however, cater to outside tourists. With the exception of Saratoga, the Utah Lake resorts lacked the twin advantages of the Salt Lake resorts: corporate capital and curative/curious water. Tellingly, Saratoga—the oldest and longest-lived resort—boasted a warm spring as well as a lakefront. John Beck, a German-American Mormon businessman who made a fortune in mining, acquired this site near the outlet of the Jordan River in 1884.[7]

Saltair resort, Great Salt Lake, ca. 1900. South-facing view with north end of Oquirrh Mountains in the distance. (Used by permission, Utah State Historical Society, Salt Lake City; all rights reserved)

An active real estate developer, Beck also bought the hot springs property near Salt Lake City. Previously, Hot Springs Lake had been used for yachting in the summer, bird hunting in the fall, and ice-skating in the winter. The hot springs themselves did not have a reputation for healing like the nearby warm springs. Undeterred, Beck launched improvements and advertisements. He hired chemists to test the water, which he began to bottle and sell as a therapeutic agent. And he turned the property into a proper resort with swimming pools, dance floors, and picnic areas—all with easy railroad access. Like many other nineteenth-century resorts, this one promptly burned down. It reopened around 1900 under different management, and remained popular among locals until another fire in 1924. A third incarnation of the resort went into foreclosure in the 1940s. Then, in 1953, the Utah Highway Commission acquired the property under threat of condemnation. Today nothing remains of Beck's Hot Springs or the lakelet, which the state drained in 1915 for mosquito abatement. The site is now occupied by the interchange of U.S. Route 89, I-15, and I-215, a traffic bottleneck adjacent to an oil refinery.[8]

Salt Lake's once-celebrated warm springs did not fare much better. In its final form as "Wasatch Springs Plunge," the city-owned bathing resort featured a large indoor swimming pool. Built in 1932, the Plunge soon became a drain on city funds. Fewer and fewer residents "took the waters" as the field of medical geography declined in professional stature. In the nineteenth century, U.S. travel guides routinely printed chemical analyses of spring water in parts per thousand without any interpretation of the data; it was assumed that readers knew the medicinal properties of "carbonite of lime" and "chloride of calcium," and the relative merits of "thermal," "purgative," and "chalybeate" water. But in the first half of the twentieth century this common knowledge became esoteric as Americans placed more confidence in the pharmaceutical industry than in nature's pharmacy. Far earlier than their counterparts in continental Europe, American doctors distanced themselves from spas. Of the hundreds of mineral-spring resorts that dotted the nation in 1900, fewer than fifty remained in business by the end of World War II. The germ theory of disease incubated new anxieties about the healthfulness of water. Instead of positive mineral content, health advocates focused on negative microbial content. Cities began chlorinating their municipal water supplies. At Wasatch Springs Plunge, the sulfurized water could not be chlorinated, and the pool lacked an adequate circulation system. The sluggish, warm water offered an ideal home for *E. coli*. In September 1946 the University of Utah Medical School tested the swimming pool and declared it unfit for swimming. The water contained 6 million bacteria per cubic centimeter; the maximum standard was 200. A local newspaper called the place a "disease trap."

Acting quickly, the city's board of health closed down this "menace to health." It was an ironic, ignominious end for a water source once known as the "pool of Siloam"—a miraculous place of healing.[9]

After World War II, Salt Lake boosters turned their attention to a different form of H_2O—snow. From small beginnings, the Utah ski industry grew into a regional player by the 1970s and an international player by the 1990s. Contemporary Salt Lake City boasts a winning ski combination: multiple resorts with steep slopes and dry powder within a half-hour drive of a major airport. These selling points—and some technically legal but scandalous bribery—convinced the International Olympic Committee to choose Utah to host the 2002 Winter Olympics. The winning of the Olympic bid marked the culmination of a multidecade state-supported advertising campaign on behalf of the ski industry. Since the 1960s Utah has touted the "Greatest Snow on Earth" (a slogan that has weathered a lawsuit from Ringling Bros. and Barnum & Bailey). Since 1985, state license plates have exhorted people to "Ski Utah." Thanks to such marketing, the state's powdery snow is now widely recognized as extraordinary.

It is sociologically significant that the "Greatest Snow" has replaced the Great Salt Lake as Utah's most renowned hydrological feature. It used to be that travelers made comments like this: "Barring the singular people who inhabit it, Great Salt Lake is the curiosity of the Great Basin." Taking this point to its extreme, Benjamin G. Ferris, who briefly served as secretary of Utah Territory in the 1850s, said, "As the Great Basin is the greatest physical, so its inhabitants may be said to be the greatest moral, curiosity of the New World." These "singular" and "curious" people were variously described as theocratic, violent, and prurient, as well as industrious and persevering. The environment of Utah supposedly encouraged such traits. In the nineteenth century, Utah was often said to seem "Asiatic," an adjective of ambivalence. Positively, Utah could be likened to the Holy Land with its temple, its River Jordan, and its inland seas. Negatively, it could be likened to Turkey, the supposed home of harems and religious despotism. "Situated as the Mormons are, in a region of thermal springs," wrote one commentator, "we may expect to see them imitate the Turks and other oriental nations in the number of their baths, and their fondness for thermal bathing, as they have already imitated them in their habits of polygamy."[10]

Traces of the old anti-Mormonism persist to this day, but the environmental component has disappeared just as surely as Salt Lake's water resorts. Identity and hydrography no longer overlap. Indeed, the Great Basin hardly matters to outsider or insider conceptions of Utah. Except when the Great Salt Lake threatens the capital with flooding—as it did during the El Niño climate event of 1983–84—modern residents of the Wasatch Front evince little awareness that they live on the edge of a vast interior drainage basin. When Utahns appeal to a supraregional identity, they speak of the "Intermountain West" or the "Rocky Mountain Region." During the 2002 Olympics the global media did much to reinforce the symbolic connection between the people of Utah and the mountains of Utah. Positive evaluations far outweighed the negative. In "local color" stories, reporters portrayed Utah Mormons as oddly if admirably conformist. On television, the standard blimp's-eye-view showed downtown buildings (including the temple) backed by snowy peaks. In televised coverage of outdoor events, Utah looked like Nagano, Japan, or any other Winter Olympics venue—a generic "Alpine" or "Nordic" recreational landscape. For their part, city officials did nothing to turn the camera's gaze from east to west, from the mountains to the lake. Once a font of curiosity, the city's namesake had become a reservoir of indifference.[11]

Utah Lake also lost its salience in the postwar period. For a brief time, in the 1930s, it looked as though the lake would acquire a long-lasting tradition proportionate to the annual community hike of Mount Timpanogos. Ironically, the drought of the Dust Bowl years exposed inviting beaches at the mouth of the Provo River. Here, at the sands of Utah's Galilee, the city of Provo sponsored a large interdenominational Easter sunrise service. At its peak in 1938, about 6,000 people attended the ceremony. But then the lake rose. Organizers moved the event to the opposite side of the city, to the foothills of the Wasatch. The lake lost out to the mountains.[12]

Not long afterward the site of the best bathing resort, Geneva, underwent a total transformation: the federal government erected a colossal coal-fired steel mill as part of the war effort. Together with the Kaiser mill in Fontana, California, Geneva Steel produced the metal for the Pacific fleet. After the defeat of Japan, Geneva stayed in business as an acquired property of U.S. Steel. The impact of this industrial plant on the physical and perceived quality of Utah Lake cannot be overemphasized. Geneva Steel's skyline of blackened smokestacks eclipsed the already dimmed attractiveness of the lake. Industrial pollution—together with municipal waste and street runoff—caused the water quality of Utah Lake to deteriorate dramatically in the mid-twentieth century.

Utah Lake became the butt of local jokes, and its shoreline became a favorite dumping ground for old refrigerators, used tires, and dead engines. Its waters were described as "toxic soup." Only diehard fishers—those who would settle for carp and catfish—remained loyal to the lake. Bathers abandoned the place. Ordinary yet intimate forms of lake use also declined in the postwar age of convenience. Local Mormons no longer baptized their eight-year-old children outdoors or equipped their iceboxes with frozen chunks of the lake. The shrunken status of Utah Lake was demonstrated in the 1960s, when the Utah Travel Council divided the state into different tourist regions—"Color Country," "Castle Country," and so on. Utah County, which encompasses Utah Valley, which envelops Utah Lake, has since been known as "Mountainland."

The postwar dominance of local mountains has even extended to lake-based recreation. Twentieth-century dam building on the back (east) side of the Wasatch created a string of popular reservoirs—notably Pineview Reservoir, Jordanelle Reservoir, and Deer Creek Reservoir. Unlike shallow, turbid, algae-rich Utah Lake, these azure mountain reservoirs offer optimal conditions for motorized play. In the twentieth century, the outboard motor (developed by Ole Evinrud of

Charles Savage, "Utah Lake from Geneva (new bathing resort)," ca. 1890. West-facing view with south end of Oquirrh Mountains in the distance. (Courtesy of the Church Archives, The Church of Jesus Christ of Latter-day Saints)

Wisconsin in 1907) revolutionized aquatic recreation, allowing for new activities like waterskiing and new conveyances like jet skis. For obvious reasons, motorboaters preferred deep, unobstructed water. Given the greater attractiveness of Deer Creek Reservoir, Utah Lake could not compete for the loyalty of recreationists.

To a user group habituated to highland reservoirs, the mere turbidity of Utah Lake suggests contamination even though pollution steadily lessened in the late twentieth century. "It's like a liquid carcinogen. It smells, it's too shallow and it's just creepy," said a BYU wakeboarder in 2004. Although he lived next door to the lake, he had never visited. "But I've heard lots of stories about how gross it is," he continued. "Maybe some people like falling off their board and landing in 2 feet of muddy water. I guess I'm just a lake elitist." Although many motorboaters do in fact use Utah Lake, they presumably represent a lower economic class or at least a different cultural persuasion from the users of Deer Creek Reservoir. But even Utah Lake regulars yearn for a mountain-style lake. A 1995 survey revealed that the "most outstanding concern among visitors . . . was water quality. Again and again respondents expressed a desire for clear, clean, blue water." Boaters called on the state to dredge and dike the lake to "restore" it to its "original" condition.[13]

::: Some things can be restored more easily than others. The recreational desiccation of Utah Lake is probably only temporary. Geneva Steel closed in 2001; dismantling began in 2005. A developer bought the site. The lakefront represents the final real estate bonanza in Utah Valley. Given demographic trends, it seems inevitable that suburbs will encircle the lake in the twenty-first century. A large lakeside development begun in the 1990s has been incorporated under the retro name Saratoga Springs. With more and more people living within sight and smell of the water, Utah Lake is ready for a renewal. A harbinger came in 2006, when county officials and mayors from nine lakeside cities drafted an agreement to create a Utah Lake Commission, a public policy group dedicated to improving the resource for people and wildlife. "If we had one person [full-time employee] who gets up every morning and worries about what is happening on Utah Lake it would help a lot," said an organizer.[14]

There is plenty to worry about, starting with native fish. In former times Utah Lake teemed with trout, chubs, and suckers. The best fishing site by far was the mouth of the Provo River. The colonists of Fort Utah relied on fish as their food insurance in the decade or so it took to create a stable agricultural economy. Only then, in the 1860s, did fish become a luxury good rather than a subsistence good.

The leading commercial fisher was Peter Madsen, a Mormon convert who learned the trade in his native home, Denmark. Madsen and his sons fished in and around the mouth of the Provo for half a century and earned a reputation for honesty and good stewardship. For many years Madsen was the only licensed commercial fisher in the Provo area. He was not, however, alone on the water. Until the 1870s the territorial government did little to regulate fishing or stop poaching. And not until later did fish wardens possess true power of enforcement. "In early days it was always open season for fishing in Provo River," recalled Raymond Partridge. He described the usual tackle as hooks attached to lines of baling wire protruding from a willow pole.[15] With this barbed tool, local fishers raked the river indiscriminately. They did even more damage in the lake with fine-mesh seines. By the early 1900s, almost all of the thirteen native species faced local or total extinction.

The first and greatest casualty was the Bonneville cutthroat trout, a handsome silvery-white fish with a scattering of black spots. Its modern scientific name is *Oncorhynchus clarki utah;* in the nineteenth century people called it "lake trout" or "salmon-trout." In prehistoric times this subspecies of the western cutthroat trout enjoyed a vast habitat—Lake Bonneville. After the lake dried up, relic populations survived in various mountain streams and lakes in the eastern Great Basin. Utah Lake was the one large low-elevation habitat. In this spacious, somewhat saline, food-rich environment, cutthroats attained peak size and flavor. Champion specimens reportedly reached 25 or 30 pounds before going upriver to spawn. More typically, a mature fish weighed 3 to 10 pounds—still big enough for a hearty meal. No less an authority than David Starr Jordan—eminent ichthyologist and future Stanford president—said that "no better trout for the table exist than those of the Utah Lake variety." He and other early taxonomists drew a distinction between the lake trout and the trout in nearby mountains. The larger, less spotted lake variety traveled farther to spawn than the other cutthroats in the Bonneville Basin. "Provo River was almost black with fish in the spring," remembered one pioneer. Utah's number-one fishing enthusiast, Wilford Woodruff, called it "the best place for fishing trout I ever sa[w]." A disciple of

Izaak Walton as well as Jesus Christ, Woodruff tied and cast artificial flies even as he crossed the Plains in 1847. At the Provo River in 1863 he reeled in 15 pounds in an hour. Using a net, a neighboring man caught 2,500 pounds of trout in a single haul.[16]

Local fishers took this abundance for granted. An outsider, a government naturalist with one of the great western surveys, issued the first authoritative voice of warning. In 1872 H. C. Yarrow investigated the Utah Lake fishery and came away impressed and depressed by the lake trout. "As an article of food, its excellence is not surpassed by any fish," he wrote. The fish possessed "unique and unequaled" flavor. Miners in the new mountain mining districts of Alta and Park City paid good money for the trout. Fishmongers worked the streets of Salt Lake City. According to Yarrow, this species was of "vast economic importance." Unfortunately, increased demand encouraged increased yields by "reckless methods of fishing." Without swift and special attention, the "species must become extinct after a few years." Yarrow's guide and informant, Peter Madsen, complained about the "interlopers and law breakers" who came from Salt Lake City with fine-mesh nets. In 1864 Madsen routinely pulled in 3,500 pounds of trout at a time. By 1872, 500 pounds was considered an "enormous haul."[17]

Yarrow summarized his findings in an 1874 letter to Utah's territorial delegate, George Q. Cannon. Cannon forwarded the letter to the Utah legislature via his fellow LDS apostle, Woodruff. In his letter Yarrow acknowledged that the trout supply "appeared to be inexhaustible." But appearances could deceive. The seemingly inexhaustible fisheries of the East had proven to be vulnerable; westerners were poised to learn the same hard truth. Yarrow urged authorities to place restrictions on the hours of the day and the days of the year when trout could be caught. He also called for restrictions on mesh size. Not even minnows could escape the seines he had seen at Utah Lake. Even worse, most fishers did not return the minnows to the water. These men were "voracious in the extreme in the matter of fishing, and by their improvidence in this respect constitute a most dangerous enemy to the fishing interest of the Territory." This class of people threatened their own future with their "inordinate present gratification." Yarrow reserved his harshest words for those men who detonated "giant powder" (dynamite) in the deep river pools where the lake trout spawned.[18]

Starting in the late 1870s, the legislature experimented with fishing regulations. Seining was initially outlawed, then permitted with certain restrictions. In 1888 the legislature established a seining season for mature trout and prohibited fishers from exporting the fish to other states. In the 1890s, in the face of continuing noncompliance, the state required wardens to accompany seiners. Unfortunately, none of these measures reversed the trout decline. In the end all commercial fishing became illegal. To enforce the game laws, the state appointed a Utah County Fish and Game Commissioner. But the office was understaffed. An 1894 petition by some licensed Utah County fishers aired the "notorious fact" that trout were "constantly being clandestinely taken" out of the lake and out of the territory. Although the commissioner's five deputies arrested twenty-one miscreants in 1894, the problem did not go away. A correspondent for *Forest and Stream* believed that the commissioner—a political appointee—contributed to the problem with "voluntary ineffectual" law enforcement. Even licensed seiners flouted the spirit of the law by bringing in small but regular numbers of trout out of season. They acted with impunity because trout killed "by accident" could be sold as legal fare.[19]

While illegal and unscrupulous fishers harmed native fish populations directly, a combination of indirect factors caused as much damage. Sawmills dumped suffocating sawdust directly into tributaries. Wastewater from towns and farms and factories encouraged lake eutrophication—an overabundance of nutrients that increased algal growth and decreased the amount of oxygen in the water. Meanwhile water-powered industries like the Provo Woolen Mills chewed up fish in their millraces. As of 1894, the Provo River provided power for twenty-eight mills and foundries. Even worse, irrigation dams prevented suckers from spawning far up the Provo River. Suckers cannot jump like trout. And even overachieving trout struggled with the power dam built by Telluride Power near the mouth of Provo Canyon in 1897. According to *Forest and Stream,* "the best of the trout became exhausted in trying to leap the dam, fell back disabled among the rocks, and floated helpless down the stream. It is no exaggeration to say that, during the height of the run, a wagon load of fish was ruined in this way every day." Under pressure from upstream Wasatch County, the "soulless corporation" made improvements to its fish ladder. But the second one didn't work any better than the first. Similar problems affected the outlet of the lake, the Jordan River. A dam and pumping plant at the head of the Jordan blocked spawning fish. Even worse, the Jordan Narrows Dam affected the lake as a whole. As codified by intervalley arbitration in 1885, irrigators in Salt Lake Valley could use Utah Valley's lake as their reservoir. Consequently, the dam-managed lake rose and shrank more often and more rapidly than it would have naturally. Extreme fluctuations devastated the once-extensive near-shore aquatic vegetation, critical habitat for native fish.[20]

Of all the incidental threats, the deadliest was also the most pastoral. To the constant admiration of outside observers like Englishman Phil Robinson, Utah Mormons had trained their wild rivers into domestic rivulets:

> At first the stream where it leaves the cañon, and debouches upon the levels of the valley, is run off into canals to north and south and west (for all the streams run from the eastern range), and from these, like the legs of a centipede, minor channels run to each farmstead, and thence again are drawn off in numberless small aqueducts to flood the fields . . . But the settlement expands, and more ground is needed. So another canal taps the stream above the cañon mouth, the main channels again strike off, irrigating the section above the levels already in cultivation, and overlapping the original area at either end.

Writing in 1883, Robinson called this irrigation system "among the wonders of the West." In Provo he saw "magnificent reaches of fertile land, acres of fruit-trees, and miles of crops" made possible by a river that had been "ruthlessly distributed over the slopes."[21]

These lifegiving canals doubled as channels of death. Since most of the streamflow now ran to places other than the lake, native fish became disoriented. Multitudes of suckers and trout were sucked off course. "Until a Fish and Game department was added to the state government the irrigation canals were part of the good fishing grounds of the state," remembered Raymond Partridge. "Whenever we heard a flopping in the irrigation water we knew a nice fish was to be served for breakfast. I once caught a trout weighing ten pounds in the ditch running past my house." One of Peter Madsen's sons, George, re-membered seeing "over five hundred trout from six to eight inches long taken out of one irrigation penstock in twelve hours. They liter-ally clogged the ditches and they were considered a nuisance rather than a blessing." Other irrigators welcomed the waste as free fertilizer for their alfalfa and free food for their families. Writing in 1907, the State Fish and Game Commissioner said that many farmers "depend largely on these destructive conditions for fish food, and in conse-quence take little or no interest in screening their ditches." Irrigators also opposed canal screens because they were expensive to install— and, once installed, they had to be cleaned of branches, leaves, and debris. Wardens struggled for decades to convince irrigators to com-ply with screening regulations. In 1912 the local newspaper estimated that 75 percent of the lake's annual fish kill occurred in farm fields.[22]

Lamentably, there was nothing illegal about a different fish-killing irrigation practice: dewatering the Provo River. Utah Valley's agricul-tural sector peaked in the early 1900s, when Provo billed itself as the "Garden City of Utah." Canal companies sometimes siphoned off the river's entire flow to nourish their fields and orchards. In June 1905 a nighttime dewatering stranded a spawning run of suckers. "The sight next day was one I will never forget," recalled George Madsen. "We estimated that 1,500 tons of suckers had perished in scarcely more than two miles of the channel. In places, the fish were piled several feet deep." The stinking specter convinced canal companies to return enough water to the river to flush the fish into the lake. "This destruction occurs to some extent each year, but never before to the appalling magnitude of last season," wrote the commissioner in his biennial report.[23] The destruction reached its zenith in the 1930s as Utah Lake reached its nadir. During an intense multiyear drought, Utah Valley irrigators cut off inflow even as Salt Lake Valley irrigators continued to pump water out. Shrinking to an average depth of one foot, the lake became warmer, more saline, and less oxygenated. The trout population never recovered.

Even when a full stream of water discharged all the way down the Provo, it entered the lake as an altered and impoverished river. Originally the river's mouth had been a fecund, changeable environment—neither firmly solid nor fully liquid. The Provo River broke into several strands as it prepared to debouch. The main channel was wide; one early bridge measured 120 feet across. In this area the river frequently shifted course; water spilled into backwater marshes. In the 1850s a section of road through this ecological zone was called the "Slough of Despair" (after the *Pilgrim's Progress*). In 1855 James Farmer, an LDS convert from England, did his best to carry a surveyor's chain across the mouth of the Provo River; "very marshy very tired and weary," he wrote in his diary.[24] He had fought his way through a 12-foot-high tangle of rushes and canes. This environment does not exist today. The marshy lakeshore around the mouth of the Provo has now been stabilized; one can walk to the shoreline without getting muddy. The wetlands have been drained, the thickets have been cut, and the river has been straitjacketed. Since the mid-twentieth century, the Provo River has entered the lake through a single narrow channel. Without side channels and slow-water eddies, spawning fish like the June sucker struggle to propagate.

The new river and the new lake belong to nonnatives. In the late nineteenth and early twentieth centuries, humans introduced at least twenty-four aquatic species to the Utah Lake drainage. Begun haphazardly in the 1870s, fish planting became a professional venture in the 1890s, when the new state government became an advocate of fish culture. Game wardens worked with hatcheries to plant brook trout, brown trout, rainbow trout, graylings, and other salmonoids in the lake. None of these hatchery fish did well in the long run. Bass and perch and catfish did better. But the real success—at least in raw numbers—was unplanned. By the 1880s carp had found their way to the lake from farm ponds. Quickly they multiplied into a mighty population. In 1899 the state recorded a commercial take of 18,000 pounds of trout and 105,000 pounds of carp. Just five years later the tally was 3,100 pounds of trout and 392,325 pounds of carp.[25]

In essence, Utah Lake metamorphosed from a "game" fish habitat to a "common" fish habitat. Carp created favorable conditions for more carp. By eating plants in the already beleaguered littoral zone, carp destroyed the habitat of natives, making them easier prey for faster-growing nonnatives. Less vegetation meant more turbidity and more algae—habitat conditions that further hurt native fish. In the 1920s Utah Lake was dubbed "America's Greatest Carp Habitation." Counterintuitively, this development did not immediately decrease the commercial value of the fishery. Using railroads, fishers shipped tons of carp to coastal markets, especially Los Angeles, where Mexicans, Chinese, Japanese, and Jews valued carp as table fish. In Utah, people much preferred trout, but they became less selective during the Depression, and gratefully ate carp that the state procured for free distribution. During World War II carp offered an alternative to rationed meat. After the war, though, locals stopped eating common fish from Utah Lake. In the prosperity of postwar America, Utahns could buy frozen and farmed fish at the supermarket. Commercial fishers now sold their carp as feed for chickens and minks.[26]

In the 1950s the Utah Department of Fish and Game attempted to improve the game fishery in Utah Lake by adding white bass and walleye. Despite the new introductions, postwar residents of Utah Valley preferred to go to the high country to reel in their recreational catch. The state also stocked the reservoirs behind Deer Creek Dam and Strawberry Dam with popular fish species. Trolling for rainbow trout in the mountains became a summer tradition for many Utah Valley families. More specialized fishers—those who cast artificial flies—stopped at the Provo River below Deer Creek Dam. Rainbow trout thrived in the cold, clear water released from the depths of reservoirs. Thanks to damming and stocking, the middle Provo River earned national recognition as a "blue-ribbon" stream. This was a historic reversal. Previously the lower Provo—the stretch below the canyon, beyond the mountains, within the township—had boasted the best trout fishing.

Today Provo is a far cry from a fish town. Only a small group of carp enthusiasts—and a growing number of Latino immigrants—take advantage of no-limit fishing in Utah Lake. The activity comes with risks, however. In 2006 state toxicologists issued a "fish consumption advisory" for Utah Lake carp because of unacceptable levels of carcinogenic PCBs. An estimated 7.5 million contaminated carp accounted for 90 percent of the biomass in the lake. The state announced its intention to drastically reduce this number. Overturning historic attitudes, state and federal wildlife managers characterized introduced fish as undesirable "alien" or "invasive" species. At Utah Lake, nonnative species altered the native ecology and preyed on the June sucker, an endemic species that had nowhere else to go.

In 1986 the U.S. Fish and Wildlife Service listed the June sucker *(Chasmistes liorus)* as an endangered species. A multiagency June Sucker Recovery Implementation Program was established with funding from a "mitigation commission" attached to the Central Utah Project, a reclamation behemoth. The recovery program was simple to describe but hard to achieve: propagate suckers in hatcheries and then release them into the wild. Initially the recovery program met with general indifference and some isolated but devastating hostility. Because of their name, the suckers are often assumed to be "trash fish" (that is, bottom-feeders) when in fact they are midwater planktivores. In 1984 a sucker-hating vandal broke into a holding pen and killed eighteen mature specimens. Four years later someone clubbed to death thirty suckers—an estimated 15 percent of the wild breeding population—as they tried to spawn in the lower Provo River, a designated "critical habitat." It's possible that the perpetrator hated the federal government more than the local fish, and preferred the idea of an extinct species to a regulated one.

In the years after these acts of violence, appreciation of the sucker—and of Utah Lake in general—increased. But lake restorationists still worked against a historical accumulation of ignorance and neglect. One of the lead ecologists on the recovery team said in 1994 that the sucker "has no cultural significance to them [local Mormons], but I think it should." He explained: "If it wasn't for the June Sucker, the Mormons would have starved. That's what got them through early winters." The next year one of his graduate students tested local knowledge by handing out questionnaires at Utah Lake State Park, located at the mouth of the Provo River. Although the selection process was random, the survey pool was self-selecting in that it contained only people who cared enough about the lake to visit it. Even this user group had slight knowledge of the June sucker; 87 percent hadn't heard of *any* endangered fish in Utah Lake. The interviewees—three-quarters of whom were Mormons—were asked to respond to the statement "June suckers represent an important part of early Mormon and Native American heritage." Seven percent marked "strongly agree," 6 percent marked "strongly disagree," and an overwhelming 63 percent registered "don't know."[27]

::: Historical forgetfulness occurs among even the most history-loving people. In the post-pioneer period, Utah Mormons chose to remember the settlement-era Wasatch Oasis as an arid wasteland inhospitable to life. In other words, they helped themselves to forget.

This process began in the nineteenth century under the initiative of the church hierarchy. Recall that after research and consultation Brigham Young and his key advisors chose the Valley of the Great Salt Lake to be the center stake of Zion. They followed established trails. Upon arrival in 1847, the advance party—the Pioneer Camp of the Saints—expressed near-uniform satisfaction with the climate, soil, and water. Waist-high grass covered the northeastern floor of the valley. Except for the shortage of hardwood, the place seemed well suited for habitation. Yet as early as 1850, key members of the Pioneer Camp began telling disingenuous stories about the 1847 migration. Church leaders mythologized the Mormon Trek to build respect and authority for themselves, and cohesion and identity for the group. At annual Pioneer Day festivities, leaders such as George A. Smith repeated a version of events that in every detail contradicted the historical record:

> Without a guide, without a knowledge of the country, without reading even the notes of any traveller upon this earth, or seeing the face of a being who ever set foot upon this land, we were led by the hand of God, through His servant Brigham, threading the difficult passes of these mountains, until we set our foot upon this place, which was, at that time, a desert, containing nothing but a few bunches of dead grass, and crickets enough to fence the land. We were more than one thousand miles from where provisions could be obtained, and found not game enough to support an Indian population.[28]

This story always ended with the Mormons making the desert "blossom as the rose." The trope of arid land redemption proved irresistible even to non-Mormon outsiders. Practically every nineteenth-century travel account after the 1860s repeated the Mormons' claim that they had turned a parched, pest-infested wilderness into a garden. By the end of the century, mythology had become history. In his multivolume *History of Utah* (1892), Orson Whitney described the 1847 panorama that greeted the pioneers: "a seemingly interminable waste of sagebrush bespangled with sunflowers,—the paradise of the lizard, the cricket and the rattlesnake."[29]

Native flora and fauna played mixed roles in this religious drama. According to the hoariest of Utah pioneer stories, the "Mormon cricket" (actually a large katydid, *Anabrus simplex*—a "cross between the spider and the buffalo") resisted the domestication of the desert. In 1848 an army of these arthropods threatened destruction of the grain fields of Great Salt Lake City. Suddenly a flock of white birds appeared in the sky. These feathered angels filled their stomachs with the crickets, vomited, and came back to binge, again and again, until the plague was gone. The story of the "miracle of the seagulls" began with a kernel of truth, but that kernel sprouted into myth. In 1913 the LDS Church dedicated the Seagull Monument—surely the world's only shrine to gulls—at Temple Square, the LDS sanctum sanctorum. The monument had a clear message: the desert gave way to the garden through the combined power of providence and industry. Tellingly, the only Great Basin plant species venerated by post-pioneer Utah Mormons was a delicate flower, the sego lily *(Calochortus nuttallii)*. Early settlers ate the lily's bulbs. During the lean times of the 1850s, pioneers also gathered roots, seeds, berries, and greens. In fact Mormons ate more thistles than lilies. But only the lily—a flower that would not look out of place in a garden or bouquet—earned an honored place in memory. In 1896, the year of statehood, the Utah legislature adopted a new seal that included sego lilies. The lily became the official state flower in 1911.[30]

Utah's pioneer era was increasingly commemorated as the pioneers themselves became an older and smaller part of the citizenry. In the second half of the nineteenth century, Utah Territory became an immigrant society as it absorbed Mormon converts from Europe—some 50,000 Britons and 30,000 Scandinavians. This migratory stream peaked in the 1860s, the same decade when Utes had to exit Utah Valley. By 1890 immigrants and their children made up two-thirds of the territory's population. Having no memories of their own of the founding of Deseret, these converts relied on others for their historical awareness. As the last pioneers of '47 passed away, historically minded Utahns founded two key organizations, the State Historical Society (1897) and the Daughters of the Utah Pioneers (1901). The DUP encouraged all its members to interview old-timers and to submit family histories. These histories were published in a seemingly endless series of pamphlets and books edited by the formidable Kate B. Carter. "The first reason for writing these histories is to vindicate our pioneers," wrote Carter. The "stories are true, they are sincere and inspirational." Meanwhile the DUP erected historical markers at hundreds of sites, including a juniper near the intersection of Sixth East and Third South in Salt Lake City. This was purportedly the "lone cedar tree"—the one and only tree growing in the valley when the pioneers arrived in 1847.[31]

A hagiographic organization such as the DUP can perhaps be forgiven for believing such inspirational hokum. It's less excusable that Andrew Jenson, longtime assistant historian for the LDS Church—and thus someone who managed an unrivaled archive of primary documents—contributed to the desertification of Zion. Speaking in the Tabernacle in 1914, Jenson described the unsettled Salt Lake Valley as the "Great American Desert" and a "wilderness." Ostensibly mountain men had told Brigham Young that

> it was folly for him to think for one moment of locating white people in this valley, where a few straggling bands of Indians of the lowest grade could not get a living from the soil. Were it not for the fish found in the Utah Lake, the Timpanogos river, and other mountain streams, and what game they could find in the mountains, these natives would perish through starvation. And of course white people could not subsist on that kind of fare.[32]

Jenson knew full well that the settlers of Salt Lake and especially Provo ate native trout for decades. In fact, for a brief time as a young man he had worked as a commercial fisher at Utah Lake. As a subsequent popularizer of history, Jenson downplayed the fecundity of fresh-water Utah Lake. The barren Great Salt Lake better matched the post-pioneer obsession with wasteland imagery.

The fish of Utah Lake suffocated in collective memory despite the resuscitating efforts of Peter Madsen. In 1910 the eighty-four-year-old fisherman wrote an article for the main LDS Church periodical, *The Improvement Era*. He began by invoking the sacred bird and flower of Utah. Unlike the seagull and the sego lily, his subject was "unsung by the poet and unchronicled in the annals of the historian." He admitted that "fish is not, perhaps, as poetic a subject" as "Crickets—the Sea Gull and the Sego Lily." Even so, he offered a new phrase "as rhythmical and surely as historically important." It was "Grasshoppers—the Mullet and the Trout." Madsen shared his memories of 1855–56, when fish "played an important part in saving the people from starvation." In his quest to commemorate the fish of Utah Lake, Madsen must have had an advocate at LDS headquarters, for his article was published. However, the "miracle of the fish" did not become a standard inspirational story recited from pulpits and related around campfires. Church magazines never again mentioned the subject. No one went on to erect a monument to the Bonneville cutthroat trout.[33]

As the twentieth century unfolded, both developers and environmentalists found it useful to portray the Wasatch Front as a desert. One side could argue for more dams and aqueducts, the other for water conservation. The past and present fecundity of this oasis zone is strangely underappreciated. Very few of the millions of people who have visited the Seagull Monument have ever traveled to the mouth of the Bear River on the Great Salt Lake, one of the most important refuges for migratory birds in western North America. Instead, the lifeless Bonneville Salt Flats have become the emblematic landscape of the Great Salt Lake.

The desiccating climate of collective memory has proven to be inhospitable to Fish-Eaters as well as to fish. Over the last quarter of the nineteenth century and the first quarter of the twentieth, Lake Utes largely disappeared from the minds of Utah Valley residents. This disappearance occurred despite the rich record of intercultural relations in the 1850s. Documents from that decade favor men over women, and adults over children, but even so, they give names and voices to scores of Utes, men who come across as many-sided individuals with multiple allegiances and motives. By the 1950s, however, these men-in-full would be supplanted in memory by stock folkloric figures (nameless "bucks" who begged or marauded) and imaginary folkloric figures (especially "Utahna" or "Princess Timpanogos"). A distinctive Great Basin history would be reduced to a generic American fiction.

There was, however, an intermediate stage of consciousness, something between familiarity and estrangement. In Mormon collective memory, the Lake Utes did not wither all at once. First a large pool of historical actors was reduced to a small pool. In the process, the remaining Ute men became one-sided figures—most typically combatants. Two Utes, Washear and Walkara, received an inordinate amount of (negative) attention.

Even during his life, Washear had been an unpopular figure in Provo. This Timpanogos band leader consistently resisted Mormon encroachment. Again and again his Mormon contemporaries described him as angry and belligerent. Only George Bean reserved any kind words for the man the settlers called Squash. In his autobiography, Bean called Washear "one of my truest friends" for visiting him during his convalescence, for teaching him the Ute language, and for saving his life during an attack by another Timpanogos man. In every other reminiscence, however, Mormons turned Washear from a malcontent to a monster. In the first half of the twentieth century, local residents told stories about "Squash" kidnapping, dismembering, and even eating Mormon babies. According to a book by the DUP, Washear "had a very large head, round as a squash, and adorned by a huge mouth in which a set of teeth gleamed, a set a chimpanzee might have been proud of." In short, "Squash-Head" filled the American role of the Bloodthirsty Savage.[34]

Meanwhile Walkara filled the role of the War Chief. According to lore, this vengeful monarch of the "Ute nation" instigated the "Walker

War" (previously known as the "second Indian war" or the "Indian War of 1853"). This mischaracterization contained the slightest bit of truth. Walkara had in fact been an audacious leader of great stature, though his direct influence did not extend much beyond his band. An opportunistic man, Walkara played all sides; when it suited him, he made overtures to Mormons, New Mexicans, federal officials, and other Indians. To Brigham Young's exasperation, he acted like neither a true friend nor a true enemy. Like all other people, Walkara was complicated. White Americans did not easily accept the idea of complicated Indians, however. After Walkara's death, Mormons resolved the dissonance through character simplification.

Ironically, the one commemorative organization that paid sustained attention to Lake Utes in general—and to Walkara in particular—consisted of people who had fought them. Starting in 1894, veterans of the Nauvoo Legion began gathering for summer encampments in Utah Valley. A statewide organization, the Utah Indian War Veterans Association, coalesced six years later. The veterans' group predictably focused on memories of violence. At their annual gatherings old-timers campaigned for government pensions, swapped battle stories, and sang songs from *The Utah Indian War Songster.* In August 1903 they met at the Provo Lake Resort, where the great Mormon photographer George E. Anderson took a picture of veterans dressed up as Indians. The mnemonic efforts of the veterans outlasted their group, which died along with its last members in the 1920s. A compilation of veterans' recollections, *Indian Depredations in Utah,* served as the standard source for the history of Mormon-Indian relations throughout the twentieth century.[35]

In the memories of veterans, Walkara the War Chief had a foil: Sowiette, the Peace Chief. This character type goes back to stories of Massasoit and Squanto—the Indians who supposedly greeted the Pilgrims with open arms.[36] Of all the Utes encountered by Mormons, Sowiette best fitted the part. Unlike most Nuche leaders, Sowiette consistently spoke and acted kindly toward the settlers of Utah Valley even though he resented their presence. In 1851 he complained to a

Utah Indian War Veterans at Utah Lake, 1903. Bottom row dressed up as Indians. Photograph by George E. Anderson. (Courtesy of the Church Archives, The Church of Jesus Christ of Latter-day Saints)

non-Mormon federal agent using his rudimentary English: "American—good! Morman—no good! American—friend. Morman—Kill, Steal." Despite that general evaluation, Sowiette regularly called on Bishop Aaron Johnson of Springville. Visiting in 1855, he said through an interpreter that "he loves the mormons & their Children he feels like taking them & dangling them on his knee. would like to live here till he Dies." Sowiette did not, however, come from Utah Valley. Compared to the Timpanogos people, it was easy for Sowiette to make peace with the settlers; they had not, after all, invaded his home territory, the Uinta Basin. Sowiette traveled to Utah Lake once or twice a year to trade and fish. In 1855 he did not tarry. He left even before receiving some promised rations from the Indian agent in

Provo. When the agent overtook him on the trail, Sowiette explained that some of his boys had been stealing corn. He had decided not to risk a confrontation. In his report the agent called Sowiette's band "the most harmless and friendly of any of the Utah Indians." An impressive and impressively old person, Sowiette commanded respect from Utes and non-Utes. At the 1865 Spanish Fork treaty session, Kanosh called him "the father of all the Utes." Despite being "old, poor, and blind [with] no flesh on his bones," Sowiette managed to make a speech (through interpreter George Bean) in which he said he had always been a friend to the Mormons as well as the "Americans." Brigham Young, who sat in the audience, answered aloud in the affirmative.[37]

In death Sowiette became a legendary figure. In 1884 and 1885, in the first published histories of Provo and Spanish Fork, Edward W. Tullidge included a pair of stories about the "old Indian king of the Utes." Tullidge was a small Mormon version of San Francisco's Hubert Howe Bancroft—a western businessman who wrote recent history for profit. He was not a sectarian hack. He adopted a disinterested if enthusiastic tone, and quoted primary sources at length. Unlike Bancroft, however, Tullidge did not use footnotes, and he sometimes failed to distinguish among certainty, speculation, and hearsay. From today's perspective, Tullidge's stories about Sowiette seem too good to be true. At a Ute council in 1847, supposedly, Sowiette struck down Walkara's motion to raise a Ute army to destroy the embryonic Mormon colony at Great Salt Lake City. Then, in 1850, Walkara decided to use his own men to massacre the settlers at Fort Utah (Provo). At the final hour Sowiette, the "head of the Ute nation," revealed the plan to Bishop Isaac Higbee. The peace chief even offered to defend the fort. Knowing that Sowiette would keep his word, Walkara abandoned his plan, but not before his men surrounded the fort and howled through the night.[38]

For good reason Tullidge offered no substantiation for this history. It never happened. Walkara did come to Fort Utah in 1850, but for entirely different purposes. In conjunction with the annual fish rendezvous, Walkara attended a diplomatic meeting with Brigham Young in the wake of the Mormons' recent extermination campaign against the Timpanogos Nuche. The meeting went well. Afterward the Utes "formed a semi-circle and went singing up to the fort."[39] It's possible that Tullidge interviewed a former resident of the fort who recalled this scene but forgot the context. In distant memory the happy, serenading Indians might have morphed into howling Indians on the warpath.

Tullidge's telling went on to influence the failing memories of old-timers. In his reminiscence from the 1880s, Peter Conover, one of Provo's original settlers, claimed that Sowiette warned *him* of the planned attack; Conover gave the year as 1852. Around 1890 William Thomas transcribed the reminiscence of his father, Robert, another Provo pioneer, who was "wasting away." William wrote "near as possable in the same words as he [Robert] related it unto me." However, the second-hand memoir contains whole phrases lifted from Tullidge. Perhaps the son assumed the father must have seen Sowiette thwart Walkara since he had been living at Fort Utah at the time. Remarkably, Tullidge's mnemonic influence extended beyond Utah Valley. In 1889 a newspaper in Manti, Utah, recalled the time when Sowiette saved the young settlement from the murderous machinations of Walkara. Two years later a revised version of this story, "Sowiette's Noble Act," appeared in an LDS Church magazine. According to the text, the Indian savior acted with "infinite pity and tenderness."[40]

As literary figures, Sowiette and Walkara actually worked hand in hand. By adoring and defending Mormons, the mythic Sowiette suggested that the Saints must have deserved that adoration and defense; they must have acted benevolently toward Indians. Yet by his very uniqueness, Sowiette, "the White Man's Friend," called attention to the overall hostility and degeneracy of the Utes, as personified by the mythic Walkara. Coexistence with such people was impossible; like locusts and wolves, they had to be eliminated. Of course, most settlers did not want to dwell on their own or their fathers' role in the violent dispossession of native peoples. Post-pioneer Provoans found it easier to memorialize a would-be massacre in the summer of 1850 than the discomforting alternative—the actual atrocities of their own campaign against the Timpanogos Nuche in the winter of the same year. Absurdly, the victorious invaders remembered themselves as victimized survivors. "The early history of Provo, if written, would be devoted in the main to a recital of extreme hardships, resulting from bitter and almost incessant Indian wars," editorialized the Chamber of Commerce in 1888. "While the pioneers of that place were permitted to establish themselves by a friendly arrangement with the red men, it did not long continue. The Indians soon began a characteristic and most violent warfare upon the hardy settlers."[41]

Locals even acted out Indian depredations. At Provo's Pioneer Day in 1878 about 3,000 residents turned out to see a parade, followed by

the great attraction of the day—a representation of an Indian attack on Pioneer Fort of '49, and gallant defence by the Pioneers. No sooner had the Pioneers entered the Fort than the Indians [dressed-up Mormons] encircled it on their horses, and with war whoops and yells, laying over the necks of their horses, firing their guns and shooting arrows at full speed, mingled with fierce shouts of the brave defenders, silenced occasionally by the roar of the cannon of the fort, made a scene bringing some reminiscences of an unpleasant character to the minds of some of our old residents and giving the uninitiated an idea of the mode of Indian warfare. The rear guard [of the parade] came to the rescue. Indians defeated, wounded cared for, treaty made, and the procession returns to the Bowery, where seated by the Marshal and assistants.[42]

All over the United States, white settler culture celebrated this kind of guilt displacement. Starting in the 1880s, William Cody as Buffalo

Bill made a fortune staging massacres committed by Indians. As Richard White has pointed out, it is remarkable how consistently colonizers portrayed natives as the aggressors in the theater of "inverted conquest."[43]

Until the pseudo-Indian Legend of Timpanogos became dominant in the mid-twentieth century, Walkara's siege remained the best-known "Indian story" in Utah Valley. The number of Ute warriors eventually swelled to 400. In 1931 a Utah Boy Scout committee on historical markers called for a Sowiette memorial. "There are score[s] of towns in central Utah which time and time again received succor at the hands of Sowiette," asserted the committee in the main LDS Church magazine. Finally, in 1941, the local camp of the Sons of the Utah Pioneers erected a plaque to Sowiette—still the only historical marker dedicated to Indians in Provo. The plaque reads in part: "It was here that the settlers were threatened with massacre by Chief Walker and his band of Indians, but were saved by Chief Sowiett's stern warning, 'When you attack you will find me and my braves defending.'" The quotation comes from Edward Tullidge, who apparently didn't know that Sowiette didn't speak proficient English.[44]

Tullidge's bogus history occupied a midpoint in the continuum between animate Indians and ghostly Indians. His imagined nonmassacre starring Sowiette at least echoed a real conflict; the "king of the Utes" at least derived from a real person. Regrettably, fake heritage would succeed false history. By 1949, the year of Provo's centennial, the transition from actual to fanciful, from Fish-Eaters to Mountain-Worshipers, had been realized. As part of a souvenir booklet, a Provo educator wrote a new Sowiette story that unwittingly symbolized the larger transition from lake to mountain:

> Sowiette came back. The saddle-colored old savage simply materialized out of the fog . . . "You are trying to tell what is real and lasting about this Mountain Midland in Utah," he rumbled shrewdly. "Let me help you. I was a Prominent Cit-

izen in these parts a century ago. I saw the first Mormon pioneers come, I helped them survive. I have watched the country grow. Let me be your ghost writer!

"From Heber to Nephi is a trail like a twisted thong, strung with little cities like bright beads. They lie there shining in the sun, treasures worth many bands of horses, many squaws, many rifles. Over them tower the giants of the Wasatch, throwing arms of ridges about them, sheltering them. Your people are secure and happy because you are in league with great peaks, because you are Men-Who-Are-Friendly-With-Mountains."[45]

Thus spoke the ghost of Utah Lake.

II

Making a Mountain: Alpine Play

4

Rocky Mountain Saints

From earliest times until the early twentieth century, the defining feature of Utah Valley was its lake. Abruptly, Mount Timpanogos replaced it in symbolic importance. The slippage of the lake did not reflexively cause the upthrust of the mountain, however. Three contingent factors came into play.

First, Latter-day Saints imported to Utah a symbolic tradition of mountain veneration. Nineteenth-century Utah Mormons saw themselves as the New Israel and looked for a new Mount Zion, the Temple Mount of Jerusalem. This outlook did not cause settlers to single out Timpanogos, but it predisposed them to lift their eyes unto the hills. Second, a European vogue of alpine aesthetics spread to America, and found a home in the American West after the Civil War. Third, federal surveyors assigned elevations to western summits, thereby creating an imagined geography based on altitude. In the late nineteenth century, survey data indicated—mistakenly, it turns out—that the summit named "Timpanogos Pk." was the highest point in the Wasatch Range. This scientific revelation encouraged locals to visualize a discrete mount beneath that elevation point. What had once been seen as a section of "the mountains" was reimagined as a self-contained landform. Thanks to the cult of measurement, a landmark became visible.

The sudden salience of Mount Timpanogos came at the expense of Mount Nebo, the favored mountain of pioneer-era Utah. The shrinking significance of Nebo may be used to symbolize the diminishing biblicist mountain tradition within Mormonism. Although the culture of Mount Zion contributed to the celebration of Mount Timpanogos, the advancement of "Timp" marked a change in the Mormon homeland. At the end of the nineteenth century, the LDS Church gave up its formal resistance to the federal government. Outwardly, at least, it submitted to Americanization. This profound political shift rearranged the symbolic landscape. Mount Timpanogos was no Mount Zion; it was a modern, secular, American mountain.

::: Across the world and throughout history, certain high points have signified holiness. The Aborigines of Australia have for millennia revered Uluru (or Ayers Rock), the colossal red monolith in the center of their continent. For centuries the Japanese have venerated Fujiyama. Central China contains the Five Sacred Mountains (Daoist) and the Four Famous Peaks (Buddhist). Mesopotamian kings, Egyptian pharaohs, and mesoamerican priests ordered the erection of "simulated mountains"—ziggurats or pyramids—to reach the plane of heaven. The twelve major gods of the ancient Greeks resided on Mount Olympus. The ruined temples of the Acropolis stand upon the Sacred Rock.

In Native America, sacred rocks abound. The most important medicine wheel sits atop a 9,642-foot-high peak in the Bighorn Range of Wyoming. In the Black Hills region, both Devils Tower and Bear Butte possess cosmic significance to many Plains Indian groups. One of them, the Kiowa, also reveres Rainy Mountain (in Oklahoma). Four peaks in the four cardinal directions mark the limits of Navajoland *(Dinetah)*; the southern mountain, Mount Taylor, is also sacred within Acoma, Laguna, and Zuni cultures. Tewas have their own four cardinal peaks. The Hopi maintain shrines on the San Francisco Peaks and preserve oral narratives about the creation of the holy mounts by warrior gods. The origin story of the Tohono O'odham involves southern Arizona's stunning Baboquivari Peak. While there is no archival evidence that Mount Timpanogos—or any other peak in the Wasatch Range—had spiritual significance to past Numic peoples, Sleeping Ute Mountain (in southwestern Colorado) has a long and continuing place in Southern Ute cosmology. Likewise, Mount Charleston (in southeastern Nevada) is venerated by certain bands of Western Shoshones and Southern Paiutes. The sacred peaks of California include Mount Diablo, Sutter Buttes, and Mount Shasta. In the Pacific Northwest, the great volcanoes of the Cascade Range figure into many native myths.[1]

In Judeo-Christian mythology, the attitude toward mountain peaks is positive. The one god of the Hebrews held summits with Abraham on Mount Moriah, Moses on Mount Sinai, and Elijah on Mount Carmel. The New Testament—especially the Gospel of St. Matthew—contains numerous references to lofty sites. Satan took Jesus to an "exceeding high mountain" to tempt him with an omniscient view of creation. On his own, Jesus went to the mountains to pray. It was from a mount that he preached the Beatitudes. At the end—or new beginning—of his life, Jesus again went to a mountain, where Moses and Elijah appeared to Peter, James, and John, and the voice of God came down from a cloud. According to belief, the site of the Transfiguration was Mount Tabor. Early Christians nurtured many other sacred peaks. The Coptic tradition of monasticism led devotees to seek out high caves and mountainside monasteries. In the sixth century, Byzantines built St. Catherine's Monastery beneath the mountain believed to be Sinai (also called Mount Moses or Jabal Musa). Since the ninth century, Mount Athos has provided sacred space for a cluster of Orthodox monasteries. In Catholic Europe, *montes sacros* began to be established in the fifteenth century. Montserrat, a mountain and monastery in Spain, became an important shrine to the Virgin. Other hillside Stations of the Cross served as pilgrimage sites—substitutes for a trip to the Mount of Olives and Mount Calvary.

However, medieval Europe featured unholy peaks, too. The ghost of Pontius Pilate haunted Mount Pilatus in Switzerland. Mont Blanc, the premier destination in the age of mountaineering, was earlier called Cursed Mountain. Legends from the Alps described demonic beasts infesting the icy crags. Christian theologians speculated that the Earth's mountainous terrain was a product not of the Creation but of human sin. They likened mountains to ugly imperfections of the body—warts, boils, pimples.

Clearly, a religious appreciation of specific mountains is ancient and widespread. But an *aesthetic* appreciation of mountain *ranges* is relatively new. In Europe it is positively modern. The Greeks and the Romans spent little aesthetic energy on cordilleras; their successors were even less responsive if not downright scornful. Plains and foothills supported agricultural beauty; by comparison the mountains seemed barren and unfriendly, providing haven only to bandits, heretics, pagans—even dragons. "During the first seventeen centuries of the Christian era," one scholar has noted, "'Mountain Gloom' so clouded human eyes that never for a moment did poets see mountains in the full radiance to which our eyes have become accustomed. Within a century—indeed, within fifty years—all this was changed." This revolution in landscape aesthetics was a harbinger of Romanticism. European artists and poets abandoned an aesthetic of restraint and balance to embrace vastness and irregularity. High, rugged mountains embodied this primal beauty; they could fill the mind with "an agreeable kind of horror"—an altered state of consciousness that became known as the sublime. For many eighteenth-century literati, the Alps were like a new drug.[2]

The notion of the sublime reached North America later, although certain distinctive sites such as Niagara Falls and the Natural Bridge of Virginia quickly became associated with the concept. The only British colony that could plausibly be described as alpine was sparsely settled New Hampshire. In the 1820s European-trained painters started arriving, and the state hosted the first American art colony. Some of the members of the so-called White Mountain School were also affiliated with the contemporaneous Hudson River School. The standout painter was Thomas Cole. "Mountains are the most conspicuous objects in landscape," Cole declared in his "Essay on American Scenery." While admitting that the "Switzerland of the United States" was not equal to the Alps, he defended New Hampshire. Nowhere had nature "so completely married together grandeur and loveliness—there he sees the sublime melting into the beautiful, the savage tempered by the magnificent." Other leading cultural figures, including Daniel Webster, Washington Irving, Nathaniel Hawthorne, and Ralph Waldo Emerson, made visits to New Hampshire in the 1820s and 1830s. The accommodations were primitive compared with those at Niagara Falls and Saratoga Springs, but that was the point. The White Mountains entered the Fashionable Tour because they seemed more unsettled than pastoral, more sublime than picturesque.[3]

By midcentury the scenery of New Hampshire had been tamed by railroads and hotels. Luckily for American aesthetes, a new arena for the mountainous sublime opened up: the Louisiana Purchase and later the Mexican War made the Rockies part of the United States. Overland migration in the 1840s and 1850s opened some Americans' eyes to this high country. Soon artists relocated the "Switzerland of America" from New Hampshire to Colorado. The celebrated painter Albert Bierstadt began the trend. His masterpiece of romantic extravagance, a vast canvas called *The Rocky Mountains,* caused a sensation when it went on display in New York City in 1864. Visual information on the West was then hard to come by. This situation changed, however, with the surveys of Ferdinand V. Hayden, Clarence King, George M. Wheeler, and John Wesley Powell (1867–1879). The four "Great Surveys" were congressionally funded media machines that distributed information to magazines, newspapers, and railroads. Through these outlets, government artists presented a romantic view of the mountainous West to Americans.[4]

A key artist was Thomas Moran. English-born and Philadelphia-raised, Moran studied painting in Europe from 1866 to 1870. The year after his return to America, he traveled west with Hayden on an expedition to Yellowstone. Moran's sketches and paintings helped spread the fame of the place and helped persuade Congress to pronounce it a national park. Congress later purchased Moran's monumental oil, *The Grand Canyon of the Yellowstone,* for display in the Capitol. The majestic mountain landscapes of the West provided the United States—a barely reconciled nation still reeling from the Civil War—with expedient symbolic material. The Rocky Mountains were close to heaven and far removed from the North and the South.

In fact the use of the Rockies for nationalistic purposes dated back to the early days of the sectional crisis. In 1825 the newly elected Thomas Hart Benton of Missouri spoke about the North American cordillera from the floor of the Senate. "Along the back of this ridge," he said, "the western limit of this republic should be drawn, and the statue of the fabled god, Terminus, should be raised upon its highest peak, never to be thrown down."[5] Following the prevailing philosophy of the founders, Benton argued for the advantage of small republics; excessive expansion would imperil American democracy. In time, however, Jacksonian Democrats like Benton renounced this philosophical legacy; the senator became a leading proponent of Manifest Destiny. Nature had given the United States an easy railroad route to the mouth of the Columbia River. This "American Road to India" would open up trade to the Orient and position the nation to surpass Britain as the world's leading empire.

In 1842, as a senior member of Congress, Benton arranged for his new son-in-law, John C. Frémont, to lead an expedition to survey part of this route to the Pacific. Frémont did the job and something extra. He climbed what he thought was the highest peak of what was supposed to be the highest branch of the Rockies—the Wind River Mountains of present-day Wyoming. Against instructions and good sense, Frémont, nauseous from altitude sickness, pushed himself and his men up icy cliffs with scant supplies. At the top of what was later dubbed Frémont Peak he unfurled an American flag with an eagle across the field of stars. The eagle flew above a huge swath of territory. This gesture by Frémont was emphatically expansionist, the opposite of erecting a terminus marker.[6]

He returned to Washington, D.C., to resounding acclaim. Further expeditions followed, making the "Pathfinder" a national hero. Ironically, the land that was to have served as his stepping-stone soon became a barrier. After the territorial gains of the Mexican War, the North and the South espoused different visions for the West. Most northerners believed that the region should be reserved for "free labor." The party of free labor, the Republican Party, tapped Frémont to be its first presidential candidate in 1856. Young, dashing, popular, and without much political experience, Frémont was chosen to have bisectional appeal. For campaign promotions, Republicans resurrected images of Frémont hoisting a flag in the Rockies; the flag now read, "LIBERTY." But by 1856 there were two competing definitions of liberty in America. Originally a national image, Frémont atop the mountainous West became a sectional one.

Only after the Civil War could Americans again imagine the Rockies as a unifying symbol. In 1873 members of the Hayden Expedition discovered the long-fabled Mount of the Holy Cross, a natural oddity located in the rugged Sawatch Range of central Colorado. Long after winter's last storm, snowfall persisted within two perpendicular crevices atop this pyramidal peak near the Continental Divide. At the right season it really did look like a cross; Manifest Destiny could hardly be more clearly manifested. William Henry Jackson, one of the pioneers of western photography and a sometime employee of Hayden, made a negative of the cross that became his best-selling image. He later doctored the negative to make the cross more dramatic. His colleague Thomas Moran was equally entrepreneurial; in 1874 he trekked to the peak to make sketches. The subsequent painting showed a perfect mountain-born cross floating in the clouds above a crystal waterfall. This canvas went on display at America's first world's fair, the 1876 Centennial Exhibition in Philadelphia, where a familiar nineteenth-century message—the providence of Nature's Nation—was celebrated. One didn't even have to be an American to see the painting's promotional value. In 1880 William Bell, a British investor in the Denver & Rio Grande Railroad, purchased Moran's *Mountain of the Holy Cross*. The railroad had recently constructed some posh European-style resorts at Colorado Springs. Bell owned a nearby castle, Briarhurst, where he hung the painting and gave regular viewings. Moran's depiction of water flowing from a holy peak accentuated the railroad's own advertising about the curative powers of its spas. The Denver & Rio Grande used the painting—and many other images by Moran and Jackson—in a national campaign to bring tourists and settlers to the Rockies.[7]

In the twentieth century the symbolic power of the Mount of the Holy Cross waned. As America grew more powerful and self-assured, it no longer needed an American Switzerland. The nation's new iconic landform, the Grand Canyon, was a drastic departure from European aesthetic traditions. Additionally, the "closing" of the frontier in 1890 made Manifest Destiny seem less relevant—at least in the usual sense of America's continental prerogative. The patriotic eminence of the new century, Mount Rushmore, invoked America's newly assumed *extra*continental mission. The nation's new position and role in the world were the main reason for including the face of Teddy Roosevelt, ardent imperialist and backer of the Panama Canal. In the American Century, the United States would not be satisfied merely to see itself in nature; it would *remake* nature in its own image. For various reasons, then, the Mount of the Holy Cross became more identified with Colorado than with the United States, more with Christianity than with Christian nationalism. In 1919 a local Catholic bishop floated the idea of an annual pilgrimage to the mountain. The *Denver Post* eventually took up the idea and sponsored an ecumenical pilgrimage. Coloradans made enough noise that Herbert Hoover created a national monument around the peak in 1929. Unfortunately, the right arm of the cross began to disintegrate soon afterward. Pilgrims lost interest. The mountain's monument status was eventually revoked. Today the Mount of the Holy Cross is unrenowned except to hikers.[8]

A second, more secular mountain promoted by the Denver & Rio Grande proved more enduring over the twentieth century. Pikes Peak, which rises above Colorado Springs and the Garden of the Gods, stands out as the oldest tourist mountain in the West. It is sometimes called America's Mountain because of its association with "America the Beautiful," the song that nearly became the national anthem. Katharine Lee Bates composed the draft of her "purple mountain majesties" lyric while visiting Pikes Peak in 1893. The mountain's salience actually dates from the 1850s, when thousands of would-be miners rushed to the "Pike's Peak Gold Region." Many painted "Pike's Peak or Bust" or "Bound for the Peak" on their wagons. In 1871, hoping to lure tourist gold, Coloradans constructed the first of many foot trails to the mountain. A carriage road opened in 1888, followed shortly by the Manitou & Pikes Peak Cog Railway. The 14,155-foot summit became even more accessible in 1916 with the completion of an automobile road. These exhibits of the "technological sublime" probably lured as many tourists as the summit itself.[9]

Easily accessible to tourists, Pikes Peak retains a symbolic edge over most other mountains in the Rockies. It helps, too, that Pikes Peak is visible from Colorado Springs, which now sprawls across the plains. Countless Coloradans regularly view the peak from picture windows and windshields. By contrast, the Mount of the Holy Cross—now within a designated wilderness area—seems as distant as the evangelistic century that created it. You can't even see it from a highway. But farther west through the Rockies on I-70 is a mountain state where more of the older symbolism survives. In Utah, a former theocracy, the traditions of the religious mountain and the patriotic mountain have a strong, peculiar history.

::: Mountains and hills adorn the landscape of early Mormonism. The Angel Moroni appeared in Joseph Smith's bedroom in 1823 and repeated several Old Testament prophecies, including Joel 2:32—"for in Mt. Zion and in Jerusalem shall be deliverance." The angel told the teenaged Smith about the Gold Plates, a scriptural record of the ancient inhabitants of the New World. Moroni himself had been the last recordkeeper, and had buried the plates in a hill. Smith instantly recognized the place "owing to the distinctness of the vision." The hill was of "considerable size, and the most elevated of any in the neighborhood."[10] This landform—a glacial drumlin—became known as Hill Cumorah. Today it is recognized as a Mormon sacred place. Every summer the Church produces a historical pageant for thousands of mountain-state Mormons who undertake a pilgrimage to upstate New York to see a low green hill.

The first seventeen years of The Church of Jesus Christ of Latter-day Saints, founded in 1830, provide a story of successive movements and removals. The trail was supposed to have ended in Independence, Missouri, the "center place." Here in 1831 Joseph Smith dedicated a hill as a temple site. As in the Bible, the site was known as Mount Zion. But the new temple was never built. Under duress, the Mormons moved on to Illinois. In 1844, facing persecution once again, Joseph Smith made plans to flee the Mississippi River for the Rocky Mountains. Taking a cue from the prophet Isaiah, he instructed his followers to construct a sixteen-foot "ensign." Presumably he meant to fly it above a new Mount Zion. Before he could map out his move, the Prophet died at the hands of vigilantes. It fell to one of Smith's apostles, Brigham Young, to organize the trek to the West.

How did westering Saints make sense of their itinerant cosmology? Some reasoned that a settlement in the West would be one of the "corner stakes" of the great tent of Zion—the center pole still being Missouri. Others emphasized the apocryphal "Rocky Mountain Prophecy" of Joseph Smith. In 1842 the Prophet purportedly said that "the Saints would continue to suffer much affliction and would be driven to the Rocky Mountains . . . and some of you will live to go and assist in making settlements and build cities and see the Saints become a mighty people in the midst of the Rocky Mountains."[11] To members of a beleaguered, bankrupt splinter group betting everything on a chancy move to an unsettled, mountainous portion of Mexico, the Rocky Mountain Prophecy must have been encouraging.

In addition to latter-day prophecy, the emigrants looked to the Bible, and specifically to Exodus. They increasingly believed in recapitulation: Latter-day Saints, the covenant people, followed Brigham Young, the modern Moses. Brother Brigham, faced with the responsibility of determining the destination, dwelled on his predecessor's directive for a mountaintop ensign. In 1846 Young had a dream about the West and "its many beautiful hills." His record does not elaborate, but oral tradition suggests the miraculous: the spirit of Joseph Smith visited Young and showed him a hill above a valley that marked the gathering place. When Young entered Great Salt Lake Valley on 24 July 1847, he allegedly recognized the hill from his vision. There could be substance to this story. On 26 July Young and his advisors climbed a minor promontory of the Wasatch in order to visualize the layout of their new temple city. They gave the knoll (not much more than a bump) the grandiloquent name Ensign Peak and made plans to fly a massive Mormon flag from its summit. At the time, they had to make do with a handkerchief—though subsequent folklore would place a flag in Brigham's hand. Inspired with "fire in my bones," the pioneer Joel Hills Johnson penned a verse in 1852–53 that became a favorite Mormon anthem. To this day, congregations sing his words:

> High on the mountaintop a banner is unfurled.
> Ye Nations, now look up; It waves to all the world
> In Deseret's sweet, peaceful land,
> On Zion's mount behold it stand![12]

The LDS hymnal is one of the best repositories of old Mormon folk values about the high country. The latest edition (1985) retains numerous nineteenth-century mountain-themed compositions, including "Behold, the Mountain of the Lord," "For the Strength of the Hills," "Holy Temples on Mount Zion," and "Zion Stands with Hills

Surrounded." Earlier editions contain many more, such as "Give Me a Home in the Heart of the Mountains," "God Bless Our Mountain Home," "I Long to Breathe the Mountain Air," and "Proud? Yes, of Our Home in the Mountains." One Mormon convert, Charles W. Penrose, felt inspired to celebrate the Saints' "mountain retreat" even before he laid eyes on it. While still in England, he penned a favorite Utah lyric, "O Ye Mountains High." The musical setting for this and other early Mormon hymns came directly from Anglo-American Protestantism. Later, in the late 1850s, a period of "homemade music" began, and the hymnodists were at times referred to collectively as "mountain home composers."[13]

There was something misplaced about this symbolic emphasis. Utah settlers occupied the lowland as much as or more than the highland. They built their homes at the interface of plain and montane environments—usually near the mouth of a canyon—in order to tap the resources of both. The valleys supplied town sites and farm sites; the mountains supplied water and timber and range. For the most part, Mormons ignored the precious mineral resources of their mountains. The true alpine settlements of northern Utah—mining towns such as Park City—were established and run by non-Mormons (an anomalous situation that persists to this day thanks to the ski industry). Brigham Young wanted a kingdom of farmers, not one of gold seekers. Lowland farming connoted industriousness, communalism, and morality. Highland mining connoted the opposite.

Although few Mormons actually inhabited the mountains, they still claimed the moral high ground. Ecclesiastical speeches from the era of Brigham Young regularly featured elevated language; catchphrases from the official *Journal of Discourses* include "mountain air," "mountain fastnesses," "mountain kingdom," "mountain retreat," "mountain walls," and the ubiquitous "mountain home." After so many years on the move, Mormons rejoiced in the sanctuary of their "everlasting hills." Their home, sheltered like a fortress, seemed prepared by God. Elizabeth Cumming, the wife of the man sent by President Buchanan to depose Brigham Young as territorial governor, instantly recognized the draw of the place:

> The grand mountains all around us aid the imagination in its flights—and one can easily realize how an unbridled fancy can become the parent of many superstitions in the midst of such scenery—mirages abound—fantastic forms appear among, above & under the clouds which rest on the tops of the mountains, or partially descend their sides. Scenes of beauty, glory and sublimity abound. They [the Mormons] are hoping ere very long to finish their grand temple "in the mountain tops"—as commanded, they believe, by many prophecies.[14]

The leading prophecy came from Isaiah 2:2: "And it shall come to pass in the last days, that the mountain of the LORD's house shall be established in the top of the mountains, and shall be exalted above the hills; and all nations shall flow unto it." This passage had been applied metaphorically to Missouri. Yet it gained force only after the displacement of Mount Zion to the Great Basin. The words of Isaiah echoed among the rocky heights of the Wasatch Range. Mountain-based biblicism probably influenced the hilltop siting of early Mormon temples in Logan (1884) and Manti (1888). The six spires of the all-important temple in Salt Lake bring to mind mountains (whence the temple's granite came). A statue of the Angel Moroni atop the highest spire faces east toward the Wasatch, the direction of the sun's and the Son's return. Paradoxically—but what is religion without paradox?—Latter-day Saint scripture anticipates "the mountains to be made low, and for the rough places to become smooth" during Christ's 1,000-year reign.[15]

As they waited for the world's end, Utah Mormons came to love their mountains as fixtures of home. With each passing year the flatlands of Ohio, Missouri, and Illinois grew more distant in memory.

Mormons as a whole sometimes called themselves "Rocky Mountain Saints" to establish a distinction from the schismatic followers of Joseph Smith who had stayed in the Midwest. In the second half of the nineteenth century, most of Utah's population growth came from European conversion and natural increase. Immigrant and infant Mormons missed the midwestern phase of Mormonism; the mountainous Great Basin was the only Zion they ever knew. Eventually the Utah highland became synonymous with the Mormon homeland. Latter-day Saints saw mountains even where they didn't exist: desert settlers of southern Utah always referred to a nearby high plateau or big mesa as "the mountain." Oddly, this passion for the high country was so general as to be vague. Pioneer lyricists and orators rarely mentioned *which* mountains inspired so much feeling. "Rocky Mountain" was a symbolic term, not a site-specific toponym. Texts from the early territorial era seldom identified the names of Utah's mountain ranges, much less individual peaks.[16]

Pioneer-era references to mountains also generally lacked the vocabulary of the picturesque and the sublime. Aesthetic appreciation trailed behind religious and emotional attachment. By the 1880s, it would catch up. Both Albert Bierstadt and Thomas Moran visited the Wasatch Range after the Civil War. More to the point, Salt Lake City developed its own mini-Morans. To the surprise of many visitors, the Territory of Utah enjoyed a robust regional art scene, with studios, salons, and theaters. Salt Lake City was the one island of "culture" between Denver and San Francisco. It had a stable population of arts-loving residents, a large percentage of whom were educated immigrants from the British Isles and Scandinavia. Two of the city's leading painters, Alfred Lambourne (1850–1926) and H. L. A. Culmer (1854–1914), were English-born converts to Mormonism. Both worked as travel writers as well as landscapists and theater artists. In 1891 Lambourne produced a portfolio called *Scenic Utah* in which he praised the Wasatch as an "expression of the higher picturesque." Its "wondrous" scenes "challenge comparison with any other mountains of the West." In 1892 Culmer added to the praise with a serial called the "Mountain Scenery of Utah." His black-and-white illustrations echoed the European romantic tradition, as did his purple prose. This is how Culmer described his favorite haunt, a lake in Big Cottonwood Canyon:

> Scores of painters, from Bierstadt down, have attempted the difficult task of reproducing this delightful scene upon canvas, but the elements which contribute to its beauty are difficult for the painter to master, and they all admit having met their match in the effort. But to those who do not attempt the almost sacrilegious task of endeavoring to reproduce this scene, who go sit upon its banks and enjoy the delicious effect upon the senses which Lake Mary never fails to excite, there is no disappointment, but only rapturous sense of enjoyment which a description in words can never convey, yet which remains aglow long afterwards in the hearts of all who have once felt it.[17]

This was not the mountain language of the prophets. Rather, Culmer invoked the conventional transatlantic aestheticism, an outlook that began to appear in Mormon periodicals in the 1880s, the decade after Brigham Young's death. Pioneer Mormons—including Young himself—had resorted to Big Cottonwood Canyon as early as the 1850s. But those early outings consisted of picnicking and dancing. Culmer had different recreational preferences: sightseeing, strolling, sketching. He and other members of Salt Lake's high society frequented the alpine lakes of the upper canyon at an emerging resort called Brighton. "Resort" is a generous word; Brighton consisted of a hotel, some cabins, and some scenery. It was enough, however, to attract aesthetes like Lambourne and Culmer. These compatriots explored the high country above Brighton and named several landforms. Lake Mary acquired the company of Lake Blanche, Lake Martha, Lake Annette, and Lake Florence.

Besides sightseers, Brighton catered to miners. The resort lay midway between two new mountain mining towns, Alta and Park City. In the same era that people reimagined the Wasatch as a storehouse of scenery, the mountains became known as a storehouse of minerals. The Civil War encouraged this development. With the coming of war, the troops in charge of guarding the overland trail were recalled for combat duty. To replace them, President Lincoln called for a volunteer force. Several hundred California men—detritus of the Gold Rush—answered the summons. Under the leadership of Patrick Edward Connor, the Third California Volunteer Infantry established Fort Douglas on a bench above Salt Lake City. The troops intended to watch over Mormons as much as Indians. Colonel Connor, a Mormon-hater, believed that the best answer to the "Mormon Question" was a mining boom—one that would flood the territory with Gentile settlers. Connor encouraged his men to prospect in the hills. In short order they discovered precious metals in the Wasatch Range east of Salt Lake City and in the Oquirrh Mountains west of the city. Although Utah never became a gold-rush destination like Nevada, Connor's strategy met with some success, especially after the completion of the transcontinental railroad (1869) and various spur lines. By 1900 Utah's mines—notably the copper field at Bingham Canyon—employed thousands of non-Mormon (not to mention non-American) miners. Fifty years after the settlement of Salt Lake, the valley's tallest structure was not the temple but one of many smelters.

This change was not entirely imposed from the outside. Despite Brigham Young's zealous preference for farming over prospecting, many Mormons joined the officers of Fort Douglas in the mining districts. Starting in 1870, these freethinking Saints could read a Mormon newspaper that championed mineral development. The paper was published by a group of dissidents ("Godbeites") who challenged the all-encompassing authority of Brigham Young, particularly his control over Utah's economy. As an alternative to theocracy, these English converts envisioned a "New Movement" based on spiritualism. All of them were excommunicated.

In truth, the greatest threat to the LDS Church came not from dissidents and malcontents in the nearby mountains but from politicians on Capitol Hill. In the 1880s the Church hierarchy lost control of Utah's future when Congress in essence criminalized Mormonism by outlawing theocracy and polygamy—two core principles of the religion. Many Church leaders had to go on the lam to avoid imprisonment. Increasing the pressure, the federal government began seizing Church assets. The LDS Church finally capitulated in the early 1890s by dismantling its political party and surrendering its control of Utah public schools. Most famously, President Wilford Woodruff instructed followers to stop consecrating plural marriages. A reluctant pragmatist, Woodruff meant his 1890 edict (popularly known as the Manifesto) to be a delaying tactic. On the basis of a revelation given to Joseph Smith, many Mormons expected the Millennium to begin in 1891. Renewed expectation accompanied the dedication of the Salt Lake Temple on 6 April 1893, precisely forty years after the groundbreaking. The biblical timing was no accident: the completion of the temple seemed to fulfill Isaiah's prophecy. Christ would soon walk on the Earth; the doctrine of plural marriage would be reinstated; and the Saints would return to Missouri, the Promised Land. But the move never happened. Utah achieved its long-denied statehood in 1896, and Woodruff died shortly thereafter. In retrospect, the completion of the temple signaled not the rebirth of Zionism but its demise.[18]

After this change—what Mormon historians call "the Great Accommodation"—LDS mountain worship moved closer to the mainstream. For second-generation residents, mountains remained symbols of sanctuary, but less in the millenarian, exclusionary sense. The prophetic Ensign Peak became a patriotic landmark beginning in July 1897, the jubilee of the coming of the pioneers. To commemorate the event, community leaders erected a flagpole on the summit and flew the Stars and Stripes in a ceremony meant to demonstrate Americanism. For the newly enfranchised citizens of the forty-fifth state, the story of Brigham Young's banner assumed new significance; storytellers now insisted that Young, like John C. Frémont, had hoisted the *American* ensign. The church-run *Deseret News* promulgated this inversion of the older legend: instead of a Mormon prophet claiming the land for theocracy, Brigham Young was an American pioneer claiming the land for democracy. In the 1930s the rotunda of the Utah state capitol was completed with a wraparound mural that included a panel showing Young on the mount with Old Glory.[19]

Mormon congregations continued to sing "High on a Mountaintop," but even their songbook underwent Americanization. In the 1920s the Church gutted its old hymnal and assembled a new collection. The numerous original contributions to *Latter-day Saint Hymns* (1927) "all but abandoned the millennialism and communitarianism of the church's initial wave of hymn-text writing."[20] Meanwhile, through selective revision, the hymn committee tempered certain Mormon classics. Here is a passage from "O Ye Mountains High," before and after:

In thy mountain retreat,
God will strengthen thy feet;
~~on the necks of thy foes thou shalt tread.~~
without fear of thy foes thou shalt tread.

. . .

Thy deliv'rance is nigh,
thy oppressors shall die .
~~The Gentiles shall bow 'neath thy rod.~~
And thy land shall be freedom's abode.

What was it like for Utah Mormons to live through this transformation? Feelings ranged from excitement to relief to disbelief to demoralization.[21] Some adapted more easily than others. A story from Utah Valley about a man and a mountain illustrates this point.

Bishop John H. Koyle's life story is locally famous for being strange, but it actually recapitulates the familiar—Joseph Smith. A farmer from Spanish Fork, Koyle had a vision in 1894 in which the Angel Moroni transported him inside "the mountain" (never given a place-name by Koyle but now known on maps as Loafer Mountain).

There Moroni gave instructions for a marvelous project. Koyle would dig into the mountainside and recover a lost mine full of gold and scriptures belonging to the Nephites, one of the ancient peoples described in the Book of Mormon. By means of this buried treasure, the Saints would survive an impending worldwide economic and military crisis. America would be destroyed. Amidst the chaos, "Cities of Refuge" would arise in Utah where the righteous would live in peace and polygamy. After a number of signs confirmed his vision, Koyle went about his millennial task. He organized the Koyle Mining Company and issued stock. He called his enterprise the Relief Mine; others dubbed it the Dream Mine. Over the next fifty years, Koyle and his fellow dreamers kept digging. Even without investment returns, the farmer-prophet never lost faith. In response, the LDS Church discharged Koyle as local bishop and finally excommunicated him not long before his death in 1949. Today the mine corporation still exists on paper, and its handful of stockholders still keep the inactive "ore processing mill"—which appears more like a hillside temple—beautifully whitewashed.[22]

Modern Utah's most famous mine is worldly and exposed, the antithesis of the Dream Mine. In 1904 the copper excavation at Bingham Canyon, Utah, moved from an underground to an open-pit process. On-site engineers figured out how to recover specks of low-grade ore out of tons of waste rock, an industrial method that revolutionized mining worldwide. It required massive capitalization, but the financial returns were great. The ore from Bingham made the conductive wire that put America on the electric grid. Demand made the hole grow wide and deep. It swallowed the town of Bingham Canyon and then the canyon itself. Once called "the Hill," the mine became known as "the Pit." The Utah Copper Company (later absorbed by Kennecott) trumpeted its success in "tearing down the mountain." "Every day the earth trembles at Bingham, Utah," proclaimed a 1908 trade magazine. "Every day, there, the mountains crumble and diminish in size, and their crests are gradually sinking below their original horizon." The result was an inverted peak, an antimountain. For most of the twentieth century, it was the deepest man-made hole on Earth (about 3,000 feet at last count), a technological wonder and an ecological wreck.[23]

The Bingham copper mine is clearly visible from the summit of Timpanogos. These two mountain landmarks—one torn down (literally), one built up (metaphorically)—date from the same period. It's as if one place demanded the other. Industrialization consumed nature on the one hand and created opportunities to consume experiences of nature on the other. The main capitalist behind the Utah Copper Company, Spencer Penrose, retired to Colorado Springs, where he spent much of his fortune boosting Pikes Peak. He brought Colorado's leading mountain into the automobile age. Penrose built a vehicular road, established bus tours, and sponsored an annual car race to the summit. Down below, he rebuilt the Broadmoor Hotel into a lavish resort that boasted spectacular views of the peak. Penrose saw the future. Resort hotels, summer cabins, automobile roads, and (eventually) ski runs: these were the modern means of making mountains in the American West.[24]

In this context, Bishop Koyle of Spanish Fork seems sadly anachronistic. He drew upon a waning tradition. Just when Koyle started having visions, the era of angels came to an end. Although The Church of Jesus Christ of Latter-day Saints kept its millenarian name beyond the 1890s, "latter-day" lost its urgency. Not charisma but bureaucracy was the direction of the modern LDS Church. The ground had shifted under the feet of the Saints. Their mountain retreat now belonged to America. Unlike Koyle, the majority of Utah Mormons accepted this outcome. They were prepared for a modern mountain, something less like Ensign Peak and more like Pikes Peak.

::::   By all rights this modern mountain should not have been Timpanogos. It should have been Mount Nebo—notwithstanding its biblical name. Nebo was the one and only mountain in the Territory of Utah that appeared consistently on nineteenth-century maps. The distant runners-up were Twin Peaks and Lone Peak, both located near Salt Lake City. What made Nebo special? In part it was altitude. Early surveyors deduced (correctly) that it was the highest peak in the Wasatch, which itself was for several decades assumed (incorrectly) to be the highest range in Utah. Another key factor was geography. As the last, southernmost peak in the Wasatch, Nebo occupies the middle of the state; it has a commanding view of central Utah and the transition zone between the Great Basin and the Colorado Plateau. If the Mormons had not preemptively established Temple Square as Utah's "initial point"—the place where the east-west baseline intersects the principal meridian—federal surveyors would have chosen Mount Nebo. The mountain was in fact used as a main triangulation point and heliograph station. Nebo can be distinctly seen from far-off peaks to the north, south, east, and west. From a low vantage point, too, Nebo has an advantage over other area mountains; its line of three pyramidal summits is prominent from Point of the Mountain, the divide between Salt Lake Valley and Utah Valley. Thus whenever people travel south from Utah's capital, their first view of Utah Valley privileges Nebo's alpine crown.

Nebo had been climbed and named in 1849 by W. W. Phelps, a beloved LDS Church leader and hymnodist. In 1850, as part of Pioneer Day festivities in the Utah Valley settlement of Payson, townsfolk gathered under a bowery for feasting and toasting. Benjamin F. Stewart raised his glass and spoke these words: "The Pioneers and soldiers ever foremost in the cause of Zion: May their exaltation be like Mt. Nebo and as firm as the everlasting hills." In another area town, a Mount Nebo Literary Association was organized in 1853. Thirty years later a romantic poem about the mountain appeared in the earliest published history of Provo.[25]

Gentiles also recognized the majesty of Nebo. In 1862 the adventurer Richard F. Burton identified Nebo's "jagged cone" as the "monarch" of the "tall and bald-headed hills" of Utah Valley. Many other books from the summer-tour-among-the-Mormons genre mention the landform. "The snowy peaks of this glorious mountain glistened on

our horizon day after day," wrote Elizabeth Kane of her 1872 tour of
Utah (guided by Brigham Young himself). In the 1880s the English
traveler Phil Robinson *complained* about people's endlessly pointing
out Mount Nebo. The Denver & Rio Grande line, completed in the
same decade, contributed to the mountain's fame. The train route into
Utah Valley via Spanish Fork Canyon offered an especially dramatic
view of Nebo, which the D&RG called the "highest and grandest of
the Utah peaks" (a phrase lifted by many travel writers). One railway
passenger coming from Colorado gave praise to "the last of the great,
lone, Rocky Mountain peaks."[26]

Artists loved this mountain, too. In the company of Major John
Wesley Powell, Thomas Moran ascended Mount Nebo in 1873. George
Ottinger, first professor of drawing at the University of Deseret (forerunner of the University of Utah), sketched it as early as the 1860s.
His associate, Alfred Lambourne, included a drawing of the mountain
in his sumptuous oversized portfolio, *Scenic Utah* (1891). Both images exaggerated the height and steepness of the landform. In his accompanying text, Lambourne noted that new information showed the
Uinta Mountains to be the highest range in the state, but maintained
that Nebo remained the "loftiest spot of the Wasatch."[27]

Although altitude and geographic position were the two main reasons for Mount Nebo's prominence, its biblical name also counted for
something. The Bible was by far the most influential book in nineteenth-century America; its language permeated lives and landscapes.
Many settler groups made a nomenclatural link between the New
World and the Promised Land. For example, town-builders applied
the name Salem—the short form of "Jerusalem" and the anglicized
word for *Shalom*—from coast to coast, from Massachusetts to Oregon and points between (including Utah Valley). Thirty-nine summits
called Nebo ornament the National Map. If Mormons were unusual
in seeing themselves as Israel, they were conventional in comparing
their homeland to Palestine. The comparison actually made sense here.
In both arid regions a freshwater lake feeds a salty one via a short
river flowing between mountain valleys. Mormons recognized this

parallelism early on and renamed the Utah Outlet the Jordan. They could have gone further: they could have chosen "Lake Galilee" over Lake Utah, or "Jabbok Creek" over Mill Creek, and so on. One travel writer—a self-declared "unbelieving Gentile"—even chided the Saints for not naming their capital "New Jerusalem" and not renaming the Great Salt Lake the "Dead Sea."[28] It was the Union Pacific and the Denver & Rio Grande—not the LDS Church—that most forcefully advanced the Utah–Holy Land comparison. Countless railroad brochures praised the attractions of "America's Dead Sea." Railroads planned and financed lakeside resorts. The promise of experiencing the lake along with the prospect of seeing a Mormon harem drew up to 200,000 tourists to Salt Lake City each year by the end of the nineteenth century. To Pullman car travelers, names like Jordan and Nebo resonated. The same could not be said for names like Ensign Peak or Nephi (a town beneath Mount Nebo named after a Book of Mormon prophet). Like the restoration of polygamy, Ensign Peak represented the LDS Church's radical appropriation of biblical tradition. Mount Nebo represented a more conservative strain of usage.

It would be a mistake to say that Nebo became a dominant landmark. The point is simply that it lacked competition. As of 1900, Nebo had accumulated far more symbolism than any other alpine summit in Utah. Moreover, its emergence into prominence had come from the combined efforts of Mormons and Gentiles, artists and scientists. Ordinarily the mountain would have retained its status in the twentieth century. But Timpanogos, fifty miles to the north, supplanted Mount Nebo as the monarch of the Wasatch and soon surpassed it in symbolic importance.

This was a surprising development because "Timp" hardly existed before 1900. People didn't "see" it. References to the mountain are extremely scarce. In their expedition diary in 1776, the Spanish friars Domínguez and Escalante referred to "La Sierra Blanca de los Timpanois"—but they had the Wasatch Range in mind. Many decades later the federal Stansbury Expedition (1849–50) made passing reference to a "Timpanogos Pk." near the Timpanogos (Provo) River, but it isn't clear that Stansbury had in mind the mountain known by that name today, because he didn't mark the summit on his official map, favoring instead Lone Peak, Twin Peaks, and Mount Nebo. On the excellent 1878 map of Utah Territory that accompanied Major John Wesley Powell's *Arid Lands* report, Timpanogos was not named although six nearby peaks were. Similarly, the atlas to the Wheeler Survey (1874) showed "Nebo," "Spanish Pk," "Provo Pks," "Lone Pk," but no "Timpanogos." The King Survey (1877) went so far as to identify a "Utah Lake Region"—a region centered on the lake, bounded by Mount Nebo on the south and by the "granite body forming the mass of Lone Peak" on the north. In no way did Timpanogos define this region.[29]

It was, however, the King Survey that provided the first authenticated description of the summit of what is now known as Mount Timpanogos. Clarence King himself found "a remarkably good instance of [quartzite] intercalations" on "Tim-pan-o-gos Peak." Writing in 1869, his colleague S. F. Emmons described the steepness of the slopes and made a useful distinction between the peak and the "Timpanogos Ridge." The peak, or highest point, was part of a long, high ridge stretching between Provo Canyon and American Fork Canyon, which itself was "part of the great mountain wall, wh. bounds the Utah lake valley on the East, geologically continuous, but cut through by the streams, wh. drain the interior mountain basins enclosed by it." Grove Karl Gilbert, another government geologist, would later call this ridge the Timpanogos Front. This topographic distinction helps to explain why local people failed to mention Timpanogos in the nineteenth century. When the pioneer generation looked at Timpanogos, they saw not a discrete peak but an area of "the mountains." "Mounts" are supposed to be isolated uplifts. Nebo meets this criterion; Timpanogos does not. From Utah Valley the latter resembles a giant craggy wall whose summit cannot be distinguished.[30]

The best prephotographic image of the Timpanogos massif supports this conclusion. In 1858 Albert Tracy, a captain in the U.S. army stationed at Camp Floyd west of Utah Lake, drew a picture in his sketchbook. A talented artist, Tracy captured a panoramic view of northern Utah Valley backed by the Wasatch. In his gorgeous and remarkably realistic drawing, the only part of the high country that looks unmistakably like a mount is Lone Peak. However, Tracy did not bother to identify this high point or any other. He reserved his place-names for the water-based topography: Lake Utah, Jordan River, Battle Creek, American Fork, Provo Canyon, and Rock Canyon.

Today it's common knowledge that the eight-mile-long landmass between Provo Canyon and American Fork Canyon is "Timp." But this had to be learned. As of 1900, different parts of the massif had different names. The part most likely to be singled out was the north end (now known as North Peak). From the back side of the massif, this secondary summit seems to rise up on its own. To the extent that tourists and aesthetes contemplated Timpanogos in the late nineteenth century, they did so from this vantage point. They were able to do so because by then a narrow-gauge railroad served a mining district at the head of American Fork Canyon—itself a thing of beauty. In the 1870s enthusiasts began referring to the gorge as the "Yosemite of Utah" (a title eventually usurped by Zion Canyon). One of the two main capitalists behind the railroad and mine was named Aspinwall. Like any good capitalist, he received an honorific place-name: the north peak became Mount Aspinwall. Meanwhile the summit point— which, like Mount Aspinwall, looks like a mount only from the back side—came to be called Monument Peak. Neither name was well known to valley farmers and townsfolk. When range surveyor Alfred Potter toured Utah in 1902, he reported that locals near the town of Pleasant Grove referred to the alpine ridge as Snow Mountain.[31]

The ridge was just as likely to have gone unnamed—even by land examiners from the Cadastral Survey of the General Land Office. This federal agency established township and range lines and recorded observations about each rectangular survey township on the U.S. checkerboard grid. Typically, examiners returned to the same coordinates in successive years to follow the progress of homesteaders. The survey that encompassed Timpanogos was performed first in 1871, then re-

peated in 1877, 1881, 1895, 1900, 1914, and beyond. The original
field notes excluded the mountain altogether because none of the land
was arable. In 1877 the surveyor described a "high mountain" composed of a "succession of perpendicular cliffs" that were "impossible
to measure up with a chain." His map was a nonstarter—entirely
blank except for a sawmill and a pine grove at the lower extremity of
the page (showing a short section of Provo Canyon). More thorough
surveying in 1900 still ignored the nonproductive slopes: "It is very
high, steep, rugged, and (considered as a whole) is a series of granite cliffs and ledges. It is impossible for cattle to get on to it, and is,
therefore, not even valuable for grazing purposes." The resulting map
showed the canyon and the foothills in sharp detail but again left the
alpine region—twelve whole sections—blank except for the words

Albert Tracy, *View from Upper Camp Floyd,* two-part pencil sketch, 31 July 1858. The page break cuts the Timpanogos massif in two. Lone Peak is located on the far left. (Albert Tracy Papers, Manuscripts and Archives Division, The New York Public Library, Astor, Lenox and Tilden Foundations)

"granite cliffs & ledges." Finally, fourteen years later, the same assayer, a local man, found a name for this worthless line of cliffs: "Mt. Timpanogos."[32]

Something important happened between 1900 and 1914: the people of Utah Valley began to visualize a mountain. This perceptual innovation had some topographic basis. As seen from its highest point, the massif does appear to be a land unit distinct from other sections of the Wasatch. As more and more local recreationists climbed the summit, this aerial visualization became normalized. From the perspective of the valley, too, the massif has certain distinguishing features.

Because of its castellated front, Timpanogos holds snow longer than other sections of the Wasatch Range visible from the valley. The Timpanogos massif is also distinctive in that it rests on a northwest-southeast axis, whereas the main stem of the range runs north-south. Because of its orientation, the mountain looks most impressive from easternmost Utah Valley, away from the lakeshore and the historic north-south thoroughfare. And it happens that the valley's most important city—the city that went on to sponsor annual community hikes on "Timp"—is located in that sector. Provo's view of the mountain has improved over time. Originally Provo (Fort Utah) was located beside the lake. A few years later, when it came time to build municipal buildings, the settlers chose higher and firmer ground a mile or so to the east. A town square—now called Pioneer Park—was established. By the last quarter of the nineteenth century, the city center had migrated once again; the former "Main Street" had become Fifth West. Today's main street—now called University Avenue—boasts a commanding view of Timpanogos due north. From this vantage, unlike from the shoreline, the high peaks of the Wasatch due east of Provo cannot be seen; the eastern foothills block the view. As seen from downtown, the Timpanogos massif stands without peer. The impressiveness of the mountain as seen from Provo is in part an optical illusion, again because of the peculiar axis of the massif. Although the ridge trends northwest-southeast, it *appears* that it trends east-west—perpendicular to the main stem of the mountains, and parallel to the baseline of the city. That dramatic illusion is made possible by an isolated northern foothill, Big Baldy (elevation 8,756 feet), which "balances" the visual composition—if Provo's view is imagined as a painting or a photograph.

First people must want to imagine. There has to be a cultural viewpoint to match the physical one. Downtown Provo existed for some fifty years before the city began to advertise itself in relation to the mountain. One of the first locally published references comes from 1910, when William Wilson released a new edition of his pictorial guide to Provo and its leading citizens. Opposite the page devoted to a

former mayor appeared a picture of "TIMPANOGUS [*sic*], THE MOUN-
TAIN OF PERPETUAL SNOW." A subsequent section on scenery and
recreation failed to mention the mountain, however. This was not an
especially grand beginning to a mountain love affair. However, within
twenty years "Timpanogus" would become "Timp" thanks to people
like Wilson, who wrote a revealing poem, "The Lay of the Provo
Booster":

> I am a jolly "Booster" from a hustling, bustling town
> That flies the flag of PROGRESS and will never pull it down.
> We are never quite contented 'lest we all get out and "root"
> For our water, land and climate, and some other things to
>   boot.[33]

In America, progress has always been measured by arithmetic. The
higher the number, the better. The possible categories are endless:
population size, assessed property valuation, sewer mileage, and so
on. Boosters in Provo eventually figured out that the snowy mountain
to the north—or, more precisely, the height of its summit—was measurably worth rooting for.

Paradoxically, the advancement of Mount Timpanogos resulted in
part from its earlier subordination to Mount Nebo. Nebo was first
surveyed scientifically by the Wheeler Survey, which published its
height as 11,992 feet in 1874. Two years later, in the atlas to the King
Survey, Timpanogos Pk. received its first published height: 11,957
feet. Members of the King Survey believed they had determined the
true high point of the Wasatch. They didn't bother resurveying Nebo,
because it fell below the 40th Parallel and outside their purview. In
fact both the Wheeler and the King surveys produced inflated elevations of the two mountains. A more accurate determination of Nebo's
height came in the summer of 1878, when the U.S. Coast and Geo-
detic Survey established a benchmark on the mountain. A C&GS
team made its way east along the 39th Parallel through the Great Basin, measuring mountains as it went. John Muir, the Apostle of the

Mountains, came along as a guest. It was Muir's second trip in two years to Utah; on both trips he seems to have climbed Mount Nebo. The survey team established a vertical angle benchmark on the southernmost of the mountain's three distinct summits. The C&GS calculated the south summit's height at 11,877 feet—a figure outstandingly close to today's computed height. It was important for the C&GS to establish an accurate benchmark on Nebo because the mountain had been chosen as one of the primary triangulation sites for Utah and Nevada; that is, its elevation would be used to determine other elevations. Timpanogos had no such importance to surveyors; it didn't receive a revised elevation (11,750 feet) until 1946. Thus its inflated height persisted on maps long after Nebo's had been corrected. Over time this miscalculation acquired folk legitimacy. In the early twentieth century local people forgot that Mount Nebo had been considered the highest mountain in the Wasatch, even the highest mountain in the state.[34]

All of this would have been academic if Americans didn't care about altitudes. But they did and they do. There is a long history of measuring a mountain's worth in feet.

::: In the early decades of the nineteenth century, New Hampshire had bragging rights to the highest peak in the United States. Although the premier summit of the so-called Presidential Range had been named after a Virginian—George Washington—southern partisans longed to have a higher point below the Mason-Dixon Line. In 1835 Professor Elisha Mitchell of the University of North Carolina tested these hopes in the Black Mountains, a spur of the Appalachians. He used the method of extrapolating elevations from differences in barometric pressure at different locations. His calculations were hardly definitive but exact enough for him to announce that North Carolina owned the prize. The supposed high point became known as Mount Mitchell. There the matter rested for two decades until one of Mitchell's former students, Thomas Clingman, took his own barometric readings in the Black Mountains and made it known that he had discovered the true high point, which he christened after himself. Professor Mitchell became defensive about his work and returned to the high country in 1857 to vindicate his name. Near a waterfall at dusk, the old man fell to his death. In truth, he had been wrong, yet the tragedy guaranteed him posthumous glory. People started calling Clingman's Peak "Mitchell's High Peak" to distinguish it from the existing Mount Mitchell.[35]

A similar story—minus the loss of life—played out in the American West after the Civil War. It centers upon Clarence King, the dashing geologist who may have been the first person to climb Timpanogos Peak, and whose survey established its inflated height. Earlier King had worked for the California Geological Survey, run by J. D. Whitney. In 1864 King helped to map the southern Sierra Nevada, the highest and roughest part of the range. King resolved to climb the apex. He and a companion made their way to what they thought might be the highest mountain (today's Mount Tyndall) only to spy a cluster of loftier peaks ahead. Against the explicit instructions of their modest chief, the survey crew named the tallest one—what was sure to be the tallest in the United States—Mount Whitney. Unfortunately, they ran out of time to climb it. Later that summer King got permission to return, but he failed to find a way to the summit. He returned to the lowland, where his career got the best of him. In 1867 he won control of his own western survey at the impossibly early age of twenty-five. Not until 1871 did he find time to make another attempt at Mount Whitney. The third time seemed charmed: he and a mountaineering friend conquered the summit of what they—and the people of Owens Valley below—believed to be Whitney. But King's own memory and sense of direction had tricked him. He had in fact climbed what he himself had earlier named Sheep Rock. As long as it lasted, King's ignorance was bliss. He wrote a thrilling chapter about his alpine exploit in an instant classic, *Mountaineering in the Sierra Nevada* (1872), a work that combined aesthetic, scientific, and recreational appreciations of mountains into a new "geological sublime."

He and his contemporary John Muir—another writer-scientist-hiker of the Sierras—defined the modern American way to see a mountain.[36]

Youthful and brash, King rubbed many people the wrong way. In August 1873, geologist W. A. Goodyear was delighted to present a paper—"On the Situation and Altitude of Mount Whitney"—that cut King down to size. Goodyear demonstrated that the peak so famously climbed by King was not in fact the peak King had named Mount Whitney. Chagrined, King rushed from Washington, D.C., to California. In just one month he managed to cross the breadth of the United States and to scale its brow. But the effort came too late. Three parties of locals—including some anglers, of all people—narrowly beat him to the prize. For some years residents of the Owens Valley worked to keep the name Mount Whitney attached to the false high point so that the apex could be called Fisherman's Peak. The proposal died. False Whitney/Sheep Rock eventually became Mount Langley, a peak that few climb today. Who among the hundreds of lottery-winning permit holders who go up neighboring Mount Whitney each summer can name the second or third highest points in the Sierra Nevada?

The allure of elevations is irrational but strong. It inspires mania and clubbishness. Easterners who climb the correct tally of peaks can join the Northeast 111 Club, the New England Four Thousand Footer Club, the Catskill 3500 Club, or the Adirondack Forty-sixers. The more exclusive Highpointers Club is reserved for those who have stood on the highest summits of all fifty states. On the Web and in guidebooks, one can find directions to the highest points of all 3,142 counties in the United States. In the twentieth century, Coloradans took "peak-bagging" to new heights. The Centennial State contains fifty-four peaks above 14,000 feet, more than the other high states (Alaska, California, Washington) combined. The Colorado Mountain Club created the geographic concept of the "Fourteener" in 1914; the term became colloquial in the 1970s. Hard-core peak-baggers work to climb all fifty-four Fourteeners in a lifetime—or in one continuous stretch. The record holders for the "Grand Slam" have done it in just over two weeks. Purists not only climb each peak but also force themselves to gain at least 3,000 feet in elevation from each starting point. The number of Fourteeners has fluctuated; controversy exists about the definition of a peak versus a subpeak. Bagging Colorado's Fourteeners has become so popular and banal that crowd-averse and thrill-seeking climbers have switched to the winter Grand Slam, or the Thirteeners, or the state's 100 highest. In order to collect more peak experiences, cultish hikers have created new lists based on the measure of "prominence," the height of a summit relative to its surrounding terrain. For example, Utah has over eighty peaks with a prominence of 2,000 feet or more.[37]

These imagined geographies can have real effects. A mountain of 14,005 feet will undergo a far greater ecological impact from human use than a mountain of 13,995 feet. Everything would be different on the metric system, of course. In North America, meters don't make good mountains. The 4,000-meter standard encompasses far too many peaks; 5,000 meters includes far too few. Besides, there is something appropriate about measuring ambulatory feats in feet. In England—the progenitor of this system of measurement—the threshold for greatness is a mere 1,000 feet. Across the Atlantic, in New England, the bar is raised to 4,000 feet. Farther west, in the Sierras and the Rockies, the magic number goes up to 14,000. In the Great Basin, dozens of ranges climax at 10,000 or 11,000 feet, but only a handful exceed 12,000.

It's a shame, really, that the eastern escarpment of the Basin, the Wasatch Range, lacks a 12,000-foot peak. No wonder Provo boosters in the 1910s rounded up the already erroneous elevation of Timpanogos from 11,957 to an even 12,000. By the 1920s that number inched up further, to 12,008. Apocryphally, the extra 8 feet came from the stone (later metal) monument on the summit of "Monument Peak." Didn't the "highest" peak of the Wasatch Range deserve to be as high as possible? Although the Wasatch is actually only the fifth highest range in Utah, it exceeds all others in symbolic importance. The overwhelming majority of the state's residents have and always will live in the shadow of the Wasatch. Thus the leading mountain of the Wasatch is automatically the leading mountain of Utah. The only peak that remotely challenges the current status of Timpanogos is the state's highest elevation—a 13,528-foot peak in the Uintas named after none other than Clarence King.

Mountains don't have feelings, but if they did, we might feel pity for Mount Nebo, the true high point of the Wasatch. Today it is familiar without being renowned, admired without being adulated. Call it chance or contingency: at the moment Utahns became interested in making a modern mountain, the obvious choice—the scientific choice—was Timpanogos Pk. Like a capable older son upstaged by his prodigious baby brother, Mount Nebo lost its footing.

5

Hiking into Modern Times

Soon after Mount Timpanogos received its identity as the highest mountain in the Wasatch, recreationists started coming. In the 1910s Eugene "Timpanogos" Roberts, athletics director at Brigham Young University, inaugurated a collegiate tradition of hiking to the summit. Roberts had partners in the promotion of alpine play. The federal government enhanced the mountain's recreational stature in 1922 by creating Timpanogos Cave National Monument. The (re)discovery of these caverns reinforced the new perceptual status of the mountain. Local communities seized on "Timp" for promotional use. They hoped to make themselves into something like Portland, Oregon, and their mountain into something like Portland's Mount Hood. In Utah Valley, civic boosterism transformed Roberts' collegiate hikes into the Annual Timpanogos Hike—a mass event the likes of which have never been seen in America before or since. Hikers by the thousands made a cumulative imprint. They solidified "Timp" as a major landmark. By the time the mountain's elevation was revised downward in the 1940s, altitude no longer mattered. The mountain had become known for being known, loved for being loved, hiked for being hiked.

*   *   *

⣿ Hiking grew out of pleasure walking, a cultural invention the English had perfected by 1800. The idea that walking up steep mountains could be pleasurable developed over the nineteenth century in tandem with industrialization. To be precise, two varieties of alpine recreation developed—hiking and mountaineering. The latter showed off the technical side of walking. Mountaineering demanded special equipment and training for negotiating extreme conditions of steepness, altitude, and ice. Most histories of the sport begin with the first ascent of Mont Blanc in 1786. The subsequent story is a breathless if tedious chronology of Firsts. The golden age of firsts was the 1860s, when British mountaineers invaded the Alps and conquered scores of "virgin peaks." England remained the hub for mountaineers through World War I. English alpinists belonged to clubs that lived up to the ideal of clubbishness. Status meant everything. All-male sportsmen-aristocrats from the Alpine Club of London took their exploits very seriously, as did their nation. English mountain climbing had nationalistic and (especially in India) colonial and racial overtones. Anglo-Saxon men were not the only ones drawn to the heights, however. Soon after Japan's imperial expansion in the 1890s, Japanese elites became interested in climbing and praising the rooftop of their nation. They redefined the discontinuous mountain peaks of central Honshu (site of the 1998 Winter Olympics) as a discrete region, the "Japanese Alps."[1]

Early American exploits in mountaineering also exhibited nationalism, even imperialism. The climbers were associated with the army. In 1806 Lieutenant Zebulon Pike tried (and failed) to climb the peak in New Spain that now bears his name. In 1820 a member of Major Stephen Long's expedition took the honor. Captain Benjamin Bonneville climbed a high peak in the Wind River Mountains in the 1830s only to be bested in the same range by Lieutenant John C. Frémont in the 1840s. Surprisingly, the top early example of an American conquest of an alpine mountain comes from Mexico. After the Mexican War ended, U.S. troops continued to occupy Mexico City until a treaty could be signed and ratified. In 1848, to counter the boredom of prolonged victory, some American soldiers decided to scale the two most symbolic mountains in Mexico—indeed, two of the most prominent mountains in North America—Popocatepetl (17,887 feet) and Citlaltepetl (18,701 feet). They planted the Stars and Stripes in the realm of Aztec gods.[2]

Back in the States, civilians came late to the tournament of mountaineering, and with limited glory. The cordilleras of the American West were generally too brown and bare for alpinists' tastes. Since glaciers defined "alpine" landscapes, only the Cascades held much allure. Fittingly, Americans made their strongest pretensions toward mountaineering in the Pacific Northwest. Seattle produced a group called The Mountaineers (1907), an offshoot of an earlier club, The Mazamas, based in Portland. The Mazamas (an arcane word for mountain goats) required its members to have scaled a mountain with a permanent ice shield over 7,000 feet. In 1894, preparatory to the first Mazamas convention—on top of 11,235-foot Mount Hood—founders issued "a cordial invitation" by way of newspapers to "all mountain-climbers and lovers of nature." One hundred ninety-three prospective members (155 men and 38 women) met for a "mountain banquet" on the summit.[3]

An open-invitation event for Oregon nature lovers? This was in fact a world away from European mountaineering. Despite its (modest) skill requirement, The Mazamas was more of a hiking club. The distinction turned on attitude as well as technique. Whereas mountaineering produced Famous Men who loved climbing, hiking produced co-ed groups who loved mountains. Whereas mountaineering brought out imperial and national feelings, hiking brought out regional and local feelings. Famous Men blazed routes—the ultimate being the north face of Everest. Hiking groups constructed trails—the ultimate being the Appalachian Trail. Whereas mountaineers wrote technical accounts of their manly conquests, hikers wrote comparatively effeminate nature poems and natural history essays. In the United States, scientist Clarence King, author of *Mountaineering in the Sierra Nevada,* and naturalist John Muir, author of *The Mountains of Califor-*

nia, embodied this division. Not coincidentally, Muir cofounded the Sierra Club. He and his friends liked to hike in groups; they didn't usually seek solitude. The Sierra Club staged annual summer High Trips for enormous parties. Likewise, The Mazamas sponsored mass hikes, often accompanied by singing, lecturing, and picnicking. Climbing a mountain could be an act of conviviality.[4]

In the United States, mountain pedestrianism began in New England. Starting in the 1820s, elite Bostonians began coming to the White Mountains. The high society of New York gravitated to resorts in the Catskills and eventually the Adirondacks. The vacation fad peaked in the 1850s, when railroads improved access. Railroad patrons imported a romantic view of mountains; most felt content to gaze upon the peaks. Those who actually climbed a summit—usually a landmark like Mount Washington—went for the view. The trip was about the visual experience on top, not the physical effort en route. Many opted to ride a horse and spend the night in a furnished summit house. Only after the hiatus of the Civil War did modern hiking emerge. When New England's mountain tourism reemerged in the 1870s, the elites shared their turf with a new breed of visitor, the middle-class camper. A postwar enthusiasm for urban pedestrianism spread to the mountains. About a dozen hiking clubs formed in New England in the two decades after the war. The most enduring, the Appalachian Mountain Club (AMC), dates to 1876. AMC hikers resembled weekend adventurers more than aesthetes. They preferred little-known peaks to Thoreau's Mount Washington or Emerson's Grand Monadnock.[5]

If European mountaineering had a golden age, so did American hiking. From roughly 1900 to World War II, scores of hiking groups followed the AMC's example. New York City alone contained about seventy-five clubs. In the West, the movement began in the coastal urban centers—Seattle, Portland, San Francisco, and Los Angeles. The Bay Area boasted the Sierra Club (1892), the Tamalpais Conservation Club (1912), the Tourist Club (1912), the California Alpine Club (1914), the Contra Costa Hills Club (1920), and the Berkeley Hiking

Club (1922). It's no accident that universities—notably Berkeley and Stanford—incubated hikers. In the United States, most hikers came from the ranks of the urban white-collar Progressive middle class. Unlike mountaineering, which was an end in itself, hiking often served as a vehicle for Progressive causes such as education and conservation.[6]

Hiking reached its zenith just as automobiles came of age. The introduction of cars led to a distinction between trails and roads. Before, hikers and ramblers used the same dirt paths as carriages. After, as automobiles claimed the main thoroughfares and turned them into modern roads, hikers moved to the mountains and forests. Motorists liked oiled surfaces; hikers preferred to move on earth. The threat of automobiles inspired the incipient wilderness movement, which led to the protection of many off-road areas suitable for hiking. Motoring and hiking were not fundamentally at odds, however. For recreationists, cars allowed unprecedented access to mountainous areas. Foresters responded by building new trails.[7]

More often than not, the interests of urban hikers and urban developers overlapped. In Denver, for example, members of the commercial elite launched an effort in 1910 to create a system of parks in the foothills of the Rockies. To great acclaim, Frederick Law Olmsted Jr. designed roads and trails for the Mountain Parks Committee. The ubiquitous Olmsted firm did similar work for Seattle. That city celebrated its coming of age with the Alaska-Yukon-Pacific Exposition in 1909; the main axis of the exposition campus—now the University of Washington—was aligned with Mount Rainier. Meanwhile, down the Pacific coast, Berkeley, Oakland, and Los Angeles established hillside parks in the early twentieth century. Los Angeles' 3,000-acre Griffith Park is perhaps best known today as the home of the "HOLLYWOOD" sign, which, when erected in 1923, said "HOLLYWOODLAND"—an advertisement for a real estate development. The sign conveys a far-reaching point: in the American West, mountains and cities have often been defined together.

Consider the story of William Gladstone Steel (1854–1934), the "Father of Crater Lake" and the founder of The Mazamas. Steel linked the industrial promise of Portland and the primitive promise of the Cascades. Working against agricultural interests, Steel lobbied in Washington for the creation of the Cascade Forest Reserve (1893) and its eventual enlargement (1907). Steel's interest in federal conservation complemented his interest in urban boosterism. An active real estate developer, Steel and some partners homesteaded at the base of Mount Hood with the intention of building a resort connected to Portland via a railroad. The Mount Hood Improvement Company ended in failure, but in other ways Steel helped to cement the connection between Portland and Mount Hood that lasts to this day. He and others went to elaborate efforts to illuminate the snow-covered volcano on Fourth of July eves with incendiary explosions. After repeated misfires, a team led by Steel lit up the mountain in 1887 with 100 pounds of "red fire" aligned toward the city. (This holiday practice continued intermittently through the 1970s.) Steel and The Mazamas worked for better city access to the mountain, constructed trails around it, and guided summertime hikes to its summit. The modern meaning of Mount Hood—a scientifically interesting, federally managed marvel of nature preserved for urban recreationists—did not exist before Steel. As one of his contemporaries said, Steel "knows all about the mountains, he all but made 'em."[8]

Steel had a counterpart in Utah. Eugene Roberts, athletics director at Brigham Young University, all but made Mount Timpanogos. More precisely, he remade the mountain into "Timp" by means of an annual mass hike. But whereas Steel promoted Mount Hood from a commercial pulpit, Roberts promoted "Timp" from an educational one. Roberts drew inspiration from the Mountaineer and the Hiker, as well as two other figures: the Athlete and the Pilgrim.

::: Roberts was born in 1880. His hometown, Provo, contained only about 5,000 inhabitants, but it functioned as the political and commercial heart of Utah's leading agricultural county. The "Garden City of Utah" had also just emerged as an educational center. A branch of the territorial University of Deseret opened here in 1870. Five years later, Brigham Young bought out the branch to establish a denominational academy. "Previously society in Provo had been very rough," wrote a local historian in 1885. "The popular saying of the early times, 'Provo or hell!' well illustrated the condition of society in the city, which is now specially known as the University city of Utah." The completion of the Utah Southern Railroad in the 1870s and the Denver & Rio Grande in the 1880s vastly improved access to Provo, which became the gateway to the newly developed Tintic Mining District (in adjacent Juab County); these things gave Provo a cosmopolitan patina. Young Eugene appreciated this more than most children his age. Since his father ran the leading hotel in town, Roberts encountered outsiders on a frequent basis. Federal marshals on the hunt for polygamists stayed at the Hotel Roberts, as did minstrel performers and rough elements. In his reminiscence, Eugene claimed he saw three or four suicide victims while working in the hotel.[9]

Violence of a different sort pervaded his childhood. Roberts became enamored with the "manly art of self-defense" and participated in local prize bouts as well as pickup fights in vacant lots. His early hero was Willard Bean, the "Mormon Cyclone," one of the best amateur boxers in Utah, who operated a sports training center out of a church gym in Provo. Boxing wasn't the half of it: Roberts lived to be physical. As a youth he became proficient in baton twirling and tightrope walking; he even considered becoming a circus performer. Instead he became a coach. Looking back, Roberts attributed a life-changing influence to his seventh- and eighth-grade teacher, Joseph B. Walton, who happened to be one of Utah's first specialists in physical education.

In 1900 PE had a much broader mandate than today. To its exponents, PE was not a school course but a course of life. Walton ran his class according to a ten-part "Day's Order": memorization exercises interspersed by calisthenics, gymnastics, and marching. He was part of an athletics craze in late nineteenth-century America. Health reformism went back to the Jacksonian period, but diet and sexual behavior initially overshadowed exercise. Later, middle-class Protestant reformers turned to "physical culture." Its main philosophy—muscular Christianity—came from Britain; its main activity—gymnastics—came from Germany. The most famous by-product, the Young Men's Christian Association, appeared in England in 1844 and in America in 1851. As the century wore on, physicians added science to the movement. Out of "physical culture" came "physical education." Whereas muscular Christianity presumed a relationship between health and character, PE tried to prove it physiologically. Physical educators raised concerns about urbanism's degenerative effects (physical and moral) on the "white race." PE promised to turn this process around. "We are soldiers of Christ," a spokesperson for the movement wrote in 1902. "We would bring in a higher kingdom of man, regenerate in body; make it more stalwart, persistent, enduring, taller, with better hearts, stomachs, nerves, and more resistful to man's great enemy—disease."[10]

This was the kind of education Eugene Roberts craved. When he entered Brigham Young Academy in 1898, he immediately organized a petition to build a gymnasium. It took four years, but Roberts' campaign yielded results. Over the same four years, Roberts failed to get his two-year degree. He may not have been an academician, but he excelled at college life. He served as president of his class, president of the athletics association, lead editor and cartoonist for the newspaper, and quarterback of the intramural team.

With energy and enthusiasm that set him apart from other students, Roberts was a natural recruit for Brigham Young Academy's South American Expedition. The quixotic dream of academy president Benjamin Cluff, the expedition intended to go to Colombia to uncover the remains of the ancient city Zarahemla, described in the Book of Mormon. Fifteen young men participated. In 1900, after a triumphal tour through Utah, Cluff's caravan rolled into Arizona, where everything fell apart. Cluff went ahead to Nogales to clear passage with Mexican officials, but he actually spent more time at the polygamist Colonia Juárez, Chihuahua. There he took the opportunity to marry a third wife (believing that the 1890 edict against polygamy applied only to Mormons within the United States). Meanwhile the rest of the party languished for a month on the other side of the border. Cluff had instructed the boys to go out and proselytize, but they wound up dating local girls. After an investigation, the LDS Church withdrew its support of the expedition and ordered the students to go home. Cluff soldiered on. When he finally returned—without any Book of Mormon relics—the Church essentially fired him from the academy. He ended up moving to Colonia Juárez.[11]

In his autobiographical material, Roberts says little about his involvement in this fiasco except that he managed to pick a fight with a "half-breed" in Nogales. As a Mormon, he must have found the expedition demoralizing. As an athlete, however, Roberts considered it (in retrospect) a valuable experience. The outdoor skills he learned on the way to the border allowed him to make a second, more successful expedition. This time he didn't go with local Church members but with associates of Harvard University. In 1902 Professor William Morris Davis, America's premier geographer, stopped in Provo on his way to the Grand Canyon for a seven-week gentlemen's vacation. While in Provo he gave a series of lectures at Brigham Young Academy and lodged at Hotel Roberts, where he met Eugene. Impressed with the boy, Davis extended him an invitation. The next two months brought sheer delight to Roberts as he explored the North Rim in the company of elite eastern intellectuals.

After his twin adventures Roberts reentered school. Before he could finish, however, he ran out of money. In 1903, for want of better opportunities, he began a three-year stint as an elementary-school teacher in Provo. Each summer, to recuperate, he went to an environment more to his liking. He pitched a tipi in Provo Canyon, which was then developing into a getaway for Wasatch Front professionals. In 1905 a girls' group camped next to Roberts, and he wound up guiding them up the North Fork of Provo Canyon to a waterfall below Timpanogos Pk. Delighted by the experience, he looked for other groups to lead; some he guided to the top of the mountain. Roberts had made his first ascent the year before in the company of John C. Swensen, an instructor at Brigham Young Academy, and one of the first people to climb the mountain for fun.

Roberts' life soon took an important detour: in 1906 he was "called on a mission" (to use the Mormon phrase). In today's missionary program, nineteen-year-old boys submit applications before receiving their call. In Roberts' day, calls could come unsolicited, even to older men with families. Roberts was not yet married, but he did have a fiancée. After some negotiation, Church authorities allowed him to get married and take his wife on the outbound voyage as a honeymoon, with the understanding that she would return before the mission proper began. Roberts never intended to keep this bargain. He traveled to Niagara Falls and then Manhattan, where he and his wife boarded an ocean liner for England, his assigned destination. There, at an organizational meeting, he heard the director of the German-Swiss mission district asking for volunteers to go to Germany, where Mormon proselytizing was then illegal. The newlyweds jumped at the chance. Their illicit adventure was cut short, however, when Sytha Roberts became pregnant. In 1907 the couple moved to a safer country, Switzerland, where their baby was born. Not long afterward Mrs. Roberts returned to America with the child. Eugene remained behind.

True to form, he combatted loneliness with activity. Not content with an ascetic mission life, he took every opportunity to attend concerts, lectures, and tours. As a regional supervisor in the Swiss Mission, he gave himself the freedom to travel without a missionary companion. Elder Roberts was by today's standards a deviant Mormon: an individualist and (at the beginning) an agnostic. He lived through Mormonism's transformation when zealotry gave way to pragmatism. In May 1908, at a conference for missionaries, he dropped a "bomb-shell" during a lecture on "New Methods of Presenting the Gospel to the Public." Roberts called for leaflets and lessons dealing with "LIVE ISSUES." "While Switzerland is waging a battle against ALCOHOL and Drugs," he remembered saying, "we missionaries are delivering from door to door tracts on Baptism for the Dead. We should work shoulder-to-shoulder with the good people in other churches for the genuine WELFARE of the PEOPLE." He wanted the missionaries to keep quiet about Mormon temple rites and to speak up about the Word of Wisdom (the LDS food and drink code)—a more salable, mainstream topic in an era of transatlantic prohibition. After some heated discussion, his motion passed. Roberts himself composed the new tract, "Alcohol and the Human Life," which told the story of Mormonism in an "indirect" way.[12]

Roberts stayed physically active, too. He fought a boxing match with another missionary—"the melee of the ministers"—using mission headquarters as the venue. And he climbed mountains. Being in the heart of the Alps, he encountered a "continual parade of tourists from America." The ones from Utah sought out missionaries to be their guides. In this way Roberts was able to continue his avocation. He even got the chance to show the Alps to Utah senator Reed Smoot. Climbing mountains with Utahns naturally reminded him of home. Reminiscing later, Roberts said, "Every time I ascended a Swiss mountain I could not help contrasting it with our own TIMPANO-GOS."[13] The Wasatch massif was equally scenic and much more accessible and climbable. The well-developed Swiss tourism industry gave him ideas—as did the pilgrimage to Einsiedeln, the holiest Catholic site in central Europe. What impressed him most was the nighttime procession by candlelight to a nearby hill (probably a Station of the Cross). Combining various Swiss and Utahn influences, Roberts developed the idea of a quasi-pilgrimage for hikers to the highest point of the Wasatch.

Upon his return in December 1908, Roberts was in no position to realize this idea. Out of financial need, he returned to teaching. After a tough year with fourth-grade "rough-necks," he resigned. Luckily, he soon got an offer to teach high school PE, German, and English. To "bone up" on English he signed up for some summer courses at the University of Utah, and there his life course changed. By chance he met William Gilbert Anderson, a visiting faculty member from Yale and a towering figure in the physical education movement. Sensing Roberts' potential, Anderson invited him to New Haven to be an assistant in the Yale Gymnasium. After a year's training at what was then America's premier athletics school, Roberts finally had the qualifications for the job he'd always wanted: recreational leader. Several offers came his way, but out of loyalty he returned to Brigham Young, which had recently been upgraded to a university. BYU hired Roberts to build its athletics program.

Today it's common to think of athletic directors as fundraisers whose job it is to produce winning teams to please alumni donors. Roberts was not that kind. As he recalled, his goals for the job were "HEALTH, PHYSICAL WELFARE, SOCIAL EFFICIENCY, AND RECREATION."[14] Although Roberts happily coached new team sports like football and basketball, he felt more enthusiasm for classical individual sports like track and field. He idealized athletic competitions as mini-Olympiads, "pageants of sportsmanship." One of his proudest accomplishments at BYU was the Invitational Meet and Relay Carnival. Started in 1911, this annual event drew from high schools and colleges throughout Utah and adjoining states. The most unusual aspect of the "carnival" was also the most reflective of Roberts' pedagogy. The Posture Parade featured groups of thirty-two girls walking in formations while maintaining perfect posture.

Roberts' recreational philosophy combined Christian utopianism, secular antimodernism, and Progressive scientism. "Civilization has of late progressed all too rapidly," he wrote in a 1911 piece. He decried the artificial softness of modern urban life and recommended scouting as a countermeasure. Two decades later Roberts again bemoaned the enervating effects of "Modernism" and even raised the specter of "race deterioration." (White) people were losing touch with the "original man" inside them, he warned. Fortunately, people could reconnect with their inner nature through "primitive recreative activities." But there was a catch: not all of these "original tendencies" were wholesome; some led to debauchery. Increased leisure could be both a blessing and a curse, bringing "weakness and strength, peace and despair, heaven and hell. What a responsibility." The measure of civilization was its ability to harness the primitive impulse without destroying it. This was the "problem of recreation" as Roberts saw it. It would become the paramount social issue in the day "bye and bye" when machines rendered most human labor obsolete and every day would be like Sunday. The outcome would be "chaos or the millennium." Unless civic leaders could build a "new social order" to match the advancements of the engineers, nothing would keep Americans "from dying of monotony or from destroying ourselves and our civilization through soft and senseless living." The answer, said Coach Roberts, was a "new leisure"—wholesome play that inculcated principles of good character. People could not be expected to do this by themselves, though. They needed "teachers of leisure"—people like Roberts trained in "scientific coaching."[15]

Where would such leaders come from? They, too, needed instruction. For this purpose, Roberts developed "scout leadership" and "recreational leadership" courses at BYU, where students learned to devise and direct group activities, home entertainments, and community dances. In 1920 Roberts convinced the administration to allow such courses to fulfill the university's theology requirement. The president's (apocryphal) first response was "What? You want the fox-trot to replace the Book of Mormon?" In fact Roberts had precedent on his side: since 1914 BYU had allowed theology students to visit the gymnasium once a week during class hours for "Physical Theology." Physical education was a new priority of the LDS Church. In 1907, having finally emerged from debt (a consequence of the polygamy fiasco), the Church decided to spend much of its capital on recreational infrastructure. It added "recreation halls" to all its new congregational buildings and constructed a state-of-the-art gymnasium—a "Temple of Health"—on the block adjacent to Temple Square in Salt Lake City. In 1910 the Deseret Gymnasium opened to great enthusiasm. The Church's de facto theologian, B. H. Roberts (no immediate relation), asserted from the pulpit of the Mormon Tabernacle that exclusive of the spired temples "there is no holier building erected by our hands than this other temple within shouting distance of us, which is devoted to the physical training and development of our youth."[16]

Coach Roberts transplanted this enthusiasm for recreation to the temple of the outdoors. His singular contribution was to fuse the widespread religious fad for physical education with the widespread secular fad for hiking. Everything came together in the form of a mass college ascent: a well-led group of morally and physically sound student athletes moving methodically with high purpose toward an elevated destination. Soon after landing his job at BYU, Roberts tested his idea; he led students on sunrise, sunset, and moonlight hikes to foothills in the Wasatch. Eventually, in 1912, he was ready to tackle the big one—Timpanogos.

Today it is hard for Provo residents to appreciate the novelty of this activity. As one native recalled (with only slight exaggeration),

> Utah had no tradition of mountain climbing . . . Provo citizens couldn't imagine climbing a mountain for *fun*. In the fall, yes, you went deer hunting. In December you hiked up Rock canyon for a Christmas tree. On Y Day students toted lime and water up the Y Mountain to whitewash the rocks forming the school letter. You might prospect for minerals, go fishing in the canyons, search for a lost cow—but, climbing for fun? What could you do once you got to the top? Come down. Big deal.[17]

In 1912 just getting to the Timpanogos trailhead involved a trek. The south and west faces of the massif—the sides that face Utah Valley—are far too steep for most people. Then as now, hobby hikers go to the back side (the north and east faces). Roberts' early mass hikes began with a journey by train or carriage up Provo Canyon to the small resort called Wildwood. From there people walked or rode horses up the North Fork of the canyon to Stewart Ranch, a homesteaded property on a flank of the mountain (now the location of Robert Redford's Sundance Resort). That stage might take all day

Friday. It took the entire following day to get up and down a sheep trail to the top, and one more (Sunday, without church) to return home. Total elevation gain from the valley floor exceeded 7,000 feet.

At the end of the 1912 summer school session, Roberts recruited a co-ed group of 30 or 40 students for a hike up Timpanogos. Hearing about this projected outing, university president George Brimhall called Coach Roberts into his office. The president was worried about safety, liability, and the potentially alarming matter of boys' and girls' spending two nights together. Roberts calmed Brimhall's fears, but objections from parents reduced the number of student participants. Of the 22 hikers who ultimately made the trip, at least half were instructors. They reported back positively to Brimhall, who approved the same summer hike the next year (with about 60 hikers) and the year after that (with about 200).

"With deliberate effort to build tradition," Roberts embellished the event a little more each year with bonfire programs, wake-up music, trail songs, and secret signs for hikers. By the time the coach moved to the University of Southern California in 1928, his hike had taken on a life of its own. In a subsequent how-to article for recreation professionals, Roberts identified the key elements of any successful mass hike: "first, a certain homogeneity and natural neighborliness of the people; second, inviting scenic features not too far distant from the central community; and third, a wise and enthusiastic organizing leadership."[18] Roberts had boundless energy, but he could not create "Timp" by himself. The leader needed followers. Likewise, he needed institutional support. BYU supplied a large part of that, and municipal and federal institutions made up the difference.

⁝⁝⁝ BYU's affiliation with Timpanogos was part of its larger affiliation with the high country. "We have majestic mountains back of us that can be seen to the very base by every passer-by," noted the student newspaper in 1906. "Why not fall in line and place a Y on the mountain side that will signify to citizen and tourist that, nes-

Eugene and Sytha Roberts on Mount Timpanogos, 1920. (L. Tom Perry Special Collections, Harold B. Lee Library, Brigham Young University, Provo, Utah)

tled 'neath the snowy peaks is an institution of which we are justly proud." With the help of an engineering professor, the student body did just that. After climbing the mountain front to about 6,000 feet, students used lime to burn out the shrub in the shape of a "Y." Ornamental blocks were added in 1910, when BYU acquired the land from the state. Hiking and whitewashing the "Y" quickly became a school tradition. The largest block letter in the world at the time of its construction, the "Y" stands almost 400 feet high and can be seen throughout the valley. Nationwide, only two letters preceded "Y Mountain." In 1905 students at the University of California in Berkeley and the University of Utah in Salt Lake City had constructed a "C" and a "U," respectively. Over the next ten years many more schools, including state universities in Montana, Oregon, Nevada, Wyoming, and Arizona, duplicated the deed. High school and town letters soon outnumbered the collegiate ones. The phenomenon of hillside monograms is unique to the American West, and its origin in the early twentieth century was part of a larger redefinition of western mountains. (People from Pleasant Grove eventually branded a foothill of the Timpanogos massif with a "G.")[19]

BYU also elevated itself literally. In 1911 a gift from Provo's Jesse Knight—one of a new breed, the Mormon mining magnate—allowed the main campus to move from downtown to a bench overlooking the city. Here was room to grow. People called the site Temple Hill; according to legend, Brigham Young had prophesied that a temple would be built here. To BYU boosters, the prophecy had been fulfilled. "It may not be the kind of temple that was in the minds or the dreams of the youth of that former day," said the student newspaper, but a "temple of learning" was still a temple.[20]

Provo's university also took teaching to the heights: it developed one of the first collegiate outdoor education programs, the Alpine Summer School. In 1921 the Stewart family of Stewart Ranch donated ten acres to the university (and later gave more). BYU leased some additional land from the U.S. Forest Service. The whole area was named Aspen Grove. Initially students lived in tents beneath the quaking aspens. The curriculum at the summer school included English and drama but focused on geology and botany, using Mount Timpanogos as an outdoor laboratory. Two students working for a master's in science degree completed ecology theses about the area in 1926. A leading American ecologist, Henry C. Cowles of the University of Chicago, visited the mountain with his students on at least two occasions in the 1920s. Cowles called Timpanogos "the most wonderful mountain I have ever seen, both from a geological and a botanical standpoint." He hoped the mountain could be "conserved in all its virgin loveliness as one of the nation's greatest citadels of research and learning." Summer sessions continued until 1942, interrupted by World War II. (After sitting dormant for years, Aspen Grove was revived as an alumni retreat in 1956.)[21]

The BYU faculty who helped with the Alpine Summer School overlapped with those who worked with Eugene Roberts. In the first few years the group hikes were basically field trips. Partway through the ascent, participants would stop at a limestone shelf called the Lecture Ledge to hear a geology talk. Farther up the trail, a different professor would cover ornithology. Student hikers took notes while chaperons watched. Once the group reached the alpine meadow beneath the summit, it was time for botanizing. People hiked together, rested together, learned together. One of the most enthusiastic participants was geology professor Fred Buss, who in 1916 raved about the "highest and most prominent peak of the Wasatch." Borrowing from Humboldtian science, Buss lectured that altitude equals latitude, and that "the climb to the top of Timpanogos was equivalent to a trip from their homes to Arctic Alpine regions," passing through all the intermediate vegetative zones. On Timpanogos he found ancient lake terraces, fault blocks, moraines, and a "miniature glacier (the only living glacier in the state of Utah, I believe)."[22]

Here Professor Buss let his enthusiasm get the best of him. Although the "Timpanogos Glacier" does in fact occupy a cirque beneath the summit, it is nothing more than a small semipermanent snowfield. In a 1909 report the U.S. Geological Survey lumped it with other "extinct glaciers" of the Wasatch. The distinction was lost on Buss and other "Timp" boosters, who were thrilled to discover that the mountain had a glacial history. In the nineteenth century, thanks to Louis Agassiz, glaciology had become essential to geology. The study of glaciers also satisfied the artistic eye. The European mountain aesthetic demanded ice along with crags. Glaciers were the mark of "true" alpine mountains. Taking advantage of a good thing, Eugene Roberts devised a hiking route that went up the steep "glacier." A 1915 magazine piece about Roberts' annual hike carried the title "Scaling Utah's Glacier." Sliding back down the 1,500-foot-long slope was part of the tradition—a thrilling way to end a day of learning.[23]

This opportunity for educational adventure was not restricted to students and faculty. Thanks to Roberts, the hike quickly became a Provo event. The coach reached out to the civic community in 1913 by forming a hiking group, the Timpanogos Nature Club, to assist him with the organization of the annual hike. An articulation of the club's guiding spirit comes from a 1917 information sheet featuring Roberts's distinctive use of caps:

> PURPOSE. The purpose of the big community hike is to climb Timpanogos under wholesome conditions, social and physical.
>
> ORGANIZATION. The company is divided into groups to facilitate equipping and camping. Each group selects a name, organizes its camping, etc., and develops enough group spirit to promote general fun. The ONE PREVAILING IDEA HOWEVER, SHOULD BE UNITY IN THE BIG COMPANY . . .
>
> SPIRIT. The spirit of the Timpanogos Hike has already become proverbial. Everything clean, wholesome, PROPER, and yet full of fun and genuine pleasure.[24]

As Roberts and his hiking corps claimed the mountain, they undercut the claim of the former dominant user group—ranchers. Before 1907, mountainside grazing went completely unregulated. Tens of thousands of sheep and smaller numbers of cattle grazed the mountain's flanks to the ground each summer. The town of American Fork (northwest of Provo) was the ranching center of Utah Valley. Each spring witnessed a race for the commons in the American Fork River basin, including Mount Timpanogos. Sheepherders from Utah Valley vied for "control areas," access points to canyons and ridges. Once secured, a control area would be continuously occupied—and denuded—through the season. Competition prodded ranchers to push their animals onto the mountain prematurely, when the soil was still wet and the forage still small. This abuse had direct consequences: gully erosion and floods. From the 1890s to the 1960s the American Fork River regularly overflowed with debris. All across Utah, overgrazing and deforestation contributed to catastrophic flooding in the first decades of the twentieth century.[25]

Utah recognized its problem quite late. George Perkins Marsh had drawn attention to the relationship between montane range cover and municipal water supply in his pioneering book, *Man and Nature* (1864). The Adirondack Forest Preserve (1885) originated with New York City's desire to control the upstate source of its drinking water. The national forest system—begun in 1891 and greatly enlarged by Theodore Roosevelt—likewise aimed at protecting the headwaters of the nation. Protection took the form of removing the land from potential sale and controlling its use by locals. In 1902 the chief grazing officer of the Interior Department, Albert Potter, made a 145-day tour of Utah's high country. In one particularly denuded portion of the central Wasatch, Potter quipped that the sheep looked so thin they "seemed to be living on fresh air and mountain scenery." Potter's subsequent report and recommendations led to the establishment of several new national forests in the state, including the Wasatch Forest Reserve, covering the American Fork drainage. Management of the land—including Mount Timpanogos—went to the newly created U.S. Forest Service (1905).[26]

Starting in 1907, local forest supervisors began the slow, contested process of stock reduction. Here, as throughout the West, local users influenced the early Forest Service more than the agency controlled them. Ranchers came together in 1908 to form the American Fork Grazing Association, which resisted drastic change. On the other side the Timpanogos Nature Club enlisted the help of Senator Reed Smoot—a noted conservationist as well as a Mormon apostle—to declare the central part (the hiking part) of the mountain a range-free zone in 1915. Smoot was the most visible of many Mormon urbanites who championed land conservation and city beautification in the Progressive Era. Yet Timpanogos continued to suffer. In 1923 a BYU science professor complained to the forest supervisor about "the lower cirque and the cirque near the mountain top where the grazing has been so heavy that the ground was left nearly bare of all vegetation and consequently has been gullied and washed by flood waters." He laid the blame on sheep, whose grazing "had destroyed practically every plant except weeds."[27]

This complaint spoke to the future. Use of the mountain was shifting from production to consumption, from work to play. Before the late nineteenth century, hardly any Utah residents climbed peaks above timberline. Few went to the high country at all. When they did, they worked, picking berries, felling trees, herding stock, or taking measurements. In America, camping and hiking became popular only after industrialization, urbanization, and consumerism began to remove people from a working relationship with the land. Scenery seekers created their own beautiful illusion of unworked nature. Even though Timpanogos hikers in the 1910s and 1920s began their trip next to the working Stewart Ranch, walked up a converted sheep trail, and shared the overgrazed massif with bleating flocks, they fixated on the mountain*top*—a landscape of talus and ice inhabited primarily by lichens. This sublime locale was very nearly the acme of nonproduction. The acme itself was not far way, but paradoxically deep underground—where sheep never trod—in Timpanogos Cave.

Three separate but proximate caverns (Hansen, Timpanogos, Middle) exist within the massif now known as Mount Timpanogos. In 1887 Martin Hansen discovered his namesake cave while cutting timber on the high slopes of American Fork Canyon. Soon he charged fees for tours. Hansen was another transitional figure in the mountain's history, a man who made money first from raw material and later from scenery. This transition didn't occur all at once, however. Other people began to mine Hansen Cave for onyx. Looters came, too, and the place was stripped. Even in its despoiled state, it remained a destination for locals. In 1914 some teenage boys came across a second cave entrance nearby. After exploring inside, they concealed the opening. The father of one of the boys entered a mining claim, but nothing resulted except rumors. In 1921, inevitably, the second cave was (re)discovered. Soon thereafter a Forest Service supervisor followed the clues (parked cars, fresh tracks) to the place. This forester moved to designate the cave a "public service site." Concerned that the spectacular limestone formations would be destroyed by mining or removed outright, the Forest Service moved to "protect" the cave by developing it for tourists. This idea found support among many local groups, including the Wasatch Mountain Club of Salt Lake City (1920) and the Alpine Club of Payson (1921).

It was, however, the Commercial Club of American Fork that took the most active role. American Fork (population 3,290) needed a new bragging right. The livestock center of Utah Valley was hardly prosperous. Town boosters initially referred to "their" new attraction as the "Wonder Cave." Like Hansen Cave, it was not at first associated with Mount Timpanogos; the town newspaper identified the location as "high on the spine of the Wasatch mountains near the head of American Fork canyon." The forest supervisor solicited name ideas— "Fairy Cave" and "Cave of Elves" had supporters—before deciding on Timpanogos Cave in late 1921. The name was chosen "for the reason that the cave is on the American Fork route to Mt. Timpanogos, and that by having the same name, they will advertise each other to visiting tourists." In a demonstration of the malleability of metageography, locals reimagined the south wall of American Fork Canyon (including the entrances to the caverns) as a part of "Timp." The discovery of the new cave confirmed the discovery of the mountain as an attraction.[28]

The year 1922 was a big one for Timpanogos Cave. Formal tours— complete with electric lights—began after the Forest Service opened a new access trail that rose 1,200 feet over about a mile of switchbacks. Most importantly, the place became a national monument. To end the mining threat once and for all, the Forest Service asked the executive branch to reserve the land, which President Harding did in October. However, the Park Service did not initially manage the monument, and neither did the Forest Service except in principle. The Forest Service had no money or personnel to spare, so it issued a special use permit to American Fork's Timpanogos Cave Committee to make improvements, collect fees, and conduct tours. All proceeds went toward enhancing American Fork Canyon as a tourist site. The early signs were encouraging. In 1923, the monument's first full year of operation, some 16,000 people hiked to the cave entrance, then shuffled through the damp, dark wonderland.[29]

At almost exactly the same time, American Fork Canyon gained yet another recreational facility—a church one. The confederated Mormon congregations of northwest Utah Valley—a diocese known as the Alpine Stake—decided that their young men and women needed more camp experience. The problem was assigned to the Mutual Improvement Association, the church auxiliary in charge of the youth. Once the local board of the MIA decided to build a summer camp, it secured a lease from the Forest Service for Bear Flat in the upper canyon and began construction in 1920. The site became known as Mutual Dell. For the next fifty-odd years, local MIA teenagers and their chaperons enjoyed weeklong outings that usually included a climb to the summit of Mount Timpanogos.[30]

::: This history of place-making—the fashioning of the Timpanogos massif into the landmark "Timp"—fits into several narratives: the golden age of hiking; the enthusiasm for physical education in the early twentieth century; the long-term shift from production to consumption, from outdoor work to outdoor play; and the rise of federal management of the western high country. These were national (if not international) trends, but by themselves they don't explain the rise of the "Wonder Mountain." Local contingencies must be counted. One was the supposed altitudinal superiority of the summit; another was the presence of a semipermanent snowfield that could be alleged to be a glacier. In addition, the high glacial mountain could be linked spatially to a "Wonder Cave" that became a national monument. Add to this list the proximity of a university town populated by a cohesive, homogeneous group of well-organized Mormons. Without any two of these contingencies, it's hard to imagine the mountain's becoming the landmark that it did. Of course, those contingencies did exist, and boosters took advantage of them. The pugnacious Eugene Roberts opened the way, but his hometown eventually took the lead. Whereas American Fork claimed the mountain through the cave (accessed via American Fork Canyon), Provo claimed the mountain through the hike (accessed via Provo Canyon). Some competition and resentment existed between the two towns, but in general they worked for a common cause. In turn, Salt Lake City supported its Utah Valley neighbors in the name of state tourism.

Over the first half of the twentieth century, the nature and geography of Utah tourism shifted. At the beginning the leading attractions were social landscapes: the Mormon holy city, especially Temple Square, and the resorts at the Great Salt Lake. Tourists still arrived by railroad. Gradually, however, the focus of tourism moved to the unsettled landscapes of southern Utah, especially its remarkable sandstone canyons. By 1950 most tourists came by automobile. Significantly, most of the sites for which Utah is now world-famous—Zion, Bryce, Arches—were "discovered" by promoters early in the automobile age. Mount Timpanogos was a transitional attraction: an undeveloped landform with intrinsic beauty, but a landform most noteworthy for a yearly social event. In the candid words of a 1922 brochure, "the old mountain is not much different from many other mountains of Utah . . . The hike is the feature that makes Timpanogos different."[31]

It takes more than a little chutzpah to market some "old mountain" as the Wonder Mountain. But the American West has never lacked geographic entrepreneurialism. For example, in the early twentieth century Spokane promoted itself as the hub of the "Inland Empire" even as Salt Lake City promoted itself as hub of the "Intermountain West." In 1906 Salt Lake hosted the inaugural convention of the See America First League. The league was envisioned as a sectional group of business leaders who would beckon the tourists of the East to the scenic West. For one year (1909) the Salt Lake magazine, *Western Monthly,* became the official organ of the league. A sample of article titles suggests its mission:

"American Scenery Is an Asset"
"See Europe If You Will, But See America First"
"See America, But See Utah First"
"The West Has Cities Older than the Pyramids"
"What Are You Doing to Make the West Attractive?"
"Another Pittsburgh in Utah—Why Not?"
"The Smelting Industry of Utah"
"The Bingham Mining District, Utah's Great Copper Camp"[32]

Scenery, like copper, was an extractive resource. Like smelting, tourism could help make Utah the true "Crossroads of the West" (or, as license plates would later say, the "Center of Scenic America"). The Salt Lake Commercial Club—a group tied closely to See America First—sent "expeditions" to publicize two of Utah's first three national monuments: Natural Bridges (1908) and Mukuntuweap (1909). Mukuntuweap became Zion National Park in 1919. The same year, the state legislature sent a memorial to Congress asking it to preserve (and thereby publicize) the colorful formations at Bryce Canyon. The area had been used for decades as summer cattle range, but not until 1916 did people "see" the place as summer tourist range, at which point Ebenezer Bryce—who had declared it to be "a hell of a place to lose a cow"—instantly became an antiquarian figure. The Wonder Mountain had a similar origin story: "Timpanogos served as a sheep and cattle pasture for many years before any one discovered in it any unusual charms. It was looked upon as a big, fine mountain—nothing more, until a youth [Eugene Roberts] happened by one day with a seeing eye and a responsive heart and a quickened imagination. He saw; he told others what he saw."[33]

For those with seeing eyes, the goal was clear. They wanted a mountain on par with Rainier, Hood, and Pikes Peak. The Kiwanis Club, the Rotary Club, and the Provo Commercial Club all contributed to this project. The Hotel Roberts hosted many of their meetings. At a 1921 Kiwanis luncheon, the speaker declared that with "an improved road and good advertising" Mount Timpanogos could "become even more renowned than Pikes Peak." A later headline from a Provo newspaper summarized the promise and the challenge: "COLORADO'S SCENERY IS BEATEN HERE—BUT COLORADO KNOWS HOW TO SELL MOUNTAINS." The paper tried to impress upon readers their civic duty to promote this project. "Mt. Timpanogos is rapidly taking its place in the public mind alongside of Pike's Peak and Mt. Rainier," it editorialized. "The attitude of citizens of this city will determine largely whether the old peak is going to become as famous as any peak in America or not." Most baldly, the brochure for the 1925 annual hike stated that

> scenic states are made by their people almost as much as they are made by their natural scenery . . . Many people climbed Timpanogos and thought it was just another mountain, but [Eugene Roberts and his collaborators] decided that it was a Wonder Mountain. From that time on they began to tell people that it was a Wonder Mountain and so it is a Wonder Mountain unto this day . . . Every service station man, every druggist, every garage man, every tinker and tailor, every groceryman, everybody that the tourist comes in touch with must be a votary of the mountains.[34]

These editorials echoed the words of Roberts as well as his alter ego, Harry Davidson Kemp. A prankster at heart, Roberts wrote a series of articles in a local newspaper under the persona of a famous eastern journalist visiting Provo for health reasons. Kemp/Roberts praised the mountain scenery, especially Timpanogos, but he also admonished Provoans for not doing enough to modernize and beautify their streets and buildings. The eastern tourists who would come to see the Wonder Mountain would also want to see a City Beautiful.[35]

Locals did their best to rise to the challenge. The Salt Lake Commercial Club and later the Provo Commercial Club produced promotional leaflets. Provo, the erstwhile "Garden City," began calling itself the "Hike City" in the 1920s. In June 1921 American Fork held "Timpanogos Day": 100 guests from Salt Lake City were treated to a banquet after sitting through a meeting in the tabernacle where speakers eulogized the mountain. Area boosters urged residents to send letters to distant friends telling them about the Wonder Mountain and its annual hike: "They, naturally, will tell others, and the advertising will grow as a snowball swells as it is rolled along. Do this for Timp, and Provo, and for the growth of your own business!"[36] For pride and promotion, locals invented new names for their mountain—the Wasatch Giant, King of the Wasatch, Monarch of the Mountains, Patriarch of the Mountains, Guardian of Utah Valley, Mount of the West, the Matterhorn of Utah, an Alp of America.

The alpine connection—made possible because of the "glacier"—inspired inordinate pride. "No single scenic feature in Utah offers greater possibilities for advertising the state than does the Timpanogos glacier," claimed a Provo paper in 1915. Some railroad brochures referred to the mountain as Utah's "glacier-crowned peak." One national magazine propagated an outrageous local fib: "Mount Timpanogos, beautiful and lofty peak of the Wasatch Range, is famed as the harbor of one of the few remaining glaciers of the world accessible to the traveler." The snowfield below the summit was repeatedly called the "southernmost glacier in North America" or America's only temperate-zone glacier. Even with some hyperbole allowed for, the assertion was wrong. Back in 1897 the great geologist Israel C. Russell had correctly identified the "pocket edition" glaciers in the Si-

Participants in the Annual Timpanogos Hike ascend the "glacier" in single file, date unknown. (L. Tom Perry Special Collections, Harold B. Lee Library, Brigham Young University, Provo, Utah)

erra Nevada as the southern limit of ice cover in the United States. (And don't forget Mexico.) Nonetheless, to this day the "Timpanogos Glacier" persists on maps, a relic of the hiking era.[37]

As much as boosters loved their so-called glacier, they glorified the hike up the glacier even more. They endlessly repeated claims that the Annual Timpanogos Hike ranked as the biggest hike in America, the greatest community hike in the world, and the largest "pilgrimage" to any mountain over 10,000 feet (or 12,000 feet, depending on the source). This claim was almost credible. Technically, the hike didn't qualify as a pilgrimage because there was nothing strictly religious or overtly spiritual about it; and even if it had qualified, it would have been much smaller than the pilgrimage to Fujiyama. However, I know of no single-day group climb of any high peak in all of history that surpasses the Annual Timpanogos Hike. At its mid-century apex of popularity, it attracted something like 10,000 participants. True, not all of them made it to the summit, but the cavalcade of hikers was something to crow about. BYU president George Brimhall stood on firm ground when he issued this exhortation: "Hike Timpanogos because it is one of Utah's most effective advertising agencies or as some would say, Utah's Best Boosters."[38]

⋮⋮ To understand fully how Eugene Roberts' collegiate tradition became a statewide event, we must travel through the first fifteen years chronologically. It's astonishing to see how many groups started hiking this mountain once Roberts opened their eyes.

The inaugural college hike occurred in 1912. The next year Roberts launched what would become a staple feature, a prehike evening program. Nineteen-fifteen and 1916 witnessed two big hikes, one sponsored by the BYU summer school, one sponsored by the Provo Commercial Club. Roberts led both. For the latter hike, the businessmen of Provo declared a store holiday. Also in 1915, a local troop of scouts and a local quorum of priests (Mormon teenage boys) climbed the peak. In addition to his other guiding, Roberts led the Boy Scouts of the Utah Stake MIA on a three-day Timpanogos excursion in 1916. The following year BYU and the Commercial Club decided to combine their hikes. About 350 camped at the base of the mountain, and about 200 made it to the summit, where musicians performed a serenade. In 1919 a convention of physical education directors concluded with an ascent of Mount Timpanogos. For the evening program of the subsequent Big Hike, BYU students staged a play in an improvised outdoor theater. The 1919 hike was immediately followed by two other mass climbs by a Mormon fathers/sons event and a Salt Lake Boy Scouts outing (both of which were repeated in later years). In July 1920, just before the annual event, Utahns organized two special hikes for two separate groups of conventioneers—a multistate organization of social workers and the National Education Association. On the Big Hike itself, about 250 made it to the summit while International News produced newsreel footage. At about this time the Forest Service built a second summit trail that began at the head of American Fork Canyon. Provo partisans, frustrated by the quality of their access routes, began improvements on their own. The commissioners of Utah County spent tax money to upgrade the North Fork road, and BYU students contributed labor to the Aspen Grove trail.

For the Tin Wedding Hike—the tenth annual event, in 1921—boosters wrapped Provo telephone poles in tinfoil. Local merchants advertised specials on hiking gear. The Hoover Candy Company offered "Timpanogos Bars" and "Timpanogos Salted Peanuts" for trail food. Provo businesses also participated in a storefront art contest. Utah Power & Light and Utah Valley Gas Company produced notable displays, but the Barton Furniture Company created the award-winning diorama (complete with miniature hikers). For the prehike bonfire program, a record crowd—perhaps 1,400 people—gathered at Aspen Grove. Six hundred fifty-three of them started the ascent; an airplane buzzed the 500 or so who reached the summit. The hiking throng included a big contingent from BYU's rival, the University of Utah. An overflow hike was conducted the next day. All told, more than 1,000 people—equal to 10 percent of Provo's population—reached the summit as part of the various group hikes in July 1921. The local paper showered praise upon the wedding planner: "The avocation of Director Roberts for the last fifteen years has been that of salesman and advertiser. As such he has specialized in selling Timpanogos, first to a few intimate friends, then to Provo and Utah, and finally to the entire nation."[39]

The Big Hike's eleventh year, 1922, marked the opening of the new-and-improved Aspen Grove hiking trail (finished with a Forest Service appropriation), the building of a "Greek theater" on land donated to BYU by the Stewart family, the establishment of Timpanogos Cave National Monument, the beginning of road work to connect American Fork and North Fork canyons, and the publication of *Timpa-*

nogos, Wonder Mountain, a glossy promotional booklet. In anticipation of the "Trail Christening Hike," organizers sponsored a poetry contest on the theme of the mountain (first prize: an oil painting of Timpanogos). Window displays appeared in Salt Lake as well as Provo. The Columbia Theater in downtown Provo screened a film montage about the Big Hike.

By 1921–22 the event had been fully institutionalized, but there was still opportunity for growth and embellishment. In 1924, on the night preceding the Friday-night prehike program, Provo staged a "Hiker's Frolic" downtown, including a parade, music, and dancing. Everyone was encouraged to come in "hiking costume." About 700 people showed up, including the entire Rotary Club in boots. Meanwhile in Salt Lake City the Wasatch Mountain Club held a street rally for the hike. Thanks to the Union Pacific, publicity about the 1924 hike appeared in over 200 periodicals. At the prehike program, approximately 1,500 people sat among the pines and aspens to watch the bonfire and fireworks. In 1925 the program planners introduced the "Timp Stick," a souvenir for the hiker who had traveled farthest to climb the Wasatch Giant. Over the 1920s, the prehike program got bigger and livelier. Barbershop quartets, hula dancing, stunt contests—practically anything was possible. To accommodate the celebrants, BYU opened the "Theater in the Pines" in 1926 (later upgraded by the Civilian Conservation Corps). Between 4,000 and 5,000 campers enjoyed the vaudevillian programs in 1927, 1928, and 1929. In each of these years more than 1,000 hikers made the trek, though many halted at the base of the "glacier." In 1930 organizers established an enduring tradition—"Timp Summit Club" badges for those who made it to the top. Each year featured a new design. The number of summiteers hit a prewar peak in 1932, when more than 1,400 earned a badge. Over the remainder of the 1930s, the two access roads were paved, making it easier than ever to reach the Aspen Grove trailhead. The hike had become a well-oiled event.

How did 1,000 to 2,000 hikers use a trail all at once? In single file, singing. By staying close together, Roberts explained, "all rock rolling

Collegiate hikers on the summit of Mount Timpanogos, ca. 1920s. (L. Tom Perry Special Collections, Harold B. Lee Library, Brigham Young University, Provo, Utah)

is prevented. This form of hiking is rather military and requires restraint and good fellowship on the part of those who take part." To love this mountain, one had to love other people. "Develop the social instinct on the hike," instructed one brochure. "Stay with the crowd and have a time." At 4:00 A.M. on the day of the hike, a bugle would rouse the campers, who would line up under the full moon. Once the hikers were under way, the mountain chorus line sang lyrics like "Oh, Timpanogos, mighty Timpanogos / Timpanogos, mountain that I love." The signature song began this way:

> There's a long, long trail a-winding,
> Upon Timpanogos so grand,

Where the glacier is white and gleaming
And the tall cliffs stand . . .[40]

The musical procession continued to the "glacier," at which point the large group broke into parts: some lunched, some rested, some stopped, while others made a dash for the summit.

In its hypersociability the Annual Timpanogos Hike resembled the contemporaneous mass outings of the Sierra Club and The Mazamas. Only the scale was bigger. Mormonism made the difference: Latter-day Saints do everything in groups. But despite the Mormon influence, the Big Hike did not feature anything strictly denominational. The religious references in the promotional material drew from the standard Christian lexicon. Even Eugene Roberts, a church employee who linked physical fitness with spiritual fitness, stopped short of sacralizing the mountain or the hike. Roberts liked to refer to hikers as pilgrims, but he mixed that metaphor with the language of oracles, nymphs, mountain gods, and especially Indian spirits. Of the seven poems about Mount Timpanogos published by the main LDS periodical, the *Improvement Era,* in the first half of the twentieth century, only one contained distinctive Mormon language.[41] LDS hikers did not come to Timpanogos because it was holy. Only later did local Mormons begin to sacralize this landform.

⁙ The 1940s were an unsettled time for the Timpanogos Hike and the world in general. The summit badge in 1942 featured a glowing "V" rising from a mountain; the legend read: "VICTORY WITH PHYSICAL VIGOR." During the war the prehike program went dormant, and the hiking crowd diminished. To keep some interest alive, organizers experimented with a slalom on the "glacier." Predictably it was billed as the "latest ski race in America" and the "highest ski race in America." After the Allied victory, the Big Hike resumed full stride in 1946, and reached new heights in 1947.

That year, a Provo journalist wrote an article on the history of the hike. He warned his readers that the U.S. Geological Survey was putting the finishing touches on a map that would shrink Timpanogos some 250 feet from its accepted elevation of 12,008. Yet when this change happened, nothing much changed. The mistaken figure continued to show up in print—indeed, it still appears in some encyclopedias. More to the point, local people didn't care anymore about the elevation. Timpanogos was now special for other reasons. As the journalist said, Timpanogos "has a fascination which has little to do with mere altitude." He argued that "the grip it holds upon people is no chamber-of-commerce publicity invention." True enough. But "Timp" itself was indeed a social creation. Back in the 1920s, Provo hikers boasted about that fact. They knew that they had made the mountain extraordinary. That history gave them pride: "The manner in which Mount Timpanogos found its home in Utah may be told in a word. Although others had looked at this craggy eminence, it was not until a young physical director, whose culture lies above the shoulder, as well as below, began his well known hiking parties, that appreciation of the mountain became general."[42]

By 1953, the year of Roberts' death, this awareness had largely been lost. Utahns had tried so strenuously to convince everyone of Timpanogos' natural preeminence that they came to believe it themselves. The boosterism was internalized. From one perspective, this place-making project could be considered a failure. Today "Timp" is nowhere near as prominent as Mount Rainier or Mount Hood. Few people outside Utah (excluding Mormons) have heard of it. Impressive though it is, Timpanogos is not—like the solitary cone of an ice-clad volcano—an obvious landmark to outsiders. The project exceeded the material at hand. However, compared to most western booster projects—and the U.S. West contains thousands of failed mines, abandoned farms, ghost towns, and boarded-up resorts—this project surely qualifies as a terrific success. Out of mid-grade material, boosters manufactured something fine: the best-known, best-loved mountain in Utah. The surest sign of their success was their obsolescence. By midcentury no one had to remind local people to promote

Timpanogos. There was no more need for didacticism. On the day of the 1922 annual hike, one of Provo's newspapers considered it efficacious to print a full-banner front-page image of the mountain with an explanation: "THIS IS TIMPANOGOS — WONDER MOUNTAIN OF THE WASATCH RANGE."[43] In 1997 the same paper redesigned its layout and adopted the mountain as its masthead. No caption was necessary. Everyone's eyes had been trained long before.

6

Sundance and Suburbia

In the second half of the twentieth century, Mount Timpanogos came to exemplify what land managers call the "urban-wild interface" as Utah Valley largely transformed from an agricultural (productive) landscape to a suburban (consumerist) landscape. This transformation encouraged two new iterations of mountain place attachment. The first was based in recreation—though not in hiking. The Sundance Resort, the pet project of movie star Robert Redford, opened on the massif in the 1970s. Like the larger ski industry, Sundance encouraged a year-round touristic connection between western urbanites and western mountains. The increased urbanity of Timpanogos coincided with its increased "wildness" as government officials phased out cattle grazing, introduced mountain goats, discontinued the Annual Timpanogos Hike, and designated the summit area a wilderness. Even without the hike, a local tradition of loving the mountain persisted. This love found new expression in the 1990s with the dedication of the Mount Timpanogos Temple. Through this building, local Mormon residents began to invest the landform with sacredness. In more ways than one, the built environment of the valley affected the physical environment of the mountain.

* * *

::: The Timpanogos massif suffered from various ailments as of the mid-twentieth century. The first generation of government foresters had done little to limit subalpine grazing; in fact they had allowed more grazing during World War I to increase the meat supply. Desertification was a serious threat before the Great Depression came to the rescue. When the bottom fell out of the market in the 1930s, most ranchers had no choice but to retreat from Utah's mountains. At the same time, New Deal policies and monies brought watershed conservation to Utah and Utah County—though not yet to Timpanogos. Not until the 1950s did foresters act forcefully to eliminate cattle grazing and reduce sheep permits to a minimum. Concurrently they implemented a soil restoration plan that included bulldozing contour terraces on the southwest face of Timpanogos, plugging gullies, and reseeding.[1]

With ranching under control, the Forest Service turned its attention to the impacts of recreationists. The Annual Timpanogos Hike reached maximum size in the 1960s. As it grew and grew, its character changed. The guiding influence of Eugene Roberts faded, and the boisterous side of the group experience came to dominate the hike. Roberts' program of nature-based moral education became subordinate to revelry. Instead of waiting for the traditional 4:00 A.M. brass choir wake-up call, many people took off after the evening program in a race to the summit, cutting shortcuts as they went. As early as 1937, Roberts (writing from Los Angeles) complained that the "promiscuous unorganized night climbing of the mountain at the time of the annual Timpanogos Hike destroys the essential unity of the ascension. It is almost an ABOMINATION." In 1948 a ranger complained about kids' rolling rocks into the Theater in the Pines and setting off firecrackers. This kind of behavior became widespread in subsequent decades. The 1963 hike was marred by a "pre-dawn brawl" by drunken "hoods." These "carousers" and "hooligans" disrupted the campfire program and prevented hikers from sleeping. The next year, hike officials responded with road checks. The rowdies stayed one step ahead by stashing their alcohol ahead of time. In 1966 forty-three police officers patrolled Aspen Grove. They cited twelve young men for drunkenness; one got hauled to jail.[2]

Even the well-behaved hikers created problems. A seven-mile human train left a trail of litter and waste. In one day, a throng of hikers could turn a path into parallel ruts. It could turn a meadow of paintbrush and lupine into a smelly, trampled mess. The alpine zone lacked adequate toilet facilities. To use the language of the day, Timpanogos was being "loved to death." The 1970 hike was the death knell. About 7,000 people (a record number) participated; perhaps half stood in line to stand on the summit. Through their hyperconcentrated use, hikers repeated the damage done earlier by stock animals. One ranger described the problem by way of analogy: "One cow in a pasture for 400 days is not as bad as 400 cows in a pasture for one day." Alarmed by the degradation, the Forest Service asked BYU's hike committee to call it quits. The committee complied with speed—and even a sigh of relief, considering the mounting problems with misbehavior that contradicted the image and ethos of the university and its hometown. "It has become impossible to cope with the hippie element," said Provo's mayor, theatrically. To compensate for the loss of the hike, BYU hoped to sponsor a series of smaller collegiate "excursions" to the summit. But the head ranger discouraged any mass hiking. "That old mountain just can't stand it," he said, "that is if we expect to maintain anything there."[3]

Since 1970 the high, central part of the massif—the only part that annual hikers visited—has somewhat but not entirely recovered. Even without the Big Hike, Timpanogos remains the most-walked-on mountain in Utah. Many family groups, scout groups, student groups, and church groups still make annual climbs. On any given Saturday between Independence Day and Labor Day, 1,000 to 2,000 hikers claim space on the mountain. On warm summer nights Timpanogos plays host to flashlight hiking. The full moon draws crowds to the metal hut on the summit, which often smells like urine. To educate and assist the summer crush of hikers, a group of volunteers formed the Timpanogos Emergency Response Team (TERT) in 1983. In season, these volunteers—all trained in wilderness medicine—keep positions at the two trailheads and at the foot of the "glacier." TERT volunteers have treated hundreds of injured hikers and educated many more in out-door preparedness. Timpanogos attracts many out-of-shape peak-baggers who know little about alpine hiking. "Hiking Timp has be-come a cultural phenomenon," explains one TERT veteran. "Because of the [annual] hike, Timpanogos is looked on less as a wild and dan-gerous mountain and more as part of our society. One goes onto the mountain not to seek solitude of nature but to be a part of a Utah County [rite] of passage. Hiking Timp is spoken about like a badge of honor."[4] Amateur hikers are easy victims of dehydration and expo-sure. Early in the season, snow holes and crevasses present mortal dangers. By late summer the snowbanks have melted, but thunder-storms can build unexpectedly. To offer protection, a large permanent wooden shelter was built at the base of the "glacier" in 1960. The most pernicious hazard, sliding down the "glacier," is also the most avoidable. Foolishly, many hikers bring plastic bags to reduce friction. More than one daredevil has ripped a new posterior hole on the sharp rocks that hide beneath the shallow snowfield.

In winter the summit of Timpanogos regains solitude. And certainly there are sections of the massif up- and down-ridge of the summit where few people ever go. However, Timpanogos in any season would not seem to fit the cultural or legislative definition of wilderness. Ac-cording to the Wilderness Act of 1964, a wilderness is "an area where the earth and its community of life are untrammeled by man," with the "imprint of man's work substantially unnoticeable," an undevel-oped land without "permanent improvements" that has "outstanding opportunities for solitude or a primitive and unconfined type of recre-ation."

In political practice, these stipulations sometimes function as mere guidelines. Wild or not, Mount Timpanogos joined the national wil-derness system in 1984. This was not surprising. From the beginning of the American conservation movement, high mountains have been considered the nation's "crown jewels." Most of the early national parks and most of the initial wilderness areas were established in rocky highlands, a terrain type that met the accepted criteria of sublimity and majesty. As a bonus, these alpine lands were "worthless": they had little value to timber, oil, or gas companies. Protecting icy summits has proven politically easier and more expedient than protecting forested foothills. In the 1970s Congress required the Forest Service to review its roadless landholdings for acreage eligible for wilderness designation. The initial inventory egregiously underreported the roadless acreage; under pressure, the agency did it over. Subsequently the designation of wilderness areas proceeded on a state-by-state basis. In Utah an omnibus wilderness bill was supported by the all-Republican *anti*wilderness delegation, which crafted legislation that protected high-altitude urban-proximate recreational land. More ecologically significant—and industrially valuable—forested acreage got short shrift. At 800,000 acres, the bill covered only 1.5 percent of the state, but it did recognize the alpine regions that Utah's urbanites most liked to play in, including a 10,750-acre portion of the Timpanogos massif that had previously been designated as a National Forest "Scenic Area." From "scenic" to "wild," the legal reclassifications of Mount Timpanogos said more about the developed valleys than about the undeveloped mountains.[5]

Most hikers who reach the summit of Timpanogos probably don't realize they have crossed into a wilderness area. For day users, a more visible marker of the mountain's wildness is the herd of Rocky Mountain goats that frequents the peak in the summertime. "Wild" mountains seem to deserve "wild" animals—particularly charismatic megafauna. Mount Timpanogos supports other large mammalian species, but most of them are nocturnal and prefer the cover of trees. People don't see them. In contrast, goats roam the exposed slopes as though they were born to be there. They weren't. These wild animals are as artificial as the wilderness area. State biologists introduced this nonnative species to nearby Lone Peak (Utah's first designated wilderness) in 1967 and to Timpanogos in 1981. The animals came from the surplus population at Olympic National Park, in Washington, another nonnative habitat. Over the years the Timpanogos herd has grown to about 100. A few lucky hunters draw permits each year.

With their impossibly agile feet, goats seem to be a perfect fit for a hiking mountain. As the project coordinator for the species introduction once said, "There is a certain mystique about mountain goats."[6]

⋮⋮⋮   There is also a certain mystique about movie stars, one of who transplanted himself to Timpanogos. As it turns out, the introduction of Robert Redford and his Sundance Resort has complemented the recent makeover of the mountain as a wilderness.

The story begins with two brothers, John R. Stewart and Scott P. Stewart. Their father was a surveyor for the General Land Office. Tagging along on survey trips, the teenage boys saw many parts of Utah available for homesteading. In their eyes, the most desirable acreage was the open area below the eastern peaks of the Timpanogos massif at the head of the North Fork of Provo Canyon. The brothers wanted to own it. In 1900 they filed for adjoining 160-acre homesteads. They enticed many relatives to do the same with the understanding that the plots would be sold back to John and Scott in exchange for financial stock in their land business, the North Fork Investment Company. By the beginning of World War II the brothers owned most of "Stewart Flat," some 3,500 acres. As previously mentioned, they gave a parcel to BYU to function as a summer school and a staging ground for the annual hike. On the rest of the land they tried various entrepreneurial schemes—ranching, logging, dairying, pig raising, real estate development. After the war the brothers split their landholding in two. Scott chose the more mountainous west side because his eldest son, Paul, was interested in herding and skiing, and the slopes suited both.[7]

Utahns had been flirting with skiing since the 1910s. The first true resort appeared in the late 1930s, when the all-but-ghost town of Alta (over the ridge to the north of Timpanogos) reinvented itself. Alta's transformation from mining camp to ski town was replicated at Park City—not to mention Aspen, Crested Butte, and Telluride in Colorado. In contrast, Stewart Flat lacked preexisting infrastructure.

When Paul and his brother Ray opened the Timp Haven ski area in the 1940s, they used a towrope driven by a converted truck engine. A chairlift arrived in 1953. Even with the improvement, Timp Haven was a simple, homegrown venture for local recreationists.[8]

This is how things stood in the early 1960s when a young actor, Robert Redford, took a scenic detour up the North Fork of the Provo River. Redford became familiar with the area through his college girl-friend (and first wife), a Mormon girl from a prominent Provo family. When he pulled his motorcycle into Timp Haven, Redford instantly felt desire. He bought two acres; soon he wanted more. After the success of *Barefoot in the Park* (1967) and *Butch Cassidy and the Sundance Kid* (1969), Redford bought out the Stewarts with the help of some financial partners. Redford built a house for his family over-looking his land. He renamed it Sundance. As he became one of the most sought-after movie stars of the 1970s, Redford increasingly withdrew from his first home in Manhattan to his second home at Sundance. The 3,300-acre property was an investment as well as a hideout. Unsatisfied with the short-term financial return, Redford's partners wanted to sell out. Going deeply into debt, Redford assumed sole ownership of the property. He needed to make money off the land to pay off his loan, but he didn't want to create another vulgar condo-complex. An outspoken environmentalist, Redford claimed that he bought the land "with the idea of ecology in mind." "I don't think I'm just piling up land the way some people pile up money," he said. "I'm collecting space, and space has a very deep meaning for me." One newspaper feature called the Sundance Kid a "one-man ecologi-cal posse." Redford favored words like "wild" and "virgin" to de-scribe Stewart Flat. "The intent was salvaging more than anything," he said.[9]

To his credit, development proceeded slowly and tastefully. The condos and second homes at Sundance were clustered among trees, and all featured wood exteriors. The original restaurant, the Tree Room, was actually built around a tree. No overhead power lines disrupted the mountain views. Even today the resort caters to travel connoisseurs, unlike the big, all-purpose resorts near Park City that hosted the 2002 Olympics. The parking lot at Sundance remains small. For years Redford fought against the widening of the Provo Canyon highway. "If Thoreau were alive today, he would be comfortable staying at Sundance," gushed one journalist. In 1991 *Hideaway Report*, a trade journal, named Sundance one of the "Sanctuaries of the Year." According to Redford, Sundance is less a resort than an "experimental retreat," less a place than a "vision."

> I was asked to define what we are, what Sundance is. I had to list words that define us, and words that don't . . . These are words I like: "cottage." I like "enlightenment." I like "community." I don't like "resort." I don't like "condominium." I don't like "amenities." If you had to hone it down, to describe in two words what this place is, it would be "rough elegance."[10]

This aesthetic can be observed—and purchased—via the Sundance mail-order catalog, which features luxury items like wooden bowls "carried out of the canyons on the back of a donkey" by the Tarahumara Indians of Mexico, and rustic barbed-wire cowboy art. The "Sundance look" favors nature-themed craft objects fashioned by hand. Everything seems to be one of a kind even if it's not. Everything is simple, and everything is expensive. It's something like a yuppie way of being Amish.[11]

Robert Redford used Sundance the place and Sundance the ethos to launch a pair of nonprofit organizations in 1981. The first, the Institute for Resource Management (IRM), facilitated dialogue on energy/environmental issues. Before petering out in the 1990s, IRM sponsored conferences on oil drilling in Alaska, energy extraction on the Navajo and Hopi reservations, and the U.S.-Soviet response to global warming. The power of Redford's celebrity secured the participation of tycoons and senators. But since IRM did not have mediation power, its conferences resulted in vague successes like "letters of understand-

ing" and "vision statements." The "Greenhouse Glasnost" conference came ahead of its time. Climate change did not become a matter
of political urgency until the twenty-first century. In 2005 Redford
and Sundance sponsored another conference on global warming, this
time focusing on local initiatives. Forty-six U.S. mayors as well as former Vice President Al Gore attended.[12]

Redford's other nonprofit has produced more tangible results. The
Sundance Institute originated as a series of workshops for directors,
screenwriters, film composers, and the like. Redford hoped to nurture
talent outside the cutthroat Hollywood scene. In 1984 the institute assumed management of the United States Film Festival. Renamed the
Sundance Film Festival, this annual event has become America's leading showcase for independent filmmakers. Each January, Park City,
Utah, becomes Hollywood for a week. Stars come to be stars; producers come to make speculative bids on the up-and-coming. The institute now has administrative offices in Salt Lake City and Beverly
Hills. The resort itself hosts film workshops and outdoor theater performances. These artistic activities—and the facilities that support
them—give the place a campus air in summertime. For a modest-sized
ski resort, it feels rarefied.

Sundance will never grow huge. There isn't much space, and much
of that is closed to development. In 1997 Redford founded the North
Fork Preservation Alliance to help convince adjoining landowners
to set up conservation easements. The next year he donated 860 of
his accumulated 5,000 acres to Utah Open Lands, a land trust. To
Redford Sundance represented an antidote to the obliteration of nature from his hometown, Los Angeles:

> I watched as the green, open spaces turned into concrete
> malls and freeways, and the clean, pure air turned into smog
> alerts. I watched as unbridled development became the or-
> der of the day. Oil drills appeared off the beaches, along
> with oil spills in the water and hunks of tar on the sand. The
> smell of orange blossoms turned into exhaust fumes.

I felt my home being taken away from me. I felt my roots being pulled out from under me. And I took it personally. I had to go further and further away to find places where the natural environment still existed.[13]

This dynamic can be observed in Redford's movies. In 1972 Redford starred in *Jeremiah Johnson,* a story about a taciturn mountain man who abandons civilization. The alpine scenes were shot entirely at Sundance, where the director, Sydney Pollack, built a cabin. Redford's later westerns required landscapes more spacious and wild than Timpanogos. In *A River Runs through It* (producer-director, 1992) and *The Horse Whisperer* (producer-director-actor, 1998), Redford romanced the Northern Rockies of Montana. On the big screen, this place really did look like The Last Best Place. Who wouldn't want a home—or a second or a third home—here? Western Montana looks green and empty and white (with 2 percent of its population foreign-born as of 2000), whereas southern California looks brown and congested and brown (26 percent foreign-born). In the 1990s "native" Montanans complained about the rush of "Californicators" buying up real estate. In the "New West," mountains and especially ski resorts are shelters of class and race. Places like Sundance are linked to spaces like southern California. Metropolitan Los Angeles cultivates hinterlands of retreat just as Hollywood cultivates hinterlands of fantasy. More specifically, the Sundance Resort wouldn't exist without the money of Redford and the clout of the Sundance Institute, both of which wouldn't exist without Hollywood.[14]

In short, Sundance needs its complementary opposite(s). You can't construct "rough elegance" without both worlds. Just as wilderness areas require sacrifice zones, antiurban asylums require metropolises. A high-tech corporate communications director in Orem, Utah, crows that "Sundance is only 15 minutes away from our offices, but it's really another world. We take clients up there all the time. It's self-gratifying, close, unique, intimate." The mountain resort is one of the amenities that make living in Utah Valley bearable for non-Mormons and cosmopolitans. The restaurants and day spa at Sundance are designed for worldly people. The sense of place the resort inspires is disconnected from the historic, endemic attachment of Mormons to their "mountain home." The homeowners' "community" at Sundance consists of jet-setting bilocals: members of the leisure class who can't live with or without the city. Their urbane antiurbanism is an elitist answer to the mass problem of environmental alienation. It's wonderful to "get back to the land" if you can afford to vacation in a second home in the mountains. Part-time communities like Sundance depend on the complex infrastructure of modernity such as airports. Mount Timpanogos hides these connections, however. In the shadow of the snowy massif, people see the best of themselves. "I feel the answer to our future may lie in our past," said Redford in the 1970s. "Those simple pioneer communities worked so well."[15]

There was something disingenuous about an outsider, a resort developer, nostalgically claiming the language of pioneering. Something ironic, too. Just over the mountain from Redford's refuge, the real caretakers of Utah's pioneer heritage—the descendants of the Mormon settlers—facilitated the conversion of the pioneer landscape into tract homes, malls, and freeways. Redford got to Utah just in time to see the Wasatch Front morph into the L.A. Basin of the Great Basin.

::: At first glance, the recent transformation of the Wasatch Front seems to violate core values inherited by Mormons. As late as 1949, the LDS apostle John D. Widtsoe—former president of Utah State Agricultural College and author of the once-influential *Dry Farming*—could claim that Mormonism and agrarianism were inseparable. "We Latter-day Saints are a land-loving people," he asserted. "We believe in the land. We are a land-using people." He cited a recent census indicating that 65 percent of Mormons participated in agriculture. "I hope that we as a people will not depart from that tradition," he continued. "Those who own the land and use it in the end will determine the future of mankind. It will not come from those who work in the factories or who live in crowded cities . . . We Latter-day Saints must ever remember the sanctity and the holiness of the land given us by the Father. There is safety in the land."[16]

Widtsoe died a short time later, and it's just as well that he missed the second half of the twentieth century, when Utah belatedly went the way of America. A land of producers became a land of consumers. In 1990, when the U.S. Census Bureau stopped counting farmers altogether, just 2.2 percent of Utahns found employment in "farming, forestry, and fishing occupations."

The transformation of Utah County—which basically consists of Utah Valley—illustrates the apparently irreversible trend. As of the late nineteenth century, this was Utah's leading agricultural county. Perhaps that isn't saying much. Utah has only one nature-made farming region—the Wasatch Front (sometimes called the Wasatch Oasis). Unfortunately, farmers there have always lacked a robust market, internal or external. Before the creation of the railway system, the Great Basin did not yield ready agricultural profits. On the other hand, as Brigham Young liked to say, it was a good place to make Saints. Mormons farmed for so long because there was little else to do economically, and because there seemed to be something righteous about it (especially compared to speculative mining). Farming sustained community. Like the hill country of the Upper South, Utah held on to an agrarian system of local exchange longer than would have seemed possible. But the limits of this semiarid land eventually asserted themselves. By the 1880s Utah Valley and the greater Wasatch Front had become overpopulated. To retain its people, the area had to change economically.[17]

In Charles Peterson's words, Utah's agricultural sector was "Americanized" in the 1890s: "Farming became a business rather than a way of building the Kingdom." In Utah Valley farmers shifted to cash crops, notably sugar beets and fruit trees. The largest of several sugar-beet refineries opened in Lehi in 1891. Several canneries appeared too. Commercial farmers benefited from improved railroad access (thanks to the Denver & Rio Grande) and improved internal markets (thanks to the Bingham and Tintic mining districts). New farmers also enjoyed greater autonomy. Before the 1870s, the LDS Church controlled land entry—that is, the process by which public domain became private property. The typical Utah farmer lived in a church-run village and farmed a plot in the community field. After the 1870s, farmers could stake out individual homesteads through the federal process. The federalization of land entry encouraged farmers to spread out on individual plots. Additionally, the government threw open much of the Ute Reservation to homesteaders in 1905. Many participants in this Uinta Basin land rush came from the Wasatch Front. Other previously unsettled portions of the state attracted dry farmers—a great experiment in homesteading that would fail after one generation.

Compared with other areas of the state, Utah Valley boasted an abundance of water from natural and artificial sources. In 1913 the valley started importing water from the Uinta Basin—without compensation to reservation Utes—under the auspices of the U.S. Bureau of Reclamation's Strawberry Valley Project. Farmers had enough water to invest in orchards and canneries. Row upon row of peach, cherry, apricot, and plum trees appeared on the northern and southern benches of the valley in the early 1900s. The makings of a new town materialized at "Provo Bench," where a series of homesteads dotted the main state road. The place was incorporated in 1919 as Orem—tellingly named for a non-Mormon railroad owner. Orem represented the geographic future: an American line town, not a Mormon village on a grid.[18]

In Utah County, economic Americanization eventually led away from agriculture. The first harbinger arrived in 1924 with the construction of Ironton, a giant pig-iron plant south of Provo financed by outside capital. This facility stayed open during the Depression, when the farm sector sank into the doldrums. Utah farmers became painfully aware of the downside of improved transportation: it opened up competition with more-productive farm states. Even in these lean years, however, Utah's fruit belt looked beautifully fecund. In 1938 novelist Thomas Wolfe described Utah Valley—a landscape in transition from agriculture to heavy industry—in his travel journal:

> ... now a kind of cooler sterner magic in the scenery (impassionate, granite, clearly barren in the hackled ridges of the limestone peaks, the austere blackness of the timber)—and the great valley floor burgeoning with Canaan in between— the cool flat silver of the lake at Provo and the full fat land of plenty now—cherry orchards groaning with their fruit, fields thick with grain and hay, and fertile tillages betwixt the granite semi-arid clearness of the desert peaks—Provo— its thriving look—the immense smelter plants . . .[19]

Not long after Wolfe's drive-through, Utah Valley added an even more immense industrial component to its landscape. During World War II the U.S. government financed the construction of the $190 million Geneva Steel Works on the shore of Utah Lake. The 1,600-acre site was chosen for its safe inland location, its proximity to raw materials and rail networks, and its secure water supply thanks to the recent damming of the Provo River at Deer Creek in uppermost Provo Canyon. Some 10,000 men built the plant in 1942–1944; afterward Geneva became the leading employer in the valley. In 1960 employment peaked at 7,500, or about 30 percent of all county jobs. Many of the steelworkers had been farmers. Provo, the former Garden City (and erstwhile Hike City), now called itself the "Steel Center of the West."[20]

Provo's neighbor, Orem, boomed because of Geneva. Between 1940 and 1980 the city's population doubled almost every decade, growing from 2,900 to 52,000. Thanks to its location on State Street (the predecessor of I-15) and its history of unmanaged growth, Orem became the natural site for Utah Valley's first shopping mall (1975). Tract housing kept pace with shopping centers, and by 2000 nearly all of Orem's cherry orchards had been eliminated. As of the 2000 cen-

Fritz Henle, "Farm Family against Backdrop of Geneva Works of U.S. Steel's Geneva Steel Company, Geneva, Utah," ca. 1950. (Courtesy of the Henle Archive Trust)

sus, Orem had 84,234 people compared to Provo's 105,000. Nowadays mapmakers refer to the adjoining cities as the "Provo-Orem metro area." The cities merged physically as a result of building booms in the 1970s and the 1990s, two periods of in-migration. The new residents were both historical beneficiaries of and contemporary sufferers from Geneva Steel. In winter, when high pressure caused inversion layers, the emissions from the plant sometimes obscured Mount Timpanogos completely. The air was worse than in Los Angeles in August. Yet the worst pollution was invisible: microscopic particulates known as PM-2.5 that could not be filtered by the respiratory system. Each winter local hospitals admitted a disproportionate number of children with lung ailments.

By the 1990s the economy of Utah Valley had outgrown the steel plant. After shutting down briefly in 1987, Geneva reopened under new management—and limped along for one final decade. The imminent loss of high-paying factory jobs did not bode well for local workers lacking college degrees, but the majority of valley residents looked forward to the postindustrial era. Provo now advertised itself as the center of "Software Valley." Scores of computer-related firms popped up in the last decade of the millennium. In the eyes of high-tech boosters, Geneva—the onetime economic heart of the valley—was an economic irrelevance and an environmental nuisance. Techies focused on amenities such as the cool evening breeze from Provo Canyon, the stunning vistas of snow-dappled Timpanogos from area golf courses, the Sundance resort, and the scenic "Alpine Loop" road. For many years, Orem-based WordPerfect sealed its software packaging with a sticker bearing a hologram of Mount Timpanogos. The "new economy" was ostensibly as clean as mountain snow. The combination of high-tech jobs and rapid population growth attracted admiration. In 1991 *Money* ranked Provo-Orem the number-one "Best Place to Live Now." In 1994 the same magazine called it the "Best Place in the West."[21]

The stature of "Timp" has grown with the metro area. Several important additions to the municipal infrastructure of Provo-Orem adopted the name of the totem mountain. In 1998 Orem got its own hospital—Timpanogos Regional. Provo's second high school was named Timpview; Orem's second and third were named Mountain View and Timpanogos, respectively. More schools result from more people, and more people equate to more potential acolytes for "Timp." As the productive fields and vacant lots of Provo-Orem have given way to ranch homes and office parks, the Wasatch Range and chiefly Mount Timpanogos have grown in local estimation. Many new homes feature picture windows oriented to the mountain. The West, the nation's most urbanized region, enjoys the nation's best urban views of nature. Highland watersheds double as "viewsheds." Many western cities feel less constricted and ugly than they actually are because of the prospect of mountains in the distance. Just by being in view, mountains raise the quality of life. They give definition to western residential living. Try to imagine Denver without the Front Range, Albuquerque without Sandia Crest, or Los Angeles without the San Gabriel and Santa Monica Mountains.

Brigham Young University, one of the biggest land users in Utah Valley, calls frequent attention to its mountain backdrop. The university adorns its catalogs and brochures with pictures of Timpanogos. Hundreds of thousands of Latter-day Saints from all over the United States have established a bond with "Timp" by attending college in Provo. The view of the mountain from the university has become the normative one—the controlling view seen in paintings and postcards. BYU also runs a popular alumni retreat at Aspen Grove, adjacent to Sundance. Long after the annual hike, the school remains tied to Timpanogos.

BYU has also affected the mountain indirectly by advancing the buildup of the valley. In the second half of the century, the university supplanted Geneva—which finally closed in 2001 after struggling for years to compete with foreign steel—as the valley's largest employer. Thanks to an infusion of church funding, BYU evolved from a compact training school into a sprawling research campus. During the pivotal presidency of Ernest L. Wilkinson (1951–1971), enrollment jumped from 5,000 to 25,000, with matching increases in faculty. During the same period Provo's population increased from 29,000 to 53,000—impressive, but not on the scale of BYU's growth. "No one who accepts the Restored Gospel will question the prophecies of the Prophet of the Lord that this will become the greatest University in the world," said Wilkinson in 1954.[22] Local merchants have benefited from this hubris. Much of Provo's economy centers upon housing, feeding, supplying, and entertaining the student body. BYU is also responsible for Utah County's leading position in Utah's high-tech sector. Two of the area's flagship corporations, Novell and WordPerfect (later bought by Corel), trace their origins to BYU students and faculty. Computer firms appreciate Utah County because of its labor pool of young, educated, low-wage, upright, hard-working people.

Culturally as well as economically, BYU marks the county. Like a magnet, the church university attracts LDS youth, especially those who have grown up outside of Utah without the companionship of a Mormon peer group. Church culture emphasizes early marriage, and there's no better place than Provo to find a Mormon mate. Moreover, BYU engenders larger social networks. The university hosts workshops for church employees, conferences for lay members, and camps for teens. The campus is the great crossroad for contemporary Latter-day Saints. Adjacent to the campus is the Missionary Training Center, where U.S. missionaries attend religious boot camp before departing to their assigned locale.

Clearly, the role of Utah County, particularly Provo, is crucial in the cultural life of Mormonism. Even by the standards of Utah—the most religiously homogeneous state in the Union—Utah County is sectarian: Mormons account for over 80 percent of the population here, but between 60 and 65 percent in the state as a whole. The statewide LDS share has dropped steadily since the 1990s as a result of in-migration. The exact affiliation numbers are contested; but raw numbers don't tell the whole story. LDS dominance remains indisputably overwhelming if measured by the percentage of legislators and statewide elected officials as well as by percentage of religious adherents. Nonetheless, certain neighborhoods and cities and counties have now carved out agnostic or alternative religious spaces. In northern and western Salt Lake County, for example, non-Mormons have enough mass and power to make a real mark in politics and culture. The same is not true of Utah County. Mormon-haters and Saints alike refer to the place as "Happy Valley." To an almost comic extent, non-Mormons fixate on one measure of moral homogeneity: the density of drinking establishments. Nationally, there are twenty-five for every 100,000 people; in Utah County the ratio is three per 100,000.

This culture of Utah County is self-sustaining because the people here so successfully reproduce themselves. The county has the youngest median age in Utah—and not just because of the large student population. BYU is one of the very few research universities at which strollers rival bicycles. In most years Utah County ranks as the most fecund county in the most fecund state in the nation. For theological and cultural reasons, Latter-day Saints value large families. A bastion of "family values," Utah County has become one of the most lopsidedly one-party (Republican) districts in America. The recent combination of a strong economy and a high birthrate has enabled the county to retain its prodigious natural increase. In rounded numbers, the county's population has jumped from 264,000 in 1990, to 369,000 in 2000, to 465,000 in 2006—an impressive 76 percent growth rate over a decade and a half. Since most Utah Mormons prefer to stay close to home, the postagricultural, postindustrial economy of Utah County has been a godsend.[23]

Increase has costs, of course. All of those new people demand houses and schools and stores and roads. Fields have yielded to concrete and steel. A new city, Eagle Mountain, has sprung up in Cedar Valley, west of Utah Lake. Its area is as large as Provo. South of Provo, Utah Valley retains a rural look and feel, but not for much longer if trends in population and land use continue. As low-value farmland suddenly becomes high-value real estate, few old farmers can resist the temptation to cash in. Developers await. Given local attitudes, it's highly unlikely that zoning boards or land trusts will create growth boundaries. There is no valley analogue to Robert Redford—no Mormon celebrity who has championed conservation easements. So the sprawl continues to spread southward. Since 1997—the sesquicentennial of Utah's settlement, a year that prompted much reflection about the future—the issue of land-use planning has received greater attention from state policymakers and the media. Nonetheless, it seems inevitable that by the mid-twenty-first century the old "Mormon landscape" will have entirely vanished from the Wasatch Front. Unlike the "New England village" or the "Santa Fe style," the Utah vernacular has not been celebrated and codified and protected. The buildings made of adobe, brick, and rough-hewn native stone; the ramshackle wood-and-wire fences; the fencerows of upright Lombardy poplars; the use of Fremont cottonwoods as ornamental trees; the compact villages with double-wide streets on a grid; the open irrigation ditches running along the streets; the close mixture of church lots and civic lots and vacant lots; the surrounding fields—this distinctive geographical matrix will soon be a memory or perhaps even a lost memory.[24]

For several generations, Utah Mormon culture celebrated two complementary values, communalism and agrarianism. But one meant more than the other. Community was the goal; farming was a means to that end. Mormons felt less attached to the soil than to a way of life. As their economy diversified, Mormons on the Wasatch Front gradually decoupled the two values. Tellingly, BYU dismantled its agriculture program in the first decade of the new century. Utah is going the way of many states, divided between a rural minority and a metropolitan majority. In cities like Provo, a vestige of agrarianism shows up in backyard gardens and food cellars, yet most urban Mormons readily accept the commutation of fields into neighborhoods—because they are usually *Mormon* neighborhoods, each a minicommunity. Procreation trumps preservation. The Wasatch Front is a paradox: a region full of people who revere their past but who do little to preserve the landscapes of their ancestors.[25]

This contradiction is not new; it shows up, for example, in stories told by Provo's Benjamin Bullock before his death in 1901. According to Bullock's son (who wrote it down for posterity after hearing it from his mother, who heard it from the source), the local ecclesiastical leader Abraham Smoot routinely sent a greeting party to meet the prophet Brigham Young when he traveled to Utah Valley. In this capacity Bullock met Young more than once on the Provo Bench. There, the story goes, Young would get out, stretch his legs, and talk of the future. On one occasion, reaching out his hand, he said: "Some day all of this sage brush will disappear, water will be taken out of Provo River in canals to water this land and this Bench will become a beautiful garden spot, where may kinds of delicious fruits and vegetables will be grown, and Provo and Pleasant Grove will become one solid City."[26]

According to the same source, Young also predicted the coming of Geneva Steel—the opposite of a garden. Mormons looked forward to both. And they came to pass. The bench became an orchard—and eventually a commercial strip. Contrary to the folk prophecy, agriculturalists lost their place as Provo and Pleasant Grove merged. Farmers sold out to developers. Even the LDS Church sold out. No longer do families gather to pick fruit as volunteers at church-owned "welfare farms." Hardly any Saints can their own produce anymore. On the one hand, local Mormons have abandoned a large part of their pioneer heritage. On the other hand, Latter-day Saints on the Wasatch Front have fulfilled the larger ambition of their pioneer ancestors while destroying the old Mormon landscape. If Brother Brigham could have accommodated 500,000 fellow believers in Utah Valley, would he have done it? In the twinkling of an eye.

::: Today this solid city beneath Mount Timpanogos looks much like any other suburb in postwar America except for one thing: each housing development has an accompanying Mormon ward house (akin to a parish building). By necessity the LDS Church stays active in Utah Valley real estate; in fact the Church often buys land for ward houses in anticipation of growth. To keep costs down, the Church, like any other suburban developer, builds from a few standard plans. Its congregational buildings are the architectural equivalent of chain stores. A cookie-cutter ward house and a cookie-cutter subdivision often go up simultaneously. In these cases, realtors advertise "church lots"—addresses where (Mormon) homebuyers will have the luxury of walking to church. This luxury is commonplace. In Utah Valley, it's actually a challenge to be remote from a ward house. For instance, as of 2000, at least one dozen churches stood within a three-mile radius of my childhood home near the mouth of Provo Canyon—and the neighborhood was not yet filled.

Organizationally and spatially, the LDS Church grows by replication and division, like a cellular organism. The cell, as it were, is the ward, which contains 200–500 congregants. Multiple wards can share a single church space by meeting at staggered times on Sundays. When the number of wards exceeds the scheduling capacity of the facility, a new chapel will be authorized (using general tithing funds). In related fashion, a ward's boundaries will be reduced when the ward's population exceeds the capacity of the meeting room. For example, the Edgemont Second Ward might split into the Edgemont Second and Third Wards. Several contiguous wards make up a "stake" (managed by a "stake president"), and when its number of component wards exceeds administrative capacity, the stake reproduces. Much as wards compose a stake, stakes compose a "temple district" assigned to a particular temple. Predictably, once the user population of a district exceeds the capacity of its temple, the LDS Church moves to construct a new temple.

Mormon temples differ in almost every way from Mormon ward houses. Temples are sacred and private, whereas ward houses are (comparatively) secular and public. The church doubles as a community center; it contains a chapel, a basketball court, a stage, a kitchen, a library, and a playroom, not to mention various classrooms, conference rooms, and offices. The sign out front says "VISITORS WELCOME," and visitors in street clothes wouldn't feel uncomfortable. The building deserves but does not demand reverence. In contrast, a temple features a stone-engraved inscription—"THE HOUSE OF THE LORD"—that announces its solemn purpose. These grand, oversized structures stand apart from their surroundings. They are fenced off and closed to the public; indeed they are closed to most Latter-day Saints. Only adult Mormons carrying "temple recommends" can enter. The recommend is a renewable identity card issued to a worthy member after a rigorous ecclesiastical interview. Though not open on Sundays, temples host the holiest rites of Mormonism. Templegoers perform secret ceremonies in special white clothes. Temples are also used for "baptisms for the dead" and "celestial marriages." (Mormons believe that conjugal unions sealed within a temple may endure beyond our time on Earth.) To the devout, temples are divine enclosures representing the highest in spiritual life and architectural achievement. To outsiders, most temples look like amalgams of a fairy-tale castle and a capitol building. Stunning if not lovely, they lend themselves to artistic reproduction. In the modern consumer age, they have become the leading folk symbols of Mormonism, available as engravings, prints, miniatures, magnets, and in every other possible format. Since the middle of the twentieth century, temple-themed gravestones have been a popular way for Utah Saints to remember their dead. A striking new headstone in the Salt Lake City cemetery combines motifs: it shows the spires of the Salt Lake Temple rising above the crest of Mount Timpanogos.

As symbols, temples are exceptionally powerful because of their landmark status. This fact is strikingly apparent along the Wasatch Front, where spired temples in Logan, Ogden, Bountiful, Salt Lake, South Jordan, American Fork, and Provo rival the mountains themselves as beloved landscape features. Anyone driving at night along a 100-mile stretch of I-15 rarely loses sight of at least one of these brightly illuminated buildings. In a real way, these mountainous buildings function like mountains: people use them to orient themselves, to make mental maps. And indeed many Mormons extend this practice to the whole Earth: a common wall decoration in Utah homes is a world map with pushpins identifying the locations of temples. By the end of 2000, the Church operated over 100 temples—half of them less than three years old. In 1997 the Church started building "mini-temples" beyond the Wasatch Front. It had proved impractical and prohibitively expensive to continue erecting temples on the scale of the landmark Utah structures.

Currently Utah Valley has two houses of the Lord. The first, the Provo Temple, has a spectacular mountain setting at the mouth of Rock Canyon. Opened in 1972, this facility reached capacity use by 1990 as a result of residential growth and the expansion of the Missionary Training Center and BYU. Church planners recognized that a new temple serving the boomtowns of northern Utah Valley would alleviate the crowding problem. In 1993 LDS officials broke ground in American Fork at the site of a former welfare farm. In 1996 they welcomed the faithful to the Mount Timpanogos Temple. Even before it was finished, the "Timp Temple" joined "Timp" itself as a key feature in the local symbolic landscape. LDS leaders distributed an architectural drawing of the temple-to-be to all children in the temple district with instructions to hang it by their beds. In July 1995 more than 10,000 Mormons gathered to watch a gold-leafed statue of the Angel Moroni placed atop the building's spire. Public schools released youngsters to witness the event. The next year, 158,000 people attended the dedication ceremonies.

Mormons love reciting numbers like this. Along with the tally of members and missionaries, the sum of temples is the LDS Church's favorite statistic. Many officials encourage the folk belief—often repeated uncritically by the media—that Mormonism is the "world's fastest-growing religion." Every six months at General Conference, church leaders promulgate new population figures and temple plans. The modern identity of Mormonism demands constant increase. As of 2000 the Church claimed approximately 11 million baptized members. The number of *active* members was much, much lower, but the Church did not advertise that statistic. Exaggeration notwithstanding, Mormondom has grown dramatically as a result of natural increase in Utah and conversions outside. The majority of recent conversions have occurred in Latin America. Since the 1990s the membership rolls of the LDS Church have included more people outside the United States than within. On the surface, then, Mormonism has metamorphosed from a U.S. religion to a hemispheric one. Mormonism has shed its insularity, which was most pronounced between the 1890s and the 1960s. During those decades, when the Church no longer emphasized the Zionist doctrine of gathering, fewer foreign-born converts contributed to the diversity of Utah by migrating there.

Mount Timpanogos Temple with its eponymous landform, 2006. Note the U.S. flag. (Courtesy of Wikimedia Commons, http://commons.wikimedia.org)

In the 1960s the Church developed the concept of multiple Zions and began looking outward again. The goal now was to become a world religion; the method was a standardized missionary program. To a remarkable degree, this program worked.

However, a regionalist worldview lingers among multigenerational church members in the "Book of Mormon Belt"—Utah and southeastern Idaho. Utah Saints still refer to their homeland as "Zion" (and, less commonly, "Deseret"). Here, in what geographers call the "Mormon Culture Region," the Saints remain a gathered people, and their latent ethnicity resurfaces every July at pioneer parades and Dutch-oven cookouts. The growing gap between these "ethnic" Mormon-Americans—from whom church leadership and church funding overwhelmingly draws—and the diverse group of foreign converts presents a challenge to the religion.[27]

The coexistence of an older, inward-looking church and a newer, outward-looking one was apparent at the open house of the Mount Timpanogos Temple in 1996. The Church uses such open houses as proselytizing opportunities. Anyone may take a guided tour of a temple between its completion and its dedication; many curious non-Mormons come for a look. In American Fork, nonmembers had the opportunity to talk to missionaries, watch a movie, read brochures—all of which emphasized a few simple points: *this is the church of Christ; this is the Lord's house; families can be forever.* LDS officials package these points like media professionals. The Church stays on message. Alongside this formality, however, the laity maintains its own traditions. Mormons love attending these open houses, too. Outside the white granite building in American Fork, local visitors could pick up a one-dollar commemorative edition of a local newspaper composed entirely of amateur pieces. Unlike the missionary literature, this informal publication was meant for Mormons; it had the resonance of peoplehood. The collected paintings, poems, inspirational stories, and songs (complete with piano scorings) employed ethnoregional vocabulary.

For example, one teenaged contributor wrote about "the Game": "You see, the Game was a very important, very special part of our childhood years. Its rules were completely uncomplicated—whenever we traveled anywhere in the car, the first person to see the beautiful white building and yell 'I see the temple!' won." A woman from American Fork shared her belief that the windburst that felled her favorite plum tree was providential, as it enabled her to see the Angel Moroni atop the new temple from her porch. In addition to such personal essays, the newspaper contained a pseudoscholarly piece by a local man on the many "cosmic mountain orientations" of the temple. For example, "the sun rises on April 6/7 [the Church's founding date] on the due east alignment to the central summit of Mount

Timpanogos, matching Solomon's Temple alignment to the summit of Mount of Olives on the same sunrise date." The author also found great significance in the "Indian name of the mountain," which "in the Aztecan-Nahuatl language branch can be translated as an 'exalted golden mountain across water'." He implied that the Indian descendants of the ancient Lamanites—as described in the Book of Mormon—had prepared this place for a temple.[28]

This translation of "Timpanogos" is bogus, but the temple's name *is* significant. It stands out because it commemorates a landform. Of the fifty temples built before this one, only two others have topographic names: the Salt Lake Temple (1896) and the Jordan River Temple (1981). By intention or coincidence, those names highlight the geographic analogy between Utah and the Holy Land—an interlake river nourishing a dead sea. If the Church had wanted to complete the biblical and hydrographic parallelism it would have looked to Utah's Galilee. The new sacred building at American Fork would have been named for the lake next door. It would have been called the Utah Lake Temple.

Chances are this idea never arose in the Temple Department at the Church Office Building in downtown Salt Lake City. As of the 1990s, the lake meant too little to notice, and the mountain meant too much to ignore. Besides, in its pursuit of globalization, the modern LDS Church downplays its Zionist past. Downplays rather than disavows, for the Church still needs its Utah base. As a temple name, "Timpanogos" works both ways. Many Utah Mormons continue to read local significance into Isaiah's prophecy about the "mountain of the Lord's House." Thus Mount Timpanogos *can* (to those who know and care) reference Zion; but as a mountain with a nonbiblical name that became loved through secular means in the twentieth century, it has no necessary or official connection to Zionism. Out of the present and the past, Latter-day Saints have found a way to make a Zion's mount without Mount Zion.

* * *

⁝⁝⁝ So again a paradox: even as Timpanogos became more urbane (through Sundance), it became more sacred (though the temple). At first glace, Robert Redford's resort and the LDS house of worship seem unrelated. The resort is exogenous; the temple is endogenous. The core users of the former rarely interact with the core users of the latter. Tellingly, a private, exclusive drug rehab retreat has opened next to the resort. Some local Mormons do of course ski and dine at Sundance, yet they don't define the place. The resort and the temple inhabit separate cultural worlds on separate sides of the mountain. However, these two sites of place attachment do share a connection besides Timpanogos itself. Both built environments draw sustenance from the urbanization of the American West—and the concomitant decline of its agricultural landscapes. Mormonism's interior sacred space—that of the temples—has expanded even as one of Zion's two exterior sacred spaces—farmland—has contracted. Only the sacred highland persists. As Utah Valley loses its fields and pastures, the Wasatch Range in general and Mount Timpanogos in particular grow in recreational and spiritual importance. You can get away to the mountain after work or on the weekend; and even when you can't, your spirit can be lifted by the pristine magnificence visible above the hazy valley air. Local (Mormon) residents have learned to look at "Timp" the way they look at a temple—as a refuge, a landmark, a symbol, and an inspiration. In 1980, near the end of her life, Ora Chipman, a prominent resident of American Fork, said it best: "One of the first things I do when I get up in the morning is to go to my bedroom—we have nine windows in it—and the first thing I do is go look at Timp. That's my inspiration, and I've got to hold the high standards of life because there is Timpanogos."[29] For her and countless others, the mountain is a mirror.

Despite the fact that Utah is generally hostile to land preservation and friendly to land development, Utahns have a deep regard for place. Indeed, one is challenged to name another state where the dominant population displays more "topophilia." The interesting point is this: neither the general sense of place Utah Mormons feel for their homeland nor the specific sense of place they feel for Mount Timpanogos has led to any major homegrown campaign for the preservation of vernacular landscapes or farmland or open space or wilderness. Many environmentalists speak of cultivating place attachment like raising social consciousness—a precursor to sustainability. That may be wishful thinking. After all, sense is not the same as sensibility.

III

Marking a Mountain:
Indian Play

7

Renaming the Land

Making "Timp" was a project based on visualization and recreation: getting people to see a massif as a mount and getting them to hike to the top. Marking "Timp"—filling the landform with meanings—was a related, concurrent process. As we have seen, some of the meanings involved science and religion. But the most significant meanings involved Indians—or at least an *idea* of Indians.

The "Indianness" of Mount Timpanogos begins with its name. Each day, unthinkingly, Americans utter foreign words like "Chicago," "Wyoming," "Timpanogos." Such words have been familiarized through use. Rarely do we stop to wonder what these "Indian" place-names mean. Only when place-names are considered in groups—as *genres* of naming—can we understand their cultural significance. "Indian" place-names are like old municipal monuments: we see them, we live with them, but we're not too sure how they got there. In fact, an important minority of "Indian" place-names has nothing to do with native peoples; these utterly fake, "Indian-sounding" names stand for verbal dispossession. The greater numbers of semiauthentic "Indian" place-names are also problematic, for they commemorate things like appropriation and miscommunication.

Names have been misheard, misconstrued, even misplaced. Mount Timpanogos got its name almost by accident. As appended to a peak, the Ute-derived word "Timpanogos" has come to connote Indianness rather than a particular native people. As the landmark called "Timp" took on a life of its own, so did its "Indian" name. One cultural artifact supported the other.

::: "Names are magic," wrote Whitman. "One word can pour such a flood through the soul."[1] Poets value names for their compact power. Corporations reward consultants for naming their brands and products, for consecrating them. Names are chosen—often ceremonially—to carry deep meaning. Yet names can be the emptiest of words, mere vessels for meaning. Frequently they are nonsensical; and the quantity of nonsense just increases with time. While a language adapts constantly, its names change slowly. No one speaks Anglo-Saxon anymore, yet the map of England contains countless Anglo-Saxon names. They've been left behind like the relics of Stonehenge. Names may persist in usage (or in books) long after their original associations have been lost. Some of these anachronisms acquire new resonance; the rest hang around as long as they function. They adorn and clutter our lives and landscapes.

Place-names—also called toponyms—can be divided into categories based on the type of place (landforms, geopolities, streets, structures, and so on). They can also be grouped by derivation:

Descriptive names describe something people see or otherwise sense about a place. Descriptive names may be general (Green River) or particular (Trin-Alcove Bend).

Associative names consist of at least two nouns that have a site-specific association. Thus a lake in the Sawtooth Mountains came to be called Redfish Lake for the salmon that ended their migration there.

Incident names reference a site-specific historical incident. For example, El Vado de los Padres (Crossing of the Fathers) was the spot where Domínguez and Escalante crossed the Colorado River on 7 November 1776.

Transfer names simply move the key element of an existing place-name to a new one. The Salmon National Forest is headquartered in Salmon, Idaho; both were named after the Salmon River.

Possessive names indicate possession—if not ownership—of landscape features. Lees Ferry on the Colorado River was originally operated by Emma and John D. Lee. ("Lees," not "Lee's"—officially, place-names cannot contain apostrophes.)

Inspirational names invoke the greatness of a place or celebrate the promise of a place. The Tibetan name for Mount Everest, Chomolungma, denotes the mountain as a deity. "Good" and "hope" are the commonest elements of English-language inspirational toponymy.

Three final categories deserve fuller explanation because they figure prominently in the history of "Indian" place-names:

Invented names are neologisms. In America, this practice found favor among town-builders, followed by suburban developers. Mexicali, Texarkana, and Kanorado are border towns. One of the settlers of Rolyat, Oregon, was an anagram-lover named Taylor. The founders of Minneapolis combined a Native American prefix and a Greek suffix. The name for Veyo, Utah, supposedly comes from "*v*irtue," "*e*nterprise," "*y*outh," and "*o*rder." Tolono, Illinois, is pure invention. Of the many aesthetic crimes committed by American name-coiners, the worst resulted in company-town names like Weslaco (Texas), Gamerco (New Mexico), and Upalco (Utah).

Commemorative names honor someone or something. Mount Everest is the (in)famous example, named by the British after Sir George Everest, a former surveyor-general of British India. In America, no one has been so honored as the first president, George Washington. Catholic saints and the less-than-saintly Christoforo Colombo have also been memorialized in quantity. Place-names sometimes commemorate animals and ideas, among many other things.

Assimilated names have been inherited or adopted from predecessors who spoke a different language. Rarely do the original names survive unchanged. This is especially the case when a written language encounters an oral language. Assimilation may involve translation, alphabetic representation, or visual transferal (when both languages are written in the same alphabet). Alphabetic representation can ultimately lead to phonetic transferal; for instance, an oral word initially represented as "Moskitu-auke" became "Mosquito Hawk." It's easy to find false meaning in foreign words.[2]

"Mount Timpanogos" represents the geographic transfer of an assimilated word. Only in a narrow or ironic sense, then, can it be called a native place-name. *Indianist* works better. "Mount Timpanogos" represents that group of officially sanctioned U.S. place-names that include non-English words of real or purported indigenous derivation.[3]

I focus on official names because they are the ones that appear on the National Map, and because the process of state legitimization is important. Starting around 1900, the federal government began cataloging and rationalizing the nation's names; a master list was subsequently codified through the detailed mapping of the U.S. Geological Survey. This record—the Geographic Names Information System—is a codex of awesome extent. Yet this database of 2 million terms does not include many of the indigenous place-names currently in use on Indian reservations. Nor does it include the "countercartography" of superseded Indian place-names remembered by natives long after the places in question have been seized and renamed. According to government regulation, a cartographic feature can have only one official name.[4]

Needless to say, Indian peoples did not control the process of state legitimization. Neither did they direct the creation of Indianist names, although often they supplied linguistic information. Names like "Mount Timpanogos" are outwardly bicultural, inwardly monocultural. Only in Hawai'i—an exceptional state in most respects—can one find a preponderance of indigenous names on the National Map. Of the Lower Forty-eight states, only Washington and Oregon contain concentrations of *cross*-cultural (and thereby non-Indianist) place-names. These names come out of the Chinook jargon, a lingua franca used by Indians, Britons, and early Yankees in the region. The temporary existence of the jargon marked the temporary existence of a "middle ground," a time and place when natives and invaders of approximately even power needed to try to understand each other. More typically, lopsided frontier contact promoted the demise of native languages. From a linguistic point of view, then, Indianist toponymy represents the "benevolent" side of asymmetric power relations. In the best cases, there is a direct link between an Indianist place-name and an Indian word used by Indians to denote the same place. For example, Wisconsin's Shishebogama Lake and Sissabagama Lake both come from an Ojibwa word defined as "lake with arms running in all directions."[5]

Of course, Indian words that appear in Indianist place-names are at best written approximations of speech. Phonetic notation is an art as well as a science. But precious few of the anglophone Americans responsible for Indianist place-names were linguists; most didn't even speak the source language. They tried to write down Indian words in English, a language notorious for its irregular spelling. English also places structural demands on place-names: customarily they contain two parts, a specific followed by a generic. Generics are topographic terms like "river," "run," "brook," "lake," "coulee," "wash." Even a well-represented native word must be mixed with a non-native word to create an English/Indianist toponym. Viewed as a two-part whole, a "Paiute" name like Skutumpah Creek is actually a bilingual blend.

Is there a right way to pronounce Skutumpah or Yosemite or any of the rest of these names? Timpanogos is now uttered tim-pə-noʹ-gəs. Because the word was first notated by Spaniards, it was presumably once pronounced more like tēmʹ-pä-no-gōs. Who knows how a Ute would have pronounced the source word some 200 years ago? The oral and aural parts of nomenclature are the faintest parts of a history full of silences. Since invaders did the most renaming in America, it follows that they committed the greatest errors of pronunciation.

"I've come across 140 ways to spell Kansas," writes William Least Heat-Moon, "and, if you include the confused Ac-, Es-, Ex-, Ok-, Uk- forms at times applied to the tribe, I've found 171 variations that employ every letter of the alphabet except b, f, and v. The question comes up, if whites couldn't get a three- or six-letter name correct, what else couldn't they get right?" Of course, Native Americans could garble names, too—given the opportunity. An intriguing example comes from Indian Territory (Oklahoma), where some Creeks, having been removed from Georgia, named a new settlement after a treaty signed in New York City. The name they gave was Nuyaka.[6]

In the precontact period, Native Americans seem to have shared a common attitude toward toponymy. Their place-names are preponderantly and richly descriptive, whereas Anglo-American place-names are disproportionately commemorative and possessive. These nomenclatural differences mirror different assumptions about individuality, community, and property. Linguistic structures also contributed to difference. Many indigenous languages allow place-names to combine specific and generic elements into one word that may function like an English phrase. Examples from Canyon de Chelly on the Navajo Reservation include (by way of translation) "at cottonwoods-stretch-across-in-a-line cove" and "the-elevated-elongate-rock-lies-on-its-side's ruin." These unofficial names are intimately local: they summon the geographic knowledge that comes from long-term residence. In Algonquian New England, many names identified natural features by their seasonal use-value. "The purpose of such names," writes William Cronon, "was to turn the landscape into a map which, if studied carefully, literally gave a village's inhabitants the information they needed to sustain themselves." By contrast, American settlers (and surveyors even more) seldom knew a place at the moment they christened it; naming preceded occupancy. When settlers did create descriptive names, their specifics tended to be general—Muddy Creek ad nauseam.[7]

It's important not to romanticize Amerindian place-names at the expense of Anglo-American toponymy. Settler names may lack richness and specificity, but they often possess directness, humor, and originality. Nevertheless, it seems fair to say that indigenous place-names can be uniquely powerful. For example, Bear Lodge—the Lakota name for Devils Tower—comes from a myth about a monster bear that explains the creation of the landform. Generally speaking, Amerindian groups lived in their sacred geographies—their holy lands. Their creation stories included local landscape features. Nomenclature, narrative, and environment sustained one another. Anthropologist Keith Basso has recorded conversations among reservation Apaches that consist almost entirely of uncontextualized utterances of place-names. By "speaking with names," these Apaches invoke meaningful site-specific stories. Their place-names, like the places themselves, function as mnemonics.[8] Similar incident names (historical and mythological) abounded in North America in the precontact and early contact periods.

Story-names thrive in certain social settings. Within a small, tight, place-based group—a family, clan, tribe, or sect—incident names resonate because everyone knows the story behind the name. In larger, more complex, more atomized societies, the stories tend to fade from collective memory. The National Map does, nonetheless, contain a few official names that can act as public mnemonics because of historic associations they have acquired. The most memorable associations are violent: the Alamo, Mountain Meadows, Sand Creek, Wounded Knee, Ludlow, Pearl Harbor, Waco, Oklahoma City, and Columbine are examples. Yet few people—not counting historians—could or would employ such names in conversation as narrative shorthand. The closest nonnative analogue to the Apache story-name comes from contemporary Mormonism, which has developed its own sacred American geography. Latter-day Saints can invoke early Church chronology through a canonized set of place-names: the Sacred Grove, Hill Cumorah, Kirtland, Independence, Hahn's Mill, Nauvoo, Carthage Jail, Winter Quarters, Emigration Canyon. Folded within these names are rousing, standardized stories that narrate the religion of Joseph Smith from 1820 through 1847. This sacred narrative-by-names advances to the Great Basin, then stops.

⋮⋮⋮ In the Great Basin, in 1776, a pair of Spanish priests recorded in their journal the first versions of the written word "Timpanogos." On their abortive journey from Santa Fe to Monterey, Fray Francisco Atanasio Domínguez and Fray Francisco Silvestre Vélez de Escalante rested in Utah Valley near the mouth of the Provo River. They named the locale El Valle de Nuetra Señora de la Merced de los Timpano-cuitzis. Confusingly, they also referred to the valley's inhabitants as the Timpanogotzis and the Timpanois. Clearly, they struggled to capture in letters the sound of this Southern Numic word, which has many other guises in the historical record: Timpanoags, Timpanoa-guts, Tumpanogots, Tim-pa-nogs, Timpanigos, Tin-pan-a-gos, Tim-panodes, Timpanogotzis, Timpagtzis, Timpipas, Timpana, Timpany, Tinpany, Tenpenny, Tinpannah, Timpanosis, Timponayas, Tim-pan-oie, Tim-Pa-Noy(s), Timpananunts, Tipana-nuu-ci, Timpenaguchya, Timpannyutas, Timpananute, Timpaiavats, Timpanoautzis . . . Domínguez and Escalante got around the problem by calling the natives *Lagunas* (Lake People) or *Come Pescado* (Fish-Eaters). According to the Spaniards, the locals took their name from the lake (Utah Lake), which they called Timpanogó. These lake people had neighbors to the north who lived by the "other lake" (Great Salt Lake). Contact between the two groups occurred through "the end of the gap of La Sierra Blanca de los Timpanois (which is the same one where they reside), to the north by northwest from where these are." "La Sierra Blanca" (White Mountain Range) referred to the entire mountainous area to the east of the valley. The "gap" referred to the narrows of the Jordan River through the Traverse Range—a long, low ridge that perpendicularly abuts the Wasatch Range.[9]

Although the Catholic friars earned the distinction of transcribing "Timpanogos," their mapmaking companion, Don Bernardo de Miera Y Pacheco, actually did more to popularize the place-name. In 1778 Miera produced several versions of a map depicting the area circumambulated by the expedition. On it Utah Lake and the Great Salt Lake were joined in the shape of an hourglass; the entire water-body was called Laguna de los Timpanogos. To the east, Miera drew a rugged mountain range—clearly the Wasatch—which he marked "Sierra de los Timpanogos." Miera's map became the foundation of Great Basin cartography. Alexander von Humboldt, among many others, borrowed from it; others elaborated on it. In 1819 an American cartographer published a map that showed a River Timpanogos flowing westward from the lake into San Francisco Bay. This misinformation took years to dry up. An early emigrant guide to Oregon described Lake Timpanogos as the source of one branch of the Willamette River. Not until the congressionally published cartography of David Burr (1839) and Charles Preuss (1848) was the mythical river removed. The new mapmakers erased Lake Timpanogos and replaced it with two separate water bodies, Utah Lake and Great Salt Lake. In the 1840s the mountain range to the east was alternately called the Wa(h)satch and the Timpanogos (or Timpan-ozu). The former won out, but Timpanogos found new cartographic life as the name of Utah Lake's main tributary.[10]

In 1848, responding to news of the Treaty of Guadalupe Hidalgo, which ended the Mexican War, abolitionist-poet John Greenleaf Whittier wrote a poem called "The Crisis." To describe American's sudden, problematic empire, Whittier summoned names from a map:

Across the Stony Mountains, o'er the desert's drouth and sand,
The circles of our empire touch the Western Ocean's strand;
From slumberous Timpanogos to Gila, wild and free,
Flowing down from Nuevo-Leon to California's sea;
And from the mountains of the East to Santa Rosa's shore,
The eagles of Mexitli shall beat the air no more.[11]

The "Stony Mountains" referred to the Rockies, the approximate eastern edge of the New West. The exact southern border of the war-won territory was indeed the Gila River. The northern boundary was less defined, but the Timpanogos River served as a handy topographical marker. Published to a wide audience just one year before the Mormons colonized Utah Valley, "The Crisis" may be used to symbolize the movement of "Timpanogos" from Spanish to English. The subsequent meanings accrued by the word belong to U.S. nomenclatural history.

::: Before anglophone name-givers could cover their maps with Indianist names—and they did so with abandon in the antebellum period—they had to learn to admire native languages. In the seventeenth and eighteenth centuries, educated people agreed that language reflected social progress: the more primitive a people, the more primitive their tongue. British-American commentators seldom had nice things to say about Indian speech. After John Eliot translated the Bible into a dialect of Algonquian, Cotton Mather marveled at his colleague's patience with this "tedious" language:

> if their alphabet be short, I am sure the words composed of it are long enough to tire the patience of any scholar in the world; they are *Sesquipedalia Verba* [foot-and-a-half-long words], of which their *linguo* is composed; one would think they have been growing ever since Babel . . . if I were to translate, *our loves,* it must be nothing shorter than *Noowomantammooonkanunonnash.*[12]

In Mather's Massachusetts, English nomenclature dominated the scene. This was especially true of town names. Although Puritans frequently built their settlements on the sites of Indian towns, and occasionally used the old names on a provisional basis, the final names—approved by the ecclesiastical courts or the later royal governors—

came almost exclusively from East Anglia. Only one of the sixty towns founded in Massachusetts Bay Colony before 1690 (Natick, a town established by John Eliot for "Praying Indian" converts) kept an Indian name. Indigenous nomenclature more commonly clung to natural features, especially streams and lakes. Hydrographic place-names did not receive as much governmental scrutiny; they typically emerged from local use. From the Puritan perspective, the unsettled world of nature easily accepted uncivilized names, whereas the civilized world of farms and fences deserved English names.[13]

Cotton Mather did not speak for everyone in colonial America. In 1685 William Penn (whose colony enjoyed better relations with Indians) wrote perhaps the earliest appreciation of Indian place-names. "I know not a Language spoken in Europe," he reported to his European supervisors, "that hath words of more sweetness or greatness, in Accent and Emphasis, than theirs; for Instance, *Octorockon*, *Rancocas*, *Ozicton*, *Shakamacon*, *Poquerim*, all of which are names of Places, and have Grandeur in them."[14]

The intellectual distance between those who disdained the guttural simplicity of Indian languages and those admired the euphonious simplicity of Indian languages was actually not so great. From the colonial period through the nineteenth century, Euro-American commentators agreed that native languages relied on metaphor over abstraction, evocation over description. It came down to aesthetics. Admirers heard poetry; detractors heard babble. Even detractors granted two points: Indian oratory was exceptional, and Indian nomenclature was noteworthy. Thomas Jefferson began the lionization of (male) Indian orators in 1785 with praise for the purported speech of Chief Logan. In the early national period, the "cult of the eloquent savage" attracted many more adherents. But whereas the unqualified admiration for Indian oratory focused on the *performance* of language, the qualified admiration for Indian toponymy focused on the language itself. In the early 1800s intellectuals began to rethink the relationships between language, race, and nationality. A new school of thought—represented by the Philadelphian Stephen Du Ponceau—extolled native languages as linguistic nonpareils. Du Ponceau argued for the severance of speech from mentality. Language did not reflect the inner qualities of its living speakers; instead it reflected the genius of ancient ancestors. In this sense, natives did not own their own names. Americans could appropriate them.[15]

Henry Schoolcraft, the leading investigator of native languages in the era before anthropology, advocated the selective adoption of native place-names. His advocacy was tellingly ambivalent. By his own example, Schoolcraft condoned the *invention* of "Indian" names. In 1832 Schoolcraft tramped and boated around the upper reaches of the Mississippi River as part of a government expedition. For explorers it had become an obsession to locate the "true" source of the great river. As luck would have it, Schoolcraft's detachment "discovered" the headwater lake. Then and there a flag was raised, and a name was given—Lake Itasca. Schoolcraft came up with this neologism by extracting three of five syllables from *veritas caput*, a Latin combination he took to mean "true source." Twenty years later, however, Schoolcraft the Indian authority revised his own history: "I enquired of Oza Windib the Indian name of the lake; he replied *Omushkos*, which is the Chippewa for Elk. Having previously got an inkling of some of their mythological and necromantic notions of the origin and mutations of the country, which permitted use of a female name for it, I denominated it ITASCA." Schoolcraft then appended a poem in which this "beauteous" female lake sheds tears. The sentimental writer Mary Eastman—whose husband did illustrations for Schoolcraft—later published a story about a lovesick Indian maiden named Itasca.[16]

Itasca was not unique: in other places, name preservation overlapped with name invention, and Indian ethnography blurred with Indianist fiction. Directly and indirectly, the spread of American literary romanticism encouraged Indianist place-naming. A surprising number of Indianist place-names come from literary texts. The process began with James Fenimore Cooper, whose usage of "Lake Horicon" as a substitute for Lake George found favor among New York locals. But it was Henry Wadsworth Longfellow who inspired the most Indianist names. His epic poem *The Song of Hiawatha* (1855) marked the climax of the Indianist vogue in American literature. Scores of place-names in the United States derive from Longfellow, who got most of his linguistic information from Schoolcraft, who did most of his research in the Great Lakes region. The names in question are Hiawatha (with 100+ hits spread across twenty-nine states in the current place-name database), Minnehaha (with 60+ hits spread across twenty-six states), Nokomis, Osseo, Wenonah, and Wabasso. A few of these names—those that appear in Minnesota and Wisconsin and Michigan—may have come from Indians themselves, but the spelling makes that possibility unlikely. Nokomis (a town in Wisconsin) probably comes from Longfellow. Okemos (a town in Michigan) possibly comes directly from the Ojibwa language.[17]

In the antebellum period, the loudest literary proponents of Indianist nomenclature came, like Longfellow, from New England. Not coincidentally, no other American region had more thoroughly displaced natives, their languages, and their names. In 1834 the "Sweet Singer of Hartford," Lydia Sigourney, wrote a famous poem of regret called "Indian Names":

> Ye say they all have passed away,
>   That noble race and brave,
> That their light canoes have vanished
>   From off the crested wave;
> That 'mid the forests where they roamed
>   There rings no hunter's shout,
> But their name is on your waters,
>   Ye may not wash it out.

Rappahannock and Niagara, Ontario and Ohio. To Sigourney, such names signified a partial restitution for sins committed against Indians: at least "their memory liveth on your hills."[18]

Remarkably, some of her regional contemporaries put poetry into action. Between 1846 and 1861 a professor at Amherst College orchestrated numerous rechristenings of landforms, especially hills. The Reverend Edward Hitchcock bemoaned the "flat and vulgar" names attached to the scenery of western Massachusetts. He preferred Indian and classical nomenclature. So he invented a tradition. Together with college students and local dignitaries, he would climb an area summit, and, accompanied by speeches, cheers, poems, toasts, and songs, he would bestow a new name—Mount Mettawompe, Mount Notunk, Mount Nonotuck, Mount Norwottuck, Mount Pocumtuck. In 1855, at one of these picnic celebrations, Hitchcock's students staged a meeting between an Indian and a Puritan. The mock English settler objected to the "college sprouts giving tarnation hard names to their hills and spending so much sympathy for the pesky red skins." The student dressed in feathers replied: "Pale Face, upon what right do you base your claim to this mountain, once the home of the Indian? . . . let the name which has been given this mountain summit rest upon it forever, for it is fitting there should remain behind *some* trace, *some* memorial of the dying redman."[19]

This melancholy refrain—a strain of romantic racism—would be repeated again and again in the nineteenth century. Indians die; only their names remain. It didn't much matter who the Indians were or what their names meant. However, the resting places for these names did matter. It's no accident that both Hitchcock and Sigourney focused on topography. Indian place-names, like Indians themselves, had powerful associations with nature. Only one other type of cartographic feature inspired such contemplation about Indian place-names: the polity. Oddly, the more general the polity, the more likely it was to receive an Indianism. Of American cities, perhaps one or 2 percent now have such names. Of American counties, roughly 7 percent have them.[20] By contrast, half of all American states go by Indianist names such as Utah.

::: Polity place-names carry the weight of the body politic. They identify not only a place but also a people. As such they are particularly revealing. In a federal system like the United States, state names

are as symbolic as the national name. In fact the United States technically has no name. "America" is an abbreviation of "the United States
of America," which itself is a governmental description, not a national appellation. In the early 1800s, aware of this problem, certain
Americans proposed an Indian name for the nation. Although the
idea failed, Congress did establish a pattern of bestowing Indianist
names on states.

At the 1787 Constitutional Convention in Philadelphia, delegates
were apparently too engrossed in the ideas of political science and the
business of political compromise to debate a national name. Perhaps
Jefferson, the founder with the best ear for poetry, would have raised
the issue—but he was away in France. It was Jefferson, of course, who
penned the term "the United States" in the Declaration of Independence. In 1776 this was a name of convenience, not of consecration.
Over time, however, this ad hoc name became fixed in usage. By the
time commentators raised a fuss, it was probably too late to change.
The perceived quandary was less about the name than about its deriv-
atives. As the prominent Bostonian William ("Judge") Tudor remarked
in 1799, "To denominate ourselves *Americans* instead of Englishmen,
was as incorrect as it would be for the individuals who now compose
the French Republic, to relinquish the name of Frenchmen, and call
themselves *Europeans*." Out of mocking contempt and linguistic propriety, British authors referred to the "the ci-devant [former] colonists" or "the people of the revolted colonies." For their part, name-
conscious republicans experimented with "United Statesans" and
"Usonians." The best candidate for a replacement name was "Columbia" (with its euphonious derivative, "Columbian"). Federal officials
liked the name well enough to give it to the district surrounding the
capital in 1790. Another suggestion—promoted by Jedidiah Morse in
the first American gazetteer—was "Fredonia." Morse felt that the ac-
quisition of the Louisiana Territory (1803) provided a sufficiently
symbolic moment to initiate a name change. If so, it was the last good
moment; in 1819 a different republic in America—in *South* America—claimed the name of Columbus.[21]

Nationalism affected nomenclature at the county and municipal levels, too—first with a flood of patriotic and neoclassical names, then with a stream of Indianist names. The state of New York alone acquired at least forty neoclassical town-names from the 1790s through the 1820s, including Delphi, Athens, Ithaca, Syracuse, Troy, and Rome. Eventually such names became a source of embarrassment. In 1838 a refined citizen wrote a "Treatise on the Art of Naming Places" that criticized the wanton imitation and repetition in American nomenclature. Enough with Syracuse and Springfield! "Every body who has been in Europe knows that our Indian names of places are exceedingly admired; not merely for intrinsic beauty, which they sometimes want, but as original and dignified by their associations." Admitting that Indian words frequently sounded "uncouth and dissonant," the author suggested that they be "trimmed and softened." "Such a process has actually taken place in most of our current Indian names," he correctly observed. "The object is, not to preserve the pure form of the Indian word, but to have an original, distinctive name." This sentiment shows up repeatedly in the periodical literature of the 1830s and 1840s. It was said that the "inventive genius" of Americans did not show in their place-names; Indian words, judiciously altered, could supply the need. Of all the unoriginal names, New York City evoked the most shame: America's "great mart" bore the name of a duke. Bring back *Manhattan*, the city's primal name, wrote the city's literati. (They got their wish—partially and belatedly—in 1898 with the incorporation of the five boroughs.)[22]

In the 1840s a group of Manhattanites revived the issue of national nomenclature and tied it to the contemporary vogue of Indianist naming. Washington Irving, under his nom de plume Geoffrey Crayon, announced the cause:

> We want a NATIONAL NAME. We want it poetically, and we want it politically. ["The United States"] is a clumsy, lumbering title, yet still it is not distinctive; for we have now the United States of Central America; and heaven knows how many "United States" may spring up under the Proteus changes of Spanish America . . . I want an appellation that

shall tell at once, and in a way not to be mistaken, that I be-
long to this very portion of America, geographical and polit-
ical, to which it is my pride and happiness to belong; that
I am of the Anglo-Saxon race which founded this Anglo-
Saxon empire in the wilderness; and that I have no part or
parcel with any other race or empire, Spanish, French, or
Portuguese, in either of the Americas. Such an appellation,
Sir, would have magic in it.

After this rousing overture, Irving put forward "United States of Appalachia" and the even more magical "United States of Alleghania."
Both appellations were prettied-up versions of Indian words; both referred to "that noble chain of mountains" that formed the "backbone" of the land. Such names had the "merit of originality, and of
belonging to the country; and they would remain as reliques of the native lords of the soil, when every other vestige had disappeared."
The Alleghanian Anglo-Saxons—the new lords, the new natives—deserved such names.[23]

Irving, one of America's top writers, published his proposal in *The
Knickerbocker,* the preeminent literary magazine in the country. Published in New York City, *The Knickerbocker* spoke for a loose fraternity who in their own estimation represented everything sophisticated
in America. Some of these men also belonged to the New-York Historical Society, which in 1845 created a special committee to study
Irving's proposal. The committee consisted of Charles Fenno Hoffman, David Dudley Field, and Henry Rowe Schoolcraft. Hoffman (an
editor) and Field (a lawyer) belonged to the urban elite; Schoolcraft, a
relative newcomer to the city, contributed frontier expertise. In its report, the distinguished group went through the various name possibilities. After reluctantly ruling out Columbia, the committee argued for
a name taken from one of "the eternal works of the Almighty, which
man cannot remove or change, and which belong to the whole country. It must be sought in our mountains, or our lakes, or our rivers."
But the Rockies were "too little familiar to us"; the Great Lakes might
as well be Canadian; and "Mississippi" had been claimed by a state.

That left the eastern chain of mountains. Siding with Irving, the committee offered "The Republic of Allegania." How would such a change be effected? This Whiggish group of men presented an appropriately Whiggish solution: they would communicate the subject to America's better men, who might mold the public mind; eventually Congress would rubber-stamp the change.[24]

As it happened, better men did not all agree. In the ensuing debate, "Vesperia" and "Columbia" and "Washington" were all offered as alternative names. Speaking for the Maryland Historical Society, one man defended "the United States of America" and attacked "Allegania." It was the wrong kind of Indian name, he said; it referred to a vicious and treacherous tribe that had retreated down the Mississippi River after being defeated by the more civilized Iroquois. Other correspondents ridiculed the idea of naming a country after any mountain range, much less this one ("a mere clod of earth" compared with the Alps). At a rancorous follow-up meeting, Hoffman denied that his committee ever dreamed of changing America's political name; they merely wished for a *poetical* name. British authors could fashion verse out of Albion, Anglia, Caledonia, Hibernia, and Britannia. Didn't United Statesers deserve the same?[25]

Although murmurs of complaint would persist for decades to come, the national name debate ended in 1845 without resolution. The problem was solved in another way. By virtue of its growing power, the United States came to own the word "America." Concurrently the nation came to possess much more of the continent. In 1846 the United States of America attacked the United States of Mexico. After this war of conquest, the matter of territorial and state names emerged as the leading issue of political nomenclature. The newly won *American* West needed to be organized and named. The task fell to Congress.

::: The Compromise of 1850 created the state of California and the territories of New Mexico and Utah. The Mormons had previously applied for territorial status under the name of their choosing,

Deseret. Congress overruled that choice. Until this moment it had been customary for the national legislature simply to affirm local usage. More often than not, American settlers came to call their region by the name of its major river—which usually carried an Indian name—or by its major indigenous group. Although only two of the thirteen colonies had Indianist names, nine of the next thirteen American states did; between 1791 and 1847 the Union accepted Kentucky, Tennessee, Ohio, Mississippi, Illinois, Alabama, Missouri, Arkansas, and Michigan. Without apparent intention, a naming pattern had been established. "Deseret" did not follow. The name wasn't Indian; it wasn't even American. The word came from the Book of Mormon, which Joseph Smith had translated from "Reformed Egyptian," in which "Deseret" means "honeybee." (The beehive, the state symbol of Utah, suggests industry and order, two qualities prized by Mormons.)

The origin of "Utah" is also exotic—coming from New Mexico in the Spanish period. The word derives from "Yuta," a Hispanicized version of a native word—possibly Western Apache for "one that is higher up." As early as the 1620s, the Franciscan father Gerónimo de Zárate Salmerón heard from the Jémez Indians about the "Qusutas" who lived to the mountainous north. "Qusutas" eventually became "Yutas," which until the mid-nineteenth century remained the favored exogenous term for the Southern Numic speakers now called Utes (called *Nuche* by themselves). A nineteenth-century authority defined "Yutas" as "they who live on mountains." In English-language sources, the word appeared as Eutaw, Gutah, Juta, Utaw, Ute-ah, Yiuhta, and Youta before stabilizing as Utah. Whereas the Spaniards used "Yuta" to refer to *all* Utes, the Mormons used "Utah" to exclusively refer to the Fish-Eaters. The U-word also had four geographic referents for four coextensive entities—a lake, a valley, a stake, and a county. For instance, in 1853 Brigham Young reported to the residents of Great Salt Lake City that "it is only the Utah who have declared war on Utah." Translation: only the Lake Utes have raided the settlements of Utah Valley/Stake/County.[26]

At the national level, "Utah" had a whole different meaning. To easterners, the name brought one thing to mind—a *territory* that begged the "Mormon Question." In 1857, when President Brigham Young blustered that President James Buchanan had dispatched troops to put down the Latter-day Saints, he told his followers that "they constituted henceforth a free and independent state, to be known no longer as Utah, but by their own Mormon name of Deseret." His words turned out to be hot wind: in the aftermath of the "Utah War," Mormons pursued statehood in the regular way. Multiple Deseret constitutions went to Congress, where they faced intransigent anti-Mormon opposition. In 1872, at yet another constitutional convention, Mormon delegates debated the wisdom of retaining "Deseret" when this name "might be made a basis of prejudice." Others worried that the name could be confused with "desert." Sentiment prevailed. The delegates stuck with "Deseret" because it referred to honeybees, whereas the alternative brought to mind an "insect-infested, grasshopper-eating tribe of Indians."[27]

Needless to say, by the time of statehood in 1896, Mormons had given up on "Deseret"—both the political idea and the place-name. After coming to terms with "Utah," Mormons gave it new significance. In 1923 Levi Edgar Young, head of the History Department at the University of Utah, published a history of the state in which he asserted that the Indians "tell us that their forefathers called this the land of 'Eutaw,' or 'High up.' 'Utah' means 'In the tops of the mountains.'"[28] This was a crucial semantic shift. Whereas "Yuta" had originally been a Spanish word referring to Indians who lived in a mountainous region, "Utah" now became an Indianist word for the region itself. Young's definition, "in the tops of the mountains," had scriptural resonance, as in Isaiah 2:2: "And it shall come to pass in the last days, the mountain of the LORD's house shall be established in the top of the mountains." Moving full circle from "Deseret," contemporary Mormons have been known to spread the "faith-promoting rumor" that Congress unwittingly fulfilled nomenclatural prophecy by imposing "Utah."

During its drawn-out time as a territory, Utah watched its younger neighbors Wyoming and Idaho receive state names. In these cases, too, a newly assertive Congress imposed Indianist names from afar. In 1868 the Senate debated a bill to give a temporary government to Wyoming Territory—except the bill's sponsor preferred the name Territory of Lincoln, in memory of the martyred president. But some senators objected to naming polities after *any* people; it seemed un-American. (Pennsylvania, Maryland, and Virginia predated the republic; the Territory of Washington was meant to get a different name when it achieved statehood.) Senators agreed to fall back on the system of adopting Indian names. The leading proposal, "Wyoming," came from a valley in Pennsylvania. The name had become famous through *Gertrude of Wyoming,* a poem by Thomas Campbell published in 1809. Although Campbell was a Briton, his verse found favor in America; it concerned an incident in 1778 when a large group of revolutionaries were besieged and killed by Tories and their Seneca allies. "Wyoming," a descriptor for the valley, derived from the Delaware language. Not surprisingly, the senator from Pennsylvania, Simon Cameron, commended the transfer of the name. Non-Pennsylvanians pushed for alternatives. Charles Sumner of Massachusetts argued that "we should, if possible, select names that belong to the soil; that are, if I may say so, aboriginal; that grow out of the country itself; in other words, the Indian names." Questions followed:

MR. SHERMAN.   Why not call it Cheyenne? That is the name of the Indian tribe who have from time immemorial existed there, or just south of there.

MR. NYE.   What does that name mean? What is the signification of it?

MR. SHERMAN.   I think it means snakes.

MR. NYE.   We do not want any snakes. [Laughter.]

Another senator suggested a different western tribe, the Shoshone. But that seemed too difficult to spell. Debate returned to "Cheyenne," which enjoyed the support of settlers. This name had its own spelling issues. Moreover, legislators couldn't agree whether the first syllable should be pronounced shā or shī. Even the lexical meaning was in doubt. The word had the misfortune of coming from the French. Did it mean "snakes" or "prairie dogs"? In any event, argued John Sherman of Ohio, the western map already contained too many things named Cheyenne, including the principal town of the proposed territory. "Pawnee," "Sioux," and "Arapaho" were proposed and discarded. James Nye of Nevada summed up the consensus for the original name: "If there is any name in the Indian catalogue of names that is famous in song and story and legend, if there is any Indian name that has become a common household word, it is the name Wyoming. I think there seems to be so strong an attachment to Indian names that we had better take the most euphonious one, and one with which the ear is most familiar."[29]

The debate on the floor revealed cultural contradictions. Everyone agreed that Indian names were the best names for states—but only when properly selected and applied by people with taste. These nomenclators preferred exotic names that were also familiar to American eyes and ears. Storied names were preferable. Tribal names were acceptable—but only if they referred to local (or, in a pinch, regional) Indians who had some commendable trait, like valor in the face of doom. The partiality for local names, though strong, could always be overruled by the necessity for euphony.

What made a name "euphonious"? How did beautiful "Indian names" sound? Long vowels seem to have been the key component. "Wyoming" might not have had any relation to the native peoples of that region, but it *sounded* more Indian to legislators than "Cheyenne." Furthermore, as the great name-scholar George Stewart once noted, twenty-eight of the fifty states have names that "fit in the pattern most beloved of the orator—a long word accented on the next-to-last syllable." As early as 1842, the aesthetics of Indianisms had reached the point that a literary critic could argue that indigenous place-names could be constructed out of sounds when the original names could not be recovered. Presenting "war," "ran," and "ca" as examples of euphonious syllables, the author assembled some new "Indian" names ready for a place on the map: Warranca, Warcaran, Ranwarca, Rancawar, Cawarran.[30]

As ridiculous as it may seem, Congress actually approved such a name—"Idaho." During the Civil War, with the southern opposition removed from Congress, the Republicans organized several western territories, including Colorado, Idaho, and Montana. Congress bandied about these three names: Colorado almost became Idaho, Idaho almost became Montana. In 1860, while the bill was still in committee, territorial delegate B. D. Williams changed "Colorado" (a Spanish word) to "Idaho." When a colleague in the Senate suggested this wasn't a true indigenous name, Williams did some research and learned the truth. The word and its meaning—"gem of the mountains"—had recently been invented by some mining boosters. Embarrassed, Williams restored the old name, and the territory became Colorado. "Idaho" managed to survive, however. Two years later, when a territory needed to be formed around the Boise mining district, no one disputed the indigenous origins of this euphonious name. The "Idahoax" lived on. State boosters soon elaborated on the fakery by presenting the original Indian pronunciation as "E Dah Ho," with an emphasis on the second syllable. Arapaho was given as source language, then Nez Perce, then Yakima, then Shoshone. Sure enough, the syllables "E Dah Ho" could be found in all these languages. "Sunrise" was offered as a plausible alternative translation. For the better part of a century, the native derivation of the name went unchallenged. To this day, many Idahoans will tell you that the name of their state means "gem of the mountains."[31]

But does "Idaho" still have much Indianness? That is, does the place-name evoke strong images of Indians? Not really. The same could be said of most states with Indianist names. Enough time has passed for each word to acquire other associations. Besides, as intangible entities, states don't automatically bring people to mind. Ironically, it is at the local level of polity that Indianist place-names maintain greater associations with Indian peoples. As inhabited geographies, towns and cities have more substance than states: the ghosts of former inhabitants can more easily haunt them. Furthermore, a significant number of American towns took the names of Indian personages (in contrast to the *tribal* names taken by several states). These personal-cum-place-names typically honor chieftains. For example, the current National Map contains thirty populated places named after Osceola, eleven after Pontiac, and ten after Tecumseh.[32] Nonetheless, the most evocative Indianist names—the ones that Americans still associate most strongly with natives, the ones that carry the most authenticity—do not belong to states or counties or even haunted towns. Like "Mount Timpanogos," they belong to nature.

::: Long before the national period, many of the conspicuous natural features of British North America were known by Indian names, which, through assimilation, eventually became Indianist names. Niagara was the famous example. Likewise, most of the big eastern rivers (Mississippi, Ohio, Tennessee, Susquehanna, Potomac) had native-derived names. This was not an intentional program: it just happened. But in the post–Civil War era, when Euro-Americans set about surveying and naming the Far West, Indianist naming often became deliberate. The place that inspired the most sustained deliberation was the place that supplanted Niagara Falls as the iconic example of American nature—Yosemite Valley.

The valley was "discovered" and named in 1851 when a battalion of gold miners pursued various bands of Indians who had refused to negotiate reservation treaties with federal officials. Not finding Indians, the Mariposa Battalion looked for villages and acorn caches, both of which they burned. It was winter. Through the deepening snow, a unit of the battalion went high into the hills and entered the natural stronghold of Yosemite. Around the campfire that night, as the profundity of the scene sank in, Lafayette Bunnell, the group's doctor and self-designated savant, suggested that the place be named. Everyone agreed. Fanciful, foreign, canonical, and scriptural names were offered, but Bunnell did not like any of them. He remembered remarking "that it would be better to give it an Indian name than to import a strange and inexpressive one; that the name of the tribe who had occupied it would be more appropriate than any I had heard suggested." He proposed "Yo-sem-i-ty," as "it was suggestive, euphonious, and certainly *American;* that by so doing, the name of the tribe of Indians which we met leaving their homes in this valley, perhaps never to return, would be perpetuated." Two of Bunnell's Indian-hating companions objected. A voice vote was taken; Yosemite won easily. Little did Bunnell know that Yosemite was not the name used by the valley's people for themselves. It was a pejorative term—They Are Killers—assigned by others.[33]

Bunnell himself was a reasoned and articulate racist—but no Indian-hater. Although he believed the acorn-eaters deserved to pass away, he took an intellectual interest in them. And he wasn't above feeling sympathy for individual Indians. Much of the battalion's time was spent capturing a Paiute-Miwok band leader named Tenaya. Bunnell developed enough grudging admiration for the captive that he felt moved to name a stupendous granite-rimmed lake—later one of Ansel Adams' favorite locations—after him. Informed of the commemorative naming, Tenaya was perplexed. "It already has a name; we call it Py-we-ack," he tried to explain. Bunnell told him that a new name was needed "because it was upon the shores of the lake that we had found his people, who would never return to it to live." Hearing this, Tenaya's "countenance fell and he at once left our group and joined his own family circle. His countenance as he left us indicated that he thought the naming of the lake no equivalent for the loss of his territory."[34]

This scene in the Sierras reveals the intimate connection between linguistic appropriation and physical displacement, between the creation of parks and the removal of peoples—connections that have often been elided. Bunnell articulated what was probably the mainstream Euro-American attitude toward Indian place-names, which remained affected little or not at all by literati such as Lydia Sigourney.

Most nineteenth-century Anglos did not share Walt Whitman's view that "all aboriginal names sound good." Bunnell, like the senators who chose "Wyoming," wanted it both ways: he wanted Indian names on American terms. Although he considered Indian languages to be especially well suited for describing nature, he didn't believe that every indigenous place-name should be kept as a memorial. He did his best to learn the Miwok names for the prominent features of Yosemite Valley, and then discarded most of them. It was Bunnell who gave us Vernal Falls, Mirror Lake, and El Capitan.[35]

Whereas Lafayette Bunnell was in the mainstream, many of the sightseers who followed him were not. In the 1860s, as the tourist trade picked up, innkeepers and writers of guidebooks realized that sightseers—a select, fashionable, and literate group—appreciated Indian names. So they brought back the "old" names and added new "Indian legends." For example, Bridal Veil Falls became Po-ho-no ("evil wind") and Vernal Falls became Pi-wy-ack ("shower of sparkling crystals"). One of the tourists who took the bait was Helen Hunt—soon to be known as Helen Hunt Jackson, Friend of the Indian. In an 1878 travel piece she censured Bunnell for his nomenclatural mischief. Naively, she repeated the tourist legends and defended the "original" place-names with their poetical meanings. She claimed that Indian names were "truth" and English names "lies." In response, Bunnell ridiculed the "*romantic* preserver of Indian names" and "those credulous admirers of the NOBLE RED MAN." "It is indeed a laughable idea for me to even suppose that a worm- and acorn-eating Indian would ever attempt to construct a name to mean a '*shower of sparkling crystals*'; his diet must have been improved by *modern* intelligent culture."[36]

A more dispassionate observer, the self-taught ethnologist Stephen Powers, concluded that "the Indians would be much amused if they could know what a piece of work we have made of some of their names." With a bilingual native informant known as Choko, Powers made a nomenclatural tour of the valley. Of the many remarkable names dictated by Choko, perhaps the most striking was Tu-tok-anu´-la, or "measuring-worm stone." This toponym for El Capitan, the sheerest of the sheer cliffs, derived from a legend about a pair of boys trapped on top. A number of mighty animals tried to jump to the rescue, but in the end it was the lowly earthworm, moving one small increment at a time, who accomplished the feat. (Powers likened the story to "The Tortoise and the Hare.") Asked about other legends—including "one of the inevitable lover's leap[s]"—Choko "dismissed them all with the contemptuous remark, 'White man too much lie.'" All of Choko's information seems plausible. Then again, a few years earlier, state geologist J. D. Whitney had secured a completely different definition (and pronunciation) of Totokónula from a different native speaker.[37]

In their search for pure names, Euro-Americans muddied the ground in Yosemite. By the early twentieth century, the state of knowledge over Indian place-names had become hopelessly confused. Transcriptions and inventions and mistranslations had blurred, and no one—not even the Miwok speakers who remained—seemed able or willing to get at the truth. In 1911 the travel writer J. Smeaton Chase tried to get to the bottom of the name game by holding a "philological powwow" with an Indian man who had been born in Yosemite. Through an interpreter, Chase ran down the standard list of names, hoping to corroborate their meanings. Miguel, his interpreter, averred

> that many of the Indian words which I propounded to him had no meanings whatever. One after another of them was declared to be "Just name, all same your name; not mean nothing." In vain I labored with him, refusing to believe that it could be as he said, and almost feeling the sincerity of Hiawatha himself to be hanging on the event. Now and then he would verify one of my examples, with an air so frank that I could not suppose him to be deliberately misleading me when, the next moment, he declared some supposed interpretation to be "White man story; no good." When I argued that even white men's names meant something he was

vastly interested, but became sceptical when I was at a loss to expound my own at his request. And it was not reassuring to be told, when I put it to him that, after all, the versions I proposed to him had certainly been given by some of his people, "Some time white man fool Indian; some time Indian fool white man maybe."[38]

No matter who played whom, at least there had been some communication between natives and nonnatives in Yosemite Valley. No one in Utah Valley—or a hundred other inhabited valleys—ever bothered to track down a single old Indian to ask about place-names. Only one kind of place inspired that kind of concern: the "uninhabited" national parks. In 1908 a General Land Office surveyor replaced the English names in Natural Bridges National Monument in southern Utah with names imported from the Hopi (thought to be descended from the ancients who left ruins near the bridges). In 1914 members of Denver's Colorado Mountain Club arranged for two elderly Arapahos to visit their old haunts in Rocky Mountain National Park to provide name data. The result was "one of the greatest concentrations of Indian names in one small area on the face of the U.S.A." A few years later, a protracted battle over a notorious Indianist place-name in another national park was finally resolved. In the history of Indianist toponymy, there has been nothing quite as ridiculous and revealing as the battle over "Mount Rainier–Tacoma."[39]

⁙ Rainier, one of the world's great mountains—and, like Timpanogos, an urban-affiliated landmark popular with hikers—takes its name from Rear Admiral Peter Rainier of the British Royal Navy. An undistinguished historical figure, Rainier never even sailed to the Pacific Northwest. But he had a well-traveled friend, Captain George Vancouver, who immortalized Rainier in 1792. The place-name was well established by 1853, when a starry-eyed New Englander took an adventure trip to the Oregon Country. Thomas Winthrop (a direct descendant of John Winthrop) felt overwhelmed by the mountain and underwhelmed by its name: "Kingly and alone stood this majesty, without any visible comrade or consort . . . in isolated sovereignty . . . Of all the peaks from California to Fraser River, this one before me was royalest. Mount Regnier Christians have dubbed it, in stupid nomenclature perpetuating the name of somebody or nobody. More melodiously the siwashes call it Tacoma,—a generic term also applied to all snow peaks."[40]

Winthrop would have fallen into obscurity had he not become the first officer killed in the first military engagement of the Civil War. His travel book, published posthumously, became a best-seller, especially among Union troops. In this odd way, the name Tacoma emerged as a serious contender with Rainier.

Odder still, the name debate became a municipal rivalry. Commencement City, a fledgling town on the southern end of Puget Sound, renamed itself Tacoma in 1868. Soon afterward Tacoma beat out Seattle to become the western terminus of the Northern Pacific, and the railroad announced that its promotional literature would refer to the volcano by its Indian name. Tacoma businesses followed suit, but Seattle refused to go along. A conciliatory hyphenation, "Mount Rainier–Tacoma," failed to catch on. In 1890 the name dispute went before the brand-new U.S. Board on Geographic Names. Created by executive order, the board had been envisioned as a means of harmonizing the maps of various federal agencies. It immediately found itself embroiled in this local dispute. Conservative by nature, the board ruled in favor of the existing name. This verdict did not stop Tacoma activists. Their indignation was reignited in 1899, when Congress created Mount Rainier National Park. Tacoma boosters wove conspiracy theories and impugned the patriotism of Rainier boosters. Peter Rainier was, after all, a Briton, someone who fought against the American Revolution. The jingoistic name-calling reached a high pitch during World War I, when the Washington legislature asked the board—

which had received expanded powers from Theodore Roosevelt—to reconsider the case. Both sides prepared legalistic briefs full of data supporting the correctness of their favored name.[41]

"Tacoma" lovers argued that "Rainier" was in every way a bad name—"cheap, commonplace, beefy and vulgar." Propriety demanded substitution of the original, appropriate, euphonious, ennobling place-name. Ethics demanded it too. In 1917 Tacoma's Justice to the Mountain Committee began issuing high-minded rhetoric about the "duty and privilege in helping to perpetuate one more memento of a vanishing race." "Mount Tacoma" was offered as a complement to "Seattle," which got its name from the Duwamish chief whose oratory has become the stuff of legend. Indeed, no American city has advertised its Indianness as much as Seattle. Tacoma supporters played a shrewd game by bringing Chief Seattle's daughter—as well as a purported (and probably fraudulent) nephew—to their side. It is doubtful, however, that Indians cared much about the name controversy. Restoring justice to the mountain was a far cry from restoring treaty rights. Only a white man—in this case the president of the Northwestern Federation of American Indians—could write a poem that ended with this plea: "Wilt thou not, oh Great White Father, hear thy humblest children's prayer / Let this Mountain be their Totem, change its name to be so fair?"[42]

According to the poem, "Ta-Co-Bet" meant "God's mountain." A different name-change proponent wrote a whole book called *The Mountain That Was "God."* Other translations of the name included "greatness," "the great snow," "the mountain," "snow peak," "snow-covered mountain," "heart food," "breast food," and "flowing breasts." The Justice to the Mountain Committee secured affidavits from several groups of Indians saying that Tacobet was the original name. Henry Sicade, a "modern, educated, full-blooded Indian, half Nesqually and half Klickitat," gave a speech before a hiking club in which he said that all the name variants derived from the same word, which meant "that place from whence comes the water." The source language was never clear.[43]

Publicity image of "mountain worshipers" at Mount Rainier staged by the concessionaire at the national park, 1929. (Courtesy of National Park Service, Mount Rainier National Park Archives)

For their part, defenders of the status quo argued that "Rainier" was entrenched; that it wasn't such a bad name; and that the substitute, "Tacoma," was not in fact a genuine Indian name. They speculated that Theodore Winthrop had simply invented a euphonious word. (This is not implausible. Winthrop's chapter on Mount Tacoma consisted primarily of a softly mocking Indian legend "interpreted" from the words of the dusky-eyed "Hamitchou, a frowzy ancient of the Squallyamish.") It was also suggested that Winthrop could have misheard, misinterpreted, or misapplied the Chinook jargon word *t'kope*, which means "white." Charles Conover, the longtime superintendent of the Tulalip Reservation, dismissed a Puyallup utterance, *Tah-koh-buh,* as "merely an Indian attempt to say a word they have heard the whites use." According to the superintendent—who didn't speak any native languages—any Indian could be persuaded by flattery to "doctor up stories, legends, etc., to suit the fancies and desires of those who patronize him." In addition to Conover (the star defense witness), Rainier boosters rounded up a corps of elderly "pioneers" who signed affidavits saying they had never heard "Tacoma" in the old days. Some of these old-timers asserted that Puget Sound Indians couldn't pronounce the English *m,* much less "Tacoma." As a last line of defense, Rainierites pointed out that even those who championed Tacoma as an authentic Indian place-name conceded that it was a generic term, not a unique denomination for this singular peak.[44]

In 1917 the U.S. Board on Geographic Names weighed the evidence and decided to take no action, which amounted to a victory for "Rainier." "Tacoma" true believers had a final recourse—Congress. In 1924 a Washington senator introduced a name-change resolution, which eventually passed. In the House, however, the bill died in committee. That was that. The city of Tacoma gave up. In twentieth-century America, state power trumped municipal power. The key decisions in the Rainier-Tacoma fight were made in Washington, D.C., where bureaucrats gave final approval to place-names given by locals and recorded by mapmakers. By midcentury the process of adding topographic names was basically complete; it was now a matter of cataloging, rationalizing, and occasionally revising them.

::: In this new era, native peoples have learned to use governmental tools to expunge, restore, or correct certain toponyms. In 1995 the U.S. Board on Geographic Names overturned a rule that had barred diacritical marks, special letters, or symbols to represent indigenous words in official place-names. In Canada, efforts to reinstate native toponymy have enjoyed national support; for example, part of what used to be called the Northwest Territories is now Nunavut (the

Inuktitut word for "our land"). In the United States, efforts at name revision have worked upward from the local level. The most active regions have been the Northern Plains, the Southwest, Hawai'i, and Alaska. In 1980 the park surrounding Alaska's Mount McKinley became Denali; the lofty mountain's name might have been changed too had it not been for an obstreperous congressman from President McKinley's home state, Ohio. The name McKinley, though contentious, has never attracted the same vitriol as Rainier. William McKinley was not just any middling president; he was an *assassinated* middling president. Indian activists have saved their greatest opposition for something bigger—an entire subclass of Indianist toponymy composed of "squaw" names.[45]

The etymology of "squaw" has been a matter of confusion, but it now seems certain that the source word simply meant "woman" in the Massachusett language. As a loanword in nineteenth-century American English, it became the ubiquitous synonym for a female Indian. Although it never carried the hostility of "nigger," this sexually objectifying term could imply a set of derogatory images: a fat, ugly, unclean beast of burden, or a slut. Following the Red Power movement, certain Indian activists spread the sensational and erroneous information that "squaw" originally meant "cunt." "How would whites feel if they had to live in a place called Vagina Valley?" they asked. Over 900 features on the National Map—most of them in the West—still carry the "s-word." The majority of these names are little known and relatively innocuous. The most offensive do make a direct reference to sexual anatomy, though not to the vagina. At least twenty summits in America have been given names like Squaw Tit. By contrast, when moundlike landforms have been anthropomorphized as nonracialized (white) breasts, they have received an English personal name paired with the clinical term "nipple." In this way, Maggie and Mary and Molly have breasts across the mountainous West, particularly in Utah, which has a vastly disproportionate number of nipples—over twenty.

The U.S. Board on Geographic Names reconsiders "Squaw" on a

case-by-case basis, unlike "Jap" and "Nigger," which were changed en masse to "Japanese" and "Negro" in 1947 and 1963, respectively. (The majority of "Negro" names have since been changed once more.) Acting on their own, several state legislatures have passed laws to eliminate "Squaw" names with the understanding that the board—and ultimately the mapmakers at the U.S. Geological Survey—will subsequently validate their actions. The state of Minnesota began the trend when it replaced all its "Squaw" names between 1995 and 1999. In 1997 many native groups, including the Uintah and Ouray Tribal Business Council of the Ute Indian Tribe, passed a resolution supporting the elimination of "Squaw" from the National Map. Renaming has proved to be slow and contentious because there is no obvious or universal replacement for "Squaw." Some proponents of the status quo have satirically suggested names such as "Politically Correct Creek."

Arizona provides the best-known and most recalcitrant case; there it took more than a decade to rename a single landform. The name became an issue because of its location: a minimountain called Squaw Peak rises abruptly above Phoenix, and the city has encircled it. A favorite recreation site, the mountain has become a metropolitan symbol not unlike Provo-Orem's Mount Timpanogos. The peak is visible to hundreds of thousands of metro residents, some 27,000 of whom are Native Americans. (As of 2000, 250,000 Indians called Arizona home.) Over the 1990s, a Navajo assemblyman tried repeatedly to remove the name through legislation. A bland substitute, Iron Mountain, was offered as a translation of a Pima name for the peak. Finally, in 2003, a newly elected Democratic governor rammed through a state-level name change. The political timing was perfect, as the renaming occurred right after the U.S. invasion of Iraq. The mountain was named for Lori Piestewa, an Army private who died in the war. Not only was the fallen soldier an Arizona Indian (Hopi); she was a woman—a single mother no less—who had earned the distinction of being the first Native American woman to die in combat for her country. Who could fault such a name? Well, local businesses like Squaw

Peak Retirement expressed some anger and annoyance, as did conservative commentators, who complained that the governor had pandered to "grievance groups." However, these voices of opposition carried a tone of resignation.[46]

There are many other uncontroversial summits named Squaw Peak, including one in Utah County. Though much overshadowed, physically and otherwise, by nearby Mount Timpanogos, Squaw Peak is a symbolic mountain in its own right. Reaching a height of 7,876 feet, this subpeak of the Wasatch juts out dramatically as the northern portal of Rock Canyon, a gash in the mountains east of Brigham Young University and the Provo Temple. Steep slopes of scree line the mouth of the canyon, offering an invitation to reckless scramblers. Several BYU students have died here over the years. Much earlier, this same location was a different kind of dying ground. In 1850, as part of the winter military campaign against the Timpanogos Nuche, Mormon militiamen pursued Big Elk's band to Rock Canyon. Trapped, the measles-infected Utes tried to retreat up the canyon through the thickening snow. Some made it; others died of exposure; several perished from bullet wounds. Reporting back to Brigham Young, the Mormon commander made a tally of the dead, including "one squaw killing herself falling from a precipice." This ambiguous phrase could mean accident or suicide.[47]

In general, Squaw as a place-name is nothing but false. But in this site-specific case, Squaw Peak actually has a true and tragic backstory involving the death of a real Indian woman, whereas Mount Timpanogos, a name with more authenticity, lacks any such historical associations. This fact goes against intuition, of course. There are dozens of peaks named Squaw. There's only one Timpanogos.

::: To recap: at the start of the Utah's American period, "Timpanogos" referred primarily to a river. In the latter part of the nineteenth century, federal surveyors applied the name to the summit of a massif, but "Timpanogos Pk." entered local usage slowly. "Timpanogos" was, however, a well-known name in nineteenth-century Utah; it stood out as one of the relatively few native words the settlers made an effort to remember. In 1883 a Mormon periodical published a piece that bemoaned the lost art of place-naming. Modern people lacked the expressiveness of Indians, the author complained. Referencing Lydia Sigourney, he praised the "suggestive and beautiful phraseology of a perishing race" and listed some of the "voicefully satisfying" names from the American map, including "Timpanogos of local (Utah) fame." A few years later, in a promotional booklet, the Provo Chamber of Commerce voiced regret that the Indian names for springs and creeks had not been preserved as well as "Timpanogos"; these other names "have all been superseded and their memory seems to fast be fading away, like the races to whom they were first known."[48]

Such praise ignores the fact that the first generation of settlers disliked this loanword. U.S. Captain Albert Tracy, stationed close to Utah Valley in the late 1850s, noted that the Mormons preferred to call the major river the Provo instead of the Timpanogos (as it then appeared on government maps). The name commemorated Etienne Provost, a French-Canadian fur trader who had frequented the valley in the 1820s. Perhaps the Mormon preference for this name grew out of town boosterism more than anti-Ute prejudice; in any case, the feeling was strong. Richard F. Burton, touring the territory in 1860, discovered that the "Mormons call the City *Provo,* and Gentiles [non-Mormons] prefer as a 'rile' *Timpanogos.*"[49]

Burton, a master of languages, also gave the earliest definition of the word: "From *Timpa,* a rock, and *ogwabe,* contracted to *oge,* a river, in the Yuta dialect." All sources agree on the linguistic parts—"rocks" and "river"—though they offer various English equivalents for the whole: "rock river," "rocky torrent," "water running over rocks," "water among the stones," and so on.[50] Before the establishment of the Ute reservation in 1865, the word "Timpanogos" was the self-given name of Nuche bands that used the mouth of the river as their home base. Once removed to the reservation, the remnants of these people were forced to enroll as members of the Uinta Band of the Ute Tribe. Over the same period of displacement—the last third of the nineteenth century—government mapmakers replaced "Timpanogos River" with "Provo River."

Thus by the twentieth century, when alpinists began imbuing "Timpanogos" with Indianness, the name had been shorn of all its native referents. It was ready to accept new meaning. In 1913, just one year after Eugene Roberts led his first organized hike to the top of Timpanogos, a group of Mormon gentlemen met in Salt Lake City to organize a private club. When it came to a name, they found an obvious choice:

> Timpanogos is the oldest geographical name which is related to this mountain region . . . There are authorities who assert that Timpanogos means Rock River. With this controversy, the Timpanogos Club is not concerned. We propose to give Timpanogos a significance of its own. It is our purpose that it shall denote a high quality of intellect and moral strength and become a name of distinction and honor in this mountain region.[51]

The Timpanogos Club was surely meant to counter the Alta Club, an elite business fraternity composed mainly of non-Mormons. The name "Alta" came from the rich and profane mining town in the Wasatch Mountains (now a ski resort). "Timpanogos" likewise suggested elevation—both topographic and spiritual. Early members of the Timpanogos Club included Mormon notables such as J. Reuben Clark (U.S. ambassador and Church apostle), Marriner S. Eccles (banker and Federal Reserve chairman), and Franklin S. Harris (BYU president). These men, like Eugene Roberts, represented a new era of Mormon leadership—sons of pioneers born in the last days of Deseret who came of age in the American (and Americanized) state of Utah.

In the post-Roberts era, "Timpanogos" received new definitions as well as new significances; it came to mean "sleeping princess" or "lady reclining" or "woman lying down." As demonstrated by the nomenclatural histories of Yosemite Valley and Mount Rainier, Indian names have often been "translated" to meet the fantasies and desires of those possessing the place. The following list is a small, supplementary sample:

Mississippi: "father of waters"
Alabama: "here we rest"
Minnesota: "sky-blue water"
Iowa: "beautiful land"
Illinois: "tribe of superior men"
Chicago: "something great"
Tallahassee: "hill of the sun-god"

These fanciful definitions suggest admiration for the beauty of Indian languages, an admiration that goes back to the earliest days of the United States. But there's a flip side. For every noble chief who intones, "Mother Earth," there are two drunken bucks grunting, "Ugh." In the latter vein, Americans have often told mocking anecdotes—a form of "folk etymology"—to explain inscrutable place-names. When they involve Indians, these race-baiting yarns are all of a piece: hapless Indians use pidgin English (and often bad logic as well) to create neologisms. For example, Sheboygan supposedly comes from "she boy 'gain" and Schenectady supposedly comes from "skin neck t' day." In the second half of the twentieth century some Utahns told such anecdotes about Mount Timpanogos. There was an Indian, the story goes, and he caught a goose for dinner; but after preparing the bird, it somehow got away, so the hapless buck was left holding "tin pan, no goose!"[52]

The impulse to devise folk etymologies is so strong that even explicable names get worked over. In 1947, for the centennial of the coming of the Mormon pioneers, various camps of the Daughters of the Utah Pioneers wrote histories of their home counties. Juab County's volume included a whole chapter on Mount Nebo, the old rival of Mount Timpanogos. Most of the chapter was taken up by a "true Indian legend" about a doomed Indian princess, Nebona—the implied source of the mountain's name.[53] This lame attempt to make Mount Nebo match up to "Timp" suggested both the continuing allure of Indianist names and the waning allure of old-time Mormonism. How remarkable that a book dedicated to the memory of the pioneers—people who called themselves the New Israel—could suggest that a quintessentially biblical name was an Indian word!

Not surprisingly, this fake/folk etymology did not enter local folk-lore. "Nebo" was too full of meaning to take on Indianness. "Tim-panogos," by contrast, was just empty enough. The utility of "Timpa-nogos," like many Indianist place-names, comes from its between-ness. The word stands out visually and aurally, but it doesn't stand for anything lexically. Though obviously an "Indian" word, it retains no strong connections to a historical tribe or person or event. The name evokes the legendary, the literary space between history and fiction. The Indianness of "Timpanogos" is strong yet vague. Thus the name can accommodate multiple shifting meanings. In 1998 a local woman circulated a petition to rename the Utah State Developmental Cen-ter—a facility for the retarded—as the Mount Timpanogos Center. "Developmental Center" was a recently coined euphemism that re-placed the original name, Utah State Training Center. The petitioner argued that a timeless name like Timpanogos would withstand the vagaries of political correctness. The name would also convey the proper meaning for the facility, since the mountain "stands above the center like a sentinel, guarding and protecting its residents."[54]

The strength of "Timpanogos" has grown not only qualitatively but quantitatively. Over the twentieth century, the name was trans-ferred to scores of new places. This growth can be measured in Provo-Orem business directories. In the 1890s there were no listings under "Timpanogos." An elementary school received the name in the first decade of the twentieth century, and remained the sole bearer until the 1920s. In the 1940s the diminutive "Timp" appeared as the name of a grocery store. In any given year in the middle of the century, five to ten businesses had names derived from "Timpanogos." When suburbanization took off in the 1980s, the number doubled. Many new toponyms built off of the new hybrid, "Timpview," the name of Provo's second high school (some of whose students came from a new subdivision called "Indian Hills"). At about the same time, trying to keep pace with growth, Provo's sister city added a new high school called Mountain View. Counting related names—Mountainland Pipe & Plumbing, Crestview Service, and so on—Provo-Orem hosted approximately seventy-five alpine-themed businesses as of the late 1990s. By contrast, fewer than ten business listings had lake-themed names.[55]

In other words, the water toponymy of Utah Valley reflected its diminished water landscape. Place-names may be mementos, but they don't guarantee good memory. "Utah" and "Timpanogos" are now indelible, but they do little to remind Utahns of the days when Yutas fished from Timpanogó. In 1999 a group of "mixed-blood" Indians whose tribal status had been terminated tried to resuscitate "Timpanogos" as a social name. The "Timpanogos Tribe, Snake Band of Shoshoni Indians," went to federal court asserting that they, not the Ute Tribe, had rightful claim to the Uintah-Ouray Reservation. The federal judge dismissed the case because the group had not gone through the administrative process of getting tribal recognition. Attorneys for the Utes said they had never before heard of the "Timpanogos Tribe."[56]

Meanwhile, the only vestige of the old watery meaning of Timpanogos survives not in Utah but in Oregon. In the early twentieth century a topographic engineer for the U.S. Geological Survey mapped an unnamed lake in the Cascades, the principal source of the Middle Fork of the Willamette River. Historically literate, the surveyor knew that early maps had erroneously shown the Willamette issuing from Timpanogos Lake, so he applied that name to the Oregon water body. Though not indigenous, the name may belong here as much as it does on Mount Timpanogos.[57]

Would the history of this mountain be any different with a different name? If surveyors had labeled the summit "Snowy Peak," would a tradition exist of climbing it? Would it still be a landmark? My edu-cated guess is "yes, but less so." Even with an uncooperative name, boosters probably would have singled out this mountain for its (pur-ported) height and its caverns. As luck would have it, an Indian name gave the landmark a heightened semblance of antiquity and authentic-ity. The place-name, like the place, seemed natural. Yet for boosters, "Timpanogos" did not go far enough. The name demanded a legend.

The Rise and Fall of a Lover's Leap

Timpanogos, Wonder Mountain, a promotional booklet produced in 1922 for the Annual Timpanogos Hike, included "The Story of Utahna and Red Eagle, An Indian Legend of Timpanogos, By E. L. (Timpanogos) Roberts." Roberts' story—an instant popular favorite in Utah Valley—went like this:

> The mountain god, Timpanogos, is once again angry: he brings famine to the land. The Indians must sacrifice another maiden. Through a ritual of selection, the chief's daughter, the beautiful and beloved Utahna, is chosen. Alone she goes to climb the sacred realms of the mountain. Red Eagle, a hunter from a foreign tribe, spies her on her suicide mission. He follows her to the summit, falling in love every step of the way. Apprehending the girl's intentions, Red Eagle intervenes. He pretends to be Timpanogos. The would-be deity leads Utahna partway down the mountain and into a cave. For a time, Red Eagle and Utahna live as lovers. Then one day a bear enters the cave and wounds Red Eagle. In this way Utahna learns that her lover is no

god. She nurses him from the edge of death, but then she treks to the peak again. This time she jumps. The weakened Red Eagle watches helplessly from below. He manages to retrieve the mangled body, which he carries to the cave. Red Eagle broods over his dead bride until he too succumbs. No longer angry, the real Timpanogos melds the two lovers' hearts and fastens the amalgam to the ceiling of the cave.

By today's sensibilities, this story is both corny and improper. Legends are supposed to be oral rather than written, folkloric rather than literary. And "Indian legends" must of course come from Native Americans. Not so when Roberts came of age. In the nineteenth century it was conventional for Euro-American writers to publish pseudo-Indian legends. Typically these stories concerned spectacular deaths at spectacular landmarks. The most common death-place had its own generic term, the lover's leap.[1]

The foundational landmark—the Plymouth Rock of the lover's leap—was Maiden Rock, Wisconsin. This sandstone bluff beside the upper Mississippi River was long renowned for its scenery and its story. Its legendary leaping lover, Winona, inspired Utahna and countless other suicidal Indian characters. By the mid-twentieth century, however, Maiden Rock was no longer special or storied. The rise and fall of this lover's leap represents the historical arc of literary legends. "Timp" is a relic of this topographic genre. As legendary stuff, Mount Timpanogos is merely bigger and harder than Maiden Rock. It has better resisted erosion.

::: "Legend" is a shifty word. In his *American Dictionary* (1828), Noah Webster gave this definition:

> 1. A chronicle or register of the lives of saints, formerly read at matins and at the refectories of religious houses. Hence,
> 2. An idle or ridiculous story told respecting saints.

3. Any memorial or relation.

4. An incredible, unauthentic narrative.

According to Webster, legends were inherently fake. Little did the American lexicographer know that European folklorists were working to impart authenticity to legends. These scholars divided the universe of oral narratives into three galaxies: myths, fairy tales, and legends. A myth in this context is a sacred story of creation. Myths are true (in the deepest sense) but ahistorical; they take place in that time before time. Fairy tales *(märchen)* are acknowledged fictions; they begin poetically, "Once upon a time . . ." Sometimes crude, usually fantastic, and always entertaining, fairy tales nevertheless communicate moral lessons. Legends *(sagen)* are historical. Whereas the fairytale "represents invention, the legend represents knowledge." People spread fairy tales through recitals, legends through conversation. Set in the near past with real people and local places, a legend is believable if not verifiable: "This happened to a friend of a friend . . ." Although such stories contain improbable or even supernatural elements, they assert credibility. They occupy the "twilight zone of credence and doubt."[2]

This modern definition of the legend builds on the work of the Grimm Brothers, who, ironically, transgressed their own rules: they doctored their legends as much as they collected them. Indeed, many seminal works of European folklore were partly fabricated. The invention of nation-states in the Romantic era inspired the complementary definition and elevation of national folks and folklores. In 1765 the Scotsman James Macpherson published *Poems of Ossian,* which he presented as translations of ancient Gaelic traditions. In truth his sources were partly oral, partly archival, and mostly imaginative. Finns hailed Elias Lönnrot's *Kalevala* (1835)—a compilation and embellishment of various old texts—as the rediscovery of the epic of their motherland. Similarly, most nineteenth-century American "Indian legends" are literary rather than folkloric, authorial rather than oral. Yet they are still recognizable as legends: quasi-historical narratives with some claim to authenticity. To describe such ambiguous texts, folklorist Richard M. Dorson developed the term "literary legend" (counterpoised with "folk legend")—though at other times he deployed a pejorative term, "fakelore": "Fakelore is the presentation of spurious and synthetic writings under the claim that they are genuine folklore. These productions are not collected in the field but are rewritten from earlier literary and journalistic sources in an endless chain of regurgitation, or they may even be made out of whole cloth, as in the case of several of the 'folk heroes.'"[3]

This definition applies to Paul Bunyan as well as to Utahna, though in fact frontier tall tales differ somewhat from fake Indian legends. Whereas tall tales acknowledge their farfetchedness through the stylized voicing of the author, "Indian legends" assert their credibility through the stylized effacement of the author. A good fake legend doesn't seem fake; instead, it seems incredibly authentic.

Throughout U.S. history, non-Indians (usually Anglos) have often taken it upon themselves to imagine what Indians have said, or would have said, or should have said—call it "speaking for Indians." Famous orations by chieftains—Logan's Lament, Red Jacket's Reply, Chief Joseph's Surrender, Chief Seattle's Speech—are notoriously suspect. Of course, not all recorded Indian speeches were ghostwritten. There is a separate line of cultural production—call it "translating for Indians"—for hybrid texts. For instance, no one dismisses *Black Elk Speaks* as a fraudulent representation of the Lakota elder Black Elk, even though it's now clear that the transcriber, John Neihardt, acted more as a mediator. Likewise, certain "Indian legends" are good-faith reworkings of real native lore. Published legends concerning Mount Katahdin in Maine and Mount Rainier in Washington, for example, seem to have grounding in indigenous sources. However, most "Indian legends" are examples of whites' putting stories into Indians' mouths.[4]

More than other story types, legends *take place*. The term "lover's leap" is both topographical and literary: it denotes the convergence of a landform and a motif. A lover's leap is a certain type of ledge upon which a certain type of act can be imagined. The first recorded imagining in America dates to 1729, when William Byrd led an expedition to the Blue Ridge Mountains to determine the dividing line between the colonies of Virginia and North Carolina. At the western end of the line, in the light of a clearing storm, Byrd's party enjoyed a stunning view: "One of the Southern Mountains was so vastly high, it seem'd to hide its head in the Clouds, and the West End of it terminated in a horrible Precipice, that we call'd the Despairing Lover's Leap."[5] Byrd offered no suggestion that an Indian had met her fate below the precipice. The notion would not have crossed his mind, because the age of American legends had not yet begun. Byrd's place-name *did* evoke a story, but that story came from the ancient world. Any well-read gentlemen would have caught the allusion—Sappho.

Not just any leaping lover, Sappho was the Poetess, the "tenth Muse," the analogue of Homer. Unfortunately, only fragments of her celebrated verse remain. More to the point, scant biographical evidence survives. Sappho is one of those historical figures who has no history, only legend. Her meaning is plastic. Today she is celebrated as the first female homoerotic author; in Victorian Britain and the antebellum United States, she was held up as the personification of romantic (heterosexual) love. According to legend, Sappho had unrequited feelings for a younger man. Her solution was to jump into the Ionian Sea from a cliff—the Leucadian Rock. This suicide story began with the Greeks themselves. Menander (ca. 342–292 B.C.E.) wrote a play, *The Lady from Leukas,* that dramatized Sappho's leap. Later the Roman poet Ovid retold the story. Much later, in the sixteenth century, Sappho was rediscovered and remythologized by French poets. Eventually the English got into the act, with Alexander Pope publishing a well-received verse translation of Ovid's poem in 1707. *The Spectator,* an influential daily magazine of genteel culture published between 1711 and 1714 in London, ran commentary about Sappho. Whether or not literate Englishmen of the eighteenth century took the Sappho legend seriously, it was part of their cultural vocabulary. William Byrd's library—one of the largest in the New World—included many shelves of classical texts. He also owned Basil Kennet's *Lives and Characters of the Ancient Grecian Poets* (1697), which contained a chapter on Sappho. To a degree that can scarcely be appreciated today, Greeks and Romans occupied the minds of British Americans; only the Bible surpassed the classics in importance.[6]

In the colonial period, then, the term "lover's leap" brought to mind a particular death at a particular place. Only after the Revolution, in the new United States, did explorers, surveyors, and settlers create their own generic geography of lover's leaps. In the process, they Americanized the Poetess; they created a "dark-skinned Sappho." Death-by-gravity became associated almost exclusively with Indians.

::: Explorer Zebulon Pike is best known today for his namesake, Pikes Peak, a mountain he tried and failed to climb while trespassing in New Spain. He deserves more credit for charting the upper reaches of his country's mighty river, the Mississippi. Leaving St. Louis in a keelboat in 1805, Lieutenant Pike and his men made their way upstream. In mid-September Pike's party entered Lake Pepin, a widening of the river about fifty miles downstream from the present-day Twin Cities. Impressive mounds of sandstone, the most prominent of which rose some 400 feet above the somnolent water, bound the so-called lake. A cliff-faced ledge protruded from the base of one of these mounds. Pike's company camped near the cliff after being stopped by bad weather. On the riverbank they came across one Murdock Cameron, who entertained them with stories. "I was shewn a point of rocks," Pike wrote,

> from which a Sioux woman cast herself, and was dashed into a thousand pieces, on the rocks below. She had been informed, that her friends intended matching her to a man she despised; and having [thereby] refused her the man she had chosen, she ascended the hill, singing her death song; and before they could overtake her, and obviate her purpose, she

took the lover's leap ! and ended her troubles, with her life. A wonderful display of sentiment in a savage ! Distance 3 miles.[7]

Pike described Cameron as "a man of tolerable information, but rather indolent habits; a Scotsman by birth, but an Englishman by prejudice." This was not an especially ringing endorsement of an informant. Then again, it's not clear how much weight Pike gave to Cameron's story. His retelling of it was perfunctory, even curt. It contained obvious clichés—"death song," "lover's leap," "dashed to a thousand pieces." Was Pike being ironic? His editorial comment—"a wonderful display of sentiment in a savage"—can be read as either sarcasm or sincerity.

It seems more than slightly odd that no one before Lieutenant Pike had publicized this storied rock. Lake Pepin was hardly aqua incognita. Two famous explorers had earlier described this locale. In the seventeenth century, the French Catholic Father Louis Hennepin had a run-in with natives at Lake Pepin without hearing any legend. Later, in a best-selling travel account from the eighteenth century, the British-American solider-explorer Jonathan Carver described the "pyramids of rocks" and "amazing precipices" around Lake Pepin—yet failed to single out the leaping place. Possibly the events had not yet happened. More likely, they had not yet been concocted. In any case, everyone who visited the Upper Mississippi *after* Zebulon Pike managed to hear about the suicidal Sioux at Lake Pepin. They expected to. Pike's journal reached a wide audience on both sides of the Atlantic after being published in 1810. In its review of the book, a Baltimore-based magazine called attention to the Lake Pepin story and its likeness to the Sappho legend. "It was thought that ancient Greece alone had her Leucadian rock," wrote the reviewer. "Who would have supposed that the rocks of the Mississippi were destined to be its rival: and that the rude breast of the savage should be the habitation of a heart that was to equal the desperate heroism of the Grecian poetess?"[8]

In 1817 the military explorer Major Stephen H. Long made another reconnaissance of the Upper Mississippi. In the wake of the War of 1812, the U.S. government hoped to increase its knowledge of the (Old) Northwest and to expand its presence there. Near Lake Pepin, Long took on the services of a Sioux man, Wazzecoota, or Shooter from the Pine Tree. "We were much amused by the singing of our chief, who felt a disposition to be merry after taking whiskey," wrote Long in his journal. "He occasionally stands up in the boat and harangues with a loud voice, proclaiming who he is, where he is going, and the company he is with." Some years later, an Indian agent observed that Wazzecoota was "not much respected by his own nation, and by *all* called a '*babbler.*'" In the company of this extrovert, Long floated past the "majestic bluffs" leading to "the Lover's Leap." One suspects that Major Long wanted to one-up Lieutenant Pike. Pike had heard a synopsis of the legend from a Scotsman; Long heard—or at least claimed he heard—a full version from a real-life Sioux. Of course, Wazzecoota was being paid; he may have told the white men what they *wanted* to hear. And everything Wazzecoota said went through an interpreter. On top of that, Long wrote his own transcription of the "translation." The resulting legend was highly embellished in the style of the day. The Indian maiden speaks like a courtly maiden— "You will soon have no daughter or sister to torment, or beguile with your false professions of love," and so on. The major undoubtedly hoped to publish his journal.[9]

Farther upstream Long's expedition reached the Falls of St. Anthony, a cataract on the Mississippi at present-day Minneapolis. Long found the scene "romantic in the highest degree." Here by the falls, as if to best Pike again, Long notated a second Indian legend, "the catastrophe of which [Wazzecoota's] mother witnessed with her own eyes." This place-story does not technically count as a lover's leap, but it comes very close because it involves gravity-propelled suicide. According to Long/Wazzecoota, the victim was a Sioux woman—an honorable wife with two children. Her loving but ambitious husband took another wife to elevate his status as he maneuvered to become a chief. Rather than live in polygyny, the first wife left her husband, taking the children with her. Some time later, she chose to take herself and her young ones over the falls in a canoe. After singing her death song, the Sioux mother was "instantly dashed to pieces."[10]

The next noteworthy explorer to visit the Upper Mississippi was Henry Schoolcraft. Later famous for his ethnographic work, Schoolcraft boated and trudged through the lake country in 1820 under the auspices of the War Department. In his published narrative (1821), Schoolcraft reported that his interpreter showed him the precipice on the east shore of Lake Pepin where a Sioux girl had jumped to reject her parent's marriage choice. Echoing Pike, Schoolcraft commented that "such an instance of sentiment is rarely to be met with among barbarians, and should redeem the name of this noble-minded girl from oblivion." This line of argumentation goes back to Jefferson's *Notes on the State of Virginia* (1785), in which the proud Virginian refuted the claims of a French intellectual that American Indian men "lack ardor," that "their other feelings are also cold and languid," that their "heart is icy," and that they felt "indifference to the other sex."[11]

Schoolcraft identified the passionate Sioux as "Oola-Ita *(Oo-la-i-ta)*"—a mellifluous name, but one that was soon superseded. In 1823 Stephen Long returned to the Upper Mississippi for another reconnaissance. After the trip he and his crew gathered in Philadelphia and decided to collaborate on a narrative in "popular form." The role of lead author went to William Keating, a mining engineer educated in Europe. Among the materials at his disposal, Keating had Long's unpublished 1817 journal, from which he borrowed the two death-place legends. Although Keating lifted the plotlines and even certain phrases from Long, he managed to make the legends his own (while claiming, of course, that they came directly from local Sioux guides). *Narrative of an Expedition to the Source of St. Peter's River* (1825) was the work of a smooth writer. Keating described how the ghost of "Ampota Sapa" ("Dark Day") could sometimes be heard singing a "doleful ditty" beside the Falls of St. Anthony. From his pen also came "Winona" and "Maiden's rock," the lasting names of the leaping lover and her jumping-off place.[12]

Where did Keating get "Winona"? It was in fact a Sioux word—a generic name given to firstborn daughters (who might acquire a different name later in life). But was the name native to the story? And was the story itself native? A dissonant text from the same expedition stirs doubt. Partway through their travels, Keating and company were joined by an Italian adventurer, Giacomo Beltrami, who had come to the New World on his own to look for the source of the Mississippi River. Beltrami eventually fell out with Major Long, but the Italian seems to have spent enough time with the Americans to hear the Winona legend. However, in his book, published as a series of letters to Europe, Beltrami used Schoolcraft's "Indian" name (instead of Keating's) and put it in a new plot. Oholoaïtha, a Sioux, was in love with Anikigi, a Chippewa. But her barbarous father desired no peace with his Chippewa enemies. He blocked the marriage and arranged another. On her appointed wedding day, a rebellious Oholoaïtha took the "fatal leap."[13]

In short, the testimonies of explorers about the lover's leap legend contain discrepancies. For historians, the cumulative evidence is too strong to dismiss out of hand, too weak to accept on good faith. However, for the nineteenth-century readership of government survey reports—the *National Geographic* periodicals of their day—the discrepancies didn't register. Credulous reprints and retellings of Keating's account of Maiden Rock could soon be found in such places as a women's newspaper, a family magazine, and a farmers' journal.

Certain Americans could do better than armchair exploration. Starting in the mid-1820s, those with time and money could experience the beauties of the Upper Mississippi by steamboat. Initially captains simply placed passengers amidst cargo. By the 1840s, tourists traveled on full-fledged tour lines, orchestras and cabin boys included. The river became famous for its castellated bluffs—often compared to the Rhine's—and the presence of Indians. For the enjoyment of guests, steamboat captains got in the habit of reciting the legend of Winona at Lake Pepin. The new western leg of the Fashionable Tour was made easier in 1854, when the Rock Island Railway connected Chicago to the Mississippi River. To mark the occasion, a host of dignitaries, including former president Millard Fillmore, staged a "Grand Excursion" up the nation's great stream. About forty reporters came along for the ride, and they disseminated stories about the Mississippi and its storied scenery to readers across the country. The Grand Excursion, like other tours, ended at the Falls of St. Anthony beside the developing city of Minneapolis.[14]

Emigrants joined the tourists in the 1850s. In that decade the population of Minnesota jumped from approximately 6,000 to 172,000— a land rush following the extinguishment of Indian title. Most of the newcomers arrived by steamboat. This northward, waterborne emigration was nearly as important as the more famous westward overland movements of pioneers to Oregon and Utah, and gold miners to California and Colorado. No doubt a significant percentage of the steamboat settlers heard the legends of Maiden Rock and the Falls of St. Anthony.

Even those who never floated upon the Father of Waters could witness its landmarks thanks to a vicarious method of travel: the panorama. Devised in Europe in the 1790s, the panorama evolved over the next half-century. It began as a large, circular painting mounted within a rotunda. Enveloped, the viewer circumambulated the art. Producers later improved the experience by constructing a rotating viewing platform in the center of the rotunda. They also used light effects to simulate the progression from sunrise to nightfall, and to call attention to scenes within the painting. The third version of the panorama, the kind made popular in America, anticipated the motion picture. Long canvases were unrolled from one cylinder to another on either side of a stage. Multiple reels could be shown in succession; over two or three hours, an audience might watch hundreds of yards of picture. Easily transported, the moving panorama sometimes functioned as a newsreel of military events such as the Napoleonic wars. In the United States, audiences desired most to witness their western territories, especially the valley of the Mississippi. For a nation unsure of its greatness vis-à-vis Europe, the Great River inspired great pride. To match the subject, entrepreneurial artists went to incredible lengths. In the aptly grandiloquent words of one historian,

> Imagine a man who declared that he had painted a picture three miles long and a rival artist who announced a few months later that *his* painting was four miles in length! They were liars, of course, but what magnificent lies! Try, if you will, to conceive a third man saying that his new picture of the same region was to be three times as long as that of the first producer, a fourth informing the public that he would paint a picture on one hundred thousand square feet of canvas, and a fifth intending to use twelve thousand square yards. These lies were no less than colossal and super-colossal. Clearly the men were doubly artists: they were both painters and press agents.[15]

Each of the five painters—John Banvard, John Rowson Smith, Sam Stockwell, Henry Lewis, and Leon Pomarede—had plied the river to sketch the scenery. On their boats, the artists toted Pike and Keating as well as charcoal and ink. Four of the five resulting panoramas included Lake Pepin and the Falls of St. Anthony. Night after night, the artists lectured in front of their moving rivers of painted canvas. In this way, literally hundreds of thousands of people heard about the legendary death-places of the Upper Mississippi. One spectator was Henry David Thoreau, who saw a panorama of the Rhine followed by a panorama of the Mississippi ("a Rhine stream of a different kind") that included the legend of "Wenona's Cliff."[16] The five rival panoramas toured the major cities of America and Europe before the fad waned in the early 1850s.

Although the now-forgotten panoramas probably did the most to spread the fame of Winona and Ampota Sapa, writers did their part, too. A full bibliography would run many pages. The authors include such literary notables as Lydia Maria Child, Felicia Hemans, James Athearn Jones, George Catlin, Henry Schoolcraft, and Mary Henderson Eastman.[17] In addition to these major works, the legend of Maiden Rock was summarily related in dozens of travel accounts in the quarter-century after William Keating's. No wonder that Lake Pepin was sometimes called the "Mississippi Horicon" after Lake Horicon, one of Cooper's oft-used settings. What accounts for this prodigious literary production? In the antebellum period, legends of the lover's leap—if not "Indian legends" generally—worked at least three ways. First, they played into cultural trends of Romanticism, antiquarianism, and nationalism. Second, they spoke to changing ideas about gender—including romantic love, courtship, and marriage. Third, they mediated contemporary issues of racial violence and racial guilt.

::: In the preface to *The Marble Faun* (1860), a novel set in Rome, Nathaniel Hawthorne made a famous apologia:

> No Author, without a trial can conceive of the difficulty of writing a romance about a country where there is no shadow, no antiquity, no mystery, no picturesque and gloomy wrong, nor anything but a commonplace prosperity, in broad and simple daylight, as is happily the case with my native land ... Romance and poetry, like ivy, lichens, and wall-flowers, need Ruin to make them grow.

This was a major problem for American authors of Hawthorne's generation—those who came of age well after the Constitution and long before the Civil War. Could a nation with no "usable" past support the romance, the new favored idiom of literature? In 1822 W. H. Gardiner stated the problem in an influential review of *The Spy*, James Fenimore Cooper's second book, and his first set in America. "But where are your materials for the higher order of fictitious composition?" Gardiner asked. Using vertiginous language, he wondered how, without "gorgeous palaces and cloud capped towers," without "monuments of Gothic pride, mouldering in solitary grandeur," without any such "romantic associations"—how could you "plunge your reader, in spite of reason and common sense, into the depths of imaginary woe and wonder?" Happily, there was a way out of this un-Gothic depression. "A little paradoxically perhaps," Gardiner exhorted authors to "go back to the days when things were newer—but not so quiet as they now are." He suggested that America had three epochs worthy of the romance: the presettlement Indian days, the colonial Indian wars, and the Revolution.[18]

The poets James Eastburn and Robert Sands had led the way with *Yamoyden* (1820), a romantic retelling of King Philip's War, the bloody frontier conflict between Puritans and Algonquians. The poem was a hit. Sensing the zeitgeist, Cooper moved from *The Spy* to his famous Leather-Stocking Tales. *The Last of the Mohicans* (1826) serves as the early bookend of the Indianist period in American literature, the late bookend being Longfellow's *Song of Hiawatha* (1855). During the nearly three decades in between, hundreds of Indian-themed plays and novels and stories and poems appeared in the United States. The majority of these works broke from the old literary mold—the captivity narrative—and portrayed natives more fully and sympathetically, if no less stereotypically.[19]

European Romanticism influenced this nativist turn. As a subject, "the Indian" lent himself well to romantic characterization. He was, according to Anglo-American treatments, guided by emotion and instinct, two good romantic traits. By nature—indeed, by *Nature*—he seemed to be brooding and woodsy. He lived amid wild and rugged scenes. The uninhibited life of the noble savage was never far from death, a favorite subject of Romanticists. Self-inflicted death was especially romantic; literary works about suicide had burgeoned in eighteenth-century Europe. The early modern period witnessed a general reevaluation of self-murder. Previously thought of as a sin and a crime (for which the body of the deceased could be desecrated, and the family of the deceased could be punished), self-murder was secularized and decriminalized. In eighteenth-century England, as romantic love became a marital ideal, newspaper coverage of lovesick suicides became "intolerably tedious." In this context, Johann Wolfgang von Goethe wrote *The Sorrows of Young Werther* (1774), a novel about a poet who ends his life because his love for a married woman can never be fulfilled. (Interestingly, Goethe incorporated his own translation of the pseudofolkloric *Poems of Ossian* into the novel's climactic scene.) This hyperromantic book found sensational and controversial success; as "Werther Fever" spread across western Europe, dozens of young people committed copycat suicides.[20]

Other European luminaries more directly propelled the literary interest in indigenes. In 1801 and 1802 the famed French author François-René de Chateaubriand published two popular romantic stories about doomed Indian love affairs amid the forests of the New World. But it was Sir Walter Scott, an author who never wrote about America, who most inspired Americans to compose Indian-themed romances. Scott's hugely successful romances and ballads of the Scottish highlands (for example, *Lady of the Lake,* 1810) provided a template: rugged landscapes, native characters, and local plots drawn from folklore or the not-so-distant past. "The appearance of a new tale from [Scott's] pen caused a greater sensation in the United States than did some of the battles of Napoleon, which decided the fate of thrones and empires," recalled one American author. Predictably, James Fenimore Cooper became known as the "American Scott."[21]

Canonization generally favors novels over stories and poems. Even today, Cooper looms large, and his shadow obscures his contemporaries who wrote short fiction—especially "sketchbooks" and magazine pieces. Legends fitted the demands of these new and phenomenally popular print formats. With their local settings and local characters set in historical time, legends shared some kinship with the romance. In both genres, the Indian was an obvious subject. However, the American romantic vogue transcended the Indian; books like James Hall's *Legends of the West* (1832) and Chandler Robbins Gilman's

Legends of a Log Cabin (1835) featured a variety of legendary characters—natives, soldiers, voyageurs, preachers, and pioneers. Washington Irving, the only legend-writer who went on to be canonized, evoked the ghostly Dutchness of New York in *The Sketch Book of Geoffrey Crayon*. "Rip Van Winkle" and "The Legend of Sleepy Hollow" didn't require the Indian past to create imaginary woe and wonder. The Hudson Valley Dutch could *function* like Indians—faintly mysterious pre-English-settlement inhabitants. When legend-writers called on Indians, they usually had a specific purpose: the romanticization of natural scenes. Whereas "Dutch" legends suited abandoned farmhouses and shady lanes, "Indian" legends suited landforms.[22]

In contemporaneous New England, Puritans populated the ghost-world of legends as much as Indians. Of the numerous Yankee legend-writers, John G. C. Brainard (1790–1828) and John Greenleaf Whittier (1807–1892) rank highest. Their inspiration had as much to do with the present as the past. They wrote their legends in the midst of the "market revolution," when so many of their region's native-born Protestant youth, seeing no future in farming, moved to industrializing cities to work for wages alongside Irish immigrants. In this context of change, antiquarianism blossomed, as did regionalism. Yankees worked to reinvent "New England" even as they sensed its identity slipping away. The emblematizing of the central village and the sacralization of Plymouth Rock (itself an invention) came out of this moment. This regionalist project was pervasive: almost every town in New England became the subject of its own monograph. Usually these town histories contained long sections on Indians, as well as local legends in prose or poetry.[23]

Literature could be used in the service of nationalism as well as in the service of regionalism. Throughout the New World, postcolonial authors turned to the legendary form. Legends could provide a sense of antiquity in the absence of a deep history. Some legend-writers went so far as to claim native peoples as fictive ancestors. As Henry Schoolcraft wrote in 1846: "They [the Indians] are relatively to us what the ancient Pict and Celt were to Britain or the Teuton, Goth and Magyar to continental Europe." Schoolcraft's interests led him to write Indian romances and, more famously, to collect, edit, and anthologize native folklore. (The latter project was aided by his mixed-blood Ojibwa wife.) Much like the Grimms of Germany, Schoolcraft reworked his tales in order to express their "true spirit and meaning." He did this by "expunging passages, where it was necessary to avoid tediousness of narration, triviality of circumstances, tautologies, gross incongruities, and vulgarities." In turn, Longfellow reworked School-craft to create *The Song of Hiawatha,* a nationalistic poem whose structure mimicked the Finnish pseudonational epic, the *Kalevala.* Even so, Longfellow professed in opening that "these legends and traditions" have been transcribed "from the lips of Nawadasha, the musician, the sweet singer."[24]

This disingenuous self-effacement was characteristic of antebellum legendry. Euro-Americans frequently presented legends both as old traditions (from the lips of a dying generation) and as contemporary fictions (from the pens of an up-and-coming generation). Thus the works could be doubly nationalistic—providing evidence of a profound preliterary past and a vibrant literary present. Writing the preface to Mary Eastman's *Dahcotah* (1849), the noted author Caroline Kirkland pronounced that Indians "live poetry; it should be ours to write it out for them." She asserted the "unquestioned right" of "Americans" to appropriate the superstitions and legends of Indians. Decrying the "parrotism" and "servile imitation" of U.S. writers, Kirkland urged them to utilize native material. She praised Eastman's ethnography—recording stories "from the very lips of the red people as they sat around her fire"—and also her artistry. It was *her* language that had "something of an Ossianic simplicity and abruptness, well suited to the theme."[25]

According to Kirkland, the native material for a national literature included not only Indians but also the "splendid prospects" and "sublime features of our country." Over time, literate citizens naturalized the relationship between romantic legends and romantic landmarks:

one national form demanded the other. Tourist sites like the Falls of St. Anthony and the Natural Bridge of Virginia doubled as patriotic sites. Above all, the nationalistic generation of writers praised its riverine scenery—especially that of the Niagara, the Lower Hudson, and the Upper Mississippi. These three waterways inspired more legends per mile than any other parts of the country. In addition to the great rivers, the highlands of New England inspired a concentration of legends. In 1824 Monument Mountain, Massachusetts, became a lover's leap thanks to a poem by the esteemed William Cullen Bryant. The next year a youthful Longfellow—who also penned a lover's leap poem—wrote rhyming couplets about an Indian chief, Jeckoyva, who fell to his death from a peak "near the White Mountains." More famously, in 1830 Lydia Maria Child used New Hampshire's Chocorua Peak as the setting for an Indian legend about the fall of another chief; her story went on to enter local folklore. The Old Man of the Mountain received a (non-Indian) legend from Hawthorne in 1850.[26]

"The Legend of the Mountain," an offering in an 1843 gift-book (a popular form of anthology typically bought around the end-of-year holidays), explains the connection between romantic literature and nationalistic landmarks better than any other text. A didactic story about a story, it begins with father and son stepping out for a walk. The son is feeling "out of sorts," and he expresses his feelings in this outburst: "Don't you think, father, that we live in a dreadfully stupid part of the country; if we walk out, there is nothing to see. Now if we lived on the banks of the River Rhine, where there is a castle with a legend at every point, there would be some fun." Cheerfully the father suggests that they use their wits to create some equally good legends; a nearby mountain offers a proper subject. The boy likes the idea: "O let me have the legend, papa, I am sure I shall like the mountain a great deal better if it has one." On demand, the father tells a story about an ancient race of giants ruled by a greedy king named Agiococook, who is turned to stone after losing a challenge to the sun. Afterward the grateful son says, "Well, then, father, I do not see but if people had time to make legends about our country, it would be as romantic as those across the water."[27]

⸪ Although literary trends can be used to explicate the rise of legends, pseudo-Indian legends, and legendary landforms in general, the popularity of the lover's leap—the story type that eventually adhered to Mount Timpanogos—demands its own explanation. Why did this motif, of all the possibilities, take hold of the antebellum imagination? Several reasons cluster around gender.

Over the eighteenth and early nineteenth centuries, Euro-American fathers gradually lost control of their children's marital choices. No longer the kings of their households, fathers had to relinquish some authority over their subjects. In general, arranged marriage gave way to consensual marriage; patriarchal marriage gave way to companionate marriage. By the 1830s the parents of the groom rarely even got the chance to grant permission. The engaged couple more often consulted the bride's parents for approval—but only after the decision had been made. As Werner Sollors puts it, traditions of descent lost out to innovations of consent. The new middle-class marriage was less about old families and desirable bloodlines and more about autonomous individuals arranging their own future. Romantic love, previously unimportant to marriage, became a prerequisite. Dating and courtship emerged as modern traditions.[28]

While structural changes in the economy contributed greatly to these gender innovations, the American Revolution played some part, too. The revolution metaphorically decapitated the ultimate patriarch, the king, who lost parental control of his children, the colonies. Familial metaphors abounded in the writings of revolutionaries, who likened the social contract to the marriage contract, and the revolution to a divorce. For example, in a 1775 essay called "Reflections on Unhappy Marriages," Thomas Paine—using the revealing pseudonym "an American savage"—called for "no other ceremony than mutual affection." After the war the citizens of the new United States recognized that their consensual union was only as strong as the bonds of affection between states. To the disappointment of unhappily married women, the dissolution of actual marriages remained difficult in the early national period. Rhetorically, however, Americans had fatefully conjoined marriage with the republican concepts of liberty and the pursuit of happiness. This issue would play out in literature as well as in law. For example, the first self-consciously American play produced in the United States—Royall Tyler's popular *The Contrast* (1787)—concerned an American girl and her two suitors, a good one (an American) whom she wants to wed for love, and a bad one (an Englishman) whom her father commands her to marry as an economic arrangement.[29]

In this context, "Indian legends" about arranged marriage may be read as expressions of a collective psyche. Tales about love-struck girls who commit suicide rather than marry men they don't love resonated in a revolutionary era when ideas about marriage were changing. By this analysis, the legendary Indian maidens often functioned as stand-ins for white girls. Lewis Deffebach's now-obscure play *Oolaita* (1821) lends itself especially well to this reading. In bad Shakespearean verse, Deffebach's melodrama tells two contrasting stories. Two white youngsters, Stephen and Emelia, have married against their parents' wishes. To avoid retribution, they run away. They joke about joining the Indians. Ironically, they are ambushed and captured by some Sioux, who intend to kill them. An empathic native girl, Oolaita, intervenes to save their lives. She takes the trespassing lovers to her father, the Sioux "king." Although he doesn't believe their elopement story, he is moved by his daughter's defense of their lives. He orders the lovers to be escorted out of his territory. Meanwhile the king has betrothed his daughter to Monoma, a respected older chief. But Oolaita has already pledged her love to the young chief, Tullula. In the end, the Indian princess goes to the precipice on the shore of Lake Pepin, where, after giving a speech against arranged marriage, she leaps to her death.

This mediocre play is interesting for two reasons. First, it mentions the place-name, Lake Pepin, as if a theater audience would already know it, thus suggesting widespread knowledge of Zebulon Pike's exploration narrative. Second, with its parallel plot of the white lovers, the play is an obvious critique of arranged marriage and a rebuke to those who would oppose the new order of romantic courtship. The drama implies that rigidly traditional, backward-looking whites— those who would separate Stephen and Emelia by force and who would generally deny voluntarism—are not so different from savages. At the same time, Oolaita, in her savage devotion to love, might as well be white.

Female writers and readers seem to have been particularly drawn to the sentimental formula of an Indian girl trapped in a bad marriage. In their desire for greater autonomy in a man's world, authors such as Lydia Maria Child may have wistfully identified with the character of the "Indian wife." Moreover, the topics of marriage and morality— unlike explicitly political topics—fell within the "sphere" of women. Finally, the motif of the lover's leap lent itself well to the genres of short fiction and poetry, both of which accommodated the space constraints of periodicals, the main forum for women's literature in the early 1800s.

The most famous woman to write about a legendary Indian wife was a Briton, Felecia Hemans. "The Indian Woman's Death Song" appeared in her signal collection, *Records of Women* (1828). Mrs. Hemans (as she was known) was "the Poetess" of her time and place. Perhaps not surprisingly, she wrote a poem called "The Last Song of Sappho." If Hemans felt affinity for abandoned women, she had personal as well as professional reasons. Her father had deserted the family when she was a child. As a teenager, Hemans began writing poetry to earn money for the family in the absence of a male breadwinner. Eventually she married an army officer and bore five sons, only to see her husband leave her. She lived as a single woman for the rest of her life. Ironically, her own double abandonment gave her the rare independence to pursue a career writing poems about "woman's weary lot." Hemans churned out sentimental verse in order to pay for her sons' education as they prepared to leave home. In *Records of Women*, half the poems end with the death of a woman. William Keating, whom Hemans referenced by way of an epigraph, inspired the verses about a wronged Indian wife steering her canoe over the Falls of St. Anthony. The New World setting implied the universality of the female burden. Across the globe—at least in Victorian literature—women paid for strength and independence with grief.[30]

Hemans was an inspiration to her counterparts in America. "More than any other female poet of the motherland, she has been naturalized in our new western world," wrote Lydia Sigourney. In time the same Sigourney earned the sobriquet "Mrs. Hemans of America." Fittingly, Sigourney wrote her own legendary poem about an Indian maiden going over a waterfall in a canoe, though the setting was not the Mississippi River but the Niagara. In her poem, a French-Canadian man becomes an honorary member of the Sioux people (who, it should be said, never lived near Niagara Falls). This fur trader woos the chieftain's daughter, Oriska. For her beloved, Oriska maintains a lovely house in the European style. Yet the "smooth Canadian" eventually abandons Oriska and their young boy. Years later an impoverished Oriska finds her former lover on his wedding night. He tells the "dark woman" to go away. Rebuffed, Oriska takes herself and her little one over the lip of the falls.[31]

The mighty drop of the Niagara River has always brought mortality to mind. Visitors here have told stories about ill-fated Indians since the earliest days of tourism. For our purposes, the most interesting fact is that the conventional protagonist switched genders over the first half of the nineteenth century. The original story was more morbid than sentimental. It concerned a hapless—and, in most versions, intoxicated—Indian man who fell asleep in a canoe, which then became unmoored above the falls. By the time the man awoke, it was too late to paddle to safety. Immediately resigned to his fate, he sat up stoically to meet the abyss—though sometimes not before taking a final swig of whiskey. As recounted by dozens of travel writers, this story came across as a dubious history rather than a believable legend from the lips of Indians. Certainly it had literary potential. In 1810 New York City mayor DeWitt Clinton suggested that it "would form a good subject for a poem." Yet to my knowledge only one author felt inspired to give it poetic treatment. When it came to Indian-themed literary legends about death-places, American authors preferred female fatalities. At Niagara the change began in 1825. That year, in the first book of verse published in Canada, James Lynne Alexander wrote about an Indian girl who took the lover's leap near Niagara Falls to avoid an unwanted marriage. The 1830s saw some transitional poems about Indian lovers who died together beside the falls. Finally, in 1848, a female poet wrote perhaps the first over-the-falls legend with a female lead. Sigourney's "Oriska" followed the next year. In the second half of the nineteenth century, the chieftain's daughter completely eclipsed the drunken man in the canoe. The norms of American legendry compelled a sex change for Niagara's victim, who eventually became known as the "Maid of the Mist."[32]

The symbolic Indian female—usually a "queen" or "princess" or "chieftain's daughter"—has a deep American history. The image of the Indian queen was used as an emblem of the New World as early as the sixteenth century. As a graphic, the Indian princess became a symbol of the British colonies around 1765 (when the serious troubles with the crown began); after the revolution she stood for the United States until the Hellenic Columbia supplanted her around 1815. Meanwhile, in U.S. literature, the character of the Indian princess represented a set of high virtues: virginity, purity, and morality. Her signature act (like Oolaita or the quasi-legendary Pocahontas and Sacagawea) was to intercede to save a white person. The ideal Indian princess was of course young and beautiful—and light-complected. After hearing the legend of princess Winona, a midcentury traveler to Minnesota complained that the "copper-headed maidens must have degenerated since those days, as I saw none to whom could be ascribed any higher species of romance than eating hominy with the fingers, and smearing the hair, coarse and harsh as a horse's mane, with possum fat and red lead." This was the other half of the picture: the racist stereotype of the princess required the racist stereotype of the squaw. Dark and stout, the squaw was a beast of burden or a whore, the repository of her tribe's inferiorities. By contrast, the princess was superior to her people, and worked as a civilizer, or a savior, or a martyr.[33]

In nineteenth-century legendry, these overtones of feminized Christianity were sometimes turned into the main melody. In 1857 Mrs. Harriet E. Bishop recounted a version of the Maiden Rock legend—a "tale of the heart"—that praises the determination of Winona to kill herself rather than break her pledge to the man she loves. The tragedy is part of God's plan. The surviving lover, heartbroken, goes wandering and comes across a preacher. Born again, the Indian man goes "forth to tell the wonderful story of Calvary to others of his tribe." In 1872 a women's periodical published a different legend that rose to the level of Christian fantasy. "In every age, and from every race," it began, "God has called for those who have represented the high and holy nature of normal womanhood, women whose pure, spiritual longings, whose grand aspirings, whose seraphic genius, no night of barbarism or of superstition could obscure. Such a one was Winona." The text presents Winona as a disciple of Osseo, an aged prophet of the Sioux who has converted long ago to Christianity. But the rest of the tribesmen reject Osseo's wisdom. Rather than become a slavelike wife, Winona takes the lover's leap, only to have the arms of the river lift her up. The "consecrated maiden" moves to the East and becomes a civilizing schoolteacher for Indians near Niagara.[34]

This moralizing legend about Indians was written by a white Christian woman for other white Christian women in a periodical published by the Methodist Episcopal Church. Feminized Protestantism in nineteenth-century America stressed the innate superior virtue of the fair sex. Through their dependent roles as wives and mothers, Christian women claimed expansive moral authority; the most powerful and politically active women of the age were also "womanly."

From their base in Christianity, they worked for abolition, women's rights, and public health, among other things. As mothers to the world, female moral reformers worked to "save" ignorant immigrants, abused prostitutes, and heathen Indians. These missionaries of domesticity were also active as writers and readers. For this group, then, Indian women were important both as missionary objects and as rhetorical tools. The sacrifices of princesses like Winona pointed to the virtue of all women; and the predicament of nameless squaws pointed to the need for greater womanly influence.

After William Keating, the most influential recounting of the Winona legend appeared in Mary Henderson Eastman's *Dahcotah* (1849), a book that advocated missionary work among the Sioux. An army wife, Eastman spent several years at Fort Snelling on the Mississippi River in Minnesota, where she became friends with missionaries; there she also had frequent contact with Dakota (eastern Sioux) women. Although she found them dirty and ugly, Eastman "could not despise them: they were wives and mothers—God had implanted the same feelings in their hearts as mine." She was appalled by the condition of her spiritual sisters, who seemed to toil nonstop yet receive no gratitude from their men. Eastman claimed that she often reproved the Indian husbands, who, like the Turks, were self-styled "lords of creation." However, she "never dared to instill such insubordinate notions into the heads of my Sioux female friends, lest some ultra 'brave,' in a desperate rage, might substitute the tomahawk for the log [as a weapon]." Eastman hoped that Dakota men could be reformed a bit before their inevitable extinction. Regardless, their negative example had rhetorical value. The patriarchs of the Sioux might be excused for their "cruel, vindictive, and ferocious" acts; they were heathens, after all. What, Eastman asked, was the excuse of *civilized* men for their similar behavior toward women? Although she didn't share it with her readers, Eastman had personal, painful insight into white men and Indian women. When she got to Fort Snelling, she encountered a mixed-race child of her husband. On a previous tour of duty, the then-unmarried Seth Eastman had formed a liaison with a Dakota woman. Their child, Mary Nancy, was known as Winona. "Eastman's squaw" (as the Indians called Mary Henderson) apparently became friendly with her husband's other woman, hard though that must have been.

Eastman felt closer to a different Sioux woman, whom she called Checkered Cloud. It was from her lips that Eastman ostensibly heard most of the legends. Although Eastman edited the stories and freely translated them, she claimed to be "faithful to the spirit of her recitals." Can we accept Eastman's word? It's possible that her informant—this "medicine woman," this "great legend-teller of the Dahcotahs," this "prophetess of the forest"—was an invention or a composite character. The figure of the storytelling crone is a common literary device—one that had in fact just been used by another chronicler of Winona. In any case, Eastman enhanced the credibility by describing Checkered Cloud's appearance in some detail. Cannily, she acknowledged the existence of other versions of the Maiden Rock legend while positioning hers as the most authentic:

> Almost every one has read it a dozen times, and always differently told. Some represent the maiden as delivering an oration from the top of the rock, long enough for an address at a college celebration. It has been stated that she fell into the water, a circumstance which the relative situation of the rock and river would render impossible. Writers have pretended, too, that the heroine of the rock was a Winnebago. It is a mistake, the maiden was a Dahcotah. It was from the Dahcotahs that I obtained the incident, and they believe that it really occurred. They are offended if you suggest the possibility of its being a fiction.[35]

Eastman kept to the plot established by Pike and elaborated by Long and Keating. Refined without being ornate, Eastman showed more lit-

THE LOVER'S LEAP.

Depiction of Winona's leap from Maiden Rock in the 1857 edition of George Catlin's *Letters and Notes on the Manners, Customs, and Traditions of the North American Indians.*

erary restraint than most of her predecessors. For added authenticity, she followed "The Maiden's Rock" with news of a corroborating event "a short time ago" when "a very young girl hung herself, rather than become the wife of a man who was already the husband of one of her sisters." Eastman noted that hanging was "almost invariably" the method of suicide for Sioux women. Yet Eastman undercut her credibility with three legends in the same collection featuring three separate suicidal females—one who leaps off a cliff, one who goes over the Falls of St. Anthony in a canoe, and one who jumps into a waterfall after stabbing herself. When push came to shove, literary convention trumped tribal convention.[36]

When and if—and this is a big if—Sioux women hanged themselves over marriage, they probably did not mean to protest male domination. Sioux culture allowed for three marriage types: elopement, mutual agreement, and purchase. To be purchased was an honor. To be a second wife was not uncommon and not necessarily undesirable. Among the nomadic western Sioux (especially Lakotas), polygyny became more pervasive—and the work of wives more demanding—during the boom in the buffalo robe trade; wives, who made the robes, could function as investments for wealthy Plains Indian men. On the whole, nineteenth-century Sioux marriage customs were more flexible than contemporaneous Euro-American customs. The behavior of the legendary Winona seems unwarranted, since Sioux divorce was a straightforward procedure that could be initiated by either the husband or the wife.[37]

In other words, Euro-Americans—especially middle-class Protestant women—projected their own gender roles onto the Dakotas. This tendency becomes obvious in Mary Eastman's second collection of legends. Most of the 1852 gift-book called *The Iris* was devoted to Dakota "traditions" written by Mary and illustrated by her husband, Seth (an accomplished artist who had earlier contemplated doing a Mississippi River panorama, and who later did illustrations for Henry Schoolcraft). Mary prefaced "The Lover's Leap: or, Wenona's Rock" with a strongly pro-woman, vaguely anti-Indian statement. "In an enlightened country, woman is not considered as being only created to perform the household duties of a wife and mother." Among the vanishing Indian nations, however, "she is still a slave." Eastman then went on to narrate a *completely new version* of the Lake Pepin legend.

It begins with Wenona happily married at age fourteen. But when she fails to produce a child, her husband drinks, takes a new wife, and begins to beat the first one. Despite it all, Wenona (a bit like Eastman) stands by her man. The story ends: "Wherever is man, with his proud, exacting spirit, there is woman, with her devoted and enduring love . . . Wenona's Rock will stand, as long as the world lasts, a monument in memory of woman's love."[38]

Inexplicably, Eastman did not say when or why *this* Wenona took the lover's leap. Nor did she acknowledge the discrepancy between this legend and her previously published one. The existence of two Wenonas demonstrates the rhetorical malleability of the Indian: he— or she—could be a metaphor, a mirror, or simply the Other as whites worked out their gender issues in literature.

Eastman, like many other white women of her era, could be both protofeminist and paleoracist. Tellingly, her identification with "enslaved" women did not extend to black female slaves. The same year that her second Wenona legend appeared, Eastman published a hastily written novel that directly rebutted *Uncle Tom's Cabin*. It was called *Aunt Phillis's Cabin*. In other nineteenth-century texts, expressions of concern for Indian women turned into attacks on Indian people. A good example comes from the vaunted Swedish novelist Fredrika Bremer, who made a two-year tour of America. In 1850 she visited Lake Pepin and the Falls of St. Anthony and heard both legends. Writing about the falls in *The Homes of the New World* six years later, Bremer asserted that Sioux women often killed themselves when faced with arranged marriage or polygyny. To Bremer this was "strong evidence in favor of the pure feminine nature of these poor women." She didn't second-guess those who made the fatal choice: better to be dead than to live with your nose and ears chopped off— the supposed punishment for disobeying the will of the Indian patriarch. After reciting the legend of Ampota Sapa, Bremer made a summary judgment: "that cruel race which scalps children and old people, and which degrades women to beasts of burden, may as well move off into the wilderness, and leave room for a nobler race. There is, in reality, only a higher justice in it."[39]

No man could have been more blunt.

⋮⋮⋮ Bremer's comment about the justice of Indian removal leads to the third and final main function of pseudo-Indian legends in the early to mid-nineteenth century. This function is the hardest to demonstrate because it involves group psychology. Nonetheless, it appears that death-place legends—of which the lover's leap was the preeminent type—became popular in part because they suggested a reason and a justification for the decline of Indians, a decline that could be blamed on Indians themselves. That is, legends may have displaced admissions of racial responsibility and expressions of racial guilt. Nineteenth-century white Americans rarely told stories—factual or legendary—about inflicting violence on native peoples. More often, their history books recounted Indian massacres of whites, and their literary legends told how Indians died on their own.

In art and literature, the figure of the dying Indian predates the era of legends. A genre piece, the death song, goes back to the 1780s. A poem called "The Death-Song of a Cherokee Indian" (also called the "The Death-Song of Alknomook") became a transatlantic favorite and was set to music many times. In this first-person lyric, a wounded and captured Cherokee warrior looks forward to a noble death; he will not complain despite torture by his tribal enemies. The words are spectral: the all-but-dead speaker looks forward to joining his father's spirit in the distant land. This presentation was typical. In the literature of the early republic, Euro-Americans repeatedly imagined natives as ghosts, thereby practicing a literary form of removal.[40]

Real Indians could disrupt the imagination, however. The Indian wars following the revolution—culminating in Tecumseh's alliance—reminded whites that Indians would not give up the ghost without a fight. In the 1830s Indian issues moved to the forefront of national debate when President Andrew Jackson advanced the policy of Indian Removal. The policy was portrayed as a humanitarian effort to give new homes to eastern Indians. Yet even apologists could see that fraud and theft and violence abetted relocation. In particular, the Cherokees of Georgia were flagrantly robbed. Although they took their case to the Supreme Court and won, they still lost their homeland. More losses awaited the Cherokees on their devastating journey to the Plains—the Trail of Tears.

Indian Removal prompted substantial soul-searching among many American citizens, including women's activists and the literati. It is no coincidence that the highpoint of Indianist literature coincided exactly with the highpoint of Indian Removal. The famed William Cullen Bryant, a supporter of Indian Removal, wrote numerous elegiac Indian poems, including a lover's leap legend, between 1821 and 1832. A famous "Indian play"—indeed, one of the great sensations of nineteenth-century American drama—hit the stage in 1829. *Metamora; or, The Last of the Wampanoags* was a legendlike retelling of the seventeenth-century King Philip's War. The play turned New England's Indians into tragic heroes. A star vehicle for Edwin Forrest, America's leading actor, *Metamora* inspired theatrical imitations, dime novels, and rhyming books. As Jill Lepore writes, "*Metamora* was just one of dozens if not hundreds of literary productions by which the fate of the Cherokees, Choctaws, Seminoles, Creeks, and Chickasaws was made acceptable to the American public by virtue of its very inevitability." Last King of the Lenapes, Last of the Mohicans, Last of the Wampanoags, Last of the Cherokees: all Indians eventually sang their Death Song.[41]

It's possible that authors and readers of "Indian legends" felt pangs of guilt about the removal policy and its effect on natives. If so, legends about suicidal Indians may have assuaged those pangs by creating a literary and topographical memorial to the removed; by allowing an exercise in empathy for Indian characters; and by shifting attention from white-on-Indian violence to self-inflicted Indian violence.

Of course, this kind of psychological reading is most convincing when it can be personally or locally grounded. The best local example comes from old Habersham County, Georgia, which abutted the Cherokee Nation in the 1820s. This part of Georgia had been opened to settlement (by lottery) in 1819 following a land cession coerced from the Cherokees. Habersham County—specifically the Nacoochee Valley—was the origin point of the gold rush of 1828-29, the event that heralded the dissolution of the remaining Cherokee Nation. One of the original white settlers, Edward Williams, supplied miners with grain. His son, George, went on to become a merchant, traveler, and author. In his book, *Sketches of Travel in the Old and New World* (1871), George Williams wrote several letters about his home, Nacoochee. Exhuming the memory of the Cherokees, he lamented that their burial mounds had all been plowed, leaving "no proud monument." There was, however, Mount Yonah, a solitary summit at the southern end of the Blue Ridge Mountains. As a child, Williams climbed this "stupendous pile of granite" several times a week in summer; old Indian trails led to the summit. As he recalled, "This guardian of the valley became as familiar to me as the face of my beloved mother."[42] He remembered, too, that community groups celebrated holidays such as Independence Day and Christmas on top of Mount Yonah. Thanks to these mountain devotees, Mount Yonah became a legendary spot. The legend—popularized by Williams though not invented by him—tells of an illicit intertribal love affair between Nacoochee ("Evening Star," a Cherokee princess) and Sautee (a brave from the enemy Choctaws). The lovers elope only to be pursued by a war party sent by the bride's father. The trackers find Sautee and barbarously execute him by throwing him from the mountain. After watching, Nacoochee follows Sautee into the spirit world by taking the lover's leap.

In *Sketches of Travel*, Williams' telling of the legend immediately followed an extended passage on the extinction of America's Indians. Remarkably, Williams said nothing specific about the unfair treaties forced upon the Cherokees or about the avaricious whites who seized the farmhouses of the Civilized Tribes; instead he made a vague reference to the Cherokees being "driven from their cherished hunting grounds." His remorse was intense yet removed:

> The dreadful work which was commenced by the Pilgrim Fathers centuries ago; an extermination which has been unceasingly kept up in the name of Christianity ! is fast blotting from the earth a great family of populous nations. At the last day, when Gabriel sounds his trumpet to awake the slumbering dead, and the great book is opened, nations and governments, as well as individuals, will call upon the mountains to fall upon them, that they and their sins may be hidden from the Judge that sitteth on the Throne.[43]

Then, *with the very next sentence,* Williams began the story of the doomed lovers Nacoochee and Sautee. The juxtaposition of jeremiad and legend is startling. Could it be that Williams (subconsciously) called upon Mount Yonah to hide the sins of town fathers? Could it be that a violent local legend attributed to Indians substituted for a violent local history belonging to whites? Certainly it appears that Williams used the legend to mask his own fear of spiritual retribution.

Georgia is not unique. In his survey of pseudo-Indian legends from across the United States, Francis A. de Caro has discerned a template to what he calls the "folklore of guilt." The template begins with a premise: "There were noble Indians." Then comes the drama of destruction. The noble Indians were destroyed by one of three things: "treacherous, evil, barbaric Indians" or "barbaric tribal codes and customs" or "natural calamities." Finally, a touch of retribution: if the noble Indians were destroyed by their own traditions or by others' aggressions, the traditionalists or the aggressors may also die. "Surely the legends might perform a wish-fulfillment function," writes de Caro; "they represent a projection of what we wish had been the true historical record, that the Indians had conveniently 'self-destructed.'" Two other lover's leaps from postremoval Cherokee country—Tallulah

Falls, Georgia (the "Niagara of the South"), and Noccalula Falls, Alabama—may have functioned in this way, with falling Indians taking the place of the fallen. A variety of legendary death-places seem to confirm de Caro's interpretation. For example, the *entire* Biloxi tribe purportedly committed mass suicide at Pascagoula Bay, Mississippi. In Illinois, Starved Rock—a scenic bluff above the Illinois River that is now a popular state park—was the supposed location of a lover's leap *and* the mass destruction of the last tribe of the Illinois Indians, who were besieged by the vengeful Potawatomi. The former site of a French fort, Starved Rock did in fact have a violent history, but it was a very complicated history. With fake legends, Euro-Americans could turn complicated violence into simple barbarism, and victims into perpetrators.[44]

The propensity of legendary Indians to die off becomes even more striking when we compare the lover's leap to a related motif, the prodigious jump. Legends of this type relate marvelous athletic feats by runners or horseback riders; the protagonists survive death-defying jumps over chasms and torrents. In other words, white heroes survive where Indian lovers die. This story type goes back to Europe; Scotland, for example, contains such places as the Soldier's Leap, Randolph's Leap, McGregor's Leap, and Rob Roy's Leap. In America, the foundational legends concern white men—soldiers or Indian killers—escaping from Indians.[45] Legendary sites include Brady's Leap (of Captain Samuel Brady) on the Cuyahoga River, Ohio; Peabody's Leap (of Timothy Peabody), Lake Champlain, New York; Rogers Rock (where Major Robert Rogers jumped), Lake George, New York; and The Images (where Captain Frye jumped), Sebago Lake, Maine.

The perpetually falling Indian—a trope that suggested racial weakness—became so familiar that authors could reference it ironically. An 1843 gift-book story, "The Lover's Leap," played with readers' expectations; it was not a conventional "Indian legend." Instead, the story concerned a seventeenth-century settler who boldly built his homestead on an isolated knoll, Rock Nest, above the Connecticut River near Springfield, Massachusetts. This settler had a fair-haired daughter, Grace. One night, a hundred bloodthirsty Indians besieged Rock Nest. All but Grace fell victim to the tomahawk. Luckily for her, an English rider—a man unsubtly named Lovell—fetched her away and led his black steed across the "unfordable and bridgeless river." This inversion of the formula reached its apotheosis in Texas, where, in the later part of the century, the state secretary of the Independent Order of Odd Fellows wrote a legend about a cowboy named Lover who found safety from murderous Indians by leaping from a cliff, catching a tree branch, and swinging to the ground. All this happened near Palo Pinto, he said. The exact spot, Lover's Retreat, was the anti–lover's leap. In legend as in life, white men had certain advantages. Better to be Mr. Lover than the loveless Winona.[46]

::: After the 1850s, legend production increased quantitatively but dropped precipitously in quality. Before, serious authors wrote legends; Indians and "Indian legends" could be the stuff of important national literature. After, legends became the domain of local enthusiasts, commercial hacks, and tourism boosters. In 1858 the New York literary magazine *The Knickerbocker* mocked the popularity of Hiawatha by printing a satirical poem by "our friend, the writer of *'Weenonah, ye Exceedynglie Sorrowfull Legende of ye Lake Pepin.'"*[47]

On the Upper Mississippi, signs of legend fatigue initially appeared in the immediate aftermath the Civil War, when tourist traffic resumed. The citizens of Minnesota were temporarily averse to the romanticization of the Sioux because the state had gone through its own internecine conflict in the midst of the national one. The "Sioux Uprising" of 1862 led to the deaths of hundreds of settlers—for which the Sioux were punished with select executions and mass expulsions. In this context, a correspondent for the *Ladies' Repository* took a river trip in 1865. At Lake Pepin, she reported, the captain couldn't bear to read the legend one more time, so he handed the text to a passenger and begged him to do it. During the recital the captain "shed derisive squints" even as a refined female passenger soaked in the melancholy. Afterward, he broke the silence:

> "The precise date of that transaction was while Noah was building the ark, and I wish most heartily that when that squaw jumped off there the whole race had gone in after her." Fixing a glance of haughty sarcasm upon the romancing lady, he inquired, "Who was that chap Longfellow made such a fuss about[?]"
>
> "Hiawatha," she replied in an injured tone, giving the continental sound to all the vowels.
>
> "Yes, well, I haven't heard Longfellow quoted much since the massacre, and I guess you can buy his book pretty cheap now up the river [in Minneapolis]."[48]

Widespread emigration to Minnesota resumed around 1869, and it became acceptable again to romanticize Sioux people—at least the legendary ones. A settlers' guide from 1869 repeated the legend of Lake Pepin before noting that "quite a village has sprung up" nearby.[49] The settlement was called Maiden's Rock. Another area village had already taken the name Winona.

This Dakota name traveled far; today there are municipalities called Winona in Arkansas, Arizona, Idaho, Kansas, Michigan, Minnesota, Missouri, Mississippi, New Hampshire, New York, Ohio, South Carolina, Tennessee, Texas, Virginia, Washington, and West Virginia. This wide distribution suggests the former pervasiveness of the lover's leap legend. The smaller number of towns named Wenona/Wenonah could have derived from the legend or from Longfellow; Wenonah was the name of Hiawatha's mother. It's likely that the two legendary women got mixed up in people's minds, and that Winona became a generic "Indian" name. As a suicidal or doomed maiden, Winona eventually showed up at the falls of the Merrimac River, New Hampshire, and a cliff near Junction, Texas, among other places.

Other leaps did not inspire any character names—or texts—at all. The toponym was enough. Numerous river towns reflexively christened new crossings "Lovers Leap Bridge." Any good precipice might be called Lover's Leap, just as any misty cascade might be called Bridal Veil Falls. More than forty cliffs in the United States retain Lover's Leap as their official name. In the nineteenth century, there were many more. A list of the prominent locations would include Delaware Water Gap, Pennsylvania–New Jersey; Wissahickon Creek, Fairmount Park, Philadelphia; French Broad River, near Hot Springs, North Carolina; Chattahoochee River, near Columbus, Georgia; Tallulah Falls, northeast of Atlanta, Georgia; Illinois River, adjacent to Starved Rock near Utica, Illinois; and Mackinac Island, Michigan. Wisconsin, a state not known for its sheer terrain, acquired at least nine leaps besides Maiden Rock. Even Mammoth Cave, Kentucky, had an underground leaping spot. American sightseers expected to find legendary sites on their tours just as they expected to find hotel accommodations. An 1870 visitor to the Natural Bridge of Virginia talked about the "celebrated Lover's Leap" opposite the famous formation. "That any one ever leaped from this point, is not claimed, nor even supposed," he wrote. The name had become narrative shorthand, a substitute for a story everyone knew by heart. But that story was no longer about Sappho. She, like the classics in general, faded from American consciousness over the 1800s. A generic Indian princess took her place.[50]

Among the Gilded Age cosmopolitan set, Winona became a source of skepticism, ridicule, or bemused curiosity. Her leap seemed banal, like El Dorado or Captain Kidd's treasure. However, among the homegrown literary talent of the Upper Midwest—poets who published in Minneapolis instead of Boston, New York, or Philadelphia— the legend of Lake Pepin remained a favorite literary subject. The plot ossified, but certain details varied. Winona's leap was said to have happened around 1700 or 1785 or 1800 or even 1820. Sometimes the maiden landed in water, sometimes on rock; one periodical even published two contradictory stories in two consecutive years.[51]

Regardless of literary value, the lover's leap retained commercial value. "Good Indian legends can be grown in almost any locality with a little care and attention," read a 1903 editorial on the tourism industry. "It adds an interest to a very ordinary cliff to know that a persecuted and necessarily beautiful Indian maiden leaped thence to her death." The Far West, because of its late incorporation into the Union, skipped the sincere, literary phase of legend-making and went straight to the cynical, commercial one. An amusing example comes from a now forgotten California attraction: Gilroy Hot Springs. One promoter of the springs was also a druggist. He hoped to lure people with his eucalyptus salve (twenty-five cents per box), the healing sulfur waters, and also the romantic tragedy of Juanita, the Indian Princess. A booklet about Juanita's fatal leap included pharmaceutical advertisements. Tourist-patients could buy "Magic Headache Powder," "Magic Toothache Drops," and various other remedies—but nothing to cure lovesickness.[52]

At Niagara Falls, entrepreneurs perfected the tourist trap, complete with hotels, shops, theaters, an Indian village (known to have Irish employees dressed up as Indians), and an updated legend. By 1900 the Lovesick Maiden—who had earlier replaced the Drunken Buck—had fallen away to accommodate the Virgin Sacrifice. The earliest reference I have found comes from an 1868 vacation guide. In certain key details, the story resembles Eugene Roberts' Timpanogos legend: the Indians were required to propitiate the spirit of the falls with an annual sacrifice of their most beautiful maiden, who sat among fruits and flowers in a white bark canoe before being carried over "this awful portal to eternity." Sometimes this "Maid of the Mist" was called Winona/Wenona. Eventually she received a distinctive moniker: Lelawala. Gift shops sold postcards of her fatal descent—in the nude. Perhaps the story (and the image) resonated at a place where so many women lost their virginity. The modern tradition of the honeymoon began here in the Gilded Age. For the next century the Maid of the Mist Steamboat Company repeated the story of the virgin sacrifice in its promotional literature and tours. Only in 1996, after repeated complaints from local Native Americans and First Nations peoples, did the company retire the legend.[53]

Given the ludicrous proliferation of lover's leaps in the Gilded Age, it's only fitting that the era's top satirist did a send-up. Mark Twain was well acquainted with the legendary landforms of the Mississippi, having grown up in Hannibal, Missouri, a river town with its own lover's leap. In 1902 he quipped that he had known Hannibal "ever since 'Lovers' Leap' was a mole-hill and the Mississippi River a small creek."[54] Twain's brother, Orion Clemens, published a legend about the leap in 1840. During his days on the river, Twain discovered the font of such stories—Lake Pepin. In his book *Life on the Mississippi* Twain included a chapter called "Legends and Scenery," which he wrote as a conversation between himself and "an old gentleman" passenger with a repertoire of stories. At Lake Pepin, the old-timer began his recital the usual way—inflexible parents insisting on an arranged marriage. Then came the twist:

> "On reaching the rock, We-no-na ran to its summit and standing on its edge upbraided her parents who were below, for their cruelty, and then singing a death-dirge, threw herself from the precipice and dashed them in pieces on the rock below.
>
> "Dashed who in pieces—her parents?"
>
> "Yes."
>
> "Well, it certainly was a tragic business, as you say. And moreover, there is a startling kind of dramatic surprise about it which I was not looking for. It is a distinct improvement upon the threadbare form of Indian legend. There are fifty Lover's Leaps along the Mississippi from whose summit disappointed Indian girls have jumped, but this is the only jump in the lot that turned out in the right and satisfactory way."[55]

Twain's irreverence seems a world away from the mawkishness of antebellum literary legends. His dismissal of Winona matched his larger, well-known disdain for Indianist literature, including James Fenimore Cooper. Yet for all his disparagement, Twain did not give up entirely on Indian legends. His (fictional) informant, the old gentleman, admitted under examination that most legends were "exceedingly sorry rubbish," and offered Henry Schoolcraft as a corrective. In *Life on the Mississippi,* Twain went so far as to reprint two of Schoolcraft's legends—one of which had been previously adapted by Longfellow. According to Twain, Schoolcraft's legends came "directly from Indian lips."[56] Schoolcraft was not, however, the source that Twain imagined him to be. Schoolcraft reworked his material. Adding to the irony, Schoolcraft had promulgated a version of the lover's leap legend that Twain so brilliantly lampooned.

Native-born whites found it hard to let go of their fantasy Indians. A local county history from the 1880s made the obvious point that Winona could not have jumped into the water as many claimed: the bluff did not overhang the river! And the maiden could not have dashed to pieces, given all the trees. "The Indians laugh when the legend of the 'Lover's Leap' is repeated to them," the author wrote. Still, he did not want to destroy this "popular idol," because "there is too little of romance in this matter-of-fact age." Another local history—written by none other than Lafayette Bunnell, the namer of Yosemite Valley, who came from Winona, Minnesota—reported that "[my] old-time half-breed friends had declared to me that there was no authentic tradition even of such an occurrence as attaches to the 'Maiden Rock.'" Yet even the skeptical Bunnell gave the romance some credence because of Major Long's reported interaction with Wazzecoota back in 1817. No one was prepared to call Zebulon Pike, Stephen Long, and William Keating the Corps of Dishonesty. There had to be some truth at the bottom of it all.[57]

The lover's leap was easy to accept for the same reason it was hard to believe: it happened in so many places. In 1873 *Appleton's Journal* published an academic analysis of this problem of credence: "We risk little in saying that eastward of the Mississippi there is scarcely a lakeshore or a river-bank, remarkable for its precipitous and rugged beauty, where some overhanging crag is not pointed out as the scene of this tragic incident, and known as the 'Lover's Leap.'" The author continued: "Even the most firm believer in the general trustworthiness of tradition must have his faith staggered by the frequency with which this romantic suicide is said to have taken place." But instead of suggesting the obvious—that the lover's leap was a European literary motif adopted by American writers—the author went on to present a mythological explanation. The lover's leap stood for the plunging of the sun into the western horizon. The leap was like the Flood, a universal myth type: genuine folklore rather than literary invention.[58]

This approach was ahead of its time. Abandoned by serious authors (such as Twain), the genre of the local legend would in fact *become* oral literature in the twentieth century. An important transitional figure was Charles Skinner, who wrote the well-received *Myths and Legends of Our Own Land* (2 vols., 1896) and *American Myths and Legends* (2 vols., 1903). Arranged geographically, these books contained hundreds of local legends, most of which featured natural landmarks; "traditions do not thrive in brick and brownstone," he claimed. In presentation, these legend gazetteers called more attention to Skinner the editor than to Skinner the author. His legends seemed like pieces of Americana collected from the field—though in fact they came out of books, newspapers, and magazines. In a chapter called "Storied Waters, Cliffs, and Mountains," Skinner noted the improbable number of lover's leaps but said, "there is no doubt that in many instances the story antedated the arrival of the white men."[59]

In Skinner's work, Maiden Rock was merely one of dozens of lover's leaps. The place had lost its primacy. Now that tourist promoters did the main work of creating and maintaining "Indian legends," this once-famous promontory faced several disadvantages. After the Civil War, east-west railroad tourism largely obviated north-south steamboat tourism. It was no longer fashionable to tour the Upper Mississippi—especially when transcontinentals allowed access to the wonders of the Far West. Compared to the Sierras or the Rockies, the bluffs of the Mississippi lost much of their ability to impress. Maiden Rock's glory days had come and gone with the 1840s. Among artists and writers, Lake Pepin and its legend had enough residual stature to appear in William Cullen Bryant's *Picturesque America* (1874), an authoritative two-volume statement on the leading features of the American landscape. However, an 1876 tourist guide by the Chicago & Northwestern Railway Company—the only line with service to Winona, Minnesota—made no mention of Lake Pepin or Maiden Rock.

By 1900 Maiden Rock had shrunk from a national to a regional landmark. The swan song for this legendary place was, improbably, a grand opera by an Italian-American composer, Alberto Bimboni. A gala performance of Bimboni's *Winona* was staged at the Minneapolis Municipal Auditorium in 1928, two years after its premiere in Portland, Oregon. Nine thousand midwesterners assembled for the event. But Minneapolis was a little too far away from Maiden Rock to permanently revive the legend. It mattered that the lover's leap was not visible from any municipality—not even from the town Winona, which erected a statue to the Indian maiden in 1902. The rock was a river traveler's landmark, and the age of river travel had come to an end. And so this lover's leap—the All-American Lover's Leap—faded from legend to history. "There was a time when a mystic halo hung over the charming eminence known as Maiden's Rock," recalled a local Wisconsin newspaper in 1941. "But in the rushing, skeptical, irreverent present day it is just another rock-faced bluff along the Upper Mississippi."[60] As if to confirm this appraisal, the WPA's *Guide to the Badger State* (1941)—part of the series of state guides known for their wide coverage and literary quality—mentioned Maiden Rock only in passing, and said nothing about the legend. By the turn of millennium, the film actress Winona Ryder (born in Winona) was far better known than her legendary namesake.

::: That the lover's leap lost momentum in the early twentieth century is, on the face of it, surprising. The Far West had not run out of scenery; indeed, the region kept acquiring new attractions in the form of national parks and monuments. Enterprises like the Fred Harvey Company (associated with the Atchison, Topeka & Santa Fe Railway) spent considerable capital publicizing these attractions. Simultaneously, native-born whites became newly fascinated with Native Americans during an era when the "New Immigration" called into question the meaning of whiteness and indeed of Americanness. However, these people fancied Indian arts, crafts, and performances far more than pseudo-Indian place-stories. More to the point, the services that the lover's leap once performed—addressing cultural anxieties about nationhood, gender, and race—lost their relevance. In 1925 a *New York Times* writer noted approvingly that one of the new southwestern playgrounds, Utah's Zion National Park, lacked a lover's leap, and warned against the "Just Too Cuters" who might yet try to foist the hackneyed name on the astounding monolith known as the Great White Throne (a place-name that evoked a more up-to-date racialism).[61]

The larger genre of pseudo-Indian local legends sputtered on through the first quarter of the century. In this final stage, the key players were not literary or commercial figures, but urbanites, hikers, conservationists, and collegians—often a combination of all four. Urban hikers promoted the Indianness of popular peaks. This trend was especially strong in the West, where many cities symbolically annexed their neighboring peaks in the early 1900s. The Mountaineers of Seattle and The Mazamas of Portland published numerous legends about Mount Rainier in their magazines. This was not simply fakelore, however. Genuine native stories were recounted on Rainier (as well as Crater Lake and Mount Shasta). In contrast, no such stories existed at Mount Tamalpais—the favorite hiking spot for San Franciscans before World War II. Undeterred, Bay Area urbanites simply invented a legend about a sleeping Indian maiden. At Pikes Peak, meanwhile, several fake Indian legends appeared between the 1890s and 1920s thanks to promoters in Colorado Springs and Denver. This was a striking development because the Indianness of the Pikes Peak region had previously been centered on the Manitou mineral springs, each of which had an Indianist name. Literary legends about the springs went back as far as 1847.[62]

In the East, the popularization of Indianist landforms had at least one notable recurrence in the twentieth century. Millionaire Henry Shoemaker—banker, newspaperman, conservationist, and diplomat—applied his wealth and energy to promoting the cultural heritage of Pennsylvania, especially its "mountain country." He went on to become the nation's first state folklorist. Of Shoemaker's hundreds of local legends, many were in fact collected in the field. A few others were true fakelore. In 1902 he first published "The Legend of Penn's Cave," a tale about a clandestine love affair between a French trader and an Indian chieftain's daughter, Nita-nee. (Shoemaker supposedly heard the story as a child from a "full-blooded" Seneca elder.) The story ends with six of Nita-nee's brothers throwing the Frenchman off a ledge at the mouth of the cave. Princess Nita-nee went on to live a long life; as related in a different Shoemaker legend, her name found a home on Mount Nittany, the picturesque knoll adjacent to Penn State University. To this day, students, alumni, and fans of the gridiron "Nittany Lions" keep these stories alive.[63]

In Utah, at roughly the same time, different collegians adopted a different Indianist mountain. Boosters affiliated with Brigham Young University wanted to create an analogue to the modern Pikes Peak—a mountain with automobile access, hiking trails, and legendary interest. With its altitude, its "glacier," its cave, and its place-name, Mount Timpanogos already seemed like a pretty good package. An Indian legend made the package complete. Given the period—1910s–1920s—the appearance of a legend made sense. The moment was close enough to the nineteenth century; and according to nineteenth-century convention, great natural landmarks produced legends that people could read about. The process was reflexive. White Americans had been practicing this kind of writing long before Eugene "Timpanogos" Roberts. The making of "Timp" may have been a modernist project, but the impulse to give the landmark a legend was conservative.

Shoemaker and Roberts were born in the same year, 1880; both carried a nineteenth-century literary form into the new century. Of the two men, however, Shoemaker was more urbane and educated. An admirer of Charles Skinner and a self-taught folklorist, Shoemaker would have understood that the classic American lover's leap—an Indian princess jumping off a cliff—was hackneyed, and in fact he did not use the motif. Compared with Shoemaker's "The Legend of Penn's Cave," Roberts' "The Story of Utahna and Red Eagle" reads like a naively old-fashioned text.

Fittingly, then, "Timp" was the terminal leap, the last major American landform to be haunted by Winona. Even as Mount Timpanogos was becoming storied, many of its geographic antecedents were losing their legendary quality. Originally a curiosity, then a cliché, the lover's leap became a curiosity once again. The relic sites are generally linked to tourism and recreation (examples include Philmont Scout Ranch, New Mexico; Hawks Nest State Park, West Virginia; Rock City, Tennessee). At Alabama's Noccalula Falls Park and Campground, the owners have erected a precariously balanced thirteen-foot bronze statue of a Cherokee princess *in the act of jumping*. The tourism industry has nurtured leaps outside America; tropical suicide spots include Lover's Leap near Treasure Beach, Jamaica, and Two Lovers' Point at Puntan dos Amantes Park, Guam. But for every leap that has hung on, many, many more have dropped off. How many current residents of the state of New York have ever heard of the lover's leaps at Canandaigua Lake, at Little Falls, at Indian Maiden's Cliff, at Mount Utsayantha, at Raven Rock, at Spook Rock, at Gypsy Rock, or at Kaaterskill Falls? Although the *idea* of the lover's leap retains a (small) place in popular culture, the literature and the geography that once supported the idea have largely been forgotten.

In Utah Valley Eugene Roberts' "Story of Utahna and Red Eagle" was quickly superseded by oral versions of the legend. The Legend of Timpanogos thus represents a turning point in American legendry when pseudo-Indian legends stopped being literature (high or low) and started being folklore. This shift is apposite, given that this genealogy of the American lover's leap began with Zebulon Pike *listening* to a story. The chain of influence connecting Maiden Rock to Mount Timpanogos runs in a circle. Like any good history, the supposed beginning is really the end.

9

Performing a Remembered Past

The Legend of Timpanogos survived because it was embodied. People imagined the mountain itself as an Indian body, and the bodies of performers acted out the legend. After encountering the legend around a smoky campfire or deep inside the chill, damp darkness of Timpanogos Cave, many listeners became tellers, repeating the legend—performing it—to family and friends. In this way, by the mid-twentieth century Eugene Roberts' printed story was transformed into pageantry and folklore.

Formal recitals mattered, too. At two moments the Legend of Timpanogos inspired concert works—first an opera, later a ballet and an oratorio. These performance pieces grew out of a genre of Indianist music, a genre that flowered in the early twentieth century. Unlike literary legends, Indianist musical works often originated in collaboration with Native Americans. This musical history allows a different perspective on the Indianness of "Timp," which has proven both enduring and changeable. By the late 1990s, when Utahns staged back-to-back celebrations of the state centennial and the Mormon pioneer sesquicentennial, certain Utah Indians claimed the Indianness of the mountain as their own. Utes themselves were known to recite the legend. History, memory, and geography combined in unlikely ways.

⁝⁝⁝ It's said that Eugene Roberts' "Story of Utahna and Red Eagle" originated as an assembly talk. Arriving early at his engagement at Pleasant Grove High School, Roberts waited in his car. Gazing out the window at snow-covered Mount Timpanogos, he outlined the narrative. A gifted speaker, he decided to try it out on the students. Later he told an acquaintance that

> he just had the kids hanging on the edges of their seats. But instead of ending it the way he eventually did—and it wasn't too clear in his own mind at this time—he gave it kind of a gag ending, like Utahna, instead of jumping off the cliff, turned around . . . and told Red Eagle to "drop dead" or something like that. Well, he said the students were just— they were furious: this gripping story that he had told them and then he ended it on a kind of a gag note. So he went home and he told his wife and she says, "Well, you've got a good story there, it will help you promote the hike," she says. "Fix up the ending and you can promote it."[1]

In other words, Roberts wanted to be like Mark Twain; his wife told him to be like William Cullen Bryant.

Roberts had other practice to draw on. In the 1910s, as part of BYU's summer school, he often led students on moonlight hikes. At some point on the trail he would stop the group with "shhh, listen." To their surprise, the students heard the beating of a tom-tom. Roberts would train his flashlight on a rock, where a helper dressed in "Indian chief regalia" demanded to know why the students trespassed on his domain. After this prank, Roberts would regale the hikers with a legend about the terrain or the trail.[2]

Born in 1880, Roberts belonged to the first generation of Mormons in northern Utah who lived without regular contact with native peoples. He stood in contrast to his Scottish-born father, who, according to an autobiographical sketch, encountered "trouble" with Indians while crossing the plains in 1851, fought Utes in Utah Valley in 1855, and endured a brief captivity by Crows while trading in Wyoming in 1857. To the younger Roberts, a relative city slicker, this history seemed romantic. "It was but yesterday that our fathers were engaged in vigorous pioneer struggles," he wrote in 1911, the year before his father's death. "But their work is finished; they have made the desert bloom and built up a commonwealth; and their sons, lolling in comparative luxury, are gradually forgetting their debt to their fathers."[3]

That passage comes from Roberts' proposal to create a Mormon scout program. Roberts wanted the soft boys of the city to recapture the firm masculinity of the frontier. He called his proposed group the Boy Pioneers of Utah and trumpeted its potential to take Mormon youth away from "modernism" and back to "Nature and the Primitive." Clearly Roberts drew inspiration from Dan Beard, founder of the Sons of Daniel Boone (1905), whose members were called Boy Pioneers. At about the same time Ernest Thompson Seton founded the Woodcraft League of America, which stressed the craft and lore of Indians. Both organizations were absorbed by the Boy Scouts of America (BSA), founded in 1910. The LDS Church initially resisted the scouting movement because it had its own youth program, the Mutual Improvement Association (MIA). Roberts helped to sway the hierarchy. The Church started using the term MIA Scouts in 1912; soon afterward it affiliated with the BSA. By 1918 Utah had more scouts per capita than any other state.

Throughout the United States, scouts and scout leaders did not seem bothered by the inherent contradiction between playing Indian and playing pioneer. Early BSA guides included extensive how-to information on making headdresses, moccasins, tipis, arrowheads, and so on. They also contained legends, songs, and dances. Scout "lodges" sometimes staged "Indian pageants" at BSA camps—also called "Pow Wows." Boys could apply their woodcraft toward the "Indian Lore" merit badge. For senior scouts, an Indianist fraternity, the Order of the Arrow, was introduced in 1915. Utah scouts worked toward such goals even as they gathered for activities like hiking the Mormon Trail to reenact the experience of their pioneer ancestors.[4]

Scoutmaster Roberts did his own double performance by performing "Indian" legends. Even as he took the title of "chief medicine man" or "big chieftain" on his hikes, Roberts invented Indian characters that functioned as foils.[5] Where Utahna and Red Eagle had gone to die, hikers went to be renewed. Although hikers grew closer to God on the mountain, they did not mistake the mountain for a god. They, like "Indians," sensed the spiritual power of the mountain, but they did not succumb to superstition. Hikers had no fear of trespassing on hallowed ground.

Practically every U.S. national park and natural wonderland is home to dubious stories about Indians who were "afraid" to ascend some magnificent canyon or peak. At Yellowstone, tourist promoters and park rangers claimed erroneously for nearly a century that Indians never visited the thermal zones because these "devilish" places were "tabooed." Here and elsewhere, the early supporters of the national park system preferred to imagine the parks as unpeopled wilderness areas. Native Americans did more than occasionally place use restrictions on sacred sites, but colonizers paid attention—by self-admiringly transgressing "Indian tradition"—only when the restrictions concerned recreational landscapes. This attitude goes back to the beginnings of nature tourism in the United States—back to the White Mountains. Indians "entreated" the "first explorer" of New Hampshire's high peaks "not to undertake the daring feat, and thus so stir up the wrath of the Gods." Similarly, the white men who made the "first" ascent of Mount St. Helens around 1860 claimed to have ignored the superstitious warnings of their Indian guides.[6]

Most strikingly, this formulaic interaction can be found in Hazard Stevens' gripping account of the conquest of Mount Rainier. The author-explorer was the son of Isaac Stevens, the former territorial governor of Washington—a man who gained fame for negotiating treaties with Indians. Like Eugene Roberts but even more so, Hazard Stevens could never match his father's frontier experience. As part of the post-pioneer generation, he probably considered his peak experience to be the next-best thing. Takhoma (as he called it) "was a virgin peak. The superstitious fears and traditions of the Indians, as well as the dangers of the ascent, had prevented their attempting to reach the summit." Nevertheless, Stevens relied on a native guide, Sluiskin, to get him within striking distance. Supposedly Sluiskin tried to deter his client by saying that the mountain was "inhabited by an evil spirit who dwelt in a fiery lake on its summit." This spirit would "surely punish the sacrilegious attempt to invade his sanctuary." After his triumphant return from the summit, Stevens related his adventure to many friends. His story performance included a retelling of Sluiskin's "harangue."[7]

By telling legends about the trail—or *on* the trail—white hikers could both invoke Indian superstition and transgress it. They, like scouts, could internalize Indianness (with its superior vitality, strength, bravery, manliness) without the inferiority of actually being Indian. Primitivist hikers were similar yet superior to the legendary primitives who hiked.

In one case the ambivalent dual identification as Indian/hiker was performed in costume on Mount Timpanogos. Mormon Vernon Selman—a son of Mormon converts, hence the name—came to America from Wales in 1864. Around 1880 he was "called on a mission" to the reservation Utes. During twenty-two years of service, he "learned to appreciate the Redmen and his ways." Subsequently Selman retired to the Provo area, where he attended the Timpanogos Ward and became active in the Timpanogos Council of the Boy Scouts of America. He taught the boys leathercraft and other "Indian work" in the tipi he erected on his lawn. Among scouts he used his "Indian name," O-und ("The Arrow Maker"). In 1927 O-und twice led scouts to the top of Mount Timpanogos wearing moccasins and "war paint," carrying a homemade bow and arrow in hand. By playing Indian on the mountain, Selman summoned Roberts' legend. But as a white native, the seventy-four-year-old O-und was free to do what young Utahna and Red Eagle could not—come back down.[8]

The local connection between scouting and Indian play did not end with Roberts and Selman. In the 1920s Andy A. Anderson, the first executive of the Timpanogos Council, performed his own version of the Legend of Timpanogos at campfire circles.[9] The plot differs from "The Story of Utahna and Red Eagle," though it ends in essentially the same way. There is no original extant text for this legend, but the main features are clear:

> The Nez Perce are suffering from famine. The chief's son, Timpanac, travels south to the valley of the Fish-Eaters to search for aid. There he falls in love with Ucanogos, the daughter of the local chief. There are rival suitors, however. They all compete in a three-part courtship contest. The first challenge is to take down with bare hands the largest possible animal. Timpanac triumphs by dragging a grizzly bear back to camp. Next he wins a race around the lake. On the last challenge, a race to the top of the mountain, Timpanac falls prey to an ambush by his competitors. In the ensuing tussle, Timpanac falls to his death. Emerald Lake (the alpine pond beneath the summit) forms where he fell. Overcome with grief, Ucanogos climbs the mountain and lies down next to her love. Her outline can still be seen.

Interestingly, the gender of the mountain was undetermined for some time. In the years of legend formation and consolidation, hikers often referred the mountain as "Old Timp," "Mr. Timp," "King of the Wasatch," or "Patriarch of the Mountains." In his canonical text of 1922, Roberts personified the mountain as a male Indian deity. However, that same year, another hiking advocate jokingly referred to the mountain as a sarcophagus for "Timpanogess." Yet another early promoter put forward a "transformation myth" that related how Chief Timpanogos, a 200-year-old "sage and savior," was transfigured in his sleep (by an angel) into the crest of the mountain. In the end, Andy Anderson's idea of an Indian Sleeping Beauty proved to be the most unforgettable. In 1957 *Sports Illustrated* made the point in a disturbingly sexual way: the hiker who reached the summit gained "some pagan pride at having conquered the largest sleeping Indian in the world."[10]

Ideologies of race and gender have affected the anthropomorphization of landforms in the United States. White Americans have repeatedly imagined large rocks as erect white heads. Before it collapsed in 2003, the Old Man of the Mountain—the symbol of New Hampshire—was the preeminent example of this kind of *lusus naturae,* or play of nature; Mount Rushmore remains the preeminent man-made "mimetolith." Numerous localities brag about local rock profiles; for example, Millard County, Utah, has the "Great Stone Face" or "Guardian of Deseret" that looks something like Joseph Smith. Canadians boast about the Sleeping Giant of Ontario. A number of Indian men have also been projected onto the land as "Indian Head Rocks." When it comes to fossilized Indian women, however, Americans tend to see breasts or entire supine bodies. William O. Douglass, Supreme Court justice and mountaineering enthusiast, recounted a climactic adolescent experience when he conquered Washington state's Kloochman Rock, an Indian maiden with "two gnarled and chewed teats pointing to the sky." The contemporary residents of Anchorage imagine a "sleeping lady" on local Mount Susitna.[11]

Besides Mount Timpanogos, however, the best example of a rock woman is California's Mount Tamalpais, a mountain with a strikingly similar modern history. In the early twentieth century, "Mount Tam" became San Francisco's favorite hiking ground. Fake Indian legends emerged at the same time. From various vantage points in the Bay Area, residents began to see the form of a recumbent Indian; pinpointing her bosom was a test of perception. In 1921 a pageant/play inspired by this legendary maiden debuted at the Mountain Theatre, a venue near the summit. The playwright, Dan Totheroh, remembered that he "plunged into research" about the "Tamal Indians." Since this "primitive race" had left behind few artifacts, his only native material was the "Tamals' abnormal fear of the mountain top. Few, if any dared to climb the overgrown trails to the mysterious, often fog-hidden summit." Totheroh's script, *Tamalpa,* became the official play of the Mountain Theatre. Between 1921 and 1970, it was produced eight times. *Tamalpa* began with the "throbbing of tom-toms from behind the trees, growing louder as TWO INDIAN MUSICIANS come into sight, carrying tom-toms and solemnly beating them." The musicians made way for the ghost of the Last Chief. By way of prologue, he told the white audience that the mountainous profile of Tamalpa (the Indian maiden) was the only reminder of his long-vanished people.[12]

Like Mount Tamalpais, Mount Timpanogos furnished a venue for theater. During the glory years of the Annual Timpanogos Hike, mountain enthusiasts congregated at the CCC-renovated Theater in the Pines. For decades the evening program before the Big Hike concluded with a retelling of Roberts' legend and a ceremonial lighting of a bonfire. Sometimes the performance took the form of a dramatic reading—punctuated by drumming—from a script adaptation by BYU professor Carlton Culmsee. KSL, the powerful AM station owned by the LDS Church, did a live broadcast of the evening program for many years. The program sometimes featured a short community play. An ambitious stage manager once constructed a "cliff" for Utahna. When the actress leaped, the audience gasped, unable to see her land in a truck bed full of hay. After the performance of the legend, dancing co-eds in "Indian costume" (representing the "spirit of the mountain") carried flames to the giant tipi-shaped woodpile built by the Kiwanis Club. A press release from 1949 anticipated the scene: "the girls will perform a primitive-style dance . . . They will carry flames in coconut shells and simulate the rising tongues of fire by means of red and yellow colored scarves. The dance will be performed to percussive accompaniment including native tom toms." Organizers sometimes referred to the audience as "tribesmen." In ad-

A theatrical scene from an evening program before the Annual Timpanogos Hike, Aspen Grove, date unknown. (L. Tom Perry Special Collections, Harold B. Lee Library, Brigham Young University, Provo, Utah)

dition to the legend and the fire lighting, the annual program included many musical numbers, including a crowd-pleasing duet, "Indian Love Song." Back in 1927, Mormon Selman came to the program dressed in "his familiar Indian costume" and "entertained the throng" by playing an accordion, of all things. In the same decade, a musician-inventor played the "Tim-Piano-Gus," a percussive instrument made of rocks.[13]

William F. Hanson, a professor at BYU, embodied the musical dimension of "Timp." On several occasions he served as musical director for the annual hike's evening program. More notably, he composed and produced three original "Indian operas," one of them based on the legend of the mountain. Hanson was part of a larger American vogue for Indianist music. Understanding his Timpanogos opera requires background investigation into the surprisingly rich history of musical Indian play.

::::: European composers gave sound to Amerindians starting in the late seventeenth century. Purcell and Vivaldi, among others, wrote operatic works based on the confrontation between Cortés and Montezuma. Because the concept of musical authenticity was not yet important, these productions simply used costume to distinguish between Spaniards and Aztecs. If and when pre-nineteenth-century composers made "Indian" sounds, they used existing symbolic conventions: quasi-folk "peasant" motifs or quasi-exotic "Turkish" or "gypsy" motifs, usually in the service of rhythmic dance numbers. Compositional devices included G minor drones, long-short-short beats, and insistent parallel fifths in the bass. The latter two musical conventions were eventually coded as "Indian"—but not until the turn of the twentieth century. Anglo-American composers lacked an "Indian" musical idiom even though Indian themes appeared in the vocal music of the early national period. The ballad opera, a popular form of entertainment, sometimes featured Indian characters; a treatment of the Pocahontas story premiered in 1808. Composers of this period also introduced the Indian lament to popular song. Parlor pieces like "Death Song of the Cherokee Indians" multiplied fast in the early 1800s. Often they were inserted into melodramas. Although these bel canto numbers made no attempt to sound Indian, they appealed to realism by presenting an "Indian" point of view—usually by means of the first-person voice (preferably a doomed chief or princess).[14]

The popularity of the "Indian song" rose in tandem with Indianist place-names and "Indian plays," peaking in the era of Indian Removal. This cultural moment ended by the 1850s, when the melodramatic Noble Savage became an object of parody and burlesque. He did not die, however. Longfellow kept the Noble Savage alive almost single-handedly. *The Song of Hiawatha* possessed an air of ethnographic authenticity that spared it the worst—though by no means all—ridicule. The poem went on to become a great popular favorite. In highbrow circles, *Hiawatha* had a much smaller impact on literature than on music. Beginning as early as 1856, Longfellow's work inspired dozens of instrumental and vocal compositions. Like the poem itself, these settings marked a shift in Indianness from musical symbolism to musical representation. The first Hiawathesque composers did not go so far as to transcribe Indian music, but they endeavored to invent music that matched what they understood to be authentic Indian folklore.[15]

Even a foreigner, Antonin Dvořák, felt drawn to *Hiawatha*. Although his opera based on the poem was abandoned, sketches for it turned up in his "New World" symphony. At the peak of his career, Dvořák spent three years (1892–1895) as director of the National Conservatory of Music of America—a congressionally chartered school in New York City. The famous Bohemian sent shock waves through America's fledgling classical musical community by publicly challenging U.S. composers to go to their country's multiracial folk sources to invent their own national music. At this time, American classical music was centered in Boston and dominated by Anglo Protestants of the German musical persuasion. The biggest name, Edward MacDowell, disowned the influence of "slave" music. Indian music, by contrast, possessed a "manly and free rudeness." As an experiment, MacDowell incorporated native melodies into a few compositions written between 1891 and 1902. For this reason, music historians locate MacDowell at the front end of the American "Indianists."[16]

Dozens of other U.S. composers "went native" in the first decade of the twentieth century. The list includes Arthur Farwell, Charles Cadman, Henry Gilbert, Arthur Nevin, Thurlow Lieurance, Charles Sanford Skilton, Harvey Worthington Loomis, and Amy Beach. Although most of these Indianists knew one another, they did not constitute a group. None of them wrote Indianist music exclusively or even primarily. When they did turn to native sources, their motivations varied from nationalism to romantic racism to simple opportunism. What united them was their reliance on musical transcriptions of ethnographic subjects. On the continuum of Indianist music, these composers moved from musical representation to musical appropriation. They embraced authenticity.[17]

For ethnographers of the period, sonic evidence was newly important because it could finally be collected with ease. The cylinder recorder—invented by Edison in 1877, made commercially available in 1888, and perfected by the mid-1890s—transformed ethnography. Crank-wound "Ediphones" and "Graphophones" could be carried into the field along with the rewritable discs made of wax. The ease of phonographic recording belied its methodological problems. Ethnographers could not simply attend a musical gathering and record discreetly. The device had limited range. A single informant had to be cajoled to sing directly into the cylinder—even if the song was supposed to be sung communally with percussive accompaniment. The ethnographer, having paid for the song, hovered nearby to monitor the device. Many songs had to be cut short because each wax disc ran for only four to six minutes. All in all, the setting was not conducive to a natural performance.[18]

Even the best recording was a challenge to transcribe. Truth be told, transcription was *translation*. As Henry Gilbert said from experience, "Transcribing Indian melodies in ordinary musical notation is somewhat like forcing a square peg into a round hole: it can be accomplished by dint of sufficient exertion, but the original form will have suffered." Native American singing features idiosyncratic embellishments like trills, trembles, shouts, and slurs. In general, the song lines do not correspond to "major" or "minor" keys. The melodies abound with semitones—notes between the twelve chromatic notes in an octave. Precise notational systems were eventually formalized for such music, but not before an unscientific method left a mark in American popular culture. Musician John Comfort Fillmore convinced himself he could notate Indian songs using the standard five-line staff and the

Western diatonic scale. He did this by listening for intentions behind the intonations. He believed that native performers lacked the training to sing the notes they *meant* to sing. Since Indians possessed a "latent harmonic sense," Fillmore did them the favor of harmonizing their monophonic songs. The resulting transcriptions looked like piano hymns.[19]

Fillmore deserved obscurity. As luck would have it, his transcriptions were commissioned and published by the prominent ethnographer Alice C. Fletcher. Without a degree or a husband, Fletcher rose through the ranks of women's clubs to become a fellow at Harvard's Peabody Museum. In middle age she developed a fascination with native peoples, especially the Omahas. After spending mere weeks among them, she spearheaded the detribalization of their land. Like most "Friends of the Indian," she believed that native peoples needed private property to progress. The Fletcher-led allotment of the Omaha reservation in 1882 inspired the (Dawes) General Allotment Act of 1887. Strangely, after doing her best to transform the Omahas, Fletcher spent the next two decades recording their traditions, especially their music. Her invaluable collaborator was Francis La Flesche, an acculturated mixed-blood Omaha who himself became an ethnographer. For many years La Flesche lived with Fletcher in Washington, D.C., as her adopted son. Together they produced *A Study of Omaha Indian Music* for the Peabody in 1893. The report described the ceremonial context of each song along with a "transcription" by Fillmore. Fletcher mailed copies of the report to well-known composers. In 1900, aiming for a wider audience, she released an abbreviated version, *Indian Story and Song*.

Fletcher's book made a deep impression on Arthur Farwell, widely considered the founder of Indianist composition. Farwell's studies began conventionally with a multiyear pilgrimage to Germany, where he worked with Engelbert Humperdinck. In 1900, not long after his return to Massachusetts, Farwell changed course after discovering *Indian Song and Story* in a bookstore. On the piano, the Omaha songs didn't move him, but when he sang the vocal lines as he imagined an Indian would, he felt musically alive. Farwell decided it was his mission to support musical Americanism. In 1901 he founded the Wa-Wan Press—named after an Omaha ceremony—to publish all-American music. In the course of a decade thirty-seven composers, most of them up-and-coming young people, received exposure in this way. Although Farwell possessed genuine talent, in general the same cannot be said of his contributors. The Indianist movement lacked a genius, even an unrecognized genius like Charles Ives. Even at its height, many critics (and fellow composers) derided "Red Indian music." Farwell had to work as an apologist. In addition to scores, most issues of the Wa-Wan Press contained essays promulgating Farwell's musical philosophy. One of his "articles of faith" stated that "Ultimate American composition can be approached in a certain degree through the knowledge of Indian music, just as a traveler can help himself to reach the top of a mountain by means of a staff." Elsewhere he used a different metaphor: all-American music was a musical tapestry sewn from various folk sources, including Negro spirituals and cowboy songs. Indian music was the "golden thread" that tied it all together.[20]

To spread the gospel further, Farwell began working the lecture circuit in 1903 with a program called "Music and Myth of the American Indians." It included music of his own and of other Indianist composers. As a composer, Farwell specialized in "character pieces" for piano that evoked the mood of the ceremony from which the melody line originated. Unlike MacDowell, Farwell acknowledged his tribal sources. Of course, these sources came through ethnographers, especially Fletcher. When Farwell began lecturing on Indians, he had no actual experience with native peoples. In time, he claimed his own ethnographic authority, his own authenticity. On tour in Los Angeles, Farwell joined the circle of Charles Lummis, the great popularizer of the "Indian Southwest." They became friends and collaborators, and recorded native and Spanish-American music in the field.

The Indian Southwest—a touristic region centered on Santa Fe, New Mexico—attracted a series of high-art personalities who experimented with primitivism. One of these was Natalie Curtis, an eastern socialite with compositional training who contributed to the Wa-Wan Press. After developing her fascination with Indian music, Curtis traveled to the Hopi mesas with a cylinder recorder. In subsequent years she sometimes used a Hopi name and wore Hopi dress. Today her reputation rests on *The Indians' Book* (1907). Still in print, this sumptuous volume contains songs and stories adorned with original art by Native Americans. From the title on down, Curtis downplayed her active role as transcriber and translator, claiming that the book was the "direct utterance of the Indians themselves." Unlike John Comfort Fillmore, she did not harmonize the vocal lines. She implicitly encouraged white people to sing native songs rather than play piano settings. In her introduction, Curtis anticipated the imminent demise of native cultures and put forward the book as a gift—a memory piece—from traditional Indians to their soon-to-be-assimilated progeny. President Theodore Roosevelt, a family friend, praised this record of a "vanished older world."[21]

The rhetoric of the Vanishing American—as old as the United States itself—reached its zenith in the fin-de-siècle era when the aggregate native population reached its nadir. Even as U.S. government agents aggressively advanced a policy of assimilation, American cultural agents played up the romance of premodern tradition. From this confluence of tragedy and nostalgia came a monumental project by a different Curtis. Between 1907 and 1930, Edward S. Curtis produced twenty volumes of *The North American Indian,* a combination of photography and ethnography. With his camera, Curtis turned Indians into icons. Also praised by Roosevelt (and funded by J. P. Morgan), Curtis' project was the definitive statement on the Vanishing American. When, in the early stages, the photographer took his images on tour, he felt dissatisfied with their effect. The projections needed music. A contract went to Henry Gilbert of Cambridge, Massachusetts, a protégé of Edward MacDowell and a friend of Arthur Farwell. Gilbert had previously transcribed cylinder recordings for Curtis; for further inspiration, he studied the work of Alice Fletcher and Natalie Curtis. Though presented as "REAL INDIAN MUSIC," Gilbert's twenty-one background pieces employed harmonies from the "standard exotic toolbox" of Western classical music. This multimedia collaboration—titled "A Vanishing Race"—was variously described as a "musicale," "picture-opera," or "lecture-entertainment." It premiered at Carnegie Hall in 1911.[22]

As sonic entertainment, the Vanishing American turned up in many places in fin-de-siècle America—Broadway, Tin Pan Alley, the theatrical stage, and the fairground. The newly popular frontier plays and western shows were qualitatively different from the "Indian plays" of the 1830s. The dramas made reference to recent history, especially the Plains Indian wars of the 1860s and 1870s, rather than to distant events. The East no longer provided the setting. The equestrian tribesman of the Plains replaced the forest Indian as the archetypical figure. Once pacified, equestrians quickly became historic, even quaint attractions. As living, singing museum displays, western Indians appeared in the era's big fairs: the 1893 Columbian Exposition in Chicago, the 1898 Trans-Mississippi and International Exposition in Omaha, and the 1904 Louisiana Purchase International Exposition in St. Louis. Tourists left with memories; ethnographers left with cylinder recordings. Music was also an important part of Buffalo Bill's Wild West, which ran alongside the Chicago fair. The show gave Antonín Dvořák one of his few opportunities to listen to Native Americans.

Here is the ironic and distinctive feature of this musical moment: Indians cooperated in the sonic appropriation of Indianness. Many Plains Indians—especially Siouan people—willingly left home for the Wild West shows. On the reservation, white officials banned singing and dancing. Off the reservation, white audiences applauded the same singing and dancing. To the chagrin of the Indian Bureau, "Show Indians" accompanied Buffalo Bill to the great cities of America and Europe; they performed before presidents, royalty, and the pope. Neither puppets nor simple victims, Show Indians made a rational choice in a time of limited choices. Because of them, millions of non-Indians heard Indians making music in the era of western shows (1883–1933). Meanwhile, on a smaller scale, the community stage made room for native performers. The national lyceum and Chautauqua movements—community-sponsored adult education programming—still had momentum in the first decade of the 1900s. Dozens of pianists and singers gave lecture-recitals on "Indian music," which often consisted of Arthur Farwell's adaptations of John Comfort Fillmore's transcriptions of Alice Fletcher's recordings. Some of the singers, like Edna Woolley-Lieurance (wife of Indianist composer Thurlow Lieurance), were whites dressed up as Indians; but others, like Princess Watahwasso (the stage name of Lucy Nicolar, Penobscot), were real Indians who "played Indian" for white audiences.[23]

Of these sopranos, Tsianina Blackstone (Cherokee-Creek) merits special mention. Before and after World War I, Blackstone and her friend-collaborator-handler, Charles Cadman, gave some 400 "Indian Music Talks" across the country. Performing to expectations, "Princess Tsianina" (also called Tsianina Redfeather) dressed in an elaborate buckskin-and-beads outfit of her own design, and sang songs such as Cadman's "To a Vanishing Race." Yet her offstage actions belied this stereotype. While performing in Santa Fe, she called attention to the Pueblo Indians' fight for cultural self-determination. During World War I, even as Indian soldiers died for a country that hadn't yet given universal citizenship to natives, Blackstone volunteered to perform for U.S. troops in Europe. She eventually retired from music to become an advocate for Indian education.

No one appreciated Blackstone's remarkable life story more than Charles Cadman. He even wrote a one-act opera loosely based on her coming-of-age story—the first American opera with a contemporary setting to premiere at New York City's Metropolitan Opera. On the one hand, *Shanewis: The Robin Woman* realistically portrayed the mixed world inhabited by twentieth-century western Indians, for it showed the title character at home in Los Angeles as well as on the reservation. On the other hand, *Shanewis* gave white audiences a mixed message about the modernity and primitiveness of Indians. In

1926, when the Hollywood Bowl revived the opera with Tsianina Redfeather singing lead, the stage director garishly expanded the pow-wow scenes to include hundreds of Indian extras dancing around tipis and campfires in the hills beside the amphitheater.[24]

"Indian operas"—operas with native characters and at least token borrowings from ethnographic sources—came into vogue between 1910 and 1930. Of the twenty-plus operas that went into production, a conspicuous number featured women in the title role; examples are *Shanewis, Natoma, Atala, Alglala,* and *Winona.* Most were based on Indian legends. Walter McClintock, an eastern businessman who became obsessed with Montana's Blackfeet, commissioned an opera as a means of preserving their mythology. He tried to secure the services of Victor Herbert, the famous operetta composer, but settled for Arthur Nevin. The resulting opera, *Poïa,* was previewed for Theodore Roosevelt at the White House in 1907. As a stage work, it premiered in Berlin in 1910—and flopped. In fact, only two Indian operas enjoyed lasting success; both were verismo, and middlebrow artists wrote them for ready-made audiences. One was *Shanewis,* the other was *Natoma*—a work by none other than Victor Herbert. Although he had no abiding interest in Native Americans, Herbert had a canny business sense. He made his Indianist contribution in 1911 at the peak of the movement.[25]

By 1930, even radio-friendly "Indian love songs" had faded in popularity—with a few exceptions like Charles Cadman's crossover hit, "From the Land of the Sky-Blue Water," which sold well as sheet music for decades, propelled by recordings by stars such as Jeanette MacDonald, Paul Whiteman, and Bing Crosby. Cadman's symphonic works became déclassé. In the 1930s and 1940s, American classical music grew up. Ironically, the composer who garnered the greatest acclaim for creating the "American" sound—Aaron Copland—had been born to Jewish immigrants. When Martha Graham suggested a Pocahontas-like "Indian Girl" for the ballet that became *Appalachian Spring,* Copland supposedly balked: "No Indians!" Even without the support of concert halls, the orchestrated Indian found some continued life in movie theaters during the golden age of the Hollywood western. In the end, though, highbrow Indianist music proved to be far less enduring than the lowbrow "Indian sound" of the "war dance"—still a staple of cartoon shows and sporting events. In Utah, no one remembers the former fame of local opera composer, ethnographer, and Mount Timpanogos booster William F. Hanson.[26]

::: Hanson was born in 1887 to Mormon parents who had established a homestead in eastern Utah's Uinta Basin. One of the last areas of the state to be settled, the Uinta Basin felt far away from the Wasatch Front. Basin homesteaders lived next door to the Uintah-Ouray (Ute) Reservation, and Hanson had regular childhood contact with Indians—unlike his direct contemporary Eugene Roberts. For college Hanson migrated to the Wasatch Front, where he studied music at BYU. In 1906 he heard a campus lecture by Arthur Farwell that set his brain on fire. After completing his degree and serving a mission for the LDS Church, Hanson moved back to the Basin, where he looked to his Ute neighbors for musical inspiration. Convinced that Ute culture was both vibrant and moribund, he took up ethnography as his avocation. He soon "decided that, due to the vastness of the nature of the culture, the most efficient mode of transcribing and interpreting the culture was in OPERA FORM."[27]

Hanson had more enthusiasm than knowledge when it came to Indian culture. He could not have composed his first opera, *The Sun Dance,* without collaboration. The co-creator was Gertrude Simmons Bonnin—also known by her self-given name, Zitkala-Ša. A mixed-blood Nakota Sioux from South Dakota, Bonnin moved to the Uintah-Ouray Reservation in 1902 with her husband, an employee of the federal Indian Bureau. Though remembered for her autobiographical writing and pan-Indian advocacy, Bonnin earned renown in her youth as a violinist. After attending boarding school and Earlham College, she studied music in Boston, then went to Paris with the Carlisle School Indian Orchestra to perform at the Universal Exposition of

1900. In the uncultured isolation of the Uinta Basin, Bonnin probably struck up an easy friendship with William Hanson, someone who shared her love—if not her aptitude—for classical music. In the early 1910s she worked with him to adapt the Sun Dance for the musical stage.

Long practiced by the western Sioux and other Plains groups, the Sun Dance eventually spread to Shoshone bands, from whom Utes learned it. Reservation Utes began performing the Sun Dance around 1890 after discontinuing their twenty-year-old practice of the Ghost Dance. Both dances provided a feeling of renewal in a time of disintegration. For Utah's Utes, the new century brought new despair as their already confining reservation in the Uinta Basin was disassembled. Through the legal purloining called allotment, the government pressured Indian male heads of household to become small private property owners. The government then threw open the remaining tribal property—the majority of the Basin—to homesteaders. Provo served as one of the staging grounds for this rush; the government ran a land lottery here. In 1906, in the midst of the homestead invasion, several hundred White River Utes—Colorado Utes who didn't want to be in Utah in the first place—fled to South Dakota, hoping to find a better life with the western Sioux. The Sioux were not welcoming; they had problems of their own. After about a year, the "Absentee Utes" returned "home." For these and other dispirited Indians, the Sun Dance offered a restorative experience, a full-body form of religion. It was hard, however, to dance without interference. Since the 1880s the Indian Bureau and its Christian allies had worked to suppress the "pagan" ceremony.[28]

Gertrude Bonnin had no personal experience with the Sun Dance, but she knew firsthand the trauma of detribalization. As an eight-year-old, she had left the Yankton Reservation for White's Indians Manual Labor Institute in Wabash, Indiana, where the Quaker authorities cut her long hair and silenced her native tongue. Boarding schools followed the dictum (made famous by the founder of Carlisle), "all the Indian there is in the race should be dead. Kill the

Indian in him, and save the man." Not until 1932, when John Collier became commissioner of Indian Affairs, did this policy begin to be dismantled. That was far too late for Bonnin, who permanently wore the effects of her schooling. Estranged from Sioux culture, she never returned home. Yet she tried to recover her Sioux heritage, beginning with the adoption of the name Zitkala-Ša. In her published writings, Zitkala-Ša denounced Americanization and declared herself a pagan. However, she also became a vocal antipeyotist. And in private, as a Catholic, then a Christian Scientist, and ultimately a Mormon, she criticized whites *and* Indians for their lack of Christianity. In the context of her disordered religious life, her work to secularize and stage the most sacred of Sioux ceremonies looks like a staging of some inner conflict. At the same time, in the context of the Ute reservation, Zitkala-Ša's collaboration must be seen as political—especially considering that her husband worked for the Indian Bureau. Hanson seemed unaware of the larger issues at play. He sometimes referred to his collaborator as a "maiden" and a "squaw." Nonetheless, he earnestly desired to stir up appreciation for native traditions.[29]

A hybrid work, *Sun Dance Opera* juxtaposed European and Indian motifs. The libretto used a conventional operatic love triangle alongside the nonnarrative sequence of the Sun Dance ceremony. For the score, Zitkala-Ša contributed several Sioux melodies. Hanson then harmonized these vocal lines according to Western tonalities to create arias. One scholar describes the score as a "cross between a Victor Herbert operetta and the sound track to a John Ford Western." The surviving score does not, however, include all the original stage music, which was interspersed with "ad libbed" ceremonial chants by nonactor Indians accompanied only by drumming. For this reason, *The Sun Dance* was actually more authentic than any other Indian opera. At the 1913 premiere—held in Orpheus Hall in the small town of Vernal, in the Uinta Basin—dozens of local Utes filled the nonoperatic parts. The cast also included a man called "Old Sioux," an alleged 100-year-old cousin of Sitting Bull and veteran of the Battle of Little Big Horn. At subsequent runs in Provo and Salt Lake, Old

Sioux and the other "full-blooded" cast members performed dances and songs before curious white audiences. These Indians surely would not have participated without the involvement of Zitkala-Ša, the de facto producer. (Years later, drawing on greater compositional experience, Hanson revised the opera's score to make it sound more "Indian" even as he erased Gertrude Bonnin's name as co-creator.)[30]

This cross-cultural operatic event preceded the first field recordings of "traditional" Ute music. The responsible ethnomusicologist, Frances Densmore, was the most prolific of all the self-taught social scientists—most of them women—inspired to action by Alice Fletcher. After studying music at Oberlin, Densmore worked as a piano teacher, church organist, choir director, and lyceum speaker. In 1895 she started giving lectures based on *A Study of Omaha Indian Music*. To audiences of clubwomen, Densmore sang transcribed versions of Omaha songs while beating on a Chippewa drum; later she added Indianist piano pieces by Arthur Farwell to the program. In 1904 Densmore began her ethnographic career portentously by "slipp[ing] into ambush" behind Geronimo—a living museum display at the St. Louis world's fair—while he was humming. Hastily she transcribed the Apache man's melody for publication. Densmore's doggedness soon caught the attention of the Smithsonian's Bureau of American Ethnology, which became her regular sponsor. Even without academic credentials, Densmore produced more than most academics—approximately 150 publications and 3,500 sound recordings.[31]

In 1914 Densmore made the first of two visits to the Uintah-Ouray Reservation. Here, in contrast to other field sites, she felt "suspicion and opposition" among the "touchy" Utes. After she set up shop in a cottage "on a street conveniently near the trader's store" in Whiterocks, several men dropped by to harass her. Through her interpreter, Densmore told the hecklers that she wanted to preserve their melodies for posterity, and that she would pay them by the song. They laughed. Densmore placed a quarter on her Graphophone, started the machine, and announced as she left the room that the money belonged to the first person to sing into the cylinder. She returned to find that the bait had worked . . . on her interpreter. At this point, Densmore decided to use her "highest trump card" by "playing up" the fact that she had been ceremonially adopted by a noted Teton Sioux. She said that her Sioux "father" wanted her to call on Red Cap, a local Ute elder. Red Cap had been one of the principals in the abortive flight to South Dakota. When Red Cap appeared at the cabin, Densmore explained her purpose: she was "collecting the songs of the Indians for the benefit of their children and that their voices would be preserved in Washington in a great building that would not burn down." Red Cap replied that he did not sing. He would, however, bring in his best singer in return for a favor. The "wily old chief" wanted Densmore to record him *talking*, and then deliver the recording to the U.S. commissioner of Indian Affairs. As later translated, Red Cap's speech began with a message to Densmore: "This work that you are doing is very good. There are so many Ute songs that they could hardly be stopped. We Indians have songs as you white people have. Because your songs also are very old, therefore like ours they could not be stopped. Because that i[s] the Indian way it is good." Red Cap went on to say that singing and dancing made the Utes feel good and made their country good, too. Then he addressed the commissioner directly: "After you have heard our songs we hope you will not stop our singing them . . . if they were taken away from us it would not be right at all."[32]

It was an extraordinary scene: an aged, illiterate, equestrian Ute putting modern technology to his own use, using Edison's machine to give voice to the voiceless. Throughout Indian country, Densmore could not have secured as many songs as she did without some genuine native support for her technological approach to musical preservation. Indians used Densmore, and she of course used them. In 1940 she wrote a how-to letter in which she shared her techniques on "the psychology of managing the Indians so as to secure the best songs." By insensitive means Densmore created an incredible sonic archive that became a cornerstone of the Federal Cylinder Project at the Library of Congress' American Folklife Center. Since 1979 many Native Americans have used the project to recover tribal songs for use in ceremonies and powwows. It does not belittle the importance of the archive to point out that these ethnographic products from the early twentieth century are not "pure" artifacts from "primitive" cultures. Tellingly, Densmore recorded a lover's leap dirge, "Song of the Maiden's Leap," from a Lakota woman named Used-as-a-Shield. For Lakotas and Utes and other Indians of the period, the traditional danced with the modern.[33]

Another telling example: One of Frances Densmore's Ute informants also did touring gigs with William Hanson. In the 1920s, building on the local success of *Sun Dance Opera*, Hanson made a lyceum circuit of Utah with a half-dozen Ute "braves," all veterans of the opera. Hanson also brought in Mormon Selman (a.k.a. "O-und") to act as liaison and translator. The extension division of BYU sponsored this so-called Hanson Wigwam Company. All dressed in feathers, the mixed-race group—whites playing Indian alongside Indians playing Indian—gave recitals of song, dance, and legend at schools and churches and even the state capitol. Its repertoire probably included the following Hanson composition for children:

When you were about our size
Did you play Indian?
If you did we'd be surprised
If you had no fun
Hi-yi-i-i Hi-yi-i
We like to play Indian[34]

After several years of touring, Hanson desired to produce another Indian opera—this time on his own. To complement the Sioux-inspired *Sun Dance Opera*, he worked to "give the world a genuine Ute composition."[35] Hanson focused on the Bear Dance. This major Ute social and ceremonial event was (and still is) held in early spring to coincide with the emergence of bears from hibernation. The dancing, which might go on for more than a week, involved a shuffle step that mimicked the movement of bears. Participants moved within a circu-

The Hanson Wigwam Company, ca. 1925. (L. Tom Perry Special Collections, Harold B. Lee Library, Brigham Young University, Provo, Utah)

lar brush enclosure that recalled a den. Over many years, Hanson traveled to the reservation to watch this springtime event. He made notes, photographs, and phonographic recordings. After becoming a member of BYU's music department in 1924, Hanson completed *Täm-Män' Nacup (Bear Dance Opera)*. Like the earlier *Sun Dance Opera*, this work grafted a love story onto a nonnarrative staging of a festival. Once again, Hanson took native melodies and adapted them to Western meters and harmonies.

Hanson's output on the Bear Dance was not restricted to opera. He compiled his field research in the form of a master's thesis. Though written for the music department, Hanson's thesis resembled ethnography, albeit on an amateur level. Hanson fancied himself a salvage worker: "Perhaps Fate also was kind in allowing the author to live at such a time and in such a place that he could see the Ute nation in this epoch of rich ceremonial and feasting, and that he could record some of its national imaginative emotionalism before its assimilation and decease, victim of the mad rush of civilization." Like earlier anthropologists—Frank Cushing comes to mind—and subsequent "Indian hobbyists," Hanson thought he could best absorb Indian traditions by participating in them. He and some of his BYU colleagues were known to "go native" and "tear up the dust" in the Bear Dance arena. In the library copy of his thesis Hanson pasted a telling photograph, a portrait of the author wearing a buckskin suit and full headdress, playing a wooden flute beside a tipi. Hanson—who also went by Ampa-o-luta ("The First Tint of Red at Dawning") and Paree ("Big Elk")—slept in this tipi on his research trips. Hanson claimed that he could pass as an Indian because of his deep tan. His friends called him "Indian Man."[36]

For Hanson, being a weekend Indian was serious business. At his own expense, he wrote and bound a richly illustrated book of "Indian lore" for donation to BYU. *The Lure of the Wigwam* included childhood reminiscences from the Uinta Basin, vignettes from Sioux history, and more. "In presenting this collection," Hanson wrote, "it has been my desire to touch some of the chords that the Great Spirit Nature has awakened in the soul of the Indian, intimate child of the great out-of-doors, that you, too, might hear; to record his stories from his own lips some of the heart throbs of the once mighty people; to preserve in writing some of his ceremonials."[37] As the final entry in this collection of lore, Hanson included the libretto to his third and final opera, *The Bleeding Heart,* a musical retelling of the Legend of Timpanogos. The frontispiece of the libretto showed a woodcut of an Indian man raising his arms in supplication to the mountain. The storyline goes like this:

> The wrathful mountain god, Timpanogos, has brought
> famine to the valley. The Witch and Bear—intermediaries
> between the human and nonhuman worlds—inform the vil-
> lagers that only a sacrifice will appease Timpanogos. Red
> Eagle, a local brave, thinks the people should remove to the
> South Land. The chief, for his part, hopes that the praying
> of the priests and the dancing of the maidens will satisfy the

mountain god. One of the maidens, Utahna, is the chief's daughter, for whom Red Eagle feels great love. The Witch and Bear continue to insist that dancing is insufficient; one of the virgins must climb to the summit and throw herself off. Over the objections of Red Eagle, the villagers come around to this conclusion. They perform a ceremonial lottery to decide which virgin will die. Utahna draws the mark. She climbs the mountain, but Red Eagle, costumed like a god, thwarts her leap. He leads his love to the cave. Their refuge is short-lived, however. Seeing no sign of rain, the villagers make their way to the mountain to check on the sacrifice. The Witch and Bear track Red Eagle to the cave. Bear laughs: Red Eagle will suffer for his misdeeds. Red Eagle advances on Bear with a club. Before he can do much damage, the Witch puts an arrow into his heart. Meanwhile, the villagers hastily reperform the ceremony of the virgin, and compel Utahna to die. The Witch and Bear watch with derision. Utahna's forced suicide may have come too late; the mountain god appears unsatisfied. After Red Eagle bleeds to death, his heart combines with Utahna's and attaches to the cave.

The opera premiered in College Hall at Brigham Young University in 1937 with an all-white cast in redface. Unlike his two earlier self-proclaimed Indian operas, Hanson presented *The Bleeding Heart* as an "opera fantasia" about "an imaginary people who lived at the foot of Mount Timpanogos."[38] In the program notes, he credited Eugene Roberts for the storyline. Yet Hanson modified Roberts' legend considerably: he Indianized it, adding not only Indianist music and dance but also two characters inspired by native sources. In particular, the talking bear—part human, part animal, part mortal, part supernatural—suggested a Ute sensibility.

As Hanson learned from his long-term study of the Bear Dance, Utes viewed bears as sacred and familial. Ute mythology tells how a hunter learned the original dance from an bear just emerged from its den. According to one version of this myth, Bear instructed man not to kill his kind. Although it was not unknown for Utes to hunt bears in the prereservation period, the practice demanded religious care: "Ute hunters feared and respected bears for their human traits, ritually addressing them with the kin term 'Father's Sister' before taking them during hibernation."[39] The springtime Bear Dance conciliated this powerful kin member, thereby promoting health, fertility, and abundance in the coming year.

The historic Euro-American attitude toward bears could not have been more different. Utah Mormons, like every other settler group in the American West, launched vigorous extermination campaigns against coyotes, foxes, bobcats, cougars, skunks, minks, magpies, ravens, raptors, and every other kind of "waster and destroyer." As early as 1849, parties of Latter-day Saints embarked on organized vermin hunts. One of the earliest ordinances passed by the preterritorial State of Deseret set a bounty on predators. Professional animal killers numbered their prey in the thousands. Wolves and bears proved to be especially vulnerable.[40] A residue of this antipredator vitriol shows up in the two standard versions of the Legend of Timpanogos. Recall that in Eugene Roberts' story, Red Eagle battles and kills a grizzly in its subterranean lair. In the alternate version popularized by Andy Anderson, the male protagonist kills a grizzly to prove his manhood and eligibility.

The distance between historic Numic and Mormon attitudes about bears is best illustrated by a Ute legend, "The Man Who Visited Bear," collected and translated by an anthropologist in the 1930s:

> There once was a man. He was going to see his aunt. It was in winter time. His aunt was Bear. He went up there and saw his aunt at the door, standing on her hind legs. Bear didn't like this man coming to see her, that is why she reared up. Bear killed the man. There was another fellow who wanted to go see Bear. After Bear ate the first man, she came out for

air and stretched out and the second man saw her. He stood right in front of Bear. Bear liked the man. "Hello, Aunt. What are you doing?" Then he told Bear, "I came to see you, my aunt. I'm going to stay with you this winter."

So he went in and lay down. He stayed there all the time. They used to get up early in the morning. She used to dig around where she stored the berries and give the man a handful. Then it came spring. Bear said, "I guess it's time for you to leave. I am going to have my little ones." "I'll come see you again after you have them." Bear had two little cubs and then the man came to see them. "All right, you can go home, the snow is all gone now." He smelled different when he came back from Bear. He smelled sour.[41]

It's hard to imagine a legend more removed from Roberts' "Story of Red Eagle and Utahna." Both stories highlight bears, but these two bears are different beings from different worlds. One animal is a kind of person, the other is a beast. William Hanson's bear—and his larger body of work—lives at the frontier of these worlds. *The Bleeding Heart* was neither Indian nor exactly pseudo-Indian. It marked the beginning of an era in which the Legend of Timpanogos went native.

⁝⁝⁝ In 1951 the humorist Frank Sullivan wrote a piece for the *New Yorker* about a Professor W. Hungerford Quigley and his wife-assistant, Dr. Johanna Bracegirdle Quigley, authors of "The Role of the Lovers' Leap in American Folklore." While on vacation near Lake Wassamattawichez, New Hampshire, these "folklore scientists" spied "a crag that we both realized instantly might be a Lovers' Leap, and one of the most perfect we had ever encountered—sheer drop, magnificent view, parking space. It had everything!" For research purposes, they gave the leaping spot the designation Quigley 873. Their next step was to find the oldest inhabitant of the nearby village. After becoming properly intoxicated, the old-timer spun a legend about

Standin' High and Leapin' Trout, two athletic Indian lovers who completed the only successful reverse lovers' leap.[42]

With this humor piece, Sullivan poked fun at folklorists for their preoccupation with cataloging and categorizing. He had a point. With obsessive precision, folklorists assigned the lover's leap—a tale type known for its "monotonous sameness"—its own motif-index classification number, A968.2. The pioneering Texan folklorist J. Frank Dobie collected many such legends in the field, yet even he couldn't resist a dig: "When . . . settlers first moved into any part of Texas where there is a cliff, what was their initial act: to get a meal, to start out hunting for buried treasure, or to christen the cliff with a tale of lovers?" It was easy to doubt the significance of the lover's leap as a folkloric subject because most of the legendary leaps in America originated with *literary* sources, and dubious ones at that.[43]

The fake-folk Legend of Timpanogos is significant precisely because it *became* folkloric. By the time Eugene Roberts passed away in 1953, his legend no longer belonged to him. It belonged to the ordinary people who retold the story orally.[44] These people would not have been interesting to the fictional Professor Quigley, who represented the preprofessional folklorists who privileged old-time traditionalists and ethnic enclaves. In contrast, the cadre of professionals who emerged in the 1950s and 1960s from Indiana University—the first U.S. institution to grant doctorates in folklore—enlarged the meaning of "folk" to include the mass vernacular. A pair of outstanding Indiana graduates, Jan Brunvand and William A. Wilson, went on to teach in Utah, where they began building folklore archives. These professors assigned their students to find, record, and transcribe folk narratives in local circulation. To complete the assignment, students had to preface their collections with ethnographic details about themselves as well as their informants. After grading, the professors kept the projects and filed them by motif type. In this way, nearly forty reports of "Timp" performances were catalogued in the last three decades of the twentieth century.

Half of the collected narratives recognizably derive from Roberts'

"Story of Red Eagle and Utahna"—although in every instance details have been dropped or added. The key consistent element is the sacrifice of a virgin to an angry mountain god. Other versions of the legend contain a variety of plotlines: an Indian maiden commits suicide because her father won't let her marry a white fur trader; she commits suicide because she doesn't like her fiancé; she commits suicide out of grief for the loss of her love (due to intertribal warfare, a hunting accident, or murder by rival suitors); she commits suicide to protect her villagers from being detected by hostile forces; and so on. Sometimes the jumper falls directly into a cave opening. Needless to say, every version includes the death of a girl. No death, no story. Personal names vary. The doomed maiden goes by Utahna, Ucanogos, or Princess Timpanogos. Her boyfriend is by turns Red Eagle, Timpanac, Sehkona, Running Deer, and Yellow Lion.[45]

Contextual data indicate some of the leading venues for legend transmission—organized hikes, youth camps, car trips, and family gatherings. Cave tours seem most important. At Timpanogos Cave National Monument, the large aortic stalactite known as the Great Heart has for decades been backlit by a ruby-red lamp. Tour guides typically tell the Legend of Timpanogos while standing in front of the illuminated Great Heart. The lighting effect was added by popular demand; visitors wanted to *see* the "bleeding heart" in addition to hearing about it. By the 1980s the red lamp had become an embarrassment to cave managers, who eventually removed it. Pressure from repeat visitors—and the locally based seasonal rangers who lead most of the tours in the summer—prevailed on the Park Service to restore the garishness. To this day, whether they like to or not, tour guides perform the Legend of Timpanogos. Some make it pithy; some add caveats about its authenticity; some give it a humorous tone. Still others present earnest retellings. As of 2000, about 60,000 people per year toured the cave and thereby had contact with the legend. A large share of that total consisted of children. The cave is a popular destination for families and school groups.

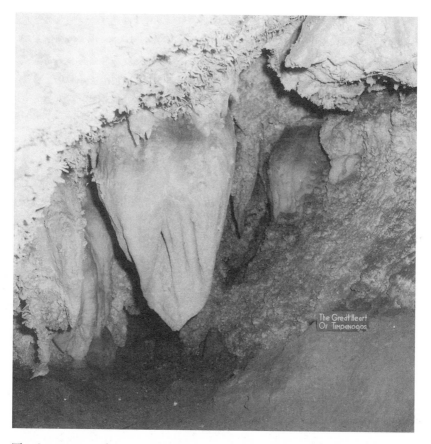

The Great Heart of Timpanogos, Timpanogos Cave National Monument, 1963.
(Special Collections Department, J. Willard Marriott Library, University of Utah)

Locals enjoy hearing the local legend, but do they believe it? At least the children do. For adults, the matter is more about playful acceptance than serious disbelief. Unlike historians, most people move comfortably between history and legend. A local "Timp" fanatic, Richard Peacock, expressed this sentiment as well as anyone. "Our experience with legends has taught us to accept them for what they are," he wrote in preface to his own retelling of the Legend of Timpanogos. "Ours is not to reason why, not to attempt to find logic in the narra-

tive, not to interpret, but to delight in the story for its own sake—
to savor the flavor of a delightful tale that inevitably mirrors many
things from the past."[46]

Yet delight by itself doesn't explain the persistence of this story. The
Legend of Timpanogos would appear to fulfill some deeper needs or
desires. Foremost, the legend functions to explain local topography
and local place-names while expressing the pride of place felt by local
residents. Every version of the Legend of Timpanogos accounts for
some landscape feature, whether it is the Great Heart or Emerald
Lake or something else. Some legends narrate two separate leaps (by
princesses from opposing tribes) and set the first at Bridal Veil Falls, a
landmark in Provo Canyon. Some tellers suggest that the Great Spirit
created the falls as a commemorative veil for the dead Indian; others
say that the leaping lover actually wore a veil. Another version of
the legend places the suicide at Squaw Peak and the entombment at
Mount Timpanogos. This legend, like most, implicitly offers a folk
derivation of "Indian" place-names.

Not only does the legend explain topography; it creates it. Thousands of people now discern an outline of an Indian woman on the
crest of the mountain. She can be seen from either side—from Heber
Valley in the north and Utah Valley in the south. The optimal vantage
point is supposedly the intersection of Eighth East and Third North in
Provo. There is, however, some disagreement over which end of the
mountain is the reclining woman's head. Not everyone can see the figure at first glance. Certain people enjoy keen eyesight: "I was always looking at it. It was comforting, solid, a big huge rock sleeping
woman. I would sit in our living room or sit on our front porch and
watch her long bumpy hair fall down as she lay with her hands across
her chest. I never quite knew if they were hands or breasts, or maybe
they were on top of each other. But she was beautiful and not dead,
just sleeping."[47]

Staring is a habit of affection. Locals love this mountain and feel
proud to claim it as part of their home. "I always watched and loved
Mt. Timpanogos as she silently watched over the valley," recalled a

local woman. "My Mother told me this story when I was a small child and the mountain became an important symbol in my life." Stories add luster to the local landscape. A popular annual event for professional storytellers hosted by the Orem Public Library since 1990 is called the Timpanogos Storytelling Festival. "Growing up in Utah we liked to say things," said a resident of Orem, "that would make Utah more interesting, whether or not they were really true. Also when we were told this legend it made us think that we had a rich heritage and we felt important. We, the girls at camp, loved to think that something so romantic had happened in Utah and was visible on the mountain."[48]

Falling in love with Mount Timpanogos may help even the newest resident to feel a bit like a native. Loving "Timp" is now local tradition. Moreover, since the "prehistoric" Indians shared the same tradition, they can be claimed as fictive kin. For instance, the Provo chapter of the Daughters of the American Revolution has named itself after Princess Timpanogos. In Richard Peacock's words, the Legend of Timpanogos reflects the "universal truths" of "our Indian brothers." Thus the legend can be used as a "tool for preserving tradition and revealing the culture of these people, for indeed, legends are told with the heart."[49]

In other words, folklore about the mountain seems to fulfill a sincere desire to "honor" Indians and to know something about their "traditions." The best evidence for this comes not from folklore archives but from the concert stage. Since 1992 the Utah Regional Ballet, based in American Fork, has staged a dance version of the Legend of Timpanogos. The troupe has even performed the ballet in international competitions. Locally, the dance has become almost as popular as *The Nutcracker*. A performance sometimes coincides with BYU's Education Week, a massive annual alumni event. In February 2002 the ballet company performed *Legend of Timpanogos* at Timpview High School as part of a cultural series sponsored by the Winter Olympics. The dance story conforms to Andy Anderson's version of the legend, although Anderson is not invoked. The director of the Utah Regional Ballet, Jacqueline Colledge, says she first heard the legend from her fourth-grade teacher. Years later, when she moved back to Utah Valley to start a dance company, she remembered the legend. She went back to her old teacher to hear the story again. Inspired, she set about creating a "signature piece" for her troupe (with her daughter cast as Ucanogos). With the help of a friend with "training in American Indian tradition," Colledge incorporated "Indian sign language" into her choreography. Although her company has advertised the ballet as a "native Nez Perce Indian story," Colledge believes that the Legend of Timpanogos originated with the Utes. Later, non-Indians adapted it. What's important now, she says, is that Native Americans reaccept the legend. In 1996 she described the goal of her ballet: "to try to unite all of us, and sense just a little bit of feeling of respect and reverence for what they [the Indians] went through and developed for all of us."[50]

Clearly, the legend fills a niche in the collective memory of local residents. For the population of Utah County—a population that in 1990 was 96 percent white and 0.7 percent Native American—the Legend of Timpanogos constitutes the most memorable "knowledge" about the Indians who once possessed this place. The legend has often appeared in the local curriculum for the fourth grade, when children study state history. Grandparents delight in telling the story to their progeny. School groups go to Timpanogos Cave, where some rangers actually act out the legend with kids. A cave tour can leave a powerful impression:

> There really were Indians living in that area and there really is a heart shape in the mountain so she felt it just had to be true. How else could this heart shape be explained? When Allyson heard the legend she felt her heart pounding and she was a little frightened thinking that Indians had died there. Since she was little, she believed the story and wanted to go out and find Indian arrowheads.[51]

In this reminiscence, an air of doubt surrounds the legend, but that doubt does not produce disbelief. To *dis*believe requires certain knowledge. The indigenous past of Utah Valley feels uncertain to most current residents. Although everyone knows that Indians must have lived here, hardly anyone outside academia knows much about them. Where are the arrowheads? Where are the remains? The Legend of Timpanogos both ameliorates and exacerbates this sense of uncertainty. As a story about long-departed Indians, it meets people's curiosity about that past, but as a *legend* it discourages further curiosity. It suggests that the documentary record about those Indians is merely fragments and shadows—*nothing but* the stuff of legends. The narrative association between Indians and death—*self-inflicted* death no less—may encourage the idea that Indians somehow disappeared on their own sometime before the white settlers arrived. To some degree, the legend obscures the role of Mormons in the displacement of Utes.

This last interpretation applies especially well to legendary Squaw Peak. It was here that a Ute woman fell and died during the Mormon-led extermination campaign of 1850. In collective memory, this one nonculpable death received disproportionate attention. In the first history of Provo, the fallen woman was identified as Big Elk's wife, "the handsomest squaw in the Ute nation." This identity cannot be corroborated, although Big Elk himself is known to have succumbed at Rock Canyon. Another source, a dubious reminiscence by a Provo pioneer, claimed that a solitary squaw (with a papoose on her back) retreated to the canyon in 1853 to avoid the fallout from an Indian offensive. There she jumped from a ledge to ensure that "she would never be taken alive by the whites who had stolen their land, killed their game, and destroyed their pony food. She had executed her protest—she was grit to the backbone. From that time to this that ledge has been known as 'Squaw Peak.'" In 1924 a local historian offered a better version of history: "Big Elk's widow, a fine-appearing, intelligent, young squaw, in attempting to climb a precipice, fell and was killed." But then the author added a contradictory footnote: "Another account ascribes the name to the tragedy of a Ute squaw's death in leaping from the peak as she was being pursued by a Snake [Shoshone] warrior after a battle between the two tribes." This pseudohistorical annotation attempted to remove Mormons from the scene altogether. Over time, collective memory finished the job. By the 1960s the predominant story about the naming of Squaw Peak was pure folklore. For example, a BYU student remembered climbing the peak when she was nine; along the way, her older brother told the tale of a "beautiful Indian squaw who fell in love with a strong Indian brave." They lived happily until "some pioneers" (not identified as Mormons) began usurping the land. The Indians went to war, the strong brave died, and the beautiful squaw threw herself from the cliff.[52]

This legend is closer to frontier folklore than to a legend attributed to Indians. In the folklore about frontier Utah, Native Americans generally appear as stock characters. The archetypal "Indian anecdotes" concern conflict or the avoidance of conflict. Pioneer settlers avoid conflict with Indians by acting fairly or charitably. Indians provoke conflict by killing, kidnapping, stealing. One of the most familiar stories concerns a threatening but comically inept "buck" trying to steal food from a cabin; a plucky pioneer wife foils his pilfering. This narrative type—still in circulation—is "true" in the sense that such confrontations must have happened at times. William A. Wilson has identified "struggles with Native Americans" as one of the three major themes in Mormon pioneer stories. "Told entirely from the settlers' point of view," he writes, "the narratives refer to Native Americans again and again in pejorative terms, as 'bucks' or 'squaws,' and depict them as less than fully human—vicious, depraved, dirty, smelly, and stupid." People who tell these stories "do not necessarily do so to deprecate Native Americans; they tell them to illustrate the heroism of their ancestors in taming this land and establishing a new Zion." Indians go hungry in these stories. They beg or maraud. As beggars they allow the pioneers to act generously; as marauders they allow the pioneers to act bravely. The narratives sidestep the reasons for the Indians' hunger.[53]

It seems puzzling that Indian anecdotes don't haunt Utah Valley nearly as much as the Legend of Timpanogos. Why would a fake legend take over a valley that witnessed so much interaction between natives and settlers? One possible reason: over time, post-pioneer generations conflated the early history of this valley with that of its geographic neighbor, Salt Lake Valley. Today, Utah Mormons endlessly repeat the "facts" that Brigham Young and his party ended their trek in a wasteland that was also a "no-man's land." This story is half true and fully misleading. As a buffer zone between Ute and Shoshone territory, Salt Lake Valley was less populated than other valleys along the Wasatch Front, but never uninhabited. And although this valley was less fertile than Utah Valley, it was hardly a sterile desert. No matter. Brigham Young's advance party has come to stand for all pioneers, and Salt Lake Valley has come to stand for the Wasatch Front. Its origin story seems to have colonized Utah Valley. More distant subregions of the state—notably San Pete Valley, San Juan County, the "Iron Mission" (Cedar City and environs), and "Dixie" (St. George and environs)—have cultivated their own pioneering stories. Compared to Utah Valley, these subregions have stronger collective memories of Indians.

Certainly Utah Valley could have acquired its own unique mythology. Provo's founding year offered the right material: a colonizing party, a fort, and an "Indian war." Perhaps Provo was settled too soon after Salt Lake. Or perhaps Provo is simply too close, physically and institutionally, to Salt Lake. These are the twin cities of Mormondom—Salt Lake the political and spiritual capital, Provo the cultural and educational capital. Students and workers commute from one valley to the other. Families overlap. In recent decades, thanks to growth, the residential and economic geographies of the valleys have merged. Although Utah Valley retains a distinct modern identity— "Happy Valley"—Utah Mormons have conflated the two places in their historical imagination. In truth, these valleys had very different histories through World War II. Among other differences, Utah Valley's record of Indian-white relations is far more extensive, intense, intimate, violent, and messy. Moreover, the pioneers of Provo were disobedient, even irreligious. Yet these may be the very reasons why the past is now obscure. It's often more desirable to misremember or forget the past than to recall it through history. History conveys responsibility. Legends, by contrast, provide antiquity without any moral strings. "Are we really forgetful," writes Carol Spindel on the subject of symbolic Indians, "or do we make a choice, albeit unconsciously, for a generic myth over the gritty ambiguities, the sandy starts and stops, and the unresolved questions that make up this particular story?"[54]

⁝⁝⁝ The ambiguity surrounding Utah's Indian past may seem odd given the LDS belief in the historicity of the Book of Mormon, a book about ancient Indians. However, the scripture is inexact about its geography, and interpretations about its setting have changed over time. Nineteenth-century Utah Saints were known to "translate" local rock art to recover messages from the old Lamanites, the original Utahns. Over the twentieth century, this geographic imagination mostly vanished. Tellingly, not one collected version of the Legend of Timpanogos refers to its characters as Lamanites or contains any other terms or metaphors from the Book of Mormon.

While the Latter-day Saints inherited from Joseph Smith an unusual racialist perspective on Native Americans, they also inherited a normative racist perspective from Euro-American culture. After Utah's territorial period, the Church stopped emphasizing the divine role of the Lamanites as a covenant people. In state politics, anti-Indian sentiment prevailed in the first half of the twentieth century. Utah was one of several western states that continued to disenfranchise Indians into the 1950s. Senator Arthur Watkins, the architect of the federal government's 1953 policy to "terminate" tribes, was a Mormon from Utah Valley. But even as racism became the dominant mode of thought, a strong undercurrent of Israelism persisted. In the 1960s and 1970s the Church refocused its attention on the promise of the

Lamanites. The key proponent was Spencer W. Kimball, longtime apostle and eventual president-prophet.

Kimball began his involvement in LDS Indian affairs in the 1940s by supervising an initiative to send Navajo children to Mormon foster homes for schooling. This ad hoc program was expanded and institutionalized in 1954. The so-called Indian Student Placement Program fell under the aegis of the Social Services Department of the LDS Relief Society, a state-licensed body. It resembled any other foster program except that the social workers were sectarian employees. Until 1972 the LDS Church used missionaries as placement recruiters. Before Indian children could be placed, they had to be baptized—formally converted. Many unbelieving parents authorized the baptism of their children merely as a means to give them an educational head start. In other words, the legal parents and the foster parents did not necessarily share the same goals for the placement children. Indian boys and girls stayed with foster families for the school year, then returned to their home reservations for the summer. The program peaked in 1970–71, when about 5,000 native children lived in Mormon homes, mostly on the Wasatch Front. By the end, more than 70,000 children had passed through the program. Indian Placement worked in tandem with Church seminaries (akin to weekday Sunday schools), which functioned as recruitment centers. An important seminary was located in Brigham City, Utah, at the Intermountain Indian School. The LDS Church ran smaller Indian seminaries at other boarding schools, on reservations, and in certain cities.[55]

Indian Seminary, like Indian Placement, fed into Indian Education at Brigham Young University—the final tier of the Church's comprehensive Indian outreach and assimilation program. Starting in 1965, BYU hired new faculty and sent recruiters to reservations across the West. One hundred forty Native Americans enrolled in the first academic year. Throughout the life of the program, the majority of the students were Navajos, but practically every western tribe was at some point represented. In the 1970s BYU boasted the largest Indian student body of any university anywhere. Enrollment topped out at around 500. Although the Indian graduation rate was low (about 20 percent), it was still the nation's best. In addition to a program of study, BYU sponsored extracurricular events through the Indian student association, Tribe of Many Feathers. Each year the university celebrated Indian Week (complete with Miss Indian BYU). The university also funded an Inter-Tribal Choir and a traveling performance group called the Lamanite Generation.[56]

In the 1970s the Lamanite Generation ended its performances with a signature song, "Go My Son," written by two students, Arliene Nofchissey (Navajo) and Carnes Burson (Ute). Using a BYU studio, the songwriters recorded the song for an LP by the same name in 1967. Done in 1960s "folk music" style, "Go My Son" encouraged Indians to climb the ladder of education. Another song, "Reservation Blues," described the "relaxed and shiftless course" of reservation life. Burson believed that each Indian student was a "desert flower" waiting to bloom. BYU gave him that opportunity, although, as luck would have it, the armed forces called him to duty shortly before he could graduate. The album notes say that he penned the following words as he flew over the Wasatch Range in a military jet: "I'm looking down on Timpanogos Mou[n]tain and the tops of our 'everlasting hills.' This is part of my promised land—a choice land—a land which I deeply love." Burson was in the vanguard. Only after the Vietnam era did an appreciable number of Utes attend Brigham Young. In 1982, for instance, 60 Utes (compared to 210 Navajos) called BYU home. But the dropout rate remained high. Between 1959 and 1985 only 17 Utes received degrees. Nonetheless, several hundred members of the Ute tribe completed extended stays in Provo and thereby became exposed or acculturated to local values like loving "Timp." Ironically, oral versions of the Legend of Timpanogos were pervasive at a time when there were more native people living in Utah Valley than at any point since the 1860s.[57]

Indian Education at BYU ended with the 1985–86 academic year, soon after President Kimball's death. Concurrently the LDS Church began to phase out the Placement Program. By 1996 nothing was left. The Church's second cycle of Lamanite redemption ended in muted disappointment, much like the first period in the mid-nineteenth century. Most Indian converts did not remain active in the Church. The downfall of George P. Lee, a Navajo protégé of Kimball, is symbolic. Lee spent years in Indian Placement, then served a mission and graduated from BYU. In 1975 he became the first Native American promoted to a high leadership position in the Church. But in 1989 he was excommunicated for unorthodox beliefs. Among other things, Lee claimed—with firm grounding in early LDS theology—that American Indians were Israelites whereas white Mormons were Gentiles. He criticized the "scriptural and spiritual extermination" of the Lamanites.[58]

Lee failed to recognize—or he recognized too well—that Mormon Israelism was in the midst of revision. In 1981 the Church quietly revised the Book of Mormon passage relating to the promise of the Lamanites: they would become "pure and delightsome" instead of "white and delightsome." More importantly, the Church began to rethink Joseph Smith's equation of modern-day Lamanites with the Indians of the United States. In the 1980s and 1990s it became conventional to regard Mesoamerica as the ancient setting of the Book of Mormon. The native and mestizo populations of Central America, especially the Yucatán and Guatemala, were thought to be the descendents of the "children of Lehi"—an alternate scriptural name. As a general descriptor, "children of Lehi" avoided the racism (if not the paternalism) historically associated with the word "Lamanite." Tellingly, BYU's Lamanite Generation was renamed "Living Legends."

This continuing shift in nomenclature and spiritual taxonomy has come partly in response to archaeological and genetic evidence about the Asiatic peopling of the Americas. It also reflects the Church's recent success proselytizing in southern Mexico. Most recently—in the face of scientific research that shows no relevant similarities between the DNA sequencing of contemporary native peoples of Israel and the Palestinian territories and of contemporary native peoples of the Americas—quasi-official Mormon apologists have adopted a more limited but more defensible fallback position: the Lamanites of Mesoamerica were eventually absorbed (genetically as well as socially) by other population groups. That's possible. The science of historical genetics is young; the evidence is sure to change. No matter what happens, however, it seems improbable that the "old" Lamanites—including the Indians of Utah—will ever fully regain their scriptural status. In 2006 the LDS church changed a key word in its publisher's introduction to the Book of Mormon; Lamanites were now described as "among the ancestors of the American Indians" instead of "the principal ancestors."[59]

::: All societies have demonstrated a facility to forget the past and also to believe what they want to about the past, even in the face of inconsistent evidence. People can create meaningful connections to olden times without formal history lessons or academic degrees. "Folk history" or "heritage" is, ironically enough, a popular research topic for professional historians. In Utah, heritage is produced and reproduced through a rich tradition of public commemoration. Latter-day Saints in the "Mormon Culture Region" (as scholars call it) are obsessed with their past. Here in "Zion" (as Utah Mormons call it), collective memory—with its omissions as well as its inclusions—works in tandem with performance.

Mormon commemoration is both annual and cyclical; it intensifies on special anniversaries. In 1947, the centennial of the Mormon pioneer trek, state and church officials dedicated a large monument at This Is the Place State Park, at the mouth of Emigration Canyon. For seventeen nights that July, a new epic outdoor play, *The Promised Valley,* was performed at the University of Utah's football stadium. The play went on to become a small-town summertime staple. The script contains just one Indian scene—a convention straight out of American pageantry—that depicts natives and settlers making peace by exchanging gifts and smoking the ceremonial pipe. The scene is listed as "optional." Inspired by *Promised Valley,* the associated communities of Castle Valley have staged the pioneer-themed Castle Valley Pageant since 1978. For the 1996 state centennial, five other Utah communities produced five new outdoor dramas.[60]

For many occasions—not just theater—Utah Mormons dress up as pioneers. LDS teenagers in Utah and Idaho are all but required to participate in at least one summer youth activity involving wagons or handcarts. Reenactments cluster in July, when about eighty cities and towns in the Mormon heartland stage Pioneer Day celebrations. Most local homes have a stash of calico. Town parades always feature costumed participants. Salt Lake City's Days of '47 Parade is the largest of these fetes—and America's third-largest annual procession, after Pasadena's Rose Parade and New York City's Thanksgiving Day Parade. In Utah, pioneer worship is a civic religion. This Is the Place State Park recently completed its transformation into a "Heritage Park" with an "Old Deseret Village" full of actors clothed in period garb.[61]

With its disproportionate focus on pioneering, the Mormon sense of the past is compressed and insular. Intentionally or not, native peoples have been pushed to the historical margins—the realm of footnotes and folklore. Utah Mormons preoccupy themselves with the narrative of *getting to* Utah. The pioneer trek is their "master commemorative narrative." They have little incentive to think about what happened here before or even afterward. Notwithstanding the achievement of "making the desert blossom as the rose," Utah's territorial period was, from a strict believer's standpoint, a debacle. Two cornerstones of Mormonism—the imminence of the Millennium and the sanctity of polygamy—wore away. After the forced Americanization of 1890, the LDS Church decided to place more emphasis on the miraculous past than on the miraculous future. Moreover, the historical emphasis was selective. The "First Vision" of Joseph Smith and the pioneer trek of Brigham Young emerged as the favored episodes for commemoration. Over the twentieth century, the Church did everything in its power to etch these episodes into collective memory. Simultaneously it did its best to erase polygamy from public consciousness. The laity abetted these efforts. As a consequence, the territorial period as a whole became indistinct. Indians faded out with the polygamists. The native peoples of the Great Basin are now doubly disadvantaged in Mormon memory: not only are the Lamanites forgettable because they didn't live up to prophecy; they are associated with a prophetic era that most Latter-day Saints would rather forget. By contrast, pioneering is a supremely usable past.[62]

The two most festive Pioneer Days thus far came in two successive years, 1996 and 1997. Both were state-sanctioned commemorative events. Nineteen ninety-six marked the centennial of Utah statehood, 1997 the sesquicentennial of Mormon colonization. As early as January 1996 it was apparent that the centennial was a warm-up for the real celebration the following year. Hispanics, blacks, Greek-Americans, and Indians all complained about the inordinate emphasis on Mormon pioneers. The chairman of the twenty-five-person Centennial Commission—twenty-four of whom were white—accused the critics of carping: "If you hung some people with a new rope, they'd complain." According to the chairman, the commission was color-blind: "I don't care whether somebody is black, white, red, or green. They're Utahns and that's all that matters." Yet when December rolled around, the public relations director for the Ute tribe looked back on the year with bitterness. "All we heard about was Mormonism and pioneers, and anything to do with Indians was a blurb," said Larry Cesspooch. "The centennial business was a slap in the face and this next one [1997] will be the other hand."[63]

The LDS Church—the de facto organizer of the sesquicentennial—tried to show sensitivity by expanding its definition of "pioneer." Anyone or any group who pressed on in the face of adversity possessed "the spirit of pioneering." Our world was full of "modern pioneers." This wasn't just lip service. The Pioneer Sesquicentennial Committee made a concerted effort to include Native Americans. However, most of the participating natives were drawn from the membership of the Church. The Sesquicentennial Committee sponsored a conference at BYU on the subject of balancing tribal beliefs and Mormonism; the event attracted some 400 Indians from all over North America. Among Utah's own tribes, the committee's overtures generated less enthusiasm. Turning down the offer of a grant initiative,

Larry Cesspooch explained, "It's like a Jew accepting money or work-ing with the Nazis now."[64]

The sesquicentennial rolled on without the Utes. A full-scale wagon train reenacted the day-by-day journey of the Pioneer Camp of the Saints, the advance party that arrived in the Valley of the Great Salt Lake on 22 July 1847. This local-interest story caught the attention of the national media. In anticipation, the Public Affairs Office of the LDS Church predistributed a special pioneer-themed CD-ROM to news bureaus. When the pioneers of 1997 descended Emigration Canyon into the valley, tens of thousands of well-wishers greeted them with cheers and hymns. The trekkers later appeared at the Days of '47 Parade, held on 24 July—Pioneer Day, a state holiday. That evening the celebration shifted to Provo, where volunteers staged a made-for-TV megapageant, "The Faith in Every Footstep Sesquicen-tennial Spectacular." This performance showed off the organizational powers of Mormons—powers put in service of a particular histori-cal memory. The Sesquicentennial Spectacular deployed four stages, 3,000 balloons, 600 flags, 200 confetti cannons, and a cast of thou-sands, including the Mormon Tabernacle Choir. The pageant went on for two successive nights at the BYU football stadium to a capacity crowd of 65,000, with simultaneous satellite broadcast to hundreds of Mormon churches on the worldwide LDS satellite network, and a tape-delay transmission on BYU's public television station.[65]

In an age of telegenic heritage, it is hard to compete against mne-monic events like the Spectacular. Nonetheless, countermemories do exist in Utah and in the nation at large. Their existence was in fact on display during the state's maligned centennial in 1996. Of the many performance pieces commissioned by the Centennial Commit-tee, two important ones transcended the de facto theme of pioneering. The first, *Dreamkeepers,* an opera, concerned the spiritual journey of a modern urban Ute woman living between cultures. Perhaps the first Indianist opera written since the 1930s, *Dreamkeepers* premiered with the Utah Opera Company in January 1996 after four years of preparation, including consultation with the Ute tribe. "Of all the things going on with the Centennial," said a member of the Ute Business Committee, "this was the only group to come to the tribe, not taking but giving something."[66]

The second work, like the first, unwittingly recapitulated the forgotten output of William Hanson. Mormon pop composer Kurt Bestor, a lifelong resident of Utah Valley, wanted to compose a serious work for orchestra and chorus. For his theme he chose his beloved peak, Mount Timpanogos, which he had only recently climbed for the first time—on Pioneer Day. Bestor approached the distinguished naturalist-writer-activist Terry Tempest Williams for a libretto. Explaining this unlikely collaboration, Williams spoke about her own tie to Timpanogos. Her grandfather, Sandy Dixon, grew up in Utah Valley, then moved to Salt Lake City, where he spent his entire adult life. When he felt the end approaching, "he wanted to move back to Orem to die in the shadow of the mountain . . . which is exactly what he did." For further inspiration, Williams stayed a week in a cabin at Robert Redford's Sundance Resort—a resort that appeals to Native America in its name, theme, and decor. Williams spent her time "just listening to the mountain." There she perceived "that it was important to go to the Ute people and ask them about the story [of the mountain]." Larry Cesspooch arranged a meeting with a tribal elder and a tribal linguist. Williams went to the reservation to request their assistance "to create a context for the legend of Timpanogos." With their permission, she incorporated many native words in her impressionistic, reverential text. The first movement narrated the creation of Mount Timpanogos by Sunawav, the Ute Creator.[67]

Timpanogos, A Prayer for Mountain Grace had its debut in July 1996. The performance received glowing praise in the state's leading newspaper. Even Larry Cesspooch was pleased. Echoing the Ute tribe's earlier reaction to *Dreamkeepers,* he welcomed this exception to the standard hoopla of 1996. The state centennial, he said, "ought to celebrate the land itself, because the land has affected everyone." He thanked Terry Tempest Williams for being the first one to finally ask Utes about *their* legend. Out of respect for the Utes, Williams made sure that the concert program included "The Real Story of Timpanogos," as related by tribal elder Ethel Grant:

> The mountains were roamed by various groups of Utes. The groups were known by nicknames. One group settled in Provo Canyon. It was plentiful country. The Utes had everything they needed, food, water, fish, deer, fruit, and berries.
>
> One day, the group decided they would move to another place. Everyone moved on with the exception of one couple who stayed with their dog. The dog was their guardian. It took care of them.
>
> Each morning, Toopanocus, the man, would go out scouting for food. The woman became suspicious of him because he was gone so much of the time. When he returned home, they would quarrel as she accused him of having another lover. A great misunderstanding took place. The man had enough.
>
> Toopanocus left with a broken heart. He went into the cave deep inside the mountain and committed suicide. Toopanocus's heart continues to bleed for her.
>
> The woman was overcome with jealousy. She climbed to the top of Bridal Veil Falls and jumped off. It is her tears that join with the waterfall today. And it is her body lying down facing the falls.[68]

Curiously, this story takes two familiar Western story motifs (Eden and the lover's leap) and adds an indigenous element, a dog guardian. The "real story" would appear to be a modern hybrid—especially given the implied reference to the Great Heart of Timpanogos. Although it's conceivable that precontact Utes knew about a cave system in American Fork Canyon, at the time there was no access to the particular chamber that houses the Great Heart.

Of course, an Indian legend doesn't have to be ancient in order to be native. Indians change, too. Like Mormons—like all societies, for that matter—Utes constantly adapt the past for present purposes. Unlike the LDS Church, however, the Ute tribe does not possess a vast archive of old documents. *Nuche* descend from an oral tradition. Unfortunately, that tradition has been weakened by demographic decline and cultural assimilation. Southern Numic faces extinction as a spoken language. In a 1996 radio interview, Clifford Duncan, a Ute historian, commented on the Legend of Timpanogos. "It may have had a Ute origin," he said, "but it's kind of changed, you know; and we don't really hang on to the stories anymore, and they begin to change. The change may have occurred once it was in the hands of the white farmers or the ranchers." Duncan might have added that many Utes have attended BYU over the years, and lived in area homes as part of the LDS Indian Placement Program, and lived on the Wasatch Front on their own. There have been ample opportunities for Indians to absorb non-Indian versions of this "Indian legend" and—should they choose—to claim it for themselves. In 2000 Larry Cesspooch came to Timpanogos Cave National Monument to tour the caverns and give a presentation to visitors. According to Cesspooch, Utes had always known about the cave. To illustrate the point, he told an amplified version of the "real" legend. Cesspooch used a different spelling for the protagonist's name—Toompunucus—and a resequenced plot. According to Cesspooch, the Ute woman committed suicide out of jealousy, and only then did Toompunucus kill himself in remorse. Cesspooch made explicit what was implied in the concert program: the Great Heart of Timpanogos is the bleeding heart of Toompunucus.[69]

It's impossible to say how old the "real" legend is, or how it came to be. There may have been numerous legends about Mount Timpanogos in circulation among Utes. Around 1980 a white man from the Uinta Basin wrote down what he claimed was a transcription of a story told by an aged Uinta Ute (no name given).[70] Although the exact words cannot be trusted, there is no reason to suspect that this white man was inventing the narrative:

The Utes are suffering from seven years of drought because the spirits are angry. The Utes move to the plains to hunt bison, but the Sioux drive them back. They return home via Provo Canyon, where a daughter of the big chief climbs a high ledge and throws herself off, praying to the spirits as she falls. Water begins gushing from her rocky grave, Bridal Veil Falls. The Utes name it Paw-Apawgi (Talking Water). The spirits lift up the girl's body and place it on the nearby mountain. She will rise again someday and lead the Utes to a world without sorrow. Her name cannot be uttered, but she goes by Too-pee-o-nuatch, The Rock Person.

Interestingly, both this legend and the "real" legend feature Bridal Veil Falls more prominently than the mountain. Perhaps the falls held special significance to The People in earlier times. Perhaps the non-Indian versions of the Legend of Timpanogos that include Bridal Veil Falls are in part derived from authentic Numic lore. Alternatively, this Ute legend may derive in whole or in part from pseudo-Indian lore. Bridal Veil Falls has been a tourist attraction since the railroad era. It appeared in guidebooks decades before Mount Timpanogos did. Fittingly, then, a fake legend about Bridal Veil Falls appeared before the Legend of Timpanogos. In 1909 *Western Monthly,* the official organ of the See America First League, published a series of "Indian legends" by J. G. Weaver highlighting scenic spots in the "Inter-Mountain West." One of these pieces was the "Ute Legend of Bridal Veil Falls," a story about Wyoakee (male) and Owasetta (female), who perform a double suicide off the falls. The 1922 pamphlet *Timpanogos, Wonder Monument*—the same pamphlet that launched "The Story of Utahna and Red Eagle"—contained a poem called "Norita: A Legend of Bridal Veil Falls." In the 1960s an entrepreneur built a restaurant above the falls approached by the Sky Ride ("Steepest Aerial Tramway in the World"), and exposed his tram-riders to another version of the fake legend. This time the doomed girl was named Noreta. In 1999 some local middle school students erected a plaque at the falls that included the legend of Norita and *Grey* Eagle.[71]

It just goes on, stories upon stories. The "real" derivation of the "real" legend will never be known for certain. Authenticity is as elusive as it is desirable, as problematic as it is powerful. To most people, though, all this doubtfulness is academic. If an Indian performs the Legend of Timpanogos as an Indian legend, then it is what it is. Only a historian would quibble if and when descendents of Utes and Mormons who long ago clashed on the shores of Utah Lake find common ground on the slopes of Mount Timpanogos. Terry Tempest Williams has said it is the "shared love and affection for Timpanogos itself . . . which binds all of us together."[72] Speaking historically, that is a fiction—yet could it become a beneficent fiction? Perhaps more of that love will move downslope to an overlooked body of water.

Notes
Acknowledgments
Index

Notes

The following abbreviations are used in the notes. In addition, in many cases I have used shortened titles for old books with elaborate title pages.

BYOF	Brigham Young Office Files, CHD
BYU	Brigham Young University
CHD	Historical Department, The Church of Jesus Christ of Latter-day Saints, Salt Lake City, Utah
DN	*Deseret News* (Salt Lake City)
JH	Journal History of The Church of Jesus Christ of Latter-day Saints
RG	Record Group, National Archives
SC-BYU	Special Collections, Lee Library, Brigham Young University, Provo, Utah
SC-USU	Special Collections, Merrill-Cazier Library, Utah State University, Logan
SC-UU	Special Collections, Marriott Library, University of Utah, Salt Lake City
SLT	*Salt Lake Tribune* (Salt Lake City)
UHQ	*Utah Historical Quarterly*
UHRC	Utah History Research Center, Salt Lake City

Introduction

1. My term "Hydraulic Age" is inspired by Donald Worster, *Rivers of Empire: Water, Aridity, and the Growth of the American West* (New York: Pantheon, 1985). For the most extreme example of the erasure of a western lake, see Wil-

liam L. Preston, *Vanishing Landscapes: Land and Life in the Tulare Lake Basin* (Berkeley: University of California Press, 1981). On the relationship between modes of production and landscape assessment, see Richard White, "'Are You an Environmentalist or Do You Work for a Living?': Work and Nature," in *Uncommon Ground: Toward Reinventing Nature,* ed. William Cronon (New York: W. W. Norton, 1995), 171–185. Interested scholars may wish to seek out my Ph.D. dissertation, "American Land Marks: A History of Place and Displacement" (Stanford, 2005), from which this book evolved. Although the dissertation contains more flaws than I care to admit, it also contains generous, even extravagant, annotations.

2. On the concepts of place and place-making, I benefited from Tim Cresswell, *Place: A Short Introduction* (Malden, Mass.: Blackwell, 2004). My understanding of "legibility" comes mainly from Kevin Lynch, *The Image of the City* (Cambridge, Mass.: MIT Press, 1960). In colloquial usage, "landmark" has four meanings: (1) a conspicuous landscape feature, (2) a boundary point, (3) a structure set aside for preservation, (4) an epochal event. I am concerned primarily with the first meaning, secondarily with the next two, and not at all with the last.

3. There are many books on the erection of U.S. landmarks (e.g., the Statue of Liberty, the Empire State Building, Hoover Dam) but few on the perceptual transformation of landforms into landmarks. One of the best is Elizabeth McKinsey, *Niagara Falls: Icon of the American Sublime* (Cambridge: Cambridge University Press, 1985). On places like El Morro, see Bruno David and Meredith Wilson, eds., *Inscribed Landscapes: Marking and Making Place* (Honolulu: University of Hawai'i Press, 2002). Throughout this book, I use "Timp" (always in quotes) to refer to the mountain as a social construction or landmark. To refer to the massif as a geomorphologic entity, I generally use "Mount Timpanogos."

4. My understanding of landscape assessment comes from diffuse sources, including the works of J. B. Jackson, Donald Meinig, Denis Cosgrove, and Anne Whiston Spirn. Specifically on the historical role of landscape assessment in the U.S. West, I relied on Anne Farrar Hyde, *An American Vision: Far Western Landscape and National Culture, 1820–1920* (New York: New York University Press, 1990).

5. Important treatments of place attachment include Yi-Fu Tuan, *Topophilia: A Study of Environmental Perception, Attitudes, and Values* (Englewood Cliffs, N.J.: Prentice-Hall, 1974); Eugene Victor Walter, *Placeways: A Theory of the Human Environment* (Chapel Hill: University of North Carolina Press, 1988); Deborah Tall, *From Where We Stand: Recovering a Sense of Place* (New York: Alfred A. Knopf, 1993); and David Butz and John Eyles, "Reconceptualizing

Senses of Place: Social Relations, Ideology and Ecology," *Geografiska Annaler, Series B, Human Geography* 79, no. 1 (1997): 1–25.

6. On the concept of space, see especially Henri Lefebvre, *The Production of Space,* trans. Donald Nicholson-Smith (Oxford: Blackwell, 1991). My understanding of metageographical inventions like the Grand Canyon was enhanced by Martin W. Lewis and Kären E. Wigen, *The Myth of Continents: A Critique of Metageography* (Berkeley: University of California Press, 1997).

7. Large-scale places—including whole regions—have also been created by and for tourism. American case studies include Dona Brown, *Inventing New England: Regional Tourism in the Nineteenth Century* (Washington, D.C.: Smithsonian Institution Press, 1995); Kathleen L. Howard and Diana F. Pardue, *Inventing the Southwest: The Fred Harvey Company and Native American Art* (Flagstaff, Ariz.: Northland Publishing, 1996); and Dydia DeLyser, *Ramona Memories: Tourism and the Shaping of Southern California* (Minneapolis: University of Minnesota Press, 2005).

8. On the cognitive and psychological dimensions of place perception, see Yi-Fu Tuan, "Visibility: The Creation of Place," in *Space and Place: The Perspective of Experience* (Minneapolis: University of Minnesota Press, 1977), 161–178; David Canter, *The Psychology of Place* (London: Architectural Press, 1977); Winifred Gallagher, *The Power of Place: How Our Surroundings Shape Our Thoughts, Emotions, and Actions* (New York: Poseidon Press, 1993); Irwin Altman and Setha M. Low, eds., *Place Attachment,* Human Behavior and Environment: Advances in Theory and Research 12 (New York: Plenum Press, 1992); and Richard C. Stedman, "Is It Really Just Social Construction? The Contribution of the Physical Environment to Sense of Place," *Society and Natural Resources* 16 (September 2003): 671–685.

9. My appreciation of the intersection of time and place owes much to Kevin Lynch, *What Time Is This Place?* (Cambridge, Mass.: MIT Press, 1972). Like landmarks, geographical regions are temporally bounded. For a useful case study of a now-defunct U.S. subregion, see Katherine G. Morrissey, *Mental Territories: Mapping the Inland Empire* (Ithaca: Cornell University Press, 1997). And for an eye-opening case study of an emerging subregion—the "Loess Hills" of western Iowa—see Peggy Petrzelka, "The New Landform's Here! The New Landform's Here! We're Somebody Now!! The Role of Discursive Practices on Place Identity," *Rural Sociology* 69, no. 3 (2004): 386–404.

10. On the grid, see Kate Brown, "Gridded Lives: Why Kazakhstan and Montana Are Nearly the Same Place," *American Historical Review* 106 (February 2001): 17–48; James C. Scott, *Seeing like a State: How Certain Schemes to Improve the Human Condition Have Failed* (New Haven: Yale University Press,

1998), chap. 1; and Roger J. P. Kain and Elizabeth Baigent, *The Cadastral Map in the Service of the State: A History of Property Mapping* (Chicago: University of Chicago Press, 1992). On the relationship between surveying and "land-marking," see D. Graham Burnett, *Masters of All They Surveyed: Exploration, Geography, and a British El Dorado* (Chicago: University of Chicago Press, 2000), esp. chaps. 4–5.

11. Meditations on place loss include Peter Read, *Returning to Nothing: The Meaning of Lost Places* (Cambridge: Cambridge University Press, 1996); Blaine Harden, *A River Lost: The Life and Death of the Columbia* (New York: W. W. Norton, 1996); Jared Farmer, *Glen Canyon Dammed: Inventing Lake Powell and the Canyon Country* (Tucson: University of Arizona Press, 1999); Erik Reece, *Lost Mountain: A Year in the Vanishing Wilderness* (New York: Riverhead Books, 2006); and Gary Paul Nabhan, "Searching for Lost Places," in *Cultures of Habitat: On Nature, Culture, and Story* (Washington, D.C.: Counterpoint, 1997), 135–151.

12. Dale McKinnon, interviewed in the documentary film *In the Light of Reverence* (2001); transcript available at http://www.sacredland.org/ITLOR_pages/transcript.html. For context, see Peter Nabakov, *Where the Lighting Strikes: The Lives of American Indian Sacred Places* (New York: Viking, 2006).

13. French sociologist Maurice Halbwachs first articulated the concept of collective memory in 1925. The recent fascination with sites of collective memory grows out of Holocaust studies and especially French studies. The seminal essay is Pierre Nora, "Between Memory and History: *Les Lieux de Mémoire*," *Representations* 26 (Spring 1989): 7–24. The scholarship on memory sites is less developed in the United States than in Europe; recent noteworthy authors include Edward T. Linenthal, John D. Seelye, and Charlene Mires. Most useful for me was Kenneth E. Foote, *Shadowed Ground: America's Landscapes of Violence and Tragedy*, rev. ed. (Austin: University of Texas Press, 2003).

14. For analyses of (urban) "placelessness," see E. Relph, *Place and Placelessness* (London: Pion, 1976); James Howard Kunstler, *The Geography of Nowhere: The Rise and Decline of America's Manmade Landscape* (New York: Simon and Schuster, 1993); and Tony Hiss, *The Experience of Place* (New York: Alfred A. Knopf, 1990).

15. Borrowing from Yael Zerubavel, we could say that Mormon pioneers possess a high "commemorative density," whereas Utah's Indians possess a low density. See *Recovered Roots: Collective Memory and the Making of Israeli National Tradition* (Chicago: University of Chicago Press, 1995), esp. chap. 1. Low density can lead to "collective amnesia" (originally a Freudian term). However, "amne-

sia" isn't exactly apropos to Utah history, because the word implies permanence or incurability. In Sam Wineburg's phraseology, the problem with Utah history is less collective amnesia than "collective occlusion"; see Wineburg, *Historical Thinking and Other Unnatural Acts: Charting the Future of Teaching the Past* (Philadelphia: Temple University Press, 2001), 242–243.

16. In scale and ambition this work bears some resemblance to W. Barksdale Maynard, *Walden Pond: A History* (Oxford: Oxford University Press, 2004), which explores large themes in U.S. history using the environmental and cultural history of one small lake in Massachusetts. More directly I took encouragement from Mark Fiege, *Irrigated Eden: The Making of an Agricultural Landscape in the American West* (Seattle: University of Washington Press, 1999), a book about little-known waterscapes in Idaho that is also about the meaning of nature; William deBuys, *Salt Dreams: Land and Water in Low-down California* (Albuquerque: University of New Mexico Press, 1999), a bottom-up environmental history; Elliott West, *The Contested Plains: Indians, Goldseekers, and the Rush to Colorado* (Lawrence: University Press of Kansas, 1998), which uses environmental and Native American history to update a canonical story from the frontier West; and Stephen J. Pyne, *How the Canyon Became Grand: A Short History* (New York: Viking, 1998), a book about topography that is also about ideas.

17. The great non-Mormon champion of Mormon history, Jan Shipps, likens the historian's American West to a "doughnut"—the hole in the center being Utah. I've also heard it said, only partly in jest, that "saintly" Utah and "sinful" Nevada cancel each other out, creating a black hole. However, there is reason for optimism given the recent appearance of bridge-building books by historians such as D. Michael Quinn, Sarah Barringer Gordon, and Kathleen Flake. Likewise, historians of Native America can no longer afford to ignore the Great Basin after the appearance of Ned Blackhawk, *Violence over the Land: Indians and Empires in the Early American West* (Cambridge, Mass.: Harvard University Press, 2006).

18. Several U.S. environmental historians—William deBuys, Nancy Langston, Donald Edward Davis, Timothy Silver, David Beesley, Christopher Johnson—have written about single mountain ranges. And local historians have produced many good books about individual landmark mountains. However, my approach to mountains more closely follows that of historical geographers such as William Wyckoff and Lary M. Dilsaver, eds., *The Mountainous West: Explorations in Historical Geography* (Lincoln: University of Nebraska Press, 1995); Kevin Scott Blake, "Mountain Symbolism and Place Identity in the Southwestern Landscape" (Ph.D. diss., Arizona State University, 1996); Veronica della Dora, "Geographies

of the Holy Mountain: Post-Byzantine and Western Representations of the Monastic Republic of Mount Athos" (Ph.D. diss., University of California at Los Angeles, 2005); Bernard Debarbieux, "The Mountain in the City: Social Uses and Transformations of a Natural Landform in Urban Space," *Ecumene* 5, no. 4 (1998): 399–431; and William R. Freudenburg, Scott Frickel, and Robert Gramling, "Beyond the Nature/Society Divide: Learning to Think about a Mountain," *Sociological Forum* 10 (September 1995): 361–392.

19. Here my work builds on Rayna Green, "A Tribe Called Wannabee: Playing Indian in America and Europe," *Folklore* 99, no. 1 (1988): 30–55; Philip J. Deloria, *Playing Indian* (New Haven: Yale University Press, 1998); Shari M. Huhndorf, *Going Native: Indians in the American Cultural Imagination* (Ithaca: Cornell University Press, 2001); and Alan Trachtenberg, *Shades of Hiawatha: Staging Indians, Making Americans, 1880–1930* (New York: Hill and Wang, 2004). On literary haunting, I consulted Judith Richardson, *Possessions: The History and Uses of Haunting in the Hudson Valley* (Cambridge, Mass.: Harvard University Press, 2003); and Renée L. Bergland, *The National Uncanny: Indian Ghosts and American Subjects* (Hanover, N.H.: University Press of New England for Dartmouth College Press, 2000). For examinations of "haunted" places in the American West, I recommend Coll Thrush, *Native Seattle: Histories from the Crossing-Over Place* (Seattle: University of Washington Press, 2007); Ann Ronald, *GhostWest: Reflections Past and Present* (Norman: University of Oklahoma Press, 2002); Drex Brooks, *Sweet Medicine: Sites of Indian Massacres, Battlefields, and Treaties* (Albuquerque: University of New Mexico Press, 1995); and Rebecca Solnit, *Savage Dreams: A Journey into the Hidden Wars of the American West* (San Francisco: Sierra Club Books, 1994).

20. I take the term "neonative" from Hal K. Rothman, *Devil's Bargains: Tourism in the Twentieth-Century American West* (Lawrence: University of Kansas Press, 1998), where it appears in a different but related context. The theme of settlers' becoming native has been examined comparatively in Thomas R. Dunlap, *Nature and the English Diaspora: Environment and History in the United States, Canada, Australia, and New Zealand* (Cambridge: Cambridge University Press, 1999). To understand the relationship between colonialism and place attachment, I also looked to Cole Harris, *The Resettlement of British Columbia: Essays on Colonialism and Geographical Change* (Vancouver: University of British Columbia Press, 1997); and Peter Read, *Belonging: Australians, Place and Aboriginal Ownership* (Cambridge: Cambridge University Press, 2000).

21. Wallace Stegner, *The Sound of Mountain Water*, rev. ed. (New York: Dutton, 1980), 38.

1. Ute Genesis, Mormon Exodus

1. J. H. Beadle, *The Undeveloped West* (Philadelphia: National Publishing, 1873), 150.

2. Donald Jackson and Mary Lee Spence, eds., *The Expeditions of John Charles Frémont*, vol. 1: *Travels from 1838 to 1844* (Urbana: University of Illinois Press, 1970), 700.

3. J. H. Simpson, *Report of Explorations across the Great Basin of the Territory of Utah* (Washington, D.C.: Government Printing Office, 1876), 32–33.

4. See David B. Madsen and David Rhode, eds., *Across the West: Human Population Movement and the Expansion of the Numa* (Salt Lake City: University of Utah Press, 1994); Warren L. D'Azevedo, *Handbook of North American Indians*, vol. 11: *Great Basin* (Washington, D.C.: Smithsonian Institution Press, 1986); and the dated but still influential Julian H. Steward, *Basin-Plateau Aboriginal Sociopolitical Groups,* Smithsonian Institution Bureau of American Ethnology Bulletin 120 (Washington, D.C.: Government Printing Office, 1938).

5. Jackson and Spence, *Expeditions of John Charles Frémont,* 702.

6. See S. Lyman Tyler, "The Myth of the Lake of Copala and the Land of Teguayo," *UHQ* 20 (October 1952): 313–329; and Joseph P. Sánchez, *Explorers, Traders, and Slavers: Forging the Old Spanish Trail, 1678–1850* (Salt Lake City: University of Utah Press, 1997), 5–13.

7. The Southern Numic word for "The People" has been spelled in various ways, including "Nooche," "Núu-ci," and "Nuuciyu." On cultural nomenclature, see James A. Goss, "The Yamparika—Shoshones, Comanches, or Utes—or Does It Matter?" in *Julian Steward and the Great Basin: The Making of an Anthropologist*, ed. Richard O. Clemmer, L. Daniel Myers, and Mary Elizabeth Rudden (Salt Lake City: University of Utah Press, 1999), 74–84. On the "speech community" and the "family cluster" among Numic peoples, see Gregory Ellis Smoak, *Ghost Dances and Identity: Prophetic Religion and American Indian Ethnogenesis in the Nineteenth Century* (Berkeley: University of California Press, 2006), chap. 1. In the anthropological literature on Utes, "band" has three distinct meanings: (1) the basic unit of society, the extended bilateral family cluster; (2) a seasonal or strategic encampment of numerous related kin groups; and (3) an environmentally bounded subculture composed of various related clusters practicing a similar subsistence strategy.

8. On nineteenth-century Ute place-names and social names, the starting source remains William R. Palmer, "Indian Names in Utah," *UHQ* 1 (January 1928): 5–26; and Palmer, "Utah Indians, Past and Present," *UHQ* 1 (April 1928): 35–52. For descriptions of fishing techniques, see Anne M. Smith, "Cultural Dif-

ferences and Similarities between Uintah and White River," in *Ute Indians II* (New York: Garland, 1974), 330; and Smith, *Ethnography of the Northern Utes,* Papers in Anthropology 17 (Albuquerque: Museum of New Mexico Press, 1974), 61–64. Dietary estimates from D'Azevedo, *Handbook of North American Indians,* 341.

9. [Don Carlos Johnson,] "Indians of Utah Valley: Incidents in Their History and Wars with the White Invader," *The Independent* (Springville, Utah), 13 February 1908, 1. On bison, see Stephen P. Van Hoak, "The Other Buffalo: Native Americans, Fur Trappers, and the Western Bison, 1600–1860," *UHQ* 72 (Winter 2004): 4–18; and Karen D. Lupo, "The Historical Occurrence and Demise of Bison in Northern Utah," *UHQ* 64 (Spring 1996): 168–180.

10. On the Timpanogos lifeway, see David Lewis, *Neither Wolf nor Dog: American Indians, Environment, and Agrarian Change* (New York: Oxford University Press, 1994), chap. 2; and Joel C. Janetski, *The Ute of Utah Lake,* University of Utah Anthropological Papers 116 (Salt Lake City: University of Utah Press, 1991), 36–40.

11. The east-west distinction was eventually replaced by a north-south distinction. In the 1880s most of the Colorado Utes were forcibly relocated to northeastern Utah alongside their Utah cousins. A smaller number of Colorado Utes were confined to reservations in southwestern Colorado. These two clusters of reservations—one to the north, one to the south—have now existed long enough that academics and natives speak of "Northern Utes" as a cultural subcategory distinct from "Southern Utes."

12. On Shoshones and the horse, see Smoak, *Ghost Dances and Identity.* For a continental overview of the horse revolution, see Colin G. Calloway, *One Vast Winter Count: The Native American West before Lewis and Clark* (Lincoln: University of Nebraska Press, 2003), chap. 6. On the Great Basin, see Demitri B. Shimkin, "The Introduction of the Horse," in D'Azevedo, *Handbook of North American Indians,* 517–524.

13. Ted J. Warner, ed., *The Domínguez-Escalante Journal: Their Expedition through Colorado, Utah, Arizona, and New Mexico in 1776,* trans. Fray Angelico Chavez (Salt Lake City: University of Utah Press, 1995), esp. 62–73.

14. Bernardo de Miera y Pacheco, report to the Sacred Royal Catholic Majesty, 26 October 1777, reprinted in *UHQ* 11, nos. 1–4 (1943): 114–120.

15. See Sánchez, *Explorers, Traders, and Slavers.*

16. On the New Mexico slave system, see James F. Brooks, *Captives and Cousins: Slavery, Kinship, and Community in the Southwest Borderlands* (Chapel Hill: University of North Carolina Press, 2002). On the slave trade in the eastern Great Basin, see especially Ned Blackhawk, *Violence over the Land: Indians and*

Empires in the Early American West (Cambridge, Mass.: Harvard University Press, 2006).

17. Charles Wilkes, "Map of Upper California by the U.S. Ex. Ex. and Best Authorities 1841," in atlas to *Narratives of the United States Exploring Expedition during the Years 1838, 1839, 1840, 1841, 1842* (Philadelphia, 1845), reprinted in Carl I. Wheat, *Mapping the Transmississippi West, 1540–1861*, vol. 2: *From Lewis and Clark to Frémont, 1804–1845* (San Francisco: Institute of Historical Geography, 1958); Jackson and Spence, *Expeditions of John Charles Frémont,* 702. "Negro" from Charles Mackay, *The Mormons: or Latter-day Saints,* 4th ed. (London: Ward and Lock, 1856), 239; "orangutans" from William Kelly, *Across the Rocky Mountains* (London: Sims and M'Intyre, 1852), 178. Simpson, *Report of Explorations,* 36.

18. Warren Angus Ferris, *Life in the Rocky Mountains,* ed. LeRoy R. Hafen, rev. ed. (Denver: Old West, 1983), 388; Dale L. Morgan, *The West of William H. Ashley* (Denver: Old West, 1964), 115; George R. Brooks, ed., *The Southwest Expedition of Jedediah S. Smith: His Personal Account of the Journey to California, 1826–1827* (Glendale, Calif.: Arthur H. Clark, 1977), 40–46. On the local fur trade, see especially John R. Alley, "Prelude to Dispossession: The Fur Trade's Significance for the Northern Utes and Southern Paiutes," *UHQ* 50 (Spring 1982): 104–123.

19. See Sánchez, *Explorers, Traders, and Slavers;* and LeRoy R. Hafen and Anne W. Hafen, *Old Spanish Trail: Santa Fe to Los Angeles* (Glendale, Calif.: Arthur H. Clark, 1954).

20. Jackson and Spence, *Expeditions of John Charles Frémont,* 695; Thomas L. Kane, "The Mormons: A Discourse Delivered before the Historical Society of Pennsylvania," copy in JH, 26 March 1850. The Journal History (JH) is a day-by-day historical scrapbook compiled by LDS Church historians. The master copy is located in CHD; microfilm copies can be found at all of Utah's major libraries. Other important primary sources on Walkara are James Linforth, ed., *Route from Liverpool to Great Salt Lake City* (London: Latter-day Saints' Book Depot, 1855), 105; and Dimick B. Huntington, *Vocabulary of the Utah and Sho-Sho-Ne or Snake Dialects,* rev. ed. (Salt Lake City: Salt Lake Herald Office, 1872), 27–29. For scholarly appraisals, see Stephen P. Van Hoak, "Waccara's Utes: Native American Equestrian Adaptations in the Eastern Great Basin, 1776–1876," *UHQ* 67 (Fall 1999): 309–330; and Ronald D. Walker, "Wakara Meets the Mormons, 1848–1852: A Case Study in Native American Accommodation," *UHQ* 70 (Summer 2002): 215–237. Needless to say, there is more than one way of representing Walkara's name. "Walker" and "Wahker" appear frequently in nineteenth-century sources. On his death and burial, see JH, 29 Janu-

ary 1855; and J. W. Gunnison, *The Mormons* (Philadelphia: J. B. Lippincott, 1860), 149.

21. Charles Dickens, "In the Name of the Prophet—Smith!" *Household Words* 8 (19 July 1851), 340, as quoted in Terryl L. Givens, *By the Hand of Mormon: The American Scripture That Launched a New World Religion* (New York: Oxford University Press, 2002), 64. In the portions of my book that concern Mormon history, I have excluded most citations of basic secondary sources because of the availability of a superb reference volume: James B. Allen, ed., *Studies in Mormon History, 1830–1997: An Indexed Bibliography* (Urbana: University of Illinois Press, 2000).

22. Richard Lloyd Anderson, "Jackson County in Early Mormon Descriptions," *Missouri Historical Review* 65 (April 1971): 270–293, quote on 286. Revelations from *The Doctrine and Covenants,* rev. ed. (Salt Lake City: The Church of Jesus Christ of Latter-day Saints, 1987), 57:3, 28:9, and 54:8.

23. *History of The Church of Jesus Christ of Latter-day Saints,* 2d ed., vol. 6 (Salt Lake City: Deseret News, 1950), 318–319.

24. Lewis Clark Christian, "Mormon Foreknowledge of the West," *Brigham Young Studies* 21 (Fall 1981): 403–415, quote on 411. Also see Ronald K. Esplin, "'A Place Prepared': Joseph, Brigham and the Quest for Promised Refuge in the West," *Journal of Mormon History* 9 (1982): 85–111.

25. Scott G. Kenney, ed., *Journal of Wilford Woodruff, 1833–1898 Typescript,* vol. 3 (Midvale, Utah: Signature Books, 1983), 187; *William Clayton's Journal* (Salt Lake City: Deseret News, 1921), 201. On ethnogenesis and recapitulation, see Jan Shipps, *Mormonism: The Story of a New Religious Tradition* (Urbana: University of Illinois Press, 1985).

26. Will Bagley, ed., *The Pioneer Camp of the Saints: The 1846 and 1847 Mormon Trail Journals of Thomas Bullock* (Spokane, Wash.: Arthur H. Clark, 1997), 209–213; *William Clayton's Journal,* 275; Willard Richards to Orson Pratt, 21 July 1847, typescript, CHD.

27. Kenney, *Journal of Wilford Woodruff,* 234; Levi Jackman, diary, MS 79, SC-BYU.

28. "Fittest" quote from Richard E. Bennett, *We'll Find the Place: The Mormon Exodus, 1846–1848* (Salt Lake City: Deseret Book, 1997), 254. "General Epistle from the Council of the Twelve Apostles to The Church of Jesus Christ of Latter Day Saints Abroad, Dispersed throughout the Earth," 23 December 1847, original in CHD.

29. Smith quoted in Bennett, *"We'll Find the Place,"* 269. See also *William Clayton's Journal,* 309; Bagley, *The Pioneer Camp of the Saints,* 232.

30. See Conevery Bolton Valenčius, *The Health of the Country: How Ameri-*

can Settlers Understood Themselves and Their Land (New York: Basic Books, 2002).

31. See Robert Bruce Flanders, *Nauvoo: Kingdom on the Mississippi* (Urbana: University of Illinois Press, 1965), 38–40, 53–54; Richard E. Bennett, *Mormons at the Missouri, 1846–1852: "And Should We Die . . ."* (Norman: University of Oklahoma Press, 1987), chap. 7.

32. William Clayton, *The Latter-day Saints' Emigrants' Guide* (St. Louis: Republican Steam Power Press and Chambers & Knapp, 1848), 20; Everett L. Cooley, "The Robert S. Bliss Journal," *UHQ* 27 (October 1959): 381–404. For a summary analysis of early pioneer perceptions of the valley, see Richard H. Jackson, "The Mormon Experience: The Plains as Sinai, the Great Salt Lake as the Dead Sea, and the Great Basin as Desert-cum-Promised Land," *Journal of Historical Geography* 18 (January 1992): 41–58.

33. Cooley, "The Robert S. Bliss Journal," 392. On healing springs, see Valenčius, *The Health of the Country*, 152–158.

34. Thomas Bullock, letter from Winter Quarters, *The Latter-day Saints' Millennial Star* (hereafter *Millennial Star*) 10 (15 April 1848): 116–119.

35. Cooley, "The Robert S. Bliss Journal," 390.

36. Willard Snow to Erastus Snow, 6 October 1847, MS 15782, CHD.

37. "Diary of the Overland Trail, 1849 and Letters, 1849–1850, of Captain David De Wolf," *Illinois State Historical Society Transactions* 32 (1925): 206; William G. Johnston, *Overland to California* (Oakland, Calif.: Biobooks, 1948), 123; Kelly, *Across the Rocky Mountains*, 161–162.

38. James Ririe quoted in *Our Pioneer Heritage* 9 (1966): 358; Thales Haskell quoted in *An Enduring Legacy* 2 (1979): 324; Cyrus Tolman quoted in ibid., 5 (1982): 179. Both *Our Pioneer Heritage* and *An Enduring Legacy* are multivolume anthologies of source material published by the Daughters of the Utah Pioneers. *Heart Throbs of the West* and *Treasures of Pioneer History* are other titles in the series, which is useful despite editorial flaws.

39. Gordon C. Cone, diary, 11 October 1849, Vault MSS 661, SC-BYU.

40. Thomas Bullock, "Celebration of the Twenty-fourth of July at Great Salt Lake City," reprinted from *Frontier Guardian*, 19 September 1849, in *Millennial Star* 11 (1 December 1849): 356. Cooley, "The Robert S. Bliss Journal," 389. The "Great" was not officially dropped from the capital's name until 1868.

41. "The Record of Norton Jacob," typescript (1949), 73, copy in UHRC; *William Clayton's Journal*, 329. After the deaths of Wanship and Goship from measles in March 1850, sources refer to the horse-owning natives of Salt Lake Valley (and adjacent Weber Valley) as "Cumumbahs" or more often "Weber Utes"—even though they were less Ute than Shoshone.

42. P. P. Pratt to Orson Pratt, 5 September 1848, reprinted in *Millennial Star* 11 (15 January 1849), 23.

43. See "Testimony of Brigham Young," 15 January 1852, reprinted in Sandra Jones, *The Trial of Don Pedro León Luján: The Attack against Indian Slavery and Mexican Traders in Utah* (Salt Lake City: University of Utah Press, 2000), 125, original in UHRC. There may have been another slave-buying episode that fall involving Wanship. The sources are reminiscent and somewhat confused; see Peter Gottfredson, *History of Indian Depredations in Utah* (Salt Lake City: Skelton, 1919), 15–18.

44. For a description of a Ute encampment, see William Henry Robinson, reminiscence, *Treasures of Pioneer History* 6: 355.

45. Lieutenant McCauley, "Notes on Pagosa Springs, Colorado," December 1878, Senate Executive Document 65, 45th Cong., 3d sess., Serial Set 1831, 4–5. On native water therapy, see Virgil J. Vogel, *Indian Medicine* (Norman: University of Oklahoma Press, 1970), 253–259. On Shoshones, see Peter Nabokov and Lawrence Loendorf, *Restoring a Presence: American Indians and Yellowstone National Park* (Norman: University of Oklahoma Press, 2004), 277–285. On Middle Park, see Samuel Bowles, *The Switzerland of North America* (Springfield, Mass.: Samuel Bowles, 1869), 72–75; and LeRoy R. Hafen and Anne W. Hafen, eds., *The Diaries of William Henry Jackson, Frontier Photographer* (Glendale, Calif.: Arthur H. Clark, 1959), 275–276.

46. George D. Smith, ed., *An Intimate Chronicle: The Journals of William Clayton* (Salt Lake City: Signature Books and Smith Research Associates, 1991), 398; Howard Stansbury, *Exploration and Survey of the Valley of the Great Salt Lake* (Philadelphia: Lippincott, Grambo, 1852), 294; Gunnison, *The Mormons,* 148. On *puwa*, see Jay Miller, "Numic Religion: An Overview of Power in the Great Basin of Native North America," *Anthropos* 78, nos. 3–4 (1983): 337–354.

47. Cyrena Merrill, autobiography (1908), MSS SC 2180, SC-BYU; John Nebeker, "Early Justice in Utah" (1884)," *UHQ* 3 (July 1930): 87. Also see Minerva Wade Hickman, autobiography, MSS SC 2314, SC-BYU.

48. Fish quote from Levi Jackman, diary, 19 April 1848; population projection from "The Record of Norton Jacob," 72.

2. Brigham Young and the Famine of the Fish-Eaters

1. Lucy Mack Smith, "Preliminary Manuscript," reprinted in *Early Mormon Documents,* ed. Dan Vogel, vol. 1 (Salt Lake City: Signature Books, 1996), 293–

294. Also see Dan Vogel, *Indian Origins and the Book of Mormon: Religious Solutions from Columbus to Joseph Smith* (Salt Lake City: Signature Books, 1986).

2. See Armand L. Mauss, *All Abraham's Children: Changing Mormon Conceptions of Race and Lineage* (Urbana: University of Illinois Press, 2003), chap. 3.

3. Richard Cummins to William Clark, 15 February 1831, reprinted in *BYU Studies* 36, no. 2 (1996–97): 234. For details see Warren A. Jennings, "The First Mormon Mission to the Indians," *Kansas Historical Quarterly* 37 (Autumn 1971): 288–299; and G. St. John Stott, "New Jerusalem Abandoned: The Failure to Carry Mormonism to the Delaware," *Journal of American Studies* 21 (April 1987): 71–85.

4. See Ronald W. Walker, "Seeking the 'Remnant': The Native American during the Joseph Smith Period," *Journal of Mormon History* 19 (Spring 1993): 1–33; Kenneth W. Godfrey, "The Zelph Story," *BYU Studies* 29 (Spring 1989): 31–56; and Lawrence Coates, "Refugees Meet: The Mormons and Indians in Iowa," ibid., 21 (Fall 1981): 491–514.

5. See Lawrence G. Coates, "Cultural Conflict: Mormons and Indians in Nebraska," *BYU Studies* 24 (Summer 1984): 275–300; Richard E. Bennett, *Mormons at the Missouri, 1846–1852: "And Should We Die . . ."* (Norman: University of Oklahoma Press, 1987), chap. 5; and Robert A. Trennert Jr., "The Mormons and the Office of Indian Affairs: The Conflict over Winter Quarters, 1846–1848," *Nebraska History* 53 (Fall 1972): 381–400.

6. Will Bagley, ed., *The Pioneer Camp of the Saints: The 1846 and 1847 Mormon Trail Journals of Thomas Bullock* (Spokane, Wash.: Arthur H. Clark, 1997), 243–244.

7. Levi Jackman, diary, MS 79, SC-BYU.

8. Oliver Huntington, diary and reminiscence, typescript, vol. 2, 52–55, SC-BYU. Also see Juanita Brooks, ed., *On the Mormon Frontier: The Diary of Hosea Stout, 1844–1861*, vol. 2 (Salt Lake City: University of Utah Press, 1964), 344–347; and D. Robert Carter, *Founding Fort Utah: Provo's Native Inhabitants, Early Explorers, and First Year of Settlement* (Provo, Utah: Provo City Corporation, 2003), 60–67.

9. Robert Glass Cleland and Juanita Brooks, eds., *A Mormon Chronicle: The Diaries of John D. Lee, 1848–1876*, vol. 1 (San Marino, Calif.: Huntington Library Press, 1955), 100–101; "refractory" quote from JH, 18 July 1848, 1.

10. "Life of James A. Little," typescript, MSS 1490, UHRC.

11. See Carter, *Founding Fort Utah*, 107–110.

12. "Provo in 1849. Pioneer Days and the Indians. Some Trying Scenes. What Caused the Ute War Now Told for the First Time," *Provo Enquirer*, 27 November

1894, clipping in Manuscript History of Provo, CHD; George Washington Bean, autobiography, 46, folder 7, MSS 1038, George Bean Papers, SC-BYU; William Thomas, "Historical Sketch and Genealogy of the Thomas's Families," 1889–1892, MA 1598, CHD; George Washington Bean, reminiscence, ca. 1892, folder 1, Bean Papers.

13. Little Chief quoted in John S. Higbee to Brigham Young, 12 April 1849, box 21, folder 16 (reel 31), BYOF. Chronology reconstructed from Oliver Huntington, diary and reminiscence, 60–64; Cleland and Brooks, *A Mormon Chronicle*, 106; and Brooks, *On the Mormon Frontier*, 351.

14. Flora Diana Bean Horne, comp., *Autobiography of George Washington Bean* (Salt Lake City: Privately published, 1945), 51; Dimick Huntington, minutes of meeting with Indians, Fort Utah, 14 May 1849, box 16, folder 17 (reel 24), BYOF.

15. George Washington Bean, autobiography; Horne, *Autobiography of George Washington Bean*, 52; Brigham Young to Isaac Higbee, 28 May 1849, box 16, folder 17 (reel 24), BYOF.

16. Parley P. Pratt to Orson Pratt, 8 July 1849, reprinted in *Millennial Star* 11 (15 November 1849): 342–343; Edward W. Tullidge, "History of Provo City," *Tullidge's Quarterly Magazine* 3 (1885): 234.

17. Quote from Lillie Jane Orr Taylor, ed., *Life History of Thomas J. Orr Jr.* (N.p.: Privately published, 1930), 17; details from Horne, *Autobiography of George Washington Bean*, 56.

18. Horne, *Autobiography of George Washington Bean*, 57–61, 100.

19. Brigham Young to Isaac Higbee, 18 October 1849, box 16, folder 18 (reel 24), BYOF. On the deteriorating situation, see LeRoy R. Hafen and Anne W. Hafen, *The Far West and Rockies*, vol. 15: *Journals of Forty-Niners: Salt Lake to Los Angeles* (Glendale, Calif.: Arthur H. Clark, 1961), 115–116; Isaac Higbee to Brigham Young, 15 October 1849, box 21, folder 16 (reel 31), BYOF; and Carter, *Founding Fort Utah*, 142–143.

20. Hafen and Hafen, *The Far West and Rockies*, 31.

21. George Mayer, reminiscences and diary, MS 1706, CHD; Statement by James Bean, 12 June 1854, in JH, 31 January 1850, 7; Brigham Young to the Brethren in the Utah Valley, 8 January 1850, box 16, folder 19 (reel 24), BYOF.

22. Thomas Bullock, "Minutes of Meeting of Brigham Young, Heber C. Kimball, George A. Smith, Ezra T. Benson, Daniel H. Wells, Joseph Young and Thomas Bullock at Parley P. Pratt's," 31 January 1850, CHD. For Young's subsequent statement of nonresponsibility, see JH, 31 January 1850, 8.

23. Howard Stansbury, *An Expedition to the Valley of the Great Salt Lake of Utah* (Philadelphia: Lippincott, Grambo, 1855), 149; J. W. Gunnison to Martha

Gunnison, Great Salt Lake City, 20 February 1850, box 1, Gunnison Papers, Henry E. Huntington Library, San Marino, Calif.

24. Daniel H. Wells, Special Order, 31 January 1850, doc. 6, box 1, folder 2 (reel 4), Territorial Militia Records, Series 2210, UHRC.

25. For an exhaustive description of this battle and the whole military campaign, see Carter, *Founding Fort Utah*, chaps. 9–11.

26. George W. Howland to Daniel Wells, 9 February 1850, doc. 19, box 1, folder 3 (reel 4), Territorial Militia Records.

27. Thomas Bullock, meeting minutes, 10 February 1850, as quoted in Carter, *Founding Fort Utah*, 198, original in CHD; "Daniel H. Wells' Narrative," *UHQ* 6 (October 1933): 124–132, quote on 126.

28. J. W. Gunnison to Martha Gunnison, Great Salt Lake City, 1 March 1850, box 1, Gunnison Papers; J. W. Gunnison, *The Mormons* (Philadelphia: J. B. Lippincott, 1860), 147. Also see Carter, *Founding Fort Utah*, 206–208.

29. Brigham Young to Daniel Wells, 14 February 1850, as quoted in Carter, *Founding Fort Utah*, 212, original in Territorial Militia Records.

30. Will Bagley, ed., *Frontiersman: Abner Blackburn's Narrative* (Salt Lake City: University of Utah Press, 1992), 170–171.

31. Julius R. (Chunky) Murray Jr., interview, 31 August 1982, Ute Indian Interview Project, Accession 853, SC-UU. March 1850 confrontation described in Horne, *Autobiography of George Washington Bean*, 63; and Thomas, "Historical Sketch and Genealogy of the Thomas's Families."

32. LaVan Martineau, *The Southern Paiutes: Legends, Lore, Language, and Lineage* (Las Vegas: KC Publications, 1992), 54. At a 1900 meeting of the Utah Indian War Veterans, it was denied that such an event ever happened; see "No Indians Beheaded," *Salt Lake Herald*, 10 August 1900, 5.

33. Casualty figures from Epsy Jane Williams, autobiography, MS 13059, CHD.

34. Scene at Fort Utah described in James Leach, reminiscences and diary, MS 1410, CHD. Scene in Great Salt Lake City described in JH, 19 February 1850; J. W. Gunnison to Martha Gunnison, 1 March 1850; George Montgomery to the Commissioner of Indian Affairs, 26 July 1850, RG 75 (Records of the Bureau of Indian Affairs), microfilm set 234 (Letters Received by the Office of Indian Affairs, 1824–81), reel 897; "Daniel H. Wells' Narrative," 126.

35. Baptisms described in Isaac Morley to Brigham Young, 20 February, 15 March, and 17 March 1850, box 22, folder 2 (reel 31), BYOF. Conversion numbers in JH, 7 July 1850. "Spirit of Lord": Brigham Young to Isaac Morley, 24 March 1850, box 16, folder 19 (reel 24), BYOF. Details about the Patsowet affair from JH, 21 April, 28 April, and 29 April 1850.

36. "Big Chief to Pe-tete-nete, Walker, Sow-ee-ette, Black Hawk, Tab-bee and other good Indian chiefs," 6 May 1850, box 16, folder 20 (reel 24), BYOF.

37. [Thomas Bullock,] "Meeting with Utes in Utah," 22 May 1850, box 74, folder 42 (reel 86), BYOF.

38. Ibid.

39. Historian's Office Journal, 22 May 1850, CR 100-1, CHD.

40. Church Historian's Office, "History of Brigham Young," vol. 7, 35–36, copy in CHD. Also see JH, 22–23 May 1850.

41. J. W. Gunnison to Martha Gunnison, 1 March 1850; Gunnison, *The Mormons*, 147.

42. JH, 7 May 1849; Cleland and Brooks, *A Mormon Chronicle*, 108.

43. JH, 20 November 1850. In August 1851 the territorial legislature petitioned President Millard Fillmore for the same. See John Alton Peterson, *Utah's Black Hawk War* (Salt Lake City: University of Utah Press, 1998), 63.

44. See Sandra Jones, *The Trial of Don Pedro León Luján: The Attack against Indian Slavery and Mexican Traders in Utah* (Salt Lake City: University of Utah Press, 2000).

45. See esp. Brian Q. Cannon, "Adopted or Indentured, 1850–1870: Native Children in Mormon Households," in *Nearly Everything Imaginable: The Everyday Life of Utah's Mormon Pioneers,* ed. Ronald W. Walker and Doris R. Dant (Provo, Utah: BYU Press, 1999), 341–357.

46. Proclamation by the Governor, 30 April 1853, *DN,* 3. For Brigham Young's recollections of the Bowman encounter, see JH, 2 May 1853; and *Journal of Discourses* 1 (1855): 104. The *Journal* was a periodical series published by the LDS Church that anthologized official sermons. The dispute over who killed Bowman went on for more than a year; see George Bean to Brigham Young, 1 May 1854, box 23, folder 10 (reel 32), BYOF.

47. Although this Arapene story went on to enter folklore, it seems well founded. See Brigham Young to the Commissioner of Indian Affairs, 28 June 1853, box 55, folder 1 (reel 66), BYOF.

48. Statement of M. S. Marlenas, 6 July 1853, box. 58, folder 14 (reel 92), Brigham Young Collection (the old arrangement of the BYOF), CHD.

49. See Howard A. Christy, "The Walker War: Defense and Conciliation as Strategy," *UHQ* 47 (Fall 1979): 395–420; and Peter Gottfredson, comp., *History of Indian Depredations in Utah* (Salt Lake City: Skelton Publishing, 1919), 43–83.

50. Walkara's letter enclosed in George Bean to Brigham Young, 1 May 1854, box 23, folder 10 (reel 32), BYOF.

51. Voyle L. Munson and Lillian S. Munson, *A Gift of Faith: Elias Hicks*

Blackburn (Eureka, Utah: Basin/Plateau Press, 1991), 43–44; Scott G. Kenney, ed., *Journal of Wilford Woodruff, 1833–1898 Typescript,* vol. 4 (Midvale, Utah: Signature Books, 1983), 272. For Walkara's feelings, see Report of G. W. Bean, 24 June 1854, box 58, folder 14 (reel 92), Brigham Young Collection (the old arrangement of the BYOF). Description of child slaves from Solomon Nunes Carvalho, *Incidents of Travel and Adventure in the Far West* (New York: Derby and Jackson, 1857), 260.

52. Brigham Young quotations from a speech on 31 July 1853 in the tabernacle in Great Salt Lake City, reprinted in *Journal of Discourses* 1 (1855): 171–172. On the Provo settlers' request and Young's response, see Peterson, *Utah's Black Hawk War,* 69–70. For critical evaluations of Mormon-Indian relations and the policies of Brigham Young, see esp. Howard A. Christy, "Open Hand and Mailed Fist: Mormon-Indian Relations in Utah, 1847–52," *UHQ* 46 (Summer 1978): 216–235; Floyd O'Neil, "The Mormons, the Indians, and George Washington Bean," in *Churchmen and the Western Indians, 1829–1920,* ed. Clyde A. Milner II and Floyd A. O'Neil (Norman: University of Oklahoma Press, 1985), 77–107; and Ronald W. Walker, "Toward a Reconstruction of Mormon and Indian Relations, 1847–1877," *BYU Studies* 29 (Fall 1989): 33–42.

53. JH, 15 August 1854.

54. "Historical Sketch and Genealogy of the Thomas's Families." For context, see Davis Bitton and Linda P. Wilcox, "Pestiferous Ironclads: The Grasshopper Problem in Pioneer Utah," *UHQ* 46 (Fall 1978): 336–355; and Jeffrey A. Lockwood, *Locust: The Devastating Rise and Mysterious Disappearance of the Insect That Shaped the American Frontier* (New York: Basic Books, 2004).

55. Rigby quoted in *Our Pioneer Heritage* 4 (1961): 251. For context, see Jill Mulvay Derr, "'I Have Eaten Nearly Everything Imaginable': Pioneer Diet," in Walker and Dant, *Nearly Everything Imaginable,* 222–247. On the contrasting foodways of Mormons and Numic peoples vis-à-vis insects, see David B. Madsen and Brigham D. Madsen, "One Man's Meat Is Another Man's Poison: A Revisionist View of the Seagull 'Miracle,'" *Nevada Historical Society Quarterly* 30 (Fall 1987): 165–181.

56. D. Robert Carter, "Fish and the Famine of 1855–56," *Journal of Mormon History* 27 (Fall 2001): 92–124, quotes from 115 and 118. This prodigiously researched article by a devoted local historian is groundbreaking.

57. George W. Armstrong to the Commissioner of Indian Affairs, 30 June 1855, in *Annual Report of the Commissioner of Indians Affairs for 1855,* House Exec. Doc. 1, no. 1, 34th Cong., 1st sess. (1856), Serial Set 840, 552–553.

58. See David L. Bigler, "Garland Hurt, the American Friend of the Utahs," *UHQ* 62 (Spring 1994): 149–170; and Beverly Beeton, "Teach Them to Till the

Soil: An Experiment with Indian Farms," *American Indian Quarterly* 3 (Winter 1977–78): 299–320. The four "Pah-ute" band names come from a map included in a letter from Hurt to Indian Commissioner George Manypenny, 3 April 1855, RG 75, microfilm set 234, reel 897.

59. I viewed a copy of the inquest verdict, dated 28 February 1856, at the American West Center, University of Utah. On the Ute attitude toward hanging, see JH, 5 March 1856.

60. Quoted in George W. Armstrong to the Commissioner of Indian Affairs, 30 September 1855, in *Annual Report of the Commissioner of Indians Affairs for 1855, 525.*

61. Kenney, *Journal of Wilford Woodruff,* 331–332; Grant speech in *Journal of Discourses* 3 (1856): 51–65; Pratt speech in ibid., 9 (1862): 178–179; Woodruff speech in ibid., 221–229.

62. "Remarks by Tow-om-bw-gah [sp?] or High Forehead, the Indian Chief, at the Bowery at Provo," 15 July 1855, interpreted by Lyman Wood, transcribed by J. Long, box 58, folder 14 (reel 92), Brigham Young Collection (the old arrangement of the BYOF).

63. "Vision of Arapine on the night of the 4th of Feb 1855," interpreted by John Lowry Jr., transcribed by George Peacock, box 74, folder 49 (reel 86), BYOF.

64. Dimick Huntington, journal, 1857–59, MS 1419 2, CHD.

65. Garland Hurt to George W. Manypenny, 2 May 1855, reprinted in *The Utah Expedition,* House Exec. Doc. 71, 35th Cong,, 1st sess. (1858), Serial Set 956, 176.

66. Springville bishop quoted in Lyndon W. Cook, ed., *Aaron Johnson Correspondence* (Orem, Utah: Center for Research of Mormon Origins, 1990), 83. On Mormons and the Indian Farm, see William G. Hartley, *My Best for the Kingdom: History and Autobiography of John Lowe Butler, a Mormon Frontiersman* (Salt Lake City: Aspen Books, 1995), 314–323.

67. Anonymous recollection quoted in *Tullidge's Histories,* vol. 2 (Salt Lake City: Edward W. Tullidge, 1889), 31.

68. Dimick Huntington, journal. For a chronology of disease, see Richard W. Stoffle, Kristine L. Jones, and Henry F. Dobyns, "Direct European Immigrant Transmission of Old World Pathogens to Numic Indians during the Nineteenth Century," *American Indian Quarterly* 19 (Spring 1995): 181–203.

69. Dimick Huntington, journal.

70. [Don Carlos Johnson,] "Indians of Utah Valley," serial, *The Independent* (Springville, Utah), 6 January–18 June 1908, quote from the 2 April issue.

71. Tintic's death reported in JH, 6 April 1859, 2; Groneman in Federal

Writers Project, WPA, Utah Pioneer Biographies, vol. 11, 181–182, copy in LDS Family History Library, Salt Lake City. On the rapes and the aftermath, see Donald R. Moorman with Gene A. Sessions, *Camp Floyd and the Mormons: The Utah War* (Salt Lake City: University of Utah Press, 1992), chap. 10.

72. A. Humphreys to Charles E. Mix, 12 November 1860, in *Report of the Secretary of the Interior,* Senate Exec. Doc. 1, 36th Cong., 2d sess. (1860), 394; Henry Martin to Office of the Superintendent of Indian Affairs, 1 October 1861, in *Report of the Secretary of the Interior,* Senate Exec. Doc. 1, 37th Cong., 2d sess. (1861), 746. Chicken quip quoted in Beeton, "Teach Them to Till the Soil," 315. Frederick W. Hatch to James Doty, 12 May 1862, RG 75, microfilm set M-834 (Records of the Utah Superintendency of Indian Affairs, 1853–70), plate 1432.

73. "Uinta Not What Was Represented," *DN,* 25 September 1861, 1.

74. "President Young's Trip to Utah County," *DN,* 14 June 1865, 293; treaty session described in O. H. Irish to the Commissioner of Indian Affairs, 9 September 1865, in *Report of the Secretary of the Interior,* House Exec. Doc. 2, 39th Cong., 1st sess. (1865), 313.

75. Treaty and treaty council minutes from RG 75, microfilm set T-494 (Documents Relating to the Negotiation of Ratified and Unratified Treaties with Various Tribes of Indians, 1801–1869), reel 8 (Unratified Treaties, 1821–65), frames 1137–51 and 1153–95.

76. Ibid., passim.

77. Sanpitch eventually signed the treaty too. See Gustive O. Larson, "Uintah Dream: The Ute Treaty—Spanish Fork, 1865," *BYU Studies* 14 (Spring 1974): 361–381.

78. J. E. Tourtellotte to the Commissioner of Indian Affairs, 20 September 1870, in *Report of the Secretary of the Interior,* House Exec. Doc. 4, 41st Cong., 3d sess. (1870), 606. On Black Hawk and the conflict named after him see Peterson, *Utah's Black Hawk War.*

79. Translation of "Sowiette" from M. S. Marlenas statement. List of names from JH, 7 July 1850.

3. The Desertification of Zion

1. Thomas Bullock, minutes, "Gathering at the Bath House to celebrate the 'Festival' of consecrating the Bath House," 27 November 1850, CHD.

2. Samuel Bowles, *Across the Continent* (Springfield, Mass.: Samuel Bowles, 1865), 98–99. On the spa tradition in America, see especially Jonathan Paul de Vierville, "American Healing Waters: A Chronology (1513–1946) and Historical

Survey of America's Major Springs, Spas, and Health Resorts Including a Review of Their Medicinal Virtues, Therapeutic Methods, and Health Care Practices" (Ph.D. diss., University of Texas at Austin, 1992); and Thomas A. Chambers, *Drinking the Waters: Creating an American Leisure Class at Nineteenth-Century Mineral Springs* (Washington, D.C.: Smithsonian Institution Press, 2002).

3. J. H. Beadle, *Life in Utah* (Philadelphia: National Publishing, 1870), 445, 247. On the Robinson homicide, the best source remains B. H. Roberts, *A Comprehensive History of The Church of Jesus Christ of Latter-day Saints,* vol. 5 (Salt Lake City: Deseret News Press, 1930), chap. 131.

4. P. Donan, *Utah—A Peep into a Mountain-walled Treasury of the Gods* (Buffalo, N.Y.: Matthews, Northup, 1891), 79. For context, see Thomas K. Hafen, "City of Saints, City of Sinners: The Development of Salt Lake City as a Tourist Attraction, 1869–1900," *Western Historical Quarterly* 28 (Autumn 1997): 343–377; and Richard H. Jackson, "Great Salt Lake City and Great Salt Lake City: American Curiosities," *UHQ* 56 (Spring 1988): 128–147.

5. Utah & Nevada Railway, *Descriptive and Historical Sketch of the Great Salt Lake, Utah Territory* (Salt Lake City: Passenger Department, 1886), copy in Bancroft Library, University of California, Berkeley; 1890 visitation estimate from *Utah: A Complete and Comprehensive Description of the Agricultural, Stock Raising and Mineral Resources of Utah,* 4th ed. (Omaha: Passenger Department of the Union Pacific Railway, 1891), 106.

6. See John D. C. Gadd, "Saltair, Great Salt Lake's Most Famous Resort," *UHQ* 36 (Summer 1968): 198–221; Nancy D. McCormick and John S. Mc-Cormick, *Saltair* (Salt Lake City: University of Utah Press, 1985); and S. Todd Shoemaker, "Saltair and the Mormon Church, 1893–1906" (Master's thesis, University of Utah, 1983). The best secondary source on the lake's resort era remains Dale Morgan, *The Great Salt Lake* (Indianapolis: Bobbs-Merrill, 1947), chap. 18.

7. See Richard S. Van Wagoner, "Saratoga, Utah Lake's Oldest Resort," *UHQ* 57 (Spring 1989): 108–124.

8. See "Our Hot Springs," *Salt Lake Herald,* copy in JH, 26 August 1888; and Louise B. Pearce, "Salt Lake City's Vanishing Hot Springs," typescript, UHRC.

9. On the numerical decline of spas, see Richard Kovacs, "The Problem of American Spas," *Journal of the American Medical Association* 127 (14 May 1945): 977. The lost geography of American spas has been examined in two fine state histories, both of which speak to national trends: Janet Mace Valenza, *Taking the Waters in Texas: Springs, Spas, and Fountains of Youth* (Austin: University of Texas Press, 2000); and Loring Bullard, *Healing Waters: Missouri's His-*

toric Mineral Springs and Spas (Columbia: University of Missouri Press, 2004). Around 2000, as part of a northern extension of Warm Springs Park, Salt Lake City exhumed and restored one of the springs along with native wetlands vegetation. Although bathing is prohibited, homeless people now take the waters.

10. T. S. Kenderdine, *A California Tramp and Later Footprints* (Newton, Pa.: Privately published, 1888), 117; Benjamin G. Ferris, *Utah and the Mormons* (New York: Harper and Brothers, 1854), 48; John Bell, *The Mineral and Thermal Springs of the United States and Canada* (Philadelphia: Parry and McMillan, 1855), 334–335. On the Orientalization of Utah and Mormonism, see Terryl L. Givens, *The Viper on the Hearth: Mormons, Myths, and the Construction of Heresy* (New York: Oxford University Press, 1997), 130–133.

11. On 2002 media coverage I relied on my own observations as well as Chiung Hwang Chen, "'Molympics? Journalistic Discourse of Mormons in Relation to the 2002 Winter Olympic Games," *Journal of Media and Religion* 2, no. 1 (2003): 29–47. My argument about the shift in symbolic emphasis from lakes to mountains agrees with Dean L. May, "Bayous, Beaches and Breaches: Human Interaction with the Great Salt Lake," in *Images of the Great Salt Lake* (Salt Lake City: Utah Museum of Fine Arts, 1996), 7–26.

12. See D. Robert Carter, "Worshiping at the Easter Cross," *Daily Herald* (Provo, Utah), 27 March 2005, F-2.

13. Laura Warner, "Utah Lake Changing with the Times," *DN*, 31 May 2004; Jessica B. Ruehrwein, "A Study of Public Attitudes and Perceptions Regarding June Suckers and Habitat Management Issues in Utah Lake, Utah" (Master's thesis, Utah State University, 1997), 87.

14. Caleb Warnock, "First Meeting of Utah Lake Commission Draws a Crowd," *Daily Herald*, 5 October 2006, C-1.

15. Raymond Partridge, "Early Days on the Provo Bench," 5–6, 20–21, typescript, MSS SC 891, SC-BYU.

16. David Starr Jordan, "Report of Explorations in Colorado and Utah during the Summer of 1889, with an Account of the Fishes Found in Each of the River Basins Examined," *Bulletin of the United States Fish Commission* 9 (1889): 34; Federal Writers Project, WPA, Utah Pioneer Biographies, vol. 28, 231, copy in LDS Family History Library, Salt Lake City; Scott G. Kenney, ed., *Journal of Wilford Woodruff, 1833–1898 Typescript*, vol. 6 (Midvale, Utah: Signature Books, 1983), 119. For biographical context, see Phil Murdock and Fred E. Woods, "'I Dreamed of Ketching Fish': The Outdoor Life of Wilford Woodruff," *BYU Studies* 37, no. 4 (1997–98): 7–47.

17. E. D. Cope and H. C. Yarrow, "Report upon the Collections of Fishes," in *Report upon Geographical and Geological Explorations and Surveys West of the*

One Hundredth Meridian, vol. 5 (Washington, D.C.: Government Printing Office, 1875), chap. 6, esp. 685–692.

18. H. C. Yarrow to George Q. Cannon, 14 January 1874; and George Q. Cannon to Wilford Woodruff et al., 5 February 1874, MSS SC 1374, SC-BYU.

19. Petition quoted in D. Robert Carter, "A History of Commercial Fishing on Utah Lake" (Master's thesis, BYU, 1969), 71; Shoshone [pseud.], "Utah Game Notes," *Forest & Stream* 43 (27 October 1896): 357. The number of arrests comes from "Fish and Game Reports," *DN,* 16 January 1895.

20. Shoshone, "June Prospects," 483. The 1894 figure comes from H. L. A. Culmer, *The Resources and Attractions of Utah as They Exist Today* (Salt Lake City: George Q. Cannon and Sons, 1894), 85. For a lake-based survey of ecological change over historical time, see Richard A. Heckman, Charles W. Thompson, and David A. White, "Fishes of Utah Lake," *Great Basin Naturalist Memoirs* 5 (1981): 107–127. A forthcoming monograph on Utah Lake by local historian D. Robert Carter promises to cover the decline of native fish in unprecedented detail; a preview of his work can been seen in *Utah Lake: Legacy* (Salt Lake City: June Sucker Recovery Implementation Program, 2003).

21. Phil Robinson, *Sinners and Saints* (Boston: Roberts Brothers, 1883), 132–133, 149.

22. Partridge, "Early Days on the Provo Bench," 20–21; Madsen quoted in "Utah Lake: America's Greatest Carp Habitation," *SLT,* 17 June 1923. *Sixth Biennial Report of the State Fish and Game Commissioner and Commissioner of State Hatcheries for the Years 1905 and 1906* (Salt Lake City: Deseret News, 1907), 9–10, copy in UHRC. "More Catfish for Utah Lake," *Provo Post,* 6 June 1912.

23. *Sixth Biennial Report,* 9–10. In recollection, Madsen may have exaggerated the poundage of dead fish; the commissioner estimated 300 tons.

24. James Farmer, diary, typescript, part 3, 32, copy in SC-BYU. I'm pleased to point out that the diarist is my great-great-grandfather.

25. Catch statistics from *Third Biennial Report of the State Fish and Game Commissioner for the Years 1899 and 1900* (Salt Lake City: Deseret News, 1901), 29; and *Fifth Biennial Report of the State Fish and Game Commissioner and Commissioner of State Hatcheries for the Years 1903 and 1904* (Salt Lake City: Star Printing, 1905), 17.

26. On welfare carp, see D. Robert Carter, "Utah Lake: A Safety Net for the Needy," *Beehive History* 27 (2001): 20–25.

27. "Can Suckers Thrive Again in Utah Lake?" *DN,* 28 August 1994; Ruehrwein, "Study of Public Attitudes and Perceptions." On the biology and hoped-for future of the fish, see June Sucker Recovery Team, "June Sucker *(Chas-*

mistes liorus) Recovery Plan," U.S. Fish & Wildlife Service, Region 6 (Denver, 1999). The Recovery Implementation Program maintains a website: www .junesuckerrecovery.org.

28. George A. Smith, 24 July 1852, *Journal of Discourses* 1 (1855): 44. Also see R. H. Jackson, "The Mormon Experience: The Plains as Sinai, the Great Salt Lake as the Dead Sea, and the Great Basin as Desert-cum-Promised Land," *Journal of Historical Geography* 18 (January 1992): 41–58.

29. Orson F. Whitney, *History of Utah,* vol. 1 (Salt Lake City: George Q. Cannon and Sons, 1892), 326–327.

30. See William Hartley, "Mormons, Crickets, and Gulls: A New Look at an Old Story," *UHQ* 38 (Summer 1970): 224–239; Brian Q. Cannon, "The Sego Lily, Utah's State Flower," *UHQ* 63 (Winter 1995): 70–84; and Jill Mulvay Derr, "'I Have Eaten Nearly Everything Imaginable': Pioneer Diet," in *Nearly Everything Imaginable: The Everyday Life of Utah's Mormon Pioneers,* ed. Ronald W. Walker and Doris R. Dant (Provo, Utah: BYU Press, 1999), 222–247.

31. Carter quoted in *Heart Throbs of the West* 1 (1939): 358. For details on the DUP and the tree, see, respectively, Norma B. Winn and Emma R. Olsen, comps., "Daughters of the Utah Pioneers through the Years," *An Enduring Legacy* 12 (1989): 93–136; and Gary Topping, "Conflict over a Mormon Symbol: A. Russell Mortensen and the Lone Cedar Tree," *Journal of the West* 37 (April 1998): 90–98. Immigration figures from Richard L. Jensen, "Immigration to Utah," in *Utah History Encyclopedia,* ed. Allan Kent Powell (Salt Lake City: University of Utah Press, 1994), 270–273.

32. Quoted in *Conference Report* (April 1914): 77–78.

33. Peter Madsen, "The Grasshopper Famine—the Mullet and the Trout," *Improvement Era* 13 (April 1910): 516–521. In 1997 the Utah legislature belatedly changed the state fish from the rainbow trout to the Bonneville cutthroat.

34. Flora Diana Bean Horne, comp., *Autobiography of George Washington Bean* (Salt Lake City: Privately published, 1945), 100–101; Emma N. Huff, comp., *Memories That Live: Utah County Centennial History* (Springville, Utah: Art City Publishing, 1947), 307–308. For stories about the inhuman cruelty of Squash, see, for example, Peter Gottfredson, *History of Indian Depredations in Utah* (Salt Lake City: Skelton Publishing, 1919), 42–43; and J. Marinus Jensen, *History of Provo, Utah* (Provo, Utah: Privately published, 1924), 105.

35. No historian has written about the Utah Indian War Veterans Association. A few details about their early history can be found near the end of Gottfredson, *History of Indian Depredations in Utah;* and in Huff, *Memories That Live,* 316–317. SC-BYU owns a copy of the *Songster* and a few related items of ephemera.

36. The sculptor Cyrus Dallin, a product of Springville, fashioned a heroic-

sized bronze of Massasoit for the tercentenary of the *Mayflower* in 1920. Ironi-cally, it has become the most prominent "Indian sculpture" in Utah. Copies of it stand outside the Utah state capitol and the Lee Library at BYU.

37. H. R. Day to Commissioner of Indian Affairs, 2 January 1852, RG 75, mi-crofilm set M-234, reel 897; Aaron Johnson to Brigham Young, 28 August 1855, box 24, folder 6 (reel 33), BYOF, CHD; George W. Armstrong to Commissioner of Indian Affairs, 30 September 1855, in *Annual Report of the Commissioner of Indian Affairs for 1855*, House Exec. Doc. 1, 34th Cong., 1st sess. (1856), 524–525; treaty council minutes from RG 75, microfilm set T-494, roll 8, frames 1153–95. Sowiette died around 1870 in the Uinta Basin, but not before meeting John Wesley Powell; see William Culp Darrah, ed., "Major Powell's Journal," *UHQ* 15, nos. 1–4 (1947): 125.

38. "History of Spanish Fork," *Tullidge's Quarterly Magazine* 3 (April 1884): 139–140; "History of Provo," ibid. (July 1884): 240–241. On Tullidge, see Davis Bitton and Leonard J. Arrington, *Mormons and Their Historians* (Salt Lake City: University of Utah Press, 1988), chap. 3. Rubbish about a Ute "royal family" lin-gered well into the twentieth century; see Conway B. Sonne, "Royal Blood of the Utes," *UHQ* 22 (July 1954): 271–276. The Shoshone leader, Washakie, functions similarly in Mormon collective memory.

39. JH, 22 May 1850.

40. Peter Wilson Conover, reminiscence, WPA typescript, copy in UHRC; Wil-liam Thomas, "Historical Sketch and Genealogy of the Thomas's Families," 1889–1892, MA 1598, CHD; "Reminiscences of the Early Days in Manti," *UHQ* 6 (October 1933): 121–122; Jennie J., "In Early Days: Sowiette's Noble Act," *Juvenile Instructor* 27 (15 December 1892): 748–749. The Manti version of the story reached its apotheosis in William H. Peterson, *The Miracle of the Moun-tains* (Manti, Utah: Privately published, 1942). A separate story about Sowiette saving a Mormon peace messenger appears in Milton R. Hunter, *Utah Indian Stories* (Springville, Utah: Art City Publishing, 1946), 32–39; and *Heart Throbs of the West* 1 (1947): 104. For a pertinent examination of false memories about Indians, see Clyde A. Milner II, "The Shared Memory of Montana's Pioneers," *Montana The Magazine of Western History* 37 (Winter 1987): 2–13.

41. [Provo] Chamber of Commerce, *Provo: The Garden City of Utah* (Omaha: D. C. Dunbar, 1888), 7.

42. Transcription of *DN* article in Manuscript History of Provo, 24 July 1878, CHD.

43. Richard White, "Frederick Jackson Turner and Buffalo Bill," in *The Fron-tier in American Culture*, ed. James R. Grossman (Berkeley: University of Califor-nia Press, 1994). In 1902 the people of Payson put on a "sham battle" with "real

Indians" for Pioneer Day; see *Heart Throbs of the West* 7 (1946): 119. This form of pageantry was widespread in Mormon Country at the time; see Eric A. Eliason, "Celebrating Zion: Pioneers in Mormon Popular Historical Expression" (Ph.D. diss., University of Texas at Austin, 1998), 167–177.

44. Vanguards-Scouts Department Committee, "Historical Markers Program (Continued)," *Improvement Era* 34 (February 1931): 234. The Sowiette plaque is located in front of the DUP museum at North Park at 500 West and 600 North in Provo. On mistaken historical markers, see James W. Loewen, *Lies across America: What Our Historic Sites Get* Wrong (New York: New Press, 1999); and Brigham D. Madsen, "The 'Almo Massacre' Revisited," *Idaho Yesterdays* 37 (Fall 1993): 54–64.

45. Carlton Culmsee, "Friendly with Mountains and Valleys," in *Provo, Utah, 1849–1949: Centennial Souvenir* (Salt Lake City: Lorraine Press, 1949), 67–68.

4. Rocky Mountain Saints

1. Studies of sacred mountains in Indian country include Kevin Blake, "Sacred and Secular Landscape Symbolism at Mount Taylor, New Mexico," *Journal of the Southwest* 41 (Winter 1999): 487–509; Blake, "Contested Landscapes of Navajo Sacred Mountains," *North American Geographer* 3, no. 1 (2001): 29–62; Linea Sundstrom, "The Sacred Black Hills: An Ethnohistorical Review," *Great Plains Quarterly* 17 (Summer/Fall 1997): 185–212; Steven M. Schnell, "The Kiowa Homeland in Oklahoma," *Geographical Review* 90 (April 2000): 155–176; and Douglas Deur, "A Most Sacred Place: The Significance of Crater Lake among the Indians of Southern Oregon," *Oregon Historical Quarterly* 103 (Spring 2002): 18–49.

2. Marjorie Hope Nicolson, *Mountain Gloom and Mountain Glory: The Development of the Aesthetics of the Infinite* (Ithaca: Cornell University Press, 1959), 3. Also see Simon Schama, *Landscape and Memory* (New York: Alfred A. Knopf, 1995), 385–513; Walter Woodburn Hyde, "The Development of the Appreciation of Mountain Scenery in Modern Times," *Geographical Review* 3 (February 1917): 107–118; and Ronald Rees, "The Scenery Cult: Changing Landscape Tastes over Three Centuries," *Landscape* 19, no. 3 (1975): 39–47. "An agreeable kind of horror" comes from a 1701 letter by Joseph Addison as quoted in Nicolson, 305.

3. Thomas Cole, "Essay on American Scenery," *American Monthly Magazine* 1 (January 1836): 1–12. On New Hampshire, see John F. Sears, *Sacred Places: American Tourist Attractions in the Nineteenth Century* (New York: Oxford University Press, 1989), chap. 4; Dona Brown, *Inventing New England: Regional*

Tourism in the Nineteenth Century (Washington, D.C.: Smithsonian Institution Press, 1995), chap. 2; Eric Purchase, *Out of Nowhere: Disaster and Tourism in the White Mountains* (Baltimore: Johns Hopkins University Press, 1999); and Christopher Johnson, *This Grand and Magnificent Place: The Wilderness Heritage of the White Mountains* (Durham: University of New Hampshire Press, 2006).

4. See Anne Farrar Hyde, *An American Vision: Far Western Landscape and National Culture, 1820–1920* (New York: New York University Press, 1990); and Patricia Trenton and Peter H. Hassrick, *The Rocky Mountains: A Vision for Artists in the Nineteenth Century* (Norman: University of Oklahoma Press, 1983).

5. Quoted in Tom Chaffin, *Pathfinder: John Charles Frémont and the Course of American Empire* (New York: Hill and Wang, 2002), 82.

6. See ibid., chap. 7; and Vernon L. Volpe, "Beyond a Literary Adventure: Bonneville's and Frémont's Conquests of the Wind Rivers," *Annals of Wyoming* 71 (Autumn 1999): 15–28.

7. See esp. Linda C. Hults, "Pilgrim's Progress in the West: Moran's *The Mountain of the Holy Cross*," *American Art* 5 (Winter/Spring 1991): 69–85.

8. See Joni Louise Kinsey, *Thomas Moran and the Surveying of the American West* (Washington, D.C.: Smithsonian Institution Press, 1992), chaps. 8 and 9; and Ferenc M. Szasz, "Wheeler and Holy Cross: Colorado's 'Lost' National Monuments," *Journal of Forest History* 21 (July 1977): 134–144.

9. On the "technological sublime," see David E. Nye, *American Technological Sublime* (Cambridge, Mass.: MIT Press, 1992).

10. "Joseph Smith—History," in *The Pearl of Great Price*, rev. ed. (Salt Lake City: The Church of Jesus Christ of Latter-day Saints, 1987), 1:41 and 1:50–51.

11. *History of The Church of Jesus Christ of Latter-day Saints*, vol. 5 (Salt Lake City: Deseret News, 1909), 85. For a corrective, see Davis Bitton, "Joseph Smith in the Mormon Folk Memory," in *Restoration Studies I, Sesquicentennial Edition*, ed. Maurice L. Draper and Clare D. Vlahos (Independence, Mo.: Temple School, 1980), 75–94.

12. See Ronald W. Walker, "'A Banner Is Unfurled': Mormonism's Ensign Peak," *Dialogue: A Journal of Mormon Thought* (hereafter *Dialogue*) 26 (Winter 1993): 71–91.

13. On Mormon hymnology, see Don B. Castleton, "The Concept of Zion as Reflected in Mormon Song" (Master's thesis, BYU, 1967), esp. chap. 5. On Penrose, see Edward A. Geary, "For the Strength of the Hills: Imagining Mormon Country," in *After 150 Years: The Latter-day Saints in Sesquicentennial Perspective*, ed. Thomas G. Alexander and Jessie L. Embry (Provo, Utah: Charles Redd

16. Gregory, interview notes; Romine, "Eugene Lusk Roberts," 178; B. H. Roberts, "Sphere of Y.M.M.I.A. Activities," *Improvement Era* 16 (January 1913): 191, 193. For context, see Richard Ian Kimball, *Sports in Zion: Mormon Recreation, 1890–1940* (Urbana: University of Illinois Press, 2003). In 1997, long after the fad for physical culture had faded, the last incarnation of the Deseret Gym was torn down to make way for a colossal auditorium called the Conference Center, a building devoted to the nonkinetic activities of sitting and listening.

17. Taylor, *Rocky Mountain Empire*, 180–181.

18. Eugene L. Roberts, "Mass Hikes," *Recreation* 30 (December 1936): 445–447.

19. Editorial, *The White and Blue*, 27 April 1906, 187. Background information drawn from "Records and Reports of the Block Y and Y Day," UA 486, SC-BYU; Gary James Bergera and Ronald Priddis, *Brigham Young University: A House of Faith* (Salt Lake City: Signature Books, 1985), 229–231; and James J. Parsons, "Hillside Letters in the Western Landscape," *Landscape* 30, no. 1 (1988): 15–23.

20. Quoted in Wilkinson, *Brigham Young University*, 405 n. 9.

21. Cowles quote from Frank Becker, "Greatest Botanical Garden in World Is Furnished by Mt. Timpanogos, It Is Said," *SLT*, 23 September 1923, 12. Also see Andrew M. Anderson, "The Brigham Young University Alpine School," *Improvement Era* 25 (October 1922): 1067–70.

22. "M.I.A. Scouts Climb Mount Timpanogos," *Provo Post*, 1 September 1916; Fred Buss, "A Brief Account of the Geology and Physiography of Mt. Timpanogos" (1916), Uinta National Forest Archives, Provo, Utah.

23. Wallace W. Atwood, *Glaciation of the Uinta and Wasatch Mountains*, U.S. Geological Survey Professional Paper 61 (Washington, D.C.: Government Printing Office, 1909); "Scaling Utah's Glacier—Mountain Timpanogas [*sic*]," *New West Magazine* 6 (August 1915): 25–26.

24. "Information and Suggestions" (1917), copy in box 8, folder 4, Wasatch Mountain Club papers, SC-UU.

25. See Andrew M. Honker, "'Been Grazed Almost to Extinction': The Environment, Human Action, and Utah Flooding, 1900–1940," *UHQ* 67 (Winter 1999): 23–47; and Charles S. Peterson, "Grazing in Utah: A Historical Perspective," *UHQ* 57 (Fall 1989): 300–319.

26. "Diary of Albert F. Potter, July 1, to November 22, 1902," photocopy in SC-USU. Also see Charles S. Peterson, "Albert F. Potter's Wasatch Survey, 1902: A Beginning for Public Management of Natural Resources in Utah," *UHQ* 39 (Summer 1971): 238–253.

27. Gary Vern Keetch, "The Changing Impact of Man in American Fork Canyon" (Master's thesis, BYU, 1968), quote on 45. On Mormon conservationists,

see Thomas G. Alexander, "Cooperation, Conflict, and Compromise: Women, Men, and the Environment in Salt Lake City, 1890–1930," *BYU Studies* 35, no. 1 (1996): 6–39.

28. "The Cave of Buried Wonders," *American Fork Citizen,* 18 December 1920, sec. 3, 1; "Natural Wonder in Wasatch Range to Be Known Hereafter as Timpanogos," *SLT,* 28 October 1921.

29. "The History of Timpanogos Cave National Monument, American Fork Canyon, Utah," photocopy of typescript, UHRC. In the 1930s the three caverns were connected with tunnels.

30. See Effie W. Adams, comp., *Mutual Dell, 1920–1973* (Pleasant Grove, Utah: Privately published, 1988), copy in SC-BYU.

31. "The Hike and E. L. Roberts," Annual Timpanogos Hike program, 1922, copy in UA 48, SC-BYU.

32. For background, see Marguerite S. Shaffer, *See America First: Tourism and National Identity, 1880–1940* (Washington, D.C.: Smithsonian Institution Press, 2001), esp. 26–39.

33. "The Hike and E. L. Roberts." On early tourism in southern Utah, see Jared Farmer, *Glen Canyon Dammed: Inventing Lake Powell and the Canyon Country* (Tucson: University of Arizona Press, 1999), esp. 10–58.

34. "Kiwanians Will Work to Popularize 'Timps,'" *Provo Post,* 7 June 1921; headline from *Daily Herald,* 11 July 1924; "Windows Are Trimmed for Timp Climb," ibid., 6 July 1924, 2; "Votaries of the Peaks," Annual Timpanogos Hike program, 1925, copy in UA 28, SC-BYU.

35. See Taylor, *Rocky Mountain Empire.*

36. "The Tin Wedding," editorial, *Provo Herald,* 13 July 1921.

37. "Mt. Timpanogos Trip Will Prove Great Success," *Provo Post,* 31 July 1915; Denver & Rio Grande Railroad, *With Nature in the Rockies,* pamphlet, n.d., copy in UHRC; "A Snow-Capped Peak of the Wasatch," *McClure's Magazine* 56 (April 1924): 97; Israel C. Russell, *Glaciers of North America* (Boston: Ginn, 1897), iii. Remarkably, the misnomer was approved by the U.S. Board on Geographic Names in 1989. Notwithstanding its name, the snowfield will surely become even less permanent in the future as a result of global warming. Not even Glacier National Park is expected to keep its bona fide glaciers.

38. George H. Brimhall, *Long and Short Range Arrows* (Provo, Utah: BYU Press, 1934), 55–56.

39. "The Tin Wedding Hike," editorial, *Provo Post,* 26 July 1921.

40. Song lyrics reproduced in various editions of the hike program located in UA 48, SC-BYU; Roberts quote from "Timp's Tin Wedding Hike to Break All Utah Mountain Climbing Records," *Provo Herald,* 11 July 1921; instructions from Annual Timpanogos Hike program, 1922.

41. The poems can be found in the following issues: November 1916, August 1922, November 1924, September 1931, July 1932, June 1935, and July 1949.

42. Theron Luke, "Annual Timpanogos Hike: Utah's Legendary Pilgrimage," *Utah Magazine* 9 (August 1947): 21; Earl J. Glade, "Climbing Timpanogos the University Way," *Provo Herald,* 20 July 1921, reprinted from *New West Magazine* 6 (August 1915): 27–28.

43. *Daily Herald,* 14 July 1922.

6. Sundance and Suburbia

1. See Michael R. Kelsey, *Climbing and Exploring Utah's Mt. Timpanogos* (Provo, Utah: Kelsey Publishing, 1989), 188–191; and John Floyd Iverson, "Mountain Surgery: A Chapter in the History of Conservation, Focusing on the Contour Trench as a Device for the Restoration of Mountain Watersheds" (Master's thesis, University of Utah, 1970). For context, see Marcus Hall, "Repairing Mountains: Restoration, Ecology, and Wilderness in Twentieth-Century Utah," *Environmental History* 6 (October 2001): 584–610.

2. "'Timpanogos' Roberts Comments on Richin's Column in Journal," news clipping, 1937, BYU Recreation Department Records, UA 563, box 1, folder 14, SC-BYU; Ralph Jensen to C. J. Hart, 22 April 1948, Charles Hart Papers, UA 561, box 5, folder 1, SC-BYU.

3. Randall L. Green, "Ecology Factors Bring Cancellation of Timp Hike," *Daily Herald* (Provo, Utah), May 1971, copy in Timpanogos Cave Scrapbook Collection, box 1, folder 13, SC-UU; "Annual Timp Hike Too Big to Handle," *DN,* 14 May 1971, A-18; "Timp Hike Not Revived, Say Forest Service, BYU," *Daily Herald,* 6 August 1971.

4. "TimpFacts," www.hobblecreekoa.com/timpfacts.htm, accessed on 4 June 2002.

5. This follows Alfred Runte's "worthless lands thesis"; see *National Parks: The American Experience,* 3d ed. (Lincoln: University of Nebraska Press, 1997). For details on the Utah bill, see *Additions to the National Wilderness Preservation System,* Hearings before the Subcommittee on Public Lands and National Parks of the Committee on Interior and Insular Affairs on H.R. 4516, U.S. House, 98th Cong., 2d sess., Serial No. 98-3, pt. 10 (Washington, D.C.: Government Printing Office, 1984).

6. John Best, "Rocky Mountain Goat Transplants Working," *Daily Herald,* 20 April 1983, 3.

7. See Justin C. Stewart, "A History of Sundance, Utah" (1987), typescript, SC-BYU; Raymond R. Stewart, "A History of Timp Haven," typescript, Timp

Haven Collection, folder 1, SC-UU; and A. Sherman Christensen, "A Story of The Mountain" (1985), typescript, Lee Library, BYU.

8. On Utah skiing, see Alan K. Engen and Gregory C. Thompson, *First Tracks: A Century of Skiing in Utah* (Salt Lake City: Gibbs Smith, 2001); and Joseph Arave, "The Forest Service Takes to the Slopes: The Birth of Utah's Ski Industry and the Role of the Forest Service," *UHQ* 70 (Fall 2002): 341–355.

9. Jack Waugh, "Robert Redford Wouldn't Have Disappointed Old Harry Longabaugh," *Los Angeles Times,* 28 February 1971. On "collecting space": Brad Darrach, "The Rocky Mountain High Life of Robert Redford," *People,* 27 October 1975, 63. "Robert Redford on Skiing in Utah," *American Airlines* (inflight magazine), n.d., copy in UHRC.

10. Jim Fergus, "Bob's World," *Outside,* December 1989, 49; quote about Thoreau from Mark Donnelly, "Robert Redford's Sundance," *Westways* 79 (March 1987): 31.

11. Liza Nicholas, "1-800-Sundance: Identity, Nature, and Play in the West," in *Imagining the Big Open: Nature, Identity, and Play in the New West,* ed. Liza Nicholas, Elaine M. Bapis, and Thomas J. Harvey (Salt Lake City: University of Utah Press, 2003), 259–271.

12. Amanda Griscom Little, "Bob Redford's Retreat," *Mother Earth News,* December–January 2006, 40–45.

13. Robert Redford, "Taking It Personally," in *Heaven Is under Our Feet,* ed. Don Henley and Dave Marsh (Stamford, Conn.: Longmeadow Press, 1991), 68.

14. For a similar reading of Sundance, see Thomas J. Harvey, "The Sundance Kid and Sundance: The West as Nature," in Nicholas, Bapis, and Harvey, *Imagining the Big Open,* 272–279.

15. WordPerfect communications director quoted in Charles Corn, "Sundance Lodge," *Forbes,* 7 December 1992, 126–127; Redford quoted in "A New Frontier Life," *House and Garden* 145 (February 1974): 62. On the dialectic of outdoor work and outdoor play, see Richard White, "'Are You An Environmentalist or Do You Work for a Living?': Work and Nature," in *Uncommon Ground: Toward Reinventing Nature,* ed. William Cronon (New York: W. W. Norton, 1995), 171–185.

16. Widtsoe quoted in Gordon Shepherd and Gary Shepherd, *A Kingdom Transformed: Themes in the Development of Mormonism* (Salt Lake City: University of Utah Press, 1984), 58. For context on Widtsoe and the Mormon ideology of agrarianism, see Donald H. Dyal, "Mormon Pursuit of the Agrarian Ideal," *Agricultural History* 63 (Fall 1989): 19–35.

17. On the economic history of Utah County, I looked to Leonard J. Arrington, "Economic History of a Mormon Valley," *Pacific Northwest Quarterly* 46 (October 1955): 97–107; Robert L. Layton, "An Analysis of Land Use in Twelve Com-

munities in Utah Valley, Utah County, Utah" (Ph.D. diss., Syracuse University, 1962); and Richard Neitzel Holzapfel, *A History of Utah County* (Salt Lake City: Utah State Historical Society, 1999). The best analysis of the practice of Mormon agrarianism happens to be a case study of a Utah Valley town: Dean L. May, *Three Frontiers: Family, Land and Society in the American West, 1850–1900* (Cambridge: Cambridge University Press, 1994).

18. Charles S. Peterson, "The 'Americanization' of Utah's Agriculture," *UHQ* 42 (Spring 1974): 108–125, quote on 122. On Utes and water, see Kathryn L. MacKay, "The Strawberry Valley Reclamation Project and the Opening of the Uintah Indian Reservation," *UHQ* 50 (Winter 1982): 68–89. On local horticulture, see Charles Hayward Wride, "The Agricultural Geography of Utah County, 1849–1960" (Master's thesis, BYU, 1961); and Gary Daynes and Richard Ian Kimball, "'By Their Fruits Ye Shall Know Them': A Cultural History of Orchard Life in Utah Valley," *UHQ* 69 (Summer 2001): 215–231.

19. Thomas Wolfe, *A Western Journal: A Daily Log of the Great Parks Trip* (Pittsburgh: University of Pittsburgh Press, 1951), 35.

20. See Leonard J. Arrington and Anthony T. Cluff, *Federally Financed Industrial Plants Constructed in Utah during World War II* (Logan: Utah State University Press, 1969); and J. R. Mahoney, "The Western Steel Industry with Special Reference to the Postwar Operation of the Geneva Steel Plant," *Utah Economic and Business Review* 3 (June 1944): 5–73.

21. On recent demographic history, see Brian W. Maxfield, "Population and Growth in Utah County, Utah, 1940 to 1980" (Master's thesis, BYU, 1981); and David L. Fuhriman, "An Examination of the Economic Growth and Demographic Changes in Utah County, 1970–1995" (Master's thesis, BYU, 1995).

22. Gary James Bergera, "Building Wilkinson's University," *Dialogue* 30 (Fall 1997): 105–133, quote on 105.

23. In addition to the U.S. Census, I consulted Cathleen D. Zick and Ken R. Smith, eds., *Utah at the Beginning of the New Millennium: A Demographic Perspective* (Salt Lake City: University of Utah Press, 2006); Tim B. Heaton, Thomas A. Hirschl, and Bruce A. Chadwick, eds., *Utah in the 1990s: A Demographic Perspective* (Salt Lake City: Signature Books, 1996); and Kathleen Flake, "The Mormon Corridor: Utah and Idaho," in *Religion and Public Life in the Mountain West: Sacred Landscapes in Transition*, ed. Jan Shipps and Mark Silk (Walnut Creek, Calif.: AltaMira Press, 2004), 91–114.

24. On the Mormon landscape, see esp. Charles S. Peterson, "Imprint of Agricultural Systems on the Utah Landscape," in *The Mormon Role in the Settlement of the West*, ed. Richard H. Jackson (Provo, Utah: BYU Press, 1978), 91–106; Richard V. Francaviglia, *The Mormon Landscape: Existence, Creation, and Perception of a Unique Image in the American West* (New York: AMS Press, 1978);

William Norton, "Mormon Identity and Landscape in the Rural Intermountain West," *Journal of the West* 37 (July 1998): 33–43; and Richard H. Jackson and Mark W. Jackson, eds., *Geography, Culture and Change in the Mormon West, 1847–2003* (Jacksonville, Ala.: National Council for Geographic Education, 2003).

25. On Utah's dearth of landscape preservationists, see John B. Wright's polemical *Rocky Mountain Divide: Selling and Saving the West* (Austin: University of Texas Press, 1993). For the larger historical debate about the compatibility of Mormonism and environmentalism, see Thomas G. Alexander, "Stewardship and Enterprise: The LDS Church and the Wasatch Oasis Environment, 1847–1930," *Western Historical Quarterly* 25 (Autumn 1994): 340–364; and Dan L. Flores, "Zion in Eden: Phases of the Environmental History of Utah," in *The Natural West: Environmental History in the Great Plains and Rocky Mountains* (Norman: University of Oklahoma Press, 2001), 124–144.

26. Ben H. Bullock, "Predictions made by President Brigham Young in the presence of my father. . ." (1952), MSS 231, SC-BYU.

27. On the cultural geography of Mormondom, the classic work is D. W. Meinig, "The Mormon Culture Region: Strategies and Patterns in the Geography of the American West, 1847–1964," *Annals of the Association of American Geographers* 55 (June 1965): 191–220. Notable follow-ups include Richard H. Jackson, "Mormon Wests: The Creation and Evolution of an American Region," in *Western Places, American Myths: How We Think about the West*, ed. Gary J. Hausladen (Reno: University of Nevada Press, 2003), 135–165; and Lowell C. "Ben" Bennion, "Mormondom's Deseret Homeland," in *Homelands: A Geography of Culture and Place across America*, ed. Richard L. Nostrand (Baltimore: Johns Hopkins University Press, 2002), 184–209.

28. Nicole Anderson, "The Game"; Ann J. Hansen, "The Unexpected Surprise"; V. Garth Norman, "The Mount Timpanogos Temple: A 'Mountain of the Lord's House,' Ancient and Modern"—all in *Mount Timpanogos Utah Temple Commemorative Edition* (American Fork, Utah: Newtah News Group, 1996), copy in author's possession.

29. Ora Chipman interviewed by Theron Luke, 10 January 1980, Mount Timpanogos Oral History Collection, UHRC. I have slightly altered the punctuation from the typescript.

7. Renaming the Land

1. Walt Whitman, *An American Primer* (Stevens Point, Wisc.: Holy Cow! Press, 1987), 18.

2. My typology builds off of George R. Stewart, *Names on the Globe* (New York: Oxford University Press, 1975), pt. 2. Other notable typologies are Ronald L. Baker and Marvin Carmony, *Indiana Place-names* (Bloomington: Indiana University Press, 1975), xii–xx; Robert Hixson Julyan, *Mountain Names* (Seattle: The Mountaineers, 1984), 4–27; and William Bright, *Native American Place-names of the United States* (Norman: University of Oklahoma Press, 2004), 9–12. An excellent technical manual on place-naming with worldwide coverage is Naftali Kadmon, *Toponymy: The Lore, Laws, and Language of Geographical Names* (New York: Vantage Press, 1997). For the American generalist, though, still nothing can match the wit and knowledge of George R. Stewart, *Names on the Land: A Historical Account of Place-Naming in the United States,* rev. ed. (Boston: Houghton Mifflin, 1958).

3. My study of Indianist toponymy excludes English-language names that originated as translations of native words, as well as the vast number of generic associative place-names concerning Native Americans. Utah alone contains 150 toponyms like "Indian Creek."

4. The Geographic Names Information System can be accessed at http:// geonames.usgs.gov. The database is still a work in progress; as of mid-2007, Phase I (based on federal sources) is complete, and Phase II (based on state and local sources) is about 90 percent complete. Phase II has added select "historical" (i.e., obsolete) and "variant" (i.e., runner-up) names to the master list.

5. Virgil J. Vogel, *Indian Names on Wisconsin's Map* (Madison: University of Wisconsin Press, 1991), 133. On cross-cultural names in the Northwest, see Douglas Deur, "Chinook Jargon Placenames as Points of Mutual Reference: Discourse, Intersubjectivity, and Environment within an Intercultural Toponymic Complex," *Names* 44 (December 1996): 291–321. My usage of "middle ground" comes from Richard White's book of the same name.

6. William Least Heat–Moon, *PrairyErth (a deep map)* (Boston: Houghton Mifflin, 1991), 120. On "Nuyaka," see Francis Lee Utley and Marion R. Hemperley, eds., *Placenames of Georgia: Essays of John H. Goff* (Athens: University of Georgia Press, 1975), 436.

7. Stephen C. Jett, *Navajo Placenames and Trails of the Canyon de Chelly System, Arizona* (New York: Peter Lang, 2001); William Cronon, *Changes in the Land: Indians, Colonists, and the Ecology of New England* (New York: Hill and Wang, 1983), 65.

8. Keith Basso, *Wisdom Sits in Places: Landscape and Language among the Western Apache* (Albuquerque: University of New Mexico Press, 1996).

9. Ted J. Warner, ed., *The Domínguez-Escalante Journal: Their Expedition through Colorado, Utah, Arizona, and New Mexico in 1776,* trans. Fray Angelico

Chavez (Salt Lake City: University of Utah Press, 1995), 70–73. Many editions of the journal erroneously identify La Sierra Blanca as Mount Timpanogos.

10. All mentioned maps and more can be found in Carl I. Wheat, *Mapping the Transmississippi West, 1540–1861,* vols. 1–2 (San Francisco: Institute of Historical Geography, 1957–58).

11. John Greenleaf Whittier, *The Early Poems of John Greenleaf Whittier* (Boston: Houghton Mifflin, 1885), 238.

12. Cotton Mather, *Magnalia Christi Americana* (1702), vol. 1 (New York: Russell and Russell, 1852), 561–562.

13. See David Hackett Fischer, *Albion's Seed: Four British Folkways in America* (New York: Oxford University Press, 1989), 36–38; William H. Whitmore, "On the Origin of the Names of Towns in Massachusetts," *Proceedings of the Massachusetts Historical Society* 12 (February 1873): 393–419; and James W. Cerny, "The Pattern of Indian-Derived Town Names in New England," *New England–St. Lawrence Valley Geographical Society Annual Meeting Proceedings* 3–4 (1973–74): 21–26.

14. William Penn, "Letter from William Penn to the Committee of the Free Society of Traders, 1683," in *Narratives of Early Pennsylvania, West New Jersey and Delaware, 1630–1707,* ed. Albert Cook Myers (New York: Charles Scribner's Sons, 1912), 230.

15. See Edward G. Gray, *New World Babel: Languages and Nations in Early America* (Princeton: Princeton University Press, 1999); William M. Clements, *Oratory in Native North America* (Tucson: University of Arizona Press, 2002); and Steven Conn, *History's Shadow: Native Americans and Historical Consciousness in the Nineteenth Century* (Chicago: University of Chicago Press, 2004), chap. 3. The phrase "cult of the eloquent savage" comes from Jill Lepore, "Wigwam Words," *American Scholar* 70, no. 1 (2001): 97–108.

16. Quote from Philip P. Mason, ed., *Schoolcraft's Expedition to Lake Itasca: The Discovery of the Source of the Mississippi* (East Lansing: Michigan State University Press, 1958), xx.

17. See Virgil J. Vogel, "Placenames from Longfellow's 'Song of Hiawatha,'" *Names* 39 (September 1991): 261–268; Vogel, *Indian Names on Wisconsin's Map,* 86–99; and John Rydjord, *Indian Place-Names* (Norman: University of Oklahoma Press, 1968), 339–346.

18. Mrs. L. H. Sigourney, *Poems* (Philadelphia: Key and Biddle, 1834), 164–166.

19. Karen Halttunen, "Mountain Christenings: Landscape and Memory in Edward Hitchcock's New England," in *New England Celebrates: Spectacle, Commemoration, and Festivity,* ed. Peter Benes (Boston: Boston University, 2002),

166–177. The prominent Bostonian Thomas Starr King rhapsodized about Indian place-names in *The White Hills* (Boston: Crosby and Nichols, 1864), 28–33, 141.

20. Joseph Nathan Kane, *The American Counties,* 4th ed. (Metuchen, N.J.: Scarecrow Press, 1983).

21. "Judge Tudor's letter on the necessity of a general name for the United States," *Monthly Anthology* 1 (May 1804): 293–297; Jedidiah Morse, *The American Gazetteer,* 2d ed. (Boston: Thomas and Andrews, 1804), v.

22. "Treatise on the Art of Naming Places," *Southern Literary Messenger* 4 (April 1838): 257–261. Also see "Aboriginal Names," ibid., 7 (July 1841): 477–479; and A. B. C., "Names of Towns in the United States," *The Knickerbocker* 9 (January 1837): 19–25. For context, see Wilbur Zelinsky, "Classical Town Names in the United States: The Historical Geography of an American Idea," *Geographical Review* 57 (October 1967): 463–495; and Zelinsky, "Nationalism in the American Place-name Cover," *Names* 31 (March 1983): 1–28.

23. Geoffrey Crayon [Washington Irving], "National Nomenclature," *The Knickerbocker* 14 (August 1839): 158–162.

24. James J. Heslin, "The Republic of Allegania: An Adventure of the New-York Historical Society," *New-York Historical Society Quarterly* 51 (January 1967): 24–44; and Homer F. Barnes, *Charles Fenno Hoffman* (New York: Columbia University Press, 1930), 158–165.

25. Heslin, "The Republic of Allegania."

26. *Relaciones by Zarate Salmeron,* trans. Alicia Ronstadt Milich (Albuquerque: Horn and Wallace Publishers, 1966), 94; Sir Richard F. Burton, *The City of the Saints* (1862), ed. Fawn M. Brodie (New York: Alfred A. Knopf, 1963), 136 and 301; Brigham Young quoted in *Journal of Discourses* 1 (1855): 167.

27. Brigham Young quoted in Will Bagley, *Blood of the Prophets: Brigham Young and the Mountain Meadows Massacre* (Norman: University of Oklahoma Press, 2002), 80. Other quotes from Dale L. Morgan, *The State of Deseret* (Logan: Utah State University Press, 1987), 113–114.

28. Levi Edgar Young, *The Founding of Utah* (New York: Charles Scribner's Sons, 1923), 3–4.

29. *Congressional Globe,* 3 June 1868, 40th Cong., 2d sess., pt. 3, 2793–96.

30. Stewart, *Names on the Land,* 314; "American Names," *United States Democratic Review* 11 (November 1842): 475–481.

31. See Merle W. Wells, "New Notes on the Word 'Idaho,'" *Idaho Yesterdays* 44 (Winter 2001): 15–17; and "Footnotes to History," ibid., 8 (Spring 1964): 33–36.

32. On "Osceola" and the issue of Indianist polity place-names in general, see Richard A. Grounds, "Tallahassee, Osceola, and the Hermeneutics of American

Place-Names," *Journal of the American Academy of Religion* 69 (June 2001): 287–322.

33. Lafayette Houghton Bunnell, *Discovery of the Yosemite and the Indian War of 1851 Which Led to That Event,* facsimile of 1911 ed. (Yosemite National Park: Yosemite Association, 1990), 62. The first edition appeared in 1880. On the meaning of "Yosemite," see L. S. Freeland and Sylvia M. Broadbent, *Central Sierra Miwok Dictionary with Texts,* University of California Publications in Linguistics 23 (Berkeley, 1960); and Sylvia M. Broadbent, *The Southern Sierra Miwok Language,* University of California Publications in Linguistics 38 (Berkeley, 1964).

34. Bunnell, *Discovery of the Yosemite,* 213–214.

35. Whitman, *An American Primer,* 18. For context, see John F. Sears, *Sacred Places: American Tourist Attractions in the Nineteenth Century* (New York: Oxford University Press, 1989), 150–155; and Delaine Fragnoli, "Naming Yosemite," *American Transcendental Quarterly* 18, no. 4 (2004): 263–275.

36. Helen Hunt, *Bits of Travel at Home* (1878; reprint, Boston: Roberts Brothers, 1893), 115 and passim; Bunnell, *Discovery of the Yosemite,* 187.

37. Stephen Powers, *Tribes of California* (1877; reprint, Berkeley: University of California Press, 1976), chap. 34; J. D. Whitney, *The Yosemite Guide-Book* (Sacramento: State of California, 1870), 16.

38. J. Smeaton Chase, *Yosemite Trails* (Boston: Houghton Mifflin, 1911), 34–35.

39. Louisa Ward Arps and Elinor Eppich Kingery, *High Country Names: Rocky Mountain National Park and Indian Peaks,* 2d ed. (Boulder, Colo.: Rocky Mountain Nature Association, 1994), 8. On the name changes in southern Utah, see H. L. A. Culmer, "Who Shall Name Our Natural Bridges," *Western Monthly* 11 (February 1910): 38–41.

40. John H. Williams, ed., *The Canoe and the Saddle or Klalam and Klickatat by Theodore Winthrop* (1863) (Tacoma: Privately published, 1913), 36.

41. See Genevieve McCoy, "'Mount Tacoma' vs. 'Mount Rainier': The Fight to Rename the Mountain," *Pacific Northwest Quarterly* 77 (October 1986): 139–149; A. D. Martinson, "Mount Rainier or Mount Tacoma?" *Columbia, the Magazine of Northwestern History* 3 (Summer 1989): 10–16; William R. Catton Jr., "The Mountain with the Wrong Name," *Etc.: A Review of General Semantics* 11 (Summer 1954): 299–304; and Stewart, *Names on the Land,* 364–372.

42. McCoy, "'Mount Tacoma' vs. 'Mount Rainier,'" 146; Thomas G. Bishop, "An Appeal to the Government to Fulfill Sacred Promises" (1915), quoted in *Brief Submitted to the United States Geographic Board . . .* (Tacoma: Justice to the Mountain Committee, 1917), 27.

43. *Brief Submitted to the United States Geographic Board,* 20. The mentioned

book is John H. Williams, *The Mountain That Was "God"* (Tacoma: Privately published, 1910).

44. Genevieve E. McCoy, "'Call It Mount Tacoma': A History of the Controversy over the Name of Mount Rainier" (Master's thesis, University of Washington, 1984), quote on 141.

45. For a survey of controversial place-names, see Mark Monmonier, *From Squaw Tit to Whorehouse Meadow: How Maps Name, Claim, and Inflame* (Chicago: University of Chicago Press, 2006).

46. My information on the name change comes from browsing the *Arizona Republic* (Phoenix), 8 April–22 April 2003. For background on the controversy, see esp. William Bright, "The Sociolinguistics of the 'S-Word': Squaw in American Placenames," *Names* 48 (September–December 2000): 207–216.

47. Daniel Wells to Brigham Young, 18 February 1850, doc. 44, Territorial Militia Records, box 1, folder 5 (reel 4), UHRC. Officially the mountain is "Squaw Mountain," but no one uses that name locally.

48. H. W. Naisbitt, "What's in a Name?" *The Contributor* 4 (July 1883): 418–420; Provo Chamber of Commerce, "Provo, the Garden City of Utah: Its Resources and Attractions" (1888), copy in LDS Church Library, Salt Lake City. Apparently it didn't occur to these authors to ask a Ute about Ute place-names or to consult the report of the Stansbury Expedition (1852), which includes a map with phonetic representations of Numic names for eight streams in Utah Valley. In the 1880s, unlike today, it would have been easy to verify these names and determine their meanings.

49. "Journal of Captain Albert Tracy," *UHQ* 13, nos. 1–4 (1945): 39; Burton, *The City of the Saints*, 371–372n.

50. See William R. Palmer, "Indian Names in Utah Geography," *UHQ* 1 (January 1928): 14.

51. "First Quadrennial of the Timpanogos Club, 1916," Timpanogos Club Papers, SC-UU.

52. "How Timpanogos got its name" (1980), folklore data sheet 5.8.1.16.5.21, Wilson Folklore Archives, SC-BYU. For context, see W. F. H. Nicolaisen, "Some Humorous Folk-Etymological Narratives," *New York Folklore* 3 (Summer–Winter 1977): 1–13; and Charles F. Hockett, "Reactions to Indian Place-names," *American Speech* 25 (May 1950): 118–121.

53. Alice Paxman McCune, ed., *History of Juab County* (Springville, Utah: Art City Publishing, 1947), 267–273.

54. Kirsten Sorenson, "New Name May Develop Again," *DN*, 19 November 1998.

55. An almost complete run of directories is available at UHRC.

56. See Gib Twyman, "Tribal Tug of War Intensifies," *DN,* 20 November 1999; and Maria Titze, "Tribe Says It's After Hunt Rights," *DN,* 8 January 2001. For context, see R. Warren Metcalf, *Termination's Legacy: The Discarded Indians of Utah* (Lincoln: University of Nebraska Press, 2002); and Parker M. Nielson, *The Dispossessed: Cultural Genocide of the Mixed-Blood Utes: An Advocate's Chronicle* (Norman: University of Oklahoma Press, 1998).

57. Lewis A. McArthur, *Oregon Geographic Names,* 4th ed. (Portland: Oregon Historical Society, 1974), 731. The Oregon place-name is spelled with a different final vowel: "Timpanogas."

8. The Rise and Fall of a Lover's Leap

1. Grady Clay, *Real Places: An Unconventional Guide to America's Generic Landscape* (Chicago: University of Chicago Press, 1994), 160, defines the lover's leap as a "special-purpose promontory" for "joint-venturing couples who have taken the wrong turns in Lovers' Lane, or for young women determined to End It All." Clay, a geographer, groups Lover's Leap with other generic locales such as Skid Row, Porno Zone, Gentrifying Neighborhood, and Vacant Lot.

2. Linda Dégh, *Legend and Belief: Dialectics of a Folklore Genre* (Bloomington: Indiana University Press, 2001), 6; Helge Gerndt as quoted in Dégh, 38.

3. Richard M. Dorson, "Fakelore," *Zeitschrift für Volkskunde* 65 (1969): 60. On European fakelore, see Allen Dundes, "Nationalistic Inferiority Complexes and the Fabrication of Fakelore: A Reconsideration of Ossian, the *Kinder- und Hausmärchen,* the *Kalevala,* and Paul Bunyan," *Journal of Folklore Research* 22 (January–April 1985): 5–18.

4. On chieftain speeches, see esp. William M. Clements, *Oratory in Native North America* (Tucson: University of Arizona Press, 2002); Edward D. Seeber, "Critical Views on Logan's Speech," *Journal of American Folklore* 60 (April–June 1947): 130–146; Harry Robie, "Red Jacket's Reply: Problems in the Verification of a Native American Speech Text," *New York Folklore* 12 (Summer–Fall 1986): 99–117; Albert Furtwangler, *Answering Chief Seattle* (Seattle: University of Washington Press, 1997); and Haruo Aoki, "Chief Joseph's Words," *Idaho Yesterdays* 33 (Fall 1989): 16–21. For examples of hybrid mountain legends, see Fannie Hardy Eckstorm, "The Katahdin Legends," *Appalachia* 16 (1924–26): 39–52; and Ella Clark, *Indian Legends of the Pacific Northwest* (Berkeley: University of California Press, 1953).

5. William Byrd, *History of the Dividing Line and Other Tracts,* vol. 1 (Richmond, Va.: Thomas H. Wynne, 1866), 131.

6. *The Spectator,* nos. 223 and 233 (1711). On the classics in America, see

Caroline Winterer, *The Culture of Classicism: Ancient Greece and Rome in American Intellectual Life, 1780–1910* (Baltimore: Johns Hopkins University Press, 2002). There was one other noteworthy lover's leap story from antiquity: Hero and Leander. Virgil and later Marlowe wrote about it.

7. Zebulon Pike, *An Account of Expeditions to the Sources of the Mississippi* (Philadelphia: C. & A. Conrad, 1810), 22.

8. Louis Hennepin, *A New Discovery of a Vast Country in America* (London, 1699); Norman Gelb, ed., *Jonathan Carver's Travels through America, 1766–1768: An Eighteenth-Century Explorer's Account of Uncharted America* (New York: John Wiley and Sons, 1993), 78; anonymous review of Pike's *Account of a Voyage up the Mississippi River, Baltimore Repertory of Papers on Literary and Other Topics* 1 (March 1811): 156.

9. "Extract of a Letter from Joseph M. Street, Indian Agent at Prairie du Chien, to the Secretary of War, dated November 15, 1827," House Document No. 277, 20th Cong., 1st sess. (1828), 15; Lucile M. Kane, June D. Holmquist, and Carolyn Gilman, eds., *The Northern Expeditions of Stephen H. Long: The Journals of 1817 and 1823 and Related Documents* (St. Paul: Minnesota Historical Society Press, 1978), passim.

10. Kane, Holmquist, and Gilman, *Northern Expeditions of Long,* passim.

11. Mentor L. Williams, ed., *Schoolcraft's Narrative Journal of Travels* (East Lansing: Michigan State University Press, 1992), 216; Thomas Jefferson, *Notes on the State of Virginia,* ed. William Peden (Chapel Hill: University of North Carolina Press, 1955), 58–59. Another commentator on aboriginal ardor in reference to a lover's leap is William L. Stone, *The Life and Times of Red-Jacket* (New York: Wiley and Putnam, 1841), 11.

12. William H. Keating, *Narrative of an Expedition to the Source of St. Peter's River,* vol. 1 (London: G. B. Whittaker, 1825), chap. 6. In a later text, Schoolcraft referred to "Olaita" as the "Docota Sappho."

13. G. C. Beltrami, *A Pilgrimage in America* (1828; reprint, Chicago: Quadrangle Books, 1962), 183–184.

14. See esp. Steven J. Keillor, *Grand Excursion: Antebellum America Discovers the Upper Mississippi* (Afton, Minn.: Afton Historical Society Press, 2004).

15. John Francis McDermott, *The Lost Panoramas of the Mississippi* (Chicago: University of Chicago Press, 1958), vii.

16. Thoreau, "Walking" (1862), in *The Major Essays of Henry David Thoreau,* ed. Richard Dillman (Albany: Whitston Publishing, 2001), 174.

17. Listed chronologically, the major works are Lewis Deffebach, *Oolaita* (Philadelphia, 1821); Felicia Hemans, "Indian Woman's Death Song," in *Records of Woman* (London, 1828); Lydia Maria Child, "The Indian Wife," in *The Leg-*

endary (Boston: Samuel G. Goodrich, 1828), 197–207; James Hall, "The Indian Maid's Death Song," in *The Western Souvenir* (Cincinnati: N. and G. Guilford, 1829); "A Legend of St. Anthony's Falls," in *The Offering, for 1829* (Cambridge, Mass.: Hilliard and Brown, 1829); James Athearn Jones, *Traditions of the North American Indians*, vol. 2 (London: Henry Colburn and Richard Bentley, 1830), 131–140; [William Snelling,] *Tales of the Northwest* (Boston: Hilliard, Gray, Little, and Wilkins, 1830); Edward Marsh Heist, "Ola-Ita: or the Sioux Girl," *Southern Literary Messenger* 3 (September 1837): 535–537; George Catlin, *Letters and Notes on the Manners, Customs, and Condition of the North American Indians*, vol. 2 (Philadelphia: Willis P. Hazard, 1857), 612–613; Barbara Hawes, *Tales of the North American Indians* (London: Longman, Brown, Green and Longmans, 1844), 130–137; Lydia Maria Child, "A Legend of the Falls of St. Anthony," reprinted in *Hobomok and Other Writings on Indians*, ed. Carolyn L. Karcher (New Brunswick, N.J.: Rutgers University Press, 1986), 202–212; Henry R. Schoolcraft, "Ampata Sapa; or, the First Wife," in *The Indian in His Wigwam* (New York: W. H. Graham, 1848), 99–100; Mary Henderson Eastman, *Dahcotah; or, Life and Legends of the Sioux around Fort Snelling* (1849; reprint, Afton, Minn.: Afton Historical Society Press, 1995); Eastman, "The Lover's Leap: or, Wenona's Rock," in *The Iris: An Illuminated Souvenir* (Philadelphia: Lippincott, Grambo, 1852), 183–190; Henry Lewis, *The Valley of the Mississippi Illustrated* (1854; reprint, St. Paul: Minnesota Historical Society, 1967); and Epes Sargent, "On Lake Pepin," in *The Knickerbocker Gallery* (New York: Samuel Hueston, 1855), 97–111. My bibliography builds upon G. Hubert Smith, "The Winona Legend," *Minnesota History* 13 (December 1932): 367–376.

18. W. H. Gardiner, review of James Fenimore Cooper's *The Spy, North American Review* 15 (July 1822): 252–253.

19. On Indians in antebellum literature, see William Herman Willer, "Native Themes in American Short Prose Fiction, 1770–1835" (Ph.D. diss., University of Minnesota, 1944); Roy Harvey Pearce, *The Savages of America: A Study of the Indian and the Idea of Civilization*, rev. ed. (Baltimore: Johns Hopkins Press, 1965), chaps. 6–7; Richard Slotkin, *Regeneration through Violence: The Mythology of the American Frontier, 1600–1860* (Middletown, Conn.: Wesleyan University Press, 1973), esp. chap. 10; Louise K. Barnett, *The Ignoble Savage: American Literary Racism, 1790–1890* (Westport, Conn.: Greenwood Press, 1975); Sherry Ann Sullivan, "The Indian in American Fiction, 1820–1850" (Ph.D. diss., University of Toronto, 1979); Sullivan, "Indians in American Fiction, 1820–1850: An Ethnohistorical Perspective," *Clio* 15 (Spring 1986): 239–257; and Klaus Lubbers, *Born for the Shade: Stereotypes of the Native American in United States*

Literature and the Visual Arts, 1776–1894, Amsterdam Monographs in American Studies 3 (Amsterdam: Rodopi, 1994).

20. "Tedious" quote from Terence R. Murphy, *Sleepless Souls: Suicide in Early Modern England* (Oxford: Clarendon Press, 1990), 292.

21. Quote from Sullivan, "The Indian in American Fiction, 1820–1850," 58.

22. See Judith Richardson, *Possessions: The History and Uses of Haunting in the Hudson Valley* (Cambridge, Mass.: Harvard University Press, 2003).

23. On Brainard and Whittier, see Richard M. Dorson, *Jonathan Draws the Long Bow: New England Popular Tales and Legends* (Cambridge, Mass.: Harvard University Press, 1946), chap. 6. On town histories, see David D. Hall, "Reassessing the Local History of New England," in *New England: A Bibliography of Its History,* ed. Roger Parks (Hanover, N.H.: University Press of New England, 1989), xix–xxxi. For national context on antiquarianism, see Lewis Perry, *Boats against the Current: American Culture between Revolution and Modernity, 1820–1860* (New York: Oxford University Press, 1993).

24. Schoolcraft quotes from Brian W. Dippie, *The Vanishing American: White Attitudes and U.S. Indian Policy* (Middletown, Conn.: Wesleyan University Press, 1982), 16–17; and Henry R. Schoolcraft, *The Myth of Hiawatha, and Other Oral Legends, Mythologic and Allegoric, of the North American Indians* (Philadelphia: J. B. Lippincott, 1856), viii. On Schoolcraft's methods, see William M. Clements, "Schoolcraft as Textmaker," *Journal of American Folklore* 103 (April–June 1990): 177–192; and Joe Lockard, "The Universal Hiawatha," *American Indian Quarterly* 24 (Winter 2000): 110–125. For hemispheric context, see David T. Haberly, "Form and Function in the New World Legend," in *Do the Americas Have a Common Literature?* ed. Gustavo Pérez Firmat (Durham, N.C.: Duke University Press, 1990), 42–61.

25. Caroline Kirkland, preface to Eastman, *Dahcotah* (New York: J. Wiley, 1849), v–xi.

26. William Cullen Bryant, "Monument Mountain" (reprinted in numerous places); Henry Wadsworth Longfellow, "Lover's Rock" and "Jeckoyva," in *The Complete Poetical Works of Longfellow,* ed. H. E. Scudder (1893; reprint, Boston: Houghton Mifflin, 1922), 648, 650; Lydia Maria Child, "Chocoruas's Curse," in *The Token; A Christmas and New Year's Present* (Boston: Carter and Hendee, 1830), 255–265; and Nathaniel Hawthorne, "The Great Stone Face," reprinted in *The Old Man's Reader: History and Legends of Franconia Notch,* ed. John T. B. Mudge (Etna, N.H.: Durand Press, 1995).

27. "The Legend of the Mountain," in *Youth's Keepsake* (Boston: T. H. Carter, 1843), 119–129. Agiococ[h]ook was one of the "Indian names" for Mount Washington.

28. See Werner Sollors, *Beyond Ethnicity: Consent and Descent in American Culture* (New York: Oxford University Press, 1986), chap. 4; Karen Lystra, *Searching the Heart: Women, Men, and Romantic Love in Nineteenth-Century America* (New York: Oxford University Press, 1989); and Ellen K. Rothman, *Hands and Hearts: A History of Courtship in America* (New York: Basic Books, 1984).

29. Jay Fliegelman, *Prodigals and Pilgrims: The American Revolution against Patriarchal Authority, 1750–1800* (Cambridge: Cambridge University Press, 1982), chap. 5; Paine quoted on 124. On marriage and divorce, see Nancy Cott, *Public Vows: A History of Marriage and the Nation* (Cambridge, Mass.: Harvard University Press, 2000), chap. 1; and Linda K. Kerber, *Women of the Republic: Intellect and Ideology in Revolutionary America* (Chapel Hill: University of North Carolina Press, 1980), chap. 6.

30. For context, see Lawrence Lipking, *Abandoned Women and the Poetic Tradition* (Chicago: University of Chicago Press, 1988).

31. Lydia Sigourney, "Memoir," in *The Poetical Works of Felicia Hemans* (Philadelphia: Porter and Coates, ca. 1860), 45; Sigourney, "Oriska" (1849), in *The Western Home* (Philadelphia: Parry and Macmillan, 1854). Like "Oriska," several versions of the Maiden Rock legend dealt with miscegenation. A common variation on the standard plot was an illicit love affair between an Indian woman and a white (French-Canadian or Anglo-American) man. This tale type never ends happily and rarely ends reproductively; either no children are produced or the children die young. Though multigenerational race-mixing is an old American story, it rarely happened in nineteenth-century U.S. literature. See Harry J. Brown, *Injun Joe's Ghost: The Indian Mixed-Blood in American Writing* (Columbia: University of Missouri Press, 2004), esp. chap. 1.

32. DeWitt Clinton, "Private Canal Journal, 1810," in *The Life and Writings of DeWitt Clinton,* ed. William W. Campbell (New York: Baker and Scriber, 1849), 130; James Lynne Alexander, *Wonders of the West* (York, Ont., 1825); Anna Blackwell, "The Legend of the Waterfall," in *The American Gallery of Art* (Philadelphia: Lindsay and Blakiston, 1848), 30–50. My knowledge about the drunken Indian story was enhanced by Paul E. Johnson, who generously provided his files on the subject. For context, see Patrick McGreevy, "Reading the Texts of Niagara Falls: The Metaphor of Death," in *Writing Worlds: Discourse, Text and Metaphor in the Representation of Landscape,* ed. Trevor J. Barnes and James S. Duncan (London: Routledge, 1992), 50–72. In Indianist literature, the male Indian suitor often dies *with* the suicidal maiden, but solo suicides by Indian men (chiefs who would rather die than surrender) are comparatively rare. How-

ever, the Indian man who falls *un*intentionally is a different story. In the words of Lora Romero, "the frequency with which Cooper's Indians plunge to their deaths from great heights is positively dumbfounding"; Romero, *Home Fronts: Domesticity and Its Critics in the Antebellum United States* (Durham, N.C.: Duke University Press, 1997), 35.

33. "Impressions of Minnesota Territory by a Pennsylvania Visitor of 1857," *Minnesota History* 46 (Summer 1979): 224. On the stereotype, see esp. E. McClung Fleming, "The American Image as Indian Princess, 1765–1783," *Winterthur Portfolio* 2 (1968): 65–81; and Rayna Green, "The Pocahontas Perplex: The Image of Indian Women in American Culture," *Massachusetts Review* 16 (Autumn 1975): 698–714.

34. Mrs. Harriet E. Bishop, *Floral Home; or, First Years of Minnesota* (New York: Sheldon, Blakeman, 1857), 219–220; Josie Keen, "Winona, a Legend of Minnesota," *Ladies' Repository,* November 1872, 339–342.

35. Eastman, *Dahcotah,* 165–166. The other storytelling crone appears in Charles Lanman, *A Summer in the Wilderness* (New York: D. Appleton, 1847), 47–50.

36. Eastman, *Dahcotah,* 169–170. Other period sources identify hanging as the gender-specific method of Sioux self-murder. See, for example, R. Eli Paul, ed., *Autobiography of Red Cloud: War Leader of the Oglalas* (Helena: Montana Historical Society Press, 1997), chap. 8. Gender-specific suicide methods were not unknown elsewhere in native America; see William N. Fenton, "A Further Note on Iroquois Suicide," *Ethnohistory* 33 (Fall 1986): 448–457.

37. See Raymond J. DeMallie, "Male and Female in Traditional Lakota Culture," in *The Hidden Half: Studies of Plains Indian Women,* ed. Patricia Albers and Beatrice Medicine (Lanham, Md.: University Press of America, 1983), 250–253.

38. Eastman, *The Iris,* 183–190.

39. Fredrika Bremer, *The Homes of the New World,* trans. Mary Howitt, vol. 2 (New York: Harper and Brothers, 1856), 29–37.

40. See G. Thomas Tanselle, "The Birth and Death of Alknomook," *Newberry Library Bulletin* 6 (May 1979): 389–401; and Renée L. Bergland, *The National Uncanny: Indian Ghosts and American Subjects* (Hanover, N.H.: University Press of New England, 2000).

41. Jill Lepore, *The Name of War: King Philips War and the Origins of American Identity* (New York: Alfred A. Knopf, 1998), 211. On Bryant, see Carl Ostrowski, "'I Stand upon Their Ashes in Thy Beam': The Indian Question and William Cullen Bryant's Literary Removals," *American Transcendental Quar-*

terly 9 (December 1995): 299–312. For literary context, see Henry Brodus Jones, "The Death Song of the 'Noble Savage': A Study in the Idealization of the American Indian" (Ph.D. diss., University of Chicago, 1924).

42. George W. Williams, *Sketches of Travel in the Old and New World* (Charleston, S.C.: Walker, Evans and Cogswell, 1871), 453.

43. Ibid., 417–418. For more on the genealogy of the legend, see John A. Burrison, "Sautee and Nacoochee: Anatomy of a Lovers' Leap Legend," *Southern Folklore* 47, no. 2 (1990): 117–132.

44. Francis A. de Caro, "Vanishing the Red Man: Cultural Guilt and Legend Formation," *International Folklore Review* 4 (1986): 74–80. Also see Jeffery Ray Jones, *Noccalula: Legend, Fact, and Function* (Collinsville, Ala.: Privately published, 1989); Kenneth W. Porter, "A Legend of the Biloxi," *Journal of American Folklore* 59 (January–March 1945): 168–173; and William Steinbacher-Kemp, "The Establishment of Starved Rock State Park," *Journal of Illinois History* 2 (Summer 1999): 123–144.

45. See Wilhelm F. H. Nicolaisen, "The Prodigious Jump: A Contribution to the Study of the Relationship between Folklore and Place-names," in *Volksüberlieferung: Festschrift für Kurt Ranke*, ed. Fritz Harkort, Karel C. Peeters, and Robert Wildhaber (Göttingen: Verlag Otto Schwartz, 1968), 531–542. I know of only one literary legend in which an Indian girl makes a prodigious jump: "The Fawn's Leap," in *The Atlantic Souvenir for 1830* (Philadelphia: Carey, Lea and Carey, 1829): 52–71.

46. "The Lover's Leap: A Tale of the Bay Province in the Olden Time," in *The Gift: A Christmas and New Year's Present* (Philadelphia: Carey and Hart, 1843), 104–130; J. Frank Dobie, ed., *Legends of Texas* (Austin: Texas Folklore Society, 1924), 159–160.

47. "Editor's Table," *The Knickerbocker* 52 (1858): 547.

48. Mary B. Janes, "Up the Mississippi," *Ladies' Repository*, August 1865, 461–464.

49. J. F. Williams, ed., *The Minnesota Guide* (St. Paul: E. H. Burritt, 1869), 30–31.

50. R. L. B., "The Natural Bridge," *Hamilton Literary Monthly*, January 1870, 178. On Wisconsin, see Dorothy Moulding Brown, "Indian Lover's Leaps in Wisconsin," *Wisconsin Archeologist* 17, no. 4 (1937): 84–87. A good descriptive listing of the major lover's leaps of New England can be found in Dorson, *Jonathan Draws the Long Bow*, chap. 5.

51. An astute reader called attention to this discrepancy in a letter published in the *Ladies' Repository* 11 (May 1873): 396. The editors replied, "We do not consider it of any serious consequence how she died."

52. "The Tourism Industry," *The Independent: A Weekly Magazine* 55 (20 August 1903): 2005; J. B. Scott, *Juanita: The Story of an Indian Princess and Tragedy of "Lover's Leap" at Gilroy Hot Sulphur Springs, California* (Salinas, Calif.: Privately published, 1901).

53. Charles H. Sweetser, *Book of Summer Resorts* (New York: "Evening Mail" Office, 1868), 72; Karen Dubinsky, *The Second Greatest Disappointment: Honeymooning and Tourism at Niagara Falls* (New Brunswick, N.J.: Rutgers University Press, 1999), esp. chap. 3. The Falls of St. Anthony lost its legendary Indian much earlier. That's because the tourist site was remade into an industrial site in 1870. Without proper scenery to support it, the legend died.

54. Rev. Henry M. Wharton, "The Boyhood Home of Mark Twain," *Century Magazine* 64 (September 1902): 675.

55. Mark Twain, *Life on the Mississippi* (Boston: James R. Osgood, 1883), 578–579. On the production of this text, see Phil Hoebing, "Legends of Lover's Leaps," *Missouri Folklore Society Journal* 21 (1999): 81–98; and Horst H. Kruse, *Mark Twain and "Life on the Mississippi"* (Amherst: University of Massachusetts Press, 1982), 113–115.

56. Twain, *Life on the Mississippi*, 580.

57. *History of Wabasha County* (Chicago: H. H. Jill, 1884), chap. 7; Lafayette Houghton Bunnell, *Winona and Its Environs on the Mississippi in Ancient and Modern Days* (Winona, Minn.: Jones and Kroeger, 1897), 164.

58. George S. Jones, "The 'Lover's Leap,'" *Appleton's Journal* 9 (22 February 1873): 262–265.

59. Charles M. Skinner, *Myths and Legends of Our Own Land*, vol. 2 (Philadelphia: J. B. Lippincott, 1896), 318. For background, see Richard M. Dorson, "How Shall We Rewrite Charles M. Skinner Today?" in *American Folk Legend: A Symposium*, ed. Wayland D. Hand (Berkeley: University of California Press, 1971), 69–88; and John Bealle, "Another Look at Charles M. Skinner," *Western Folklore* 53 (April 1994): 99–123.

60. Mrs. Eric W. Forslund and E. J. D. Larson, *Stockholm's Saga* (privately reprinted from a *Pepin Herald* serial, 7 September 1939–23 January 1941), quote on 79. On Bimboni's work, see Edward Ellsworth Hipsher, *American Opera and Its Composers* (Philadelphia: Theodore Presser, 1934), 72–76.

61. Wallace Smith, "'Just Too Cuters' Now Invade Zion Park," *New York Times*, 16 August 1925, SM-7.

62. On Tamalpais, see David Robertson, "Mt. Tamalpais: The Legendary Birth of a Holy Mountain," *California History* 70 (Summer 1991): 146–161; and Richard H. McHale, "The Legend of the Sleeping Maiden of Mount Tamalpais," manuscript, ca. 1964, Bancroft Library, University of California, Berkeley. On

Pikes Peak, see Ernest Whitney, *Legends of the Pikes Peak Region* (Denver: Chain and Hardy, 1892); Elijah Clarence Hills, "The Pike's Peak Region in Song and Myth," *Colorado College Language Series* 2 (January 1913): 165–220; and Laura T. Mecum, *Pikes Peak Yesterday and Today* (Colorado Springs: Privately published, 1926).

63. See Simon J. Bronner, *Popularizing Pennsylvania: Henry W. Shoemaker and the Progressive Uses of Folklore and History* (University Park: Pennsylvania State University Press, 1996).

9. Performing a Remembered Past

1. Mr. and Mrs. Delbert Chipman, interviewed by Theron Luke, 9 April 1979, Mount Timpanogos Oral History Collection, UHRC. I have modified the punctuation from the transcript. Luke is the speaker.

2. Gertrude Roberts Cash, "Eugene L. Roberts—A Study in Leadership," typescript, June 1959, copy in Lee Library, BYU.

3. "William D. Roberts," in *Latter-day Saint Biographical Encyclopedia,* ed. Andrew Jenson, vol. 1 (Salt Lake City: Andrew Jenson Company, 1901), 498–502; Eugene L. Roberts, "The Boy Pioneers of Utah," *Improvement Era* 14 (October 1911): 1084–92, quote on 1089.

4. On Mormon scouting, see Richard Ian Kimball, *Sports in Zion: Mormon Recreation, 1890–1940* (Urbana: University of Illinois Press, 2003), chap. 4. On the Boy Scout Association's connections to Indian play, see esp. Philip J. Deloria, *Playing Indian* (New Haven: Yale University Press, 1999), chap. 4.

5. Quotes from "Mother Luna to Be Hostess to Sturdy Hikers," *Provo Post,* 8 August 1919; and "Stage Set for Annual Pilgrimage," *Daily Herald,* 15 July 1925. Other period hikers "played Indian"; see Susan R. Schrepfer, *Nature's Altars: Mountains, Gender, and American Environmentalism* (Lawrence: University Press of Kansas, 2005), 140.

6. Benjamin G. Willey, *Incidents in White Mountain History* (Boston: Nathaniel Noyes, 1857), 44. The Mount St. Helens source is Loo-Wit Lat-Kla [pseud.], *Gold Hunting in the Cascade Mountains* (1861), Yale University Library Western Historical Series 3 (New Haven, 1957). For a refutation of the "Yellowstone taboo," see Peter Nabokov and Lawrence Loendorf, *Restoring a Presence: American Indians and Yellowstone National Park* (Norman: University of Oklahoma Press, 2004), esp. 271–285. For a fable-busting account of Indian mountaineering, see Oliver Toll, *Arapaho Names and Trails* (N.p.: Privately published, 1962), 40–41, copy in Bancroft Library, University of California, Berkeley. In the first edition of *Mountaineering in the Sierra Nevada* (1872), Clarence King

can Folklife Center, 1988), ix; Frances Densmore, *Teton Sioux Music,* Smithsonian Institution Bureau of American Ethnology Bulletin 61 (Washington, D.C.: Government Printing Office, 1918), 494–495.

34. "Playing Indian," box 1, folder 3, William Hanson Papers, MSS 299, SC-BYU.

35. Harrison R. Merrill, "Preserving the Music and Legends of the Utes for Future Generations," *DN,* 7 March 1925.

36. William Hanson, "The Lure of Tam-man Nacup" (Master's thesis, BYU, 1937), quote on x; "'Indian Love Call' Claims Profs Who Participate in Bear Dance," *Y News,* 24 April 1936, box 4, folder 7, Hanson Papers.

37. William Hanson, *The Lure of the Wigwam,* bound manuscript (ca. 1935), SC-BYU, quote from preface.

38. Program for *The Bleeding Heart,* box 5, folder 4, Hanson Papers.

39. David Rich Lewis, *Neither Wolf nor Dog: American Indians, Environment, and Agrarian Change* (New York: Oxford University Press, 1994), 28.

40. See Victor Sorensen, "The Wasters and Destroyers: Community-sponsored Predator Control in Early Utah," *UHQ* 62 (Winter 1994): 26–41. For context, see Jon Coleman, *Vicious: Wolves and Men in America* (New Haven: Yale University Press, 2004), chaps. 7–8.

41. Anne M. Smith, comp., *Ute Tales* (Salt Lake City: University of Utah Press, 1992), 9–10. The teller was Agnes Maianna (Uinta band).

42. Frank Sullivan, "Quigley 873," in *The Night the Old Nostalgia Burned Down* (Boston: Little, Brown, 1953), 11–19; originally published in the 29 December 1951 issue of the *New Yorker.*

43. Louise Pound, "Nebraska Legends of Lovers' Leaps," *Western Folklore* 8 (October 1949): 304–313, quote on 306; J. Frank Dobie, ed., *Legends of Texas* (Austin: Texas Folklore Society, 1924), 163.

44. Nonetheless, more than a few print versions appeared after Roberts—for example, Edward R. Tuttle, *The Heart of Timpanogos* (Salt Lake City: Privately published, 1957).

45. In addition to the folklore files at Utah State University and BYU (where Timpanogos legends are found in the "etiological" section), I read these separately cataloged student projects: Kris Randle, "The Lore of Mt. Timpanogos," MS 488, box 27, folder 1, SC-UU; Jennifer Christensen, "Up on Top: A Folklore Collection at Timpanogos Cave National Monument," Folklore Project 1444, SC-BYU.

46. Richard C. Peacock, *Reflections of Timpanogos* (Manti, Utah: Privately published, 1974), 3.

47. Rachel Farmer (sister of the author), personal communication.

48. Joan Peterson, "Timpanogos," folklore data sheet 5.8.1.16.5.2, SC-BYU; Trish Jensen, "Legend of Timpanogos" (1997), folklore data sheet 5.8.16.5.26, SC-BYU.

49. Peacock, *Reflections of Timpanogos,* 3, dedication.

50. Helen Forsberg, "A Native Legend of Love and Loss," *SLT,* 26 September 1997, E-1; advertisement for "Legend of Timpanogos" in author's possession; Colledge quote from *Friday Edition* news program, KUER (Salt Lake City), as aired on 16 August 1996 and recorded by the author.

51. "Utahna and the Heart of Timpanogos" (1992), folklore data sheet 5.8.1.16.5.23, SC-BYU.

52. Edward W. Tullidge, "History of Provo City," *Tullidge's Quarterly Magazine* 3 (1885): 239. George C. Scott, "In Utah County," *Our Pioneer Heritage* 3 (1960): 446; this undated reminiscence presumably comes from the late nineteenth century. J. Marinus Jensen, *History of Provo, Utah* (Provo, Utah: Privately published, 1924), 55; Susan Hansen, "How 'Squaw Peak' Got Its Name" (1968), folklore data sheet 5.8.1.15.9.1, SC-BYU.

53. William A. Wilson, "The Folk Speak: Everyday Life in Pioneer Oral Narratives," in *Nearly Everything Imaginable: The Everyday Life of Utah's Mormon Pioneer,* ed. Ronald W. Walker and Doris R. Dant (Provo, Utah: BYU Press, 1999), 485–503. For context, see Rayna D. Green, "Traits of Indian Character: The 'Indian' Anecdote in American Vernacular Tradition," *Southern Folklore Quarterly* 39 (1975): 233–262.

54. Carol Spindel, *Dancing at Halftime: Sports and the Controversy over American Indian Mascots* (New York: New York University Press, 2000), 264. Provo celebrated its 150th anniversary in 1999 with a reenactment of a wagon train from Salt Lake City, but the commemoration came too soon after 1997's extravagant Mormon Pioneer Sesquicentennial to generate much enthusiasm. The city memorialized Indians in one problematic way: a new wooden sculpture of Sowiette, the Ute leader who, according to legend, saved Fort Utah in 1850. A few years later, however, the city published an excellent history about Mormons and Utes: D. Robert Carter, *Founding Fort Utah: Provo's Native Inhabitants, Early Explorers, and First Year of Settlement* (Provo, Utah: Provo City Corporation, 2003).

55. See James B. Allen, "The Rise and Decline of the LDS Indian Student Placement Program, 1947–1996," in *Mormons, Scripture, and the Ancient World: Studies in Honor of John L. Sorenson,* ed. Davis Bitton (Provo, Utah: Foundation for Ancient Research and Mormon Studies, 1998), 85–119; Armand L. Mauss, *All Abraham's Children: Changing Mormon Conceptions of Race and Lineage* (Urbana: University of Illinois Press, 2003), chap. 4; and J. Neil Birch, "Helen

John: The Beginnings of Indian Placement," *Dialogue* 18 (Winter 1985): 119–129.

56. Virgus C. Osborne, "Indian Education at Brigham Young University, 1965–1985" (1993), MSS 2256, SC-BYU. The BYU program began under university president Ernest L. Wilkinson, a man with a deep relationship with Indians, especially Utes. In his previous career as a Washington, D.C., lawyer, Wilkinson codrafted the Indian Claims Commission Act and under its provisions helped many tribes obtain cash settlements for stolen land. The resolution of the "Big Ute Case" in 1950 brought Wilkinson renown and riches, both of which allowed him to take the BYU job in 1951. Tragically, the $32 million settlement won by Wilkinson exacerbated factionalism on the Uintah-Ouray Reservation—factionalism that played into the "termination" of the "mixed-blood" Utes. Wilkinson—a close associate of Senator Arthur Watkins as well as a close friend of Gertrude Bonnin Simmons (Zitkala-Ša)—exemplifies the distinctive mixture of paternalism, admiration, racism, and religious expectation that has long characterized the attitude of white Utah Mormons toward Native Americans.

57. Jacket notes for *Go My Son* (Provo, Utah: Blue Eagle Records, 1967), LP formerly in the author's (and grandfather's) possession, now available at the Archive of Recorded Sound, Stanford University. In sheet music form, the song is reproduced in Levine, *Writing American Indian Music,* 240–241. On Indians in Mormon music, see Michael Hicks, *Mormonism and Music: A History* (Urbana: University of Illinois Press, 1989), chap. 12; and P. Jane Hafen, "'Great Spirit Listen': The American Indian in Mormon Music," *Dialogue* 18 (Winter 1985): 133–142. Enrollment figures from Osborne, "Indian Education at Brigham Young University."

58. "The Lee Letters," *Sunstone* 13 (August 1989): 50–55. For context, see Mauss, *All Abraham's Children,* chap. 5.

59. The mesoamerican model builds on John L. Sorenson, *An Ancient American Setting for the Book of Mormon* (Salt Lake City: Deseret Book, 1985). For critiques, see esp. Simon G. Southerton, *Losing a Lost Tribe: Native Americans, DNA, and the Mormon Church* (Salt Lake City: Signature Books, 2004); and Thomas W. Murphy, "Simply Implausible: DNA and a Mesoamerican Setting for the Book of Mormon," *Dialogue* 36 (Winter 2003): 109–131.

60. Arnold Sundgaard, *Promised Valley,* simplified version (Provo, Utah: Pacific Publications, 1958), 45.

61. See Davis Bitton, *The Ritualization of Mormon History and Other Essays* (Urbana: University of Illinois Press, 1994); Eric A. Eliason, "Pioneers and Recapitulation in Mormon Popular Historical Expression," in *Usable Pasts: Traditions and Group Expressions in North America,* ed. Tad Tuleja (Logan: Utah

State University Press, 1997), 175–211; and Jessie L. Embry and William A. Wilson, "Folk Ideas of Mormon Pioneers," *Dialogue* 31 (Fall 1998): 81–99.

62. I borrow the term "master commemorative narrative" from Yael Zerubavel, *Recovered Roots: Collective Memory and the Making of Israeli National Tradition* (Chicago: University of Chicago Press, 1995). On the First Vision, see Kathleen Flake, *The Politics of American Religious Identity: The Seating of Senator Reed Smoot, Mormon Apostle* (Chapel Hill: University of North Carolina Press, 2004), chap. 5. On polygamy, see Stephen C. Taysom, "A Uniform and Common Recollection: Joseph Smith's Legacy, Polygamy, and the Creation of Mormon Public Memory, 1852–2002," *Dialogue* 35 (Fall 2002): 113–144.

63. Christopher Smith and Lili Wright, "For Plenty of Utahns, The Party Was a Dud," *SLT*, 7 January 1996; Matthew Brown, "Indians Balk at Offer to Take Part in Celebration," *SLT*, 23 December 1996.

64. Brown, "Indians Balk at Offer." On the BYU event, see Tony Yapias, "Conference Addresses the Balancing of Tribal Traditions and LDS Beliefs," *SLT*, 26 July 1997, D-1.

65. The author attended the event. Impressive though it was, the Spectacular probably had less mnemonic impact than the Church-produced film *Legacy* (1993), a dramatization of the Mormon trek. This Hollywood-style 72mm movie was viewed some five million times during its multiyear run in a specially designed theater adjacent to Temple Square.

66. Catherine Reese Newton, "Birth of a Dream: 4 Years in the Making, 'Dreamkeepers' Opens," *SLT*, 7 January 1996, E-1. To its further credit, the Centennial Committee also commissioned a new state history (Thomas Alexander's *Utah, The Right Place*) and a compilation of tribal histories: Forrest S. Cuch, ed., *A History of Utah's American Indians* (Salt Lake City: Utah State Division of Indian Affairs/Utah State Division of History, 2000).

67. Quotations from Lance S. Gudmundsen, "Concert Pays Tribute to Timpanogos," *SLT*, 7 July 1996, E-2. Also see Jerry Johnston, "Peaking for a Concert," *DN*, 7 July 1996.

68. "The Real Story of Timpanogos: Love, Jealousy, and Death, Told by Ute Elder Gramma Ethel Grant," from concert program in the author's possession.

69. Duncan, interviewed on *Friday Edition* news program, KUER (Salt Lake City), as aired on 16 August 1996 and recorded by the author. Information about Cesspooch's visit from personal communication with Suzanne Flory, Chief of Interpretation at Timpanogos Cave National Monument, December 2000.

70. George Stewart to Theron Luke, ca. 1980, Theron Luke Papers, box 3, folder 8, UHRC.

71. J. G. Weaver, "Ute Legend of Bridal Veil Falls," *Western Monthly* 10 (February 1909): 43–45; "The Legend of Bridal Veil Falls," PAM 5906, UHRC.

72. Gudmundsen, "Concert Pays Tribute to Timpanogos." I should point out that Terry Tempest Williams has done more than anyone else recently to raise the level of interest in Utah's other unloved lake—the Great Salt Lake—thanks to her popular memoir *Refuge: An Unnatural History of Family and Place* (New York: Pantheon, 1991).

Acknowledgments

The roots of this project reach back to two folklore courses I took as an undergraduate at Utah State University. Although they may not remember me, I wish to thank my teachers, Steve Siporin and Barre Toelken. Another USU professor, David Rich Lewis, has been a continuing source of encouragement and solidarity. At the University of Montana, my master's thesis advisor, Dan Flores, influenced me more than he probably realizes. I'm happy to call him my friend.

When I moved to Stanford University, I had the good fortune of working with Richard White. The quality of his scholarship is a matter of public record. For my part, I bear witness to his integrity as a teacher and mentor.

The History Department at Stanford treated me well for six years. The chair at that time, Carolyn Lougee Chappell, merits praise for her unwavering support of graduate students. The same goes for Professor Richard Roberts. Another faculty member, Zephyr Frank, supplied some welcome camaraderie. And two kindhearted administrators, Lynn Kaiser and the late Gertrud Pacheco, answered many questions and solved many problems.

In my doctoral program I made a pair of student friends who became professional and personal confidants. Rachel St. John and Matthew Morse Booker—of thee I sing! Likewise, Rebecca Lemon deserves a hymn of thanks. She knows why.

I wrote the first draft of the manuscript while in residence at the Stanford Humanities Center. For creating a hospitable environment for writers, I offer my appreciation to the center's staff, particularly to Chi Elliott. For funding my writing fellowship as well as part of my research, I acknowledge the Dean's Office of the College of Humanities and Sciences. After I left Stanford, the Huntington-USC Institute on California and the West gave me the time and space to finish the project. Many thanks to Bill Deverell of the University of Southern California and Roy Ritchie of the Huntington Library for that golden opportunity.

Revising requires help. I owe a debt to Tom Alexander, dean of Utah historians, for his careful critique of a late draft. Earlier versions were read in full by Alan Taylor, Kären Wigen, and Sam Wineburg, as well as two anonymous referees for Harvard University Press. I thank them all. For comments on specific chapters I relied upon the generosity of Veronica della Dora, Matt Klingle, Christian McMillen, Chris Morris, Judith Richardson, Jen Seltz, and Cecilia Tsu. At Harvard my vigilant editor, Kathleen McDermott, shepherded the manuscript along the lengthy path of academic publishing. Keen-eyed copyeditor Ann Hawthorne found innumerable ways to refine the final draft.

My friend and fellow cartophile, Jen Mapes, converted my hand-drawn maps into digital files. For her kindness—and for her patience with my fastidiousness—she has my heartfelt gratitude.

Historians would be lost without librarians. I praise them collectively. Also I wish to single out three for commendation. At the archives of The Church of Jesus Christ of Latter-day Saints in Salt Lake City, Bill Slaughter was a constant beacon of kindliness. At Stanford University, Mary Munill of Interlibrary Services tracked down hundreds of obscure titles with a smile. And in Room 4040 of the Lee Library at Brigham Young University—the ex-location of Special Collections—Sarah Ann Seestone treated me like the world's most valuable historian. I won't soon forget.

Finally, I wish to acknowledge in these pages the undying presence of my maternal grandfather, Walter Edward Clark, a man of the nineteenth century. From him, more than from any other person, I inherited my past.

Index